The New Press
Education Reader

Leading Educators Speak Out

EDITED BY
ELLEN GORDON REEVES

THE NEW PRESS

NEW YORK
LONDON

*To my family and friends, and to the students and teachers
I have been so fortunate to know.*

Requests for permission to reproduce selections from this book
should be mailed to: Permissions Department,
The New Press, 38 Greene Street, New York, NY 10013.

Published in the United States by The New Press, New York, 2006
Distributed by W. W. Norton & Company, Inc., New York

LIBRARY OF CONGRESS CATALOGING-IN-PUBLICATION DATA
The New Press education reader : leading educators
speak out / edited by Ellen Gordon Reeves.
p. cm.
ISBN-13: 978-1-59558-142-6 (hc.) 978-1-59558-110-5 (pbk.)
ISBN-10: 978-1-59558-142-1 (hc.) 1-59558-110-3 (pbk.)
1. Teaching.   2. Teachers.   3. Discrimination in education—United States.
4. Educational equalization—United States.   I. Reeves, Ellen Gordon.
LB7.N378 2006
371.1—dc22   2006046745

The New Press was established in 1990 as a not-for-profit alternative to the large,
commercial publishing houses currently dominating the book publishing industry.
The New Press operates in the public interest rather than for private gain, and is
committed to publishing, in innovative ways, works of educational, cultural, and
community value that are often deemed insufficiently profitable.

www.thenewpress.com

Composition by dix!
This book was set in New Baskerville

Printed in Canada

2   4   6   8   10   9   7   5   3   1

Contents

Acknowledgments

Many thanks to my colleagues at The New Press, including Jessica Colter, Sarah Fan, Nico Carbellano, and Emily Barrett for their hands-on help in preparing the manuscript. I have been privileged to work with most of the authors in this collection and I could never thank them enough for their wisdom and kindness over the years.

I am most grateful for the help and support of Alexandra and Maureen Miletta, great friends, great writers, and great teachers who most likely cannot fathom the extent of their influence.

Preface

The New Press Education Reader is a book I wish I'd had before I started teaching so many years ago, and it's a book I'd like to share with all the parents, teachers, and administrators I know and those I have yet to meet.

Part I, "On Teachers and Teaching," opens with a perennial question: what does good teaching look like? "To Be a Teacher" explores what it takes to be a great educator through interviews with a variety of experts across the United States. Kathleen Cushman and high school students from What Kids Can Do, Inc., provide another view by revealing what students look for in a teacher in "Respect, Liking, Trust and Fairness."

Diversity in the teaching pool is as important as the diversity in the student body. Lisa Delpit shares the voices of Native American and African American teachers and the challenges they face in "Teacher's Voices: Rethinking Teacher Education for Diversity," noting that the interviews "contain a gold mine of knowledge about how to educate not only teachers but children of color." Michele Foster takes a look at African American teachers in historical context, examining their unique experiences, which have been "either completely overlooked or amalgamated with those of white teachers." The section ends with two narratives—one from a third-grade teacher, one from the head of an alternative school—from Studs Terkel's *Working*, first published in 1972, revealing, for better or worse, both how much and how little have changed in our schools since then.

Although the civil rights movement brought sweeping changes in America, we are still witness to cultural conflicts and racial tensions that arise in our classrooms all too often as students and teachers struggle to understand one another. "Combating Racism and Homophobia" is the topic of Part II. Judith Rényi's "The Making of a Revolution" was written in the early 1990s, in the midst of heated public debate about multiculturalism. She discusses why there was so much discomfort with changing the curriculum, in spite of the fact that doing so would actually achieve the goals many claimed they had for all students in this country. While most standard textbooks and curricula now routinely incorporate the history, literature, and cultural traditions of a much broader range of ethnic groups, the battle is far from over. Laurie Olsen's students from the prototypical Madison High explain the distinct racial groupings and boundaries at their school. David Mura interrogates white privilege as he and his young daughter discuss Tahar Ben Jelloun's *Racism Explained to My Daughter*. Mica Pollock provides concrete ideas for combating everyday racism in schools. Antiracism, Pollock writes, "requires not treating people as race group members when such treatment harms, and treating people as race group members when such treatment assists." Michael Ford discusses homophobia, another kind of discrimination many young people must contend with. Herbert Kohl concludes with personal and pedagogical suggestions based on a lifetime spent advocating for social justice in and out of classrooms.

"Advocates for Equity: A Range of Perspectives" opens with Robert Coles sharing the voices of children in poverty. Victoria Purcell-Gates offers her considerable expertise to illuminate what we need to do to build the language skills of these children. William Ayers and Patricia Ford ask if there is a distinctly urban pedagogy, while acknowledging that the "broad outlines of what we describe . . . could productively inform teaching from the gold coast suburbs to the red hills of Georgia or the rich farmlands of the prairies." Next, Gary Orfield provides an overview of the relationship between housing and school desegregation policies in the wake of the tragic "dismantling" of *Brown v. Board of Education.* "For many school districts," he writes, "the only hope for eradicating segregation in schools lies in chipping away at segregated housing." In "What Alondra Learned" from *Final Test,* Peter Schrag observes that "adequacy" has become "the central drama in the struggle to see whether the hopes for educational opportunities for all children that were raised by the *Brown v. Board* school desegregation decision of 1954 can be fulfilled." The poorer the district and the less money a school has in its budget, the more vulnerable it is to the siren call of consumer marketers, offering computers, soda machines, television sets, field trips, and even teaching materials advertising their products and services. This is not the solution, as Susan Linn so eloquently argues in "Students for Sale: Who Profits from Marketing in Schools?"

How can we begin to address all of these pressing issues? Only through combined efforts on many fronts. While it may be intuitive that the more involved families and communities are in the education of children, the better those children will fare academically and otherwise, we now have the research to prove it. "Parent, Family and Community Involvement: The Key to Success" tells these stories and offers ways schools can facilitate productive relationships with their students' families. Anne Wheelock discusses communication with parents, particularly with regard to the issue of tracking, followed by the National Coalition of Education Activists who offer guidelines for investigating tracking in schools and school systems. At the very end, William Ayers reminds us in "Organizing and Teaching" that "teaching, like organizing, is an act of faith."

It is my hope that the voices of the teachers and students gathered here, as well as the advice and experience of so many dedicated educators and activists, will be used in the service of children until, in the words of the

Shaker hymn that was such an important part of my own schooling, "we come down where we ought to be."

Ellen Gordon Reeves
May 2006

I

On Teachers and Teaching

1

To Be a Teacher:
Experts Talk About What It Takes
To Be a Great Educator

Daniel Moulthrop, Nínive Clements Calegari, and Dave Eggers

Based on our own experiences as students, we all have a sense of what happens in the classroom. We understand the basic processes and structures: students come in, teacher takes attendance, lesson begins. But when education and cognition experts speak about effective teaching, they paint a deeper and more detailed picture. From lesson planning to delivering instructions, from greeting children at the beginning of a class to introducing a new concept, effective teachers make decisions constantly—often very rapidly and sometimes even unconsciously—to create the best learning conditions for their students.

If every student came to school ready to learn and schools were the perfect environments for encouraging learning, a teacher's job would likely be significantly easier. But students at all levels do not always arrive in class ready to learn, and schools are sometimes so large they are not able to make the individual needs of students the highest priority. Good teachers are always thinking in terms of large-scale, overarching goals, such as creating a positive classroom culture and fostering students' critical-thinking abilities. They are simultaneously moving students toward short-term, immediate goals—ensuring all students understand the instructions for that evening's Spanish homework, successfully transitioning from a lab experiment involving crickets to quiet reading time in a second-grade classroom, or making sure Anthony, who seems upset and might become disruptive, knows that his teacher cares about him and expects him to focus.

Here, a variety of experts—sociologists, cognitive scientists, education-policy thinkers—speak about the elements of effective teaching. Teaching is not just something anybody with a bachelor's degree can do. Good teaching is extremely complex, subtle, and nuanced, and it's well worth everything we can afford to spend on it.

Linda Darling-Hammond, Charles E. Docommun Professor of Education at Stanford University; Faculty Sponsor for Stanford's Teacher Education Program (STEP)

Darling-Hammond is the author or editor of nine books, including the award-winning The Right to Learn: A Blueprint for Creating Schools That Work, *and more than 200 journal articles that deal with educational reform, policy, and practice. She has served on the White House Advisory Panel's Resource Group for the National Educational Goals.*

First of all, good teachers know how to understand students' thinking: where they are, what they know, what they understand, and how they learn and perceive. They're able to plan a curriculum that starts from where kids are and gets them to where they need to go in any particular subject matter. They understand how the structure of the discipline works, and that allows them to figure out what the ideas are, the scope and sequence of what students need to encounter in order to build their knowledge so that it adds up to deeper understanding and proficiency within a discipline. That's a lot different than having an idea for a particular lesson on a particular day.

They know a lot about group dynamics, and know how to organize a large number of students, twenty or thirty students, so that they can work productively together, can learn from each other, can be presented with tasks that are interesting, engaging, and doable for them, and can accomplish those and achieve success and then build on what they know to achieve more success.

Anyone who has ever spent even two hours overseeing a child's birthday party gets a tiny glimpse of what a teacher needs to know. Most people would find it challenging even to keep kids busy and not in crisis for a couple of hours. They don't even have to ensure that the students learn anything or master new skills and proficiencies or become more socially adept or more responsible citizens. So think about what a teacher needs to know to do that. You have to think about not only being able to keep the students busy, but being able to organize them so that they get a lot of learning accomplished.

A teacher needs to know how to assess what students know and what they don't know, and what they're learning and how they're learning, so that they can use that assessment to solve problems in learning and to plan their curriculum.

Teachers need to know how people learn to read. Even a high school teacher needs to know how to help kids master both elementary and sophisticated skills in reading. Even if that teacher is a math teacher, she needs to know about literacy, because what kids can do has a great deal to do with how they can make meaning out of texts. And as many teachers find out, even some high school kids have not mastered those skills.

A teacher needs to know how students who have neurobiological differences and disabilities process information and learn, so that she can work with the 10 to 20 percent of students who have specific kinds of learning disabilities and special education needs. That may mean adapting the curriculum in a variety of ways for those students so that they can make progress. It's not enough to say, "You get it or you don't," or, "I got you the book." You have to figure out how to help everyone learn. A teacher needs to know today how to make content accessible to students who don't speak English as a first language and who may not speak English at all when they come into your classroom, how people acquire language and how you help them do that within a subject matter or field (with its own specialized language).

A teacher needs to know how to manage interpersonal relationships and dynamics among kids. For example, in any given classroom there are some students who are high-status students and other students who often get bullied or ignored by their peers, and the teacher needs to know how to help those students find a niche and a foothold so that they can be respected and become contributing members of the classroom. The teacher needs to know how to teach other kids how to consider one another respectfully, and get along and work together in productive ways.

And I'm just getting started! So much! A teacher needs to know how to collaborate with other professionals in order to build a school environment that meets all of the students' needs and allows them to have a coherent experience as they go from grade to grade and classroom to classroom and are helped by a variety of professionals.

A teacher needs to know how to work with parents and families, needs to understand different family norms and expectations and cultures and backgrounds and how to find common ground in working together on behalf of the child. A teacher needs to know how to get from parents what they know about the child, so they can be partners together. A teacher needs to know a lot about cultural context for learning because everyone's learning is shaped by their cultural expectations and experiences, and they need to know how to enquire into that because it's going to be a different set of beliefs and understanding and expectations and experiences that kids bring to classrooms in every different community.

Dan Lortie, Sociologist, Former Professor of Sociology at University of Chicago

Lortie is most famous for his book Schoolteacher: A Sociological Study, *which, though published in 1975, continues to be widely read by students of sociology and education. His current work focuses on elementary school administrators.*

The basic condition that makes the job of teachers difficult is that teachers—as persons, as individuals, and particularly in the lower grades—are trained to think that they're dealing with individual kids. But in fact they're dealing with twenty-five individual kids in each class. Somewhere in there, it is so emotionally trying that it's very hard for teachers to feel successful. There's always a sense that somehow or other, they could have done a better job.

The irony in this is that the smarter and more sensitive the teacher is, the more likely they are to feel that way. The [teachers who aren't as sensitive] think everything's great. In teaching, you have to learn to live with less than you want. Here they are, knocking themselves out for the good of these kids, and yet, somehow or other, not getting a sense of satisfaction. This is what I mean by uncertainty; it's built in. I don't think schools of education have done a good enough job preparing students for that tension of the one against the many, to develop better techniques for assessing what they have achieved. Standardized tests don't do it because teachers care about a lot of things standardized tests don't measure—cognitive things, not just affective things. Standardized tests are narrow. They differ in their utility in terms of what's being taught. It's much easier to test immediate comprehension in math than it is in social studies and art. Somewhere in there lies a difficult question to sort out.

Another complexity is the attitude of families. Willard Waller, a sociologist of education, first wrote in 1928 about this. There are several aspects of this as a problem. One is that when kids leave home for school, they move into a situation which is ordered in a universal way. It's their first experience in having to do what everyone else does. That's partly a function of schooling, to teach people how to live in an ordered world, where there are tasks that have to be done and standards you have to meet. They've got thirty kids from different families. Those families emphasize different things at home, and they've got to somehow combine and unite these kids into a working thing called a classroom, and it ain't the most natural thing in the world. It takes time, as kids go through the system, to get them grooved into the idea that, okay, I'm in Miss Jones's class, and in Miss

Jones's class, you've got to do this, you can't do that—to learn the rules and obey the rules.

Deborah Stipek, Dean, Graduate School of Education at Stanford University

Stipek studies the motivation of children, early childhood and elementary education, and school reform. She served for five years on the Board on Children, Youth and Families at the National Research Council.

One of the various difficulties is the context in which teachers teach. Especially if you're teaching in low-income schools, you have, in some states more than others and in some communities more than others, a dearth of resources, and you're trying to meet the needs of children who have very complicated teaching needs—kids who need special services, kids for whom English is a second language. They need a lot of extra help in being able to master curricula when they're getting their teaching in a language in which they're not completely proficient. Many teachers are doing that with very, very thin resources.

There are scandalous contexts in which some teachers work. You have situations where there may be one phone that teachers have available to them, down the hall, and yet we know how important it is for teachers to maintain contact with families. I've seen schools where [during their breaks] teachers are lined up to be able to make a call home to talk to a parent of a child who is having some difficulties.

Often in schools there is no place for teachers to go when they have fifteen minutes to take a breath. There's either no planning time or very little planning time. We expect teachers to individualize instruction, to develop interesting, engaging units, curriculum units, but they're front and center with a group of twenty to thirty-five kids all day long, so when are they going to develop these units? They do it on their own time, they do it on Saturdays, and weekends, and until ten, eleven, twelve o'clock at night. If you're an English teacher, or a teacher in almost any subject, being able to review students' work—to give detailed feedback to students about what they are understanding and what they are not understanding, is a critical variable in being a good teacher and acknowledged to have important implications for how well students learn. So when are teachers going to do that if they're with kids all day long?

Those who study teaching and learning are aware of this fast pace and, in different ways than those who experience it, recognize the effects this pace

has on teachers and the students they teach. Researchers like Gaea Leinhardt are keenly aware of the characteristics of good teachers, and are
adept at articulating even the most intangible elements of the job.

Gaea Leinhardt, Professor, Graduate School of Education at the
University of Pittsburgh

*Leinhardt teaches courses on how teachers and students build a common under-
standing in the classroom. She coordinates the University of Pittsburgh's Cognitive
Sciences in Education Program and is a senior scientist in the Learning Research
and Development Center.*

There are two things that make teaching extraordinarily hard. One is the
intensity of being "on" for the six and a half hours that you're on, in ways
that almost no other profession requires. You can't drop down and not pay
attention, except for very slotted times, and that comes with a specific contract arrangement. When you're with the kids, you cannot *not* be there.
That kind of intensity is quite hard. Because of the risks of not being available—the physical risks, the psychological risks, the emotional risks—you
must constantly just be there.

For me, it's a sense of changing direction all the time. We're starting a
lesson, and even if nothing is interrupting the lesson, I need to constantly
remember where we were, where we're going, and where people are with
me. How are we, as a group, evolving this understanding, and is everybody
at about the same place? It's extraordinarily intense.

Go anywhere else and compare. Go down to a courthouse and look at
judges and other professionals. All of them have breaks. Certainly, academics have breaks all the time. There are other professions where you need to
be "all there," but the duration of being "all there" is usually a little shorter.
In surgery, they don't always go back and do it the next day. They have one
operation, and they know they're going to have a long one, and they prepare for it, and everybody around them, these huge crews, are there to literally mop their brow.

The other thing is that most of us who work with our minds are allowed
to control the trajectory of a time period, whether that's a day or a week or
a month. We decide, "This is what I'm going to do today." But teachers
have a set of obligations—it could be state standards, local standards—and
they have a vision of how they're going to get there. They're barraged with
interruptions—nonstop interruptions and immediate demands. Those
can come from the hierarchy of the school, where the loudspeaker is blar-
ing every twenty minutes to tell you to come to such and such and fill out
this form and be somewhere else, or it can be very local: Johnny's dog dies

and Suzie's grandmother has cancer and Emily had nightmares all night. It doesn't matter. The immediate psychological environment is in front of you, and you have to cope with it. On a daily basis, it's very wearing.

As parents, we entrust our most precious assets to this system. Think about it: we're taking a little kid, and we're plunking him in a place that we don't know—we haven't examined the physical building—with a human being we haven't examined. We leave our darling child with this person. That person has to be very worthy, and has to be deeply moral. I don't mean to be fuzzy about that; they have to have a real commitment to acting in a humane, honest way, intellectually and in a person-to-person fashion, all the time. They can't be cranky. They can't lose it. Of course, they do, but we're really asking them not to. We're asking them to be above the fray, to be able to care in honest ways with these children, and to administer justice constantly—and in the meantime, to get something taught. It's the juggling, the interruption, the compromise with your own sense of control, that make it more complex than being an engineer who knew a lot of math and now wants to come back and stand in front of a class and teach arithmetic. It's much more complex that that.

It is being detached in the right way so you can make good, just judgment calls and so you can offer a constant optimistic vision toward the future. One of the challenges teachers of adolescents deal with is that one of the safest routes for adolescents is to withdraw, and in the kind of culture that we have now, that's actually a possibility. Someone can withdraw and still be functional. In other times and other places, withdrawing like that meant death. That's not what it means now, and you have to have teachers who are prepared to keep offering an optimistic future vision so students can keep working toward that future vision. That doesn't mean "get good grades in algebra so you can get into the calculus class so you can get into college." It means always imagining the future in all of its complexity, while having a social contract with the parents and the community that today, we're trying to get through these ideas of algebra.

David Klahr, Professor, Department of Psychology at Carnegie Mellon University

Klahr's primary goals in his research in cognitive development are to discover what children know and to explain how they come to know it. His work focuses primarily on science education.

Students often come in with misconceptions about how things work. Everyday language and scientific language have a lot of similarities. They seem similar, but they mean quite different things. A good teacher has to be sensitive, to try to figure out where the child is with respect to what they know, and not just whether they know it or not, but what do they know about this concept that's probably right, and what do they know about it that's probably wrong, and how can I build on what they know that's right, and how can I show them the parts that are wrong. That's the real difficulty.

Here's an example. You're trying to teach kids about electric circuits. When a circuit is open, no current is flowing; when it's closed, the current flows. The students are confused, because open usually refers to a situation when a door is open, and you can go through it. Closed usually means things are stopped. But in electric circuits, a closed circuit means the circuit is closed and electrons can move around that circuit. So there's a word that means almost the opposite in that context of what it means in everyday life. Kids get confused. Then you say, let's use the analogy of water flowing. That's a good one, because water flows, and electrons flow, so you think you have a nice analogy. But again, when you open the faucet, it flows, and when you close it, it doesn't flow, and this is the opposite of what happens when you open the switch and when you close the switch. That's a concept in which the terminology can drive you crazy. If a teacher isn't sensitive to that, the teacher's going to think this kid just doesn't get it. It has to be addressed directly. You have to say to the child, the reason you're confused is you're thinking of what happens in everyday language.

A lot of good teachers know their domain, and they know that kids have misconceptions. They walk around the classroom and they can look at Suzie and say she's got misconception x, and I know how to deal with that; and Joe has misconception y, and I can deal with that. It's not that formal, but that's what a really good teacher can do. That's why it's so important for teachers to know their subject matter. With twenty-five students, it can be twenty-five times as hard.

Assessment is also an important part. Teachers have to be able to figure out what kids know on a continual basis, and they need to have good, clear measures of the things they're trying to teach. Teachers face this conflict between state standards and high-stakes tests. They have to decide how to allocate their time—either to getting ready for some kind of high-stakes assessment or continuing with the unit they're trying to teach.

Steve Seidel, Director, Project Zero, Graduate School of Education, Harvard University

Project Zero supports a variety of ongoing research dedicated to "the development of new approaches to help individuals, groups, and institutions learn to the best of their capacities."

One of the big ironies is that schools are the primary institutions set up for the explicit purpose of teaching and learning, and they're very hard places to do that work. Even though that's their purpose, they're institutions, and teaching and learning are profoundly human enterprises. In so many ways, institutions don't adequately take into account the humanness of learning, of teaching, and of the significance of the relationships between people. I don't just mean between teachers and students but among students and among the adults as a community. There are a lot of human relationships in teaching and learning, and that's not always facilitated so well by the school setting. That's one of the tensions people in the profession of teaching in public schools struggle with. Often the whole time they're in their profession, they find ways to be there by negotiating between the human dimensions of real learning and real teaching and the institutional constraints of the school.

In schools, we as teachers tend to see a phenomenon like Shakespeare's sonnets and we think, this is probably a stretch for this group of thirty-five middle school students, so I'm going to simplify it in some way. Instead of twenty sonnets, I'm going to give them one. Instead of letting them really work with that one, I'm going to paraphrase it for them, or I'm going to do something that simplifies it. The intent generally comes from an understandable place, but in doing that we strip the phenomenon of its real interest and, in a sense, disrespect the complexity of the phenomenon. We also disrespect the potential capacity of these young people's minds to grasp this phenomenon and make sense of it.

So the nature of the task is to create a problem that's within—not immediately within, but potentially within—the capacity of these students to grasp and provide the support that gets them to the place where they can do that and totally respects the complexity of the phenomenon.

Making this happen in public schools takes an absolute clarity about, commitment to, and interest in the minds of your students. You have to believe that they have capable minds. It's a mind that's capable both of reason and of influence, of deep emotion and of struggling with deep emotion.

I think that's another thing that's very inhumane—schools are not particularly comfortable with emotion. A lot of teachers are not particularly comfortable with emotion because when you've got thirty-five kids coming through every hour, and you've got five, six classes a day and three to five classes to prepare for, it becomes very hard to say we're going to deal with everybody's feelings about everything. Part of what happens is that we then even strip the emotional content out of the subject matter that we're studying. Why should anybody be interested? We don't watch movies or TV that are endlessly stripped of emotion. Emotion is one of the absolutely key entry points for all of us to anything that has to do with complex human life—in history, in the arts, and so on.

Take a forty-three-minute class period. People need to come in, get settled, and talk to each other because they haven't been together, right? Some of them might have been, but a lot of them are encountering each other for the first time. There's a lot of social need. There's a need to say hello, if they've got any social relationship at all. If they don't, they need help saying hello because they're going to work together and try to identify long-term, large, project-based ideas, or this set of ideas or this material. Then, teachers need to find the discrete pieces that people can actually feel a sense of progress on, because by that time, it's really thirty to thirty-five minutes. It's basically an insane structure. But, in the real world of work, we do take time to say hello in the morning and ease in. You need to respect that.

The ability to teach specific knowledge about a certain content area—science, math, social studies—is one important skill, but just as important, or maybe even more important, is teaching children *how* to learn. We know teachers help students learn how to read, for instance, but we don't always recognize they must also teach how to *understand* what is read—a skill that becomes increasingly important for students in high school and college. The best teachers make this explicit and juggle dozens of teaching strategies simultaneously, adjusting them to the ever-shifting needs of their students.

Tom Sherman, Professor of Education and Adolescent Psychology at Virginia Polytechnic State University

Sherman is an educational psychologist who studies how children learn and how teachers can teach children to learn. He is a former public school teacher who now teaches in Virginia Tech's teacher training program, helping to train about 120 teachers a year.

One of the problems with thinking, and thinking well, is that it's not like watching Tiger Woods swing a golf club. You may not be able to do it like he does it, but at least you can see how he does it. On the other hand, if you have a student who is particularly good, you can see the outcome, but you can't see what's going on in that student's head. If you have two students, one who is a good thinker and one who is not a good thinker, the one who is not a good thinker really has no access to what the good thinker does. It looks like it's magic, or more likely, it looks like they've got something I don't have, so the student thinks, "They're smart, and I'm not."

It turns out that a lot of kids do develop that kind of a concept: You're a smart guy and I'm not. If I can figure out what you do when you solve a problem and I do those same things, most of the time, I can solve that problem, too. So the question then becomes, How do you get inside an individual's head to show how that thinking takes place? As I've said, you can model what you do, and think out loud. Instead of writing down the answer, you think through, out loud, how you got that answer. You do that in a variety of situations.

The second way is to teach the individual skills specifically. One of the key elements of sophisticated thinking is checking your work. When you think about it, if you don't know how well you've done, you really have no idea what you've done or whether you've done it well. A lot of times in school, kids are taught to wait for the teacher to tell them. It's not taught explicitly, it's just the way it works: Teachers tell you if you got it right or wrong. One of the things that teachers do that makes a big difference is asking kids, "You tell me what you got right or you tell me what you got wrong, because you really can't fix things if you don't know they're wrong." It's best to know this beforehand. That is, it's best if I know this is wrong before I submit it to my editor, or before I put an article in and it gets rejected because I didn't do it right or I didn't have the right information. The same thing is true with kids.

It turns out children who tend not to be high achievers rarely do that kind of self-checking. They look to the teacher. If you ask them, "Well, how did you do on the test?" they say, "Well, I don't know, I haven't gotten it back yet." Of course, we find that very often in higher education, where you ask students how they did on the test and they say, "How would I know? You haven't handed it back yet." You want students to say, "I think I got it," or "There was an issue, but I think I handled it." You want them to have a sense that they know how to handle the material. But that's got to be taught.

An effective teacher not only needs to be a sophisticated thinker him- or herself, but also needs to be able to model that thinking process. You have to make it transparent. Not only that, but you have to get the children to do it. In addition to that, you want children to have a variety of strategies to solve problems and address issues. A defining difference between children who are high achievers and children who are low achievers is that the low achievers have only one way of doing things. The high achievers will have several ways. If one doesn't work, they'll try another, and another. One of the things good teachers do is teach multiple strategies for addressing issues.

One of the best-known examples is this: Children who are good readers have multiple strategies for reading. They tend to read and know when they are understanding. When they are reading, they also know when they are not understanding. When they are not understanding, they have things they can do to help them understand. They may re-read. They may think, How does this relate to me? They may go back and find some material they may have read that will help them understand so they achieve comprehension. On the other hand, poor readers tend to keep on going. Oftentimes they know they don't understand. But they don't have any strategies for correcting their lack of understanding.

So the teacher's job is to teach other ways to read, other strategies for correcting a failure to comprehend. One of the most simple and effective strategies for dealing with comprehension failure is to re-read. A lot of kids think it's supposed to happen the first time. If you don't know, you don't know, and you're never going to get it—that's what they think. But if they use good reading skills, then they will understand when they read.

Another thing good teachers do is to focus on the core issues of the discipline. This helps students not just to understand the information but also to master the intellectual strategies of the discipline. Think about teaching history. In my day, if you went though history, it meant memorizing a lot of names, dates and places and thinking about the temporal relationship between them, and doing a lot of memory work—but now, sophisticated teachers are teaching students to do history. That is, to think through the interpretation of information and what the standards are for interpreting and judging information, rather than just accepting what's there. It means asking questions like, Where does this come from? What was that person thinking? Why would they have interpreted it this way? What are other ways of interpreting it? That's pretty sophisticated stuff, but it is the kind of thing that even very young kids can do, not like a PhD would, but asking the same sort of questions and dealing with the same sort of issues.

It illustrates that great teachers go beyond simply saying, "Think about it, think about it. Just sit there and think about it a minute." Well, hell, if I knew what to do, I wouldn't be sitting here not getting the answer. What does it mean to "Think about it"? So what these teachers are doing is focusing on the components of what we mean when we say "think about it" or "reflect." It might mean "Make some comparisons, create some criteria for making judgments and then apply those criteria, then determine whether you are satisfied or not satisfied," and you build those kinds of skills across time. No matter how old we get, we are still able to become better thinkers.

It's not just that a teacher's day is stressful and virtually devoid of downtime. Every moment of the teaching day, good teachers are doing a number of crucial tasks simultaneously: delivering instruction, keeping all students focused on the task at hand, assessing how well students are understanding, identifying why students are having trouble, modifying explanations and activities, making personal connections to suit the needs of different students, teaching skills that build on what students already know, and preparing them for future learning. In order to fulfill those curricular needs, a teacher must first address the immediate emotional and psychological needs of his students, which often requires that the teacher himself function as the model of moral behavior. Many teachers do this in schools that are sometimes difficult places to do that work.

Given the complexity of the job, it seems imperative to convince the most exceptional people to become teachers. Bringing the very best people to the job is a challenge, and all the recruiting tools in education won't make a real difference until one of them is competitive pay.

2

Respect, Liking, Trust, and Fairness

Kathleen Cushman

"If you see the teacher respect students,
you'll follow that role model."

In the high school classroom, respect and trust travel a two-way street between teacher and student—and have everything to do with learning.
Students say that if a teacher sets a steady example of fairness and respect,
they respond positively whether or not they like a teacher personally. If
they trust a teacher to do the job with competence and without bias, they
are willing to fulfill their part of the deal: to pay attention, do the work, and
play by the rules.

> There was this guy who coached track. If he told you to do twenty laps
> and the guys were complaining, he would say: "Okay, do five." If you
> were tired, he would say, "Okay, you can stop." He would take you out
> for pizza after practice. He was a cool coach; they all loved him. But
> when the time for the meets came, they never won anything. So they
> got a new coach. The new coach, if he says, "Do fifty laps," and they
> say, "We don't wanna," he'll say, "Oh, no? Then do fifty-two!"
> They hated him because he made them work so hard. But when the
> time for the meets came, they won every single time. They learned
> the difference between respecting and liking.   ALEXIS

> Being able to trust your teacher and be trusted is important. One stu-
> dent in my school was homeless. The principal wasn't like, "Let's go
> to your house and talk to your mom." He was like, "If you need a safe
> place to stay, I know someone you can talk to." He doesn't want you to
> feel embarrassed. When they have teacher conferences, he does not
> tell other people private things you have told him. If you're gay, if

you're getting beat up, if you're not eating, if you're dealing with identity problems, you can tell him! Because you *know* that it is affecting your work. You can talk about it with him, and he'll keep giving you chances, even if you keep messing up. If going to homework lab after school doesn't work, he'll try something else.   ALEXIS

How can new high school teachers, who sometimes look and feel quite close to their students in age, strike that balance of respect, trust, and fairness? How does mutual respect in high school show itself—and what, if anything, does it have to do with how much a student and teacher like each other? What builds trust between teachers and students, and what breaks it down? At a time when students are just developing into adults, how much leeway do they need to make mistakes?

I'm not adult enough to get a job and have my own apartment, but I'm adult enough to make decisions on my own, know right from wrong, have ideas about the world. That's why it's hard to be a teenager—it's like a middle stage.   VANCE

If I have to go to the bathroom, and you tell me not to go, I'm going to go anyway. I'm not trying to be disrespectful, but certain teachers ask me to do something that compromises myself, and I'll say no. It has its effects—then you don't call on me, or you have an expression on your face. You're attacking me back in class. You shouldn't show that it bothers you. It shouldn't have to show in front of other students. Don't ignore me. I'm a student. Yeah, I should have respected you, but you're thirty or forty years old, an adult—you should rise above it, not continue the animosity. No teacher should be rolling their eyes at me.   ALEXIS

One group of student co-authors made up the following rules of thumb they thought applied equally to teachers and students:

IF YOU'RE LOOKING FOR RESPECT . . .

Show up on time.

Take your responsibility seriously, whatever it is. Do what you agreed to do.

Don't insult people's intelligence.

Respect others' right to a separate identity, even if it's not the one you choose.

Don't assume you know everything about someone.

Be careful what you say. Don't make jokes until you know people well enough.

Do Students Need to Like a Teacher?

Everyone likes some people better than others, including students and teachers. But in general kids want teachers to put good teaching ahead of popularity.

It's okay if kids hate you at first. If you care about your teaching, we'll get past that. We're not going to be receptive to someone so quickly—we're kind of young in our thinking.   MIKA

To a certain extent you have to have a personality that students respond to. But that doesn't mean you have to be our best friend, because that will cause our education to suffer. I hate to admit it, but respect and authority are part of the job. Kids expect adults to give us directions and boundaries, but it's a balance.   VANCE

Students often like a teacher who has something in common with them, who seems approachable, or who is closer to their generation and more familiar with youth culture. Though they don't need to know a lot about a teacher's private life, they appreciate a degree of openness and humor.

I relate to one teacher well and a lot of people don't. She is somewhat like me (very sarcastic and moody at times), and I think that's why we click. We talk like we're buddies, and she's always encouraging me.

ALEXIS

The teacher should fill out the same questionnaire and share his answers with the students. Let them laugh at him a little. There's nothing like laughing at a teacher.   LAURALIZ

Liking a teacher can help with learning.

It kind of ruins a subject if you don't like the teacher. I never liked history at all. But this year I have a really cool teacher, and so even if it's hard, even if I don't do well on tests, I'm starting to like it more.

BOSUNG

I really hate calculus, but I really like the teacher so I really work hard and do my homework.   TIFFANY

I have to somewhat like the teacher to be able to learn—to know I can go to that person and ask for help when I need it, and he will be okay with it.   LAURALIZ

But most students are also ready to learn from teachers they may not like on a personal level. Whether or not they like them, they gain more from teachers who care about their material and commit themselves to students' learning.

I don't have to act like I like you, and you don't have to act like you like me, in order for me to learn and you to teach. [I don't like] the way my math teacher teaches, but I know that the way he comes into a classroom, he wants the students to leave knowing math. This makes me open my mind to what he has to say and how he's trying to say it. I'm going to learn whether or not the teacher and I are friends. As long as a teacher is real and the student is real and they are acting in a respectful way, there can be a give-and-take relationship with information.   MIKA

I liked my Spanish teacher most. She was a good teacher but she would get off the subject and talk about other things—she was very easily distracted. She was funny and I like funny teachers. But I learned more from my global studies teacher. He is a great teacher—very serious and strict. He really cares about students; you can tell he likes to teach. He sticks to the subject. It wasn't easy to distract him. When he's done with the lesson he'll make one joke and that will be it—and it will relate to the subject.   LAURALIZ

Must Teachers Like Students?

It matters to students that teachers like being in their company.

It's not as important for a teacher to like the students as it is for the students to think the teacher likes them. Students feel more comfortable and motivated in classes where they think the teacher likes them.   DARYL

But when teachers appear to like some students more than others, they feel uncomfortable, whether or not they count among the favored.

> I would rather not know if I'm a teacher's favorite. It puts me in a weird position. When we're having a test or something, other students will come up to me and say, "Why don't you ask if we can not have it—she likes you." TIFFANY

> My French teacher has a very disturbing habit of calling some of his students his "advanced" students. This gives those that are not "advanced" a feeling of lesser value, and feelings of anger come up. He creates a barrier between himself and students, and even between students in the class. BOSUNG

If teachers don't like students, the students can also tell, and it affects their learning. Even the suspicion that a teacher holds a bias sometimes grows into students feeling that they can't do anything right.

> If the teacher doesn't like you, they won't say, "You can do it," or push you to your full potential. If you miss a day at school, they won't say what you missed and help you out. MONTOYA

> My friend said one little thing, and now that's the end of her. The teacher wrote her off, so she has a 65 now and I have a 90 and we have done nothing different. LAURALIZ

Most students would rather stay somewhere in the middle, not singled out for favor or disfavor. They may not feel comfortable making a personal connection until after a course has ended.

> When I'm their student, I go to them for help and nothing else—it's just something I have. After I'm not their student anymore, I might go to them just to talk; I tell them how my new teacher is, and how I like my new class. MARIBEL

The Importance of Self-respect

Students respect teachers who are comfortable with themselves. Even when teachers come from a different background than students do, if they convey self-respect, kids will respond.

A student has enough common sense to see something in the teacher that they connect with. The teacher doesn't have to throw it to them—the student will choose to make the connection because they see it.   ALEXIS

The teacher has to not be afraid to show himself, and at the same time maintain a boundary. Don't try to look like me, talk like me, dress like me, put your hair in cornrows. The minute you try to broad-cast about yourself in order to make a connection with the kid, that's the minute it fails, because we can sniff out that kind of thing. If you just keep teaching, you will eventually reach someone. We'll put in the effort to connect with you.   VANCE

And they want teachers to act like adults, confident and authoritative.

If you start as an authority figure, the relationships will come. You can get friendly later on. And you can be friendly and still be strict. You have to let them know that you're not one of their peers.   BOSUNG

If you are too friendly with the students, when things get out of con-trol and you try to get authoritative, they're like, "yeah, whatever," and don't pay any attention.   TIFFANY

Fairness Builds Trust and Respect

Students know that by coming to school they are making a bargain with teachers,* and they want it to be a fair one. Here's how they define it:

THE BARGAIN WE MAKE WITH TEACHERS

If you will . . .	Then we will . . .
Show you know and care about the material	Believe the material can be important for us to learn
Treat us as smart and capable of challenging work	Feel respected and rise to the challenge of demanding work

(continued)

* We are grateful to Joseph McDonald at New York University for his framing of "the deal" between students and teachers in a work in progress he shared with us. It afforded an invaluable construct through which our student co-authors explored and analyzed their experiences.

THE BARGAIN WE MAKE WITH TEACHERS *(continued)*

If you will . . .	Then we will . . .
Allow us increasing independence but agree with us on clear expectations	Learn to act responsibly on our own, though we will sometimes make mistakes in the process
Model how to act when you or we make mistakes	Learn to take intellectual risks; learn to make amends when we behave badly
Show respect for our differences and individual styles	Let you limit some of our freedoms in the interest of the group
Keep private anything personal we tell you	Trust you with information that could help you teach us better

Whether they are "hard" or "easy" teachers, the adults who win students' trust and respect are the ones perceived as scrupulously fair in carrying out this usually unspoken bargain. From the very first day, students are alert to signals of whether the teacher will uphold it—and that will largely determine whether they in turn will do their part. Our students listed the following things they hope their teachers will do:

Let us know what to expect from you and the class. When you ask us about ourselves on the first day, answer our questions, too. You don't have to reveal anything you consider private (like whether you have a girlfriend or boyfriend), but we should know certain things from the start. Do you give a zero when homework is not turned in on time? Do you count class participation as part of the final grade?

SOME THINGS WE WANT TO KNOW ON THE FIRST DAY

What will we be studying or doing during this course?

What can we expect for pop quizzes, tests, essays, or projects?

Do you give a lot of homework?

What is your grading system?

Is this class going to be fun? If not, what will make it interesting?

Will you be available to help us outside class?

Know your material.

It feels like we're being punished when the teacher doesn't know the subject well enough to help students. The student has to move on the next year to a higher level, and they'll be stumped in the next year. It's kind of not fair.   ANDRES

I had a math and chemistry teacher that didn't know either subject. If you were quiet, you got an A, and if you were talking, you wouldn't do well. It kind of makes me angry in a way, because when you get to college you'll be stuck. It's okay for a teacher to learn, but they shouldn't take your time to learn it.   MAHOGANY

Push us to do our best—

I had a math teacher who was always on your case: "Write out the problem, turn in your work, you can do it." I didn't like the way he pushed me. But later I thought he was a good teacher—the little things, like "make sure you don't forget to write it all out"—those are the things you need to remember.   DIANA

My algebra teacher, when I got a C in his class, he was upset. He just pushed me to keep my head outa them boys and into the books. He made me go to tutoring after school to keep my grades up.   PORSCHE

—and push us equally.

I have a teacher who pushes the "good" students a lot more than the not-so-good students. Like when a straight-A student doesn't do the work, he'll give that person lectures, but when a lower-grade student doesn't do the work, he'll just give up, like he didn't expect it anyway.
                                                                    DIANA

Some teachers give more of themselves to students who succeed rather than fail. It feels like they're saying, "You're not worth my time because I'm dealing with students who have more potential than you." I don't feel that "go-go-go!" from them.   ALEXIS

Do your part.

You have teachers that are not even responsible. They're not even in class—they leave you there. They give you the assignment and just walk around the halls.   PORSCHE

One teacher made us redo an assignment that I was sure that I had already done, then claimed that we had done it all wrong, just to cover up for the fact that he had lost the assignments. It was an insult to my pride, a waste of time, and a blatant lie. "Because I said so," or "Because I am the teacher," are also not good explanations for punishments. Teachers must be clear and fair, or students will be hurt or angry.   BOSUNG

Make sure everyone understands. Give the slower students among us a chance without putting them on the spot.

When you have a question, it's better if the teacher comes and stands by your desk instead of saying "What do you need?" from across the room.   PORSCHE

[Some teachers] don't care whether you're smart or dumb. They don't talk to you; if you're failing a class they don't ask you "What's the matter?" They let you fail, and they don't give you makeup work.
                                                          MONTOYA

Grade us fairly.

If someone gives you a bad grade, they should tell you exactly why. We have this Spanish teacher that grades Latino kids so hard it's impossible for them to get As no matter how hard you try.   DIANA

Sometimes [favoritism] shows in their opinions on papers and comments on grades—which is the worst thing, because students always compare their grades with each other.   MARIBEL

AM I PLAYING FAVORITES? A Reflective Exercise for Teachers

Pick out a representative mix of students from your class. Using copies of this questionnaire or blank pages in a notebook or journal, answer the following questions.

Student's name _____

Things I like about the student

Personal choices (clothes, hair, posture, language, cooperation)

Academic choices (does work, participates)

_____

Things that annoy me about the student
Personal choices (clothes, hair, posture, language, rule-breaking)

_____

Academic choices (does work, participates)

_____

Positive attention I paid the student today *(check any that apply)*
☐ Called on in an encouraging way
☐ Asked how things are going
☐ Trusted with an important responsibility
☐ Asked his or her thoughts on a question that matters
☐ Acknowledged good work or helpful contribution by student
☐ Responded to something in the student's writing

Negative attention I paid the student today
☐ Used sarcasm in class to make my point with the student
☐ Criticized in class
☐ Did not offer specific encouragement to speak
☐ Imposed behavior sanctions (gave detention, sent to office, etc.)

Most recent grade(s) I gave the student_____

After you have completed the questionnaire for several students, look over the results and reflect in writing on the following questions:

Did students with lower grades have more "personal choices" that annoyed me?

Did students with higher grades receive more positive attention from me?

What could I do to increase positive attention to students whose choices annoy me?

Understand that we make mistakes.

Because of something that happened in ninth grade, she won't sit down with me and talk to me about anything. So I do the same back to her—I don't smile at her or respect her. Teachers need to make allowance for the fact that we change from year to year and even from week to week. Sometimes I'm just acting hotheaded, I need to clear the air and then come back and apologize. I can acknowledge the things I do wrong.   ALEXIS

We're some moody-ass people right now!   MIKA

We're growing.   VANCE

Don't denigrate us, especially in public.

One teacher would say out loud, "You're getting a D," or other negative things in front of other students, disrespecting them.

MAHOGANY

I respect this one teacher, but I feel like she doesn't respect me. She'll say things in front of the class that make me feel bad, like "you didn't do this" or "you did this wrong."   DIANA

Keep your biases to yourself.

This gay kid in my class was putting something on his lips, and the teacher said, "You don't need to put on lip gloss in class!" If a girl put on lip gloss in class, he wouldn't say that. Then the boys in class felt like they could laugh at that kid. If the teacher could make comments, they felt like they could, too.   TIFFANY

By the looks of a kid, some teachers think he'll be a troublemaker. People say, "They're black, they do drugs," that kind of thing. If the teacher judges kids like that, the kids start saying the teacher's racist and they have less respect for that teacher.   MARIBEL

Don't treat us like little kids.

Teenagers don't think of themselves as children, even from the ninth grade. Teachers should realize that they're working with kids who feel that they are somewhat adults and don't like to be treated as little kids, even though in actuality they are kids. In my mind you're not my parent, you're my teacher. That line goes but so far. Don't overstep your boundary.   ALEXIS

Part of a teacher's job is giving teenagers the practice at that independence—not just controlling the kids in their classes but actually giving them more ability to try things out for themselves.

MAHOGANY

Listen to what we think.

Some teachers have a way of making themselves more approachable. They do not seem like hard, old teachers who sternly instruct the class; a student can go up and carry out a conversation without feeling awkward. This gives the class a more comfortable and accepting atmosphere to learn in.   BOSUNG

Sometimes my teachers ask me things like, "What grade do you think I'm going to give you if you didn't do the work?" Then they get upset if I seem to actually be thinking of what the answer might be. A lot of times I'm not interested in the work.   DIANA

QUESTIONS WE WISH A TEACHER WOULD ASK

Would you like extra credit?

Will you be able to do homework over the weekend?

How would you like to make up your homework/projects?

How are you feeling—do you want to do your work right now, or for homework?

Do you need a ride to and from school?

Do you have lunch money?

What could I be doing to help you learn better?

Care what's going on with us.

Some teachers start to fill a void that maybe isn't being addressed at home. Teachers are our de facto parents for the seven or so hours you're with them. I don't really have a father, so I guess it's important talking to a guy who seems to know what's going on in the world, respects you, knows what's going on with you.   VANCE

School lets you find some adults you can connect with. There might be something really important, like pregnancy, that you can't talk to your parents about, but you know you have to talk to adults about. I have one of these relationships with my adviser. I think I trust him because I see him so often; he's my teacher for two classes, and I have a free [period] with him.   ANDRES

Don't betray our confidences.

You want to be able to trust a teacher. You don't want to be telling them your problem and then have them go to other teachers and say you have a problem, or tell your mom you should see a psychiatrist. Some teachers, it's like you tell them something and then there's a microphone attached to them.   PORSCHE

If you have that trust with a teacher, it could go kind of wrong. They might look down on you because you did something that you're not telling other people. It makes you wonder if it will affect how you do in their class.   ANDRES

Sometimes the chance to stand in each other's shoes can build respect between teachers and students.

In the very beginning of the class, our teacher had us write for homework one night about how we would teach a history class if we were teachers. She didn't use what I wrote down, but it got the students to recognize how hard it was to teach it.   HILARY

One day we had to plan a lesson. She gave us a topic, and we had to research it and make a lesson plan. Each day the students got to teach, and we got to see where she was coming from, in terms of having everyone in the class pay attention and learn from you. That changed our class a lot—now every time we get disruptive, she reminds us how we felt in that situation.   MAHOGANY

Fairness Affects Classroom Behavior

A teacher's fairness, trust, and respect have a lot of influence on how students feel about themselves and about their teachers. But they also have an important effect on students' behavior in the classroom.

The worst thing for a teacher is to be considered unfair, because students then try to take advantage of it. If you're the favorite one, you think you can get away with certain things. If you're the "down" one, sometimes you can shut yourself off, or try to control the class instead of the teacher.   MARIBEL

If you hurt me with your words, I'm gonna say or do something that I know is gonna hurt you.   ALEXIS

SUMMARY
HOW TO SHOW RESPECT, TRUST, AND FAIRNESS

- Let us know what to expect from you and from the class.
- Know your material.
- Push us to do our best—and push us equally.
- Do your part.
- Make sure everyone understands.
- Grade us fairly.
- Understand that we make mistakes.
- Don't denigrate us.
- Keep your biases to yourself.
- Don't treat us like little kids.
- Listen to what we think.
- Care what's going on with us.
- Don't betray our confidences.

3

Teachers' Voices: Rethinking Teacher Education for Diversity

Lisa Delpit

There can be no doubt that issues of diversity form the crux of what may be one of the biggest challenges yet to face those of us whose business it is to educate teachers. In the wake of reports proposing the complete reformation of teacher education has come a groundswell of concern about the effects of reform-related activities on the participation of ethnically and culturally diverse teachers in the workforce.[1]

Concern is not misplaced; conservative estimates suggest that black, Hispanic, Asian, and Native American children presently comprise almost 30 percent of the school-age population, and "minority" students represent a majority in all but two of our twenty-five largest cities. Furthermore, by some estimates the turn of the century will find up to 40 percent nonwhite children in American classrooms.[2] Yet the current number of teachers from nonwhite groups threatens to fall below 10 percent, and the percentage of education degrees conferred onto members of these groups decreased by more than 6 percent between 1981 and 1985; additional data suggest a continued downward trend.[3] Patricia Graham, then dean of Harvard's Graduate School of Education, put it succinctly: "Most teachers who teach today's children are white; tomorrow's teaching force will be even more so."[4]

Researchers have cited many reasons for the decline of minority participation in the teaching force—among them, the overall decline of the numbers of college-bound students from ethnic groups, the widening of professional opportunities for people of color, the increased prevalence of competency examinations, the lack of prestige for teaching as a profession, low salaries, and less than optimal working conditions. Numerous recommendations have been made to try to remedy the situation: providing increased financial aid to students of color, recruiting nontraditional college students (for example, military retirees), providing "test-wiseness" instruction to increase the passing rates on various state or institution-mandated examinations, raising teacher salaries, and restructuring schools to provide teachers with more autonomy and more opportunities for career advancement. While many of these recommendations have proven useful, the problem still exists.

In the course of defining the problem and seeking viable solutions, we in the research community have seldom looked to teachers themselves as major sources of guidance. When ethnically diverse teachers are asked to reflect on "the problem," additional dimensions come to the fore. The following personal statements were collected in the course of conducting research about the attitude of educators of color toward their preservice and in-service teacher education, and their subsequent teaching lives:

An African-American elementary teacher on her teacher education experience in a predominantly white institution:

> My teacher education was just a joke. I did everything I was supposed to do, but they weren't impressed. I was just too confident and outspoken. So I said to myself, "I guess I have to play their game." I had to shuffle my feet; Lisa, I literally had to grin and bow! And then I got an *A*. This was my freshman year. I was the only black person in the class. Coming from the inner city, where at least teachers would treat you kind of fair, I thought these people could give me constructive criticism. That's all I ever asked for. I know I'm not perfect. White people—I guess it's going to sound racist—but white people want black people to be humble, to be grateful they gave them a little bit of time. Usually I just can't do it, but I should have gotten the Academy Award for my performance [in teacher education classes]! So to me, the joke started then and went on for four years.

A Native Alaskan teacher is talking about her teacher training experiences:

> I must have heard this so many times, that Native kids are low achievers. It used to frustrate me to hear that, and here I used to think, *what they don't know.* What I thought was that these "educators" have never really been out there. They just went by what they learned from books.
>
> I had a hang-up about this for a long time. I used to try to strike back without realizing what I was saying. Finally I started to say to myself, "In order to get through this thing, I have to pass this course, even though they're talking about *me.* "
>
> This is happening in my graduate classes right now. They're talking about Native kids, and I relate it to me—"low achievers," "high

dropouts," "they don't function well academically." We are labeled right from the beginning. I hear these things about my people and I get so frustrated.

An African-American woman who left teaching talks about her cooperating teacher:

> She thought all black children were poor, but the kids in that school weren't poor. She kept talking about how we couldn't expect too much from them because they were poor. She even thought *I* was poor. She kept asking me questions like, "Is your father unemployed a lot?"

A Native Alaskan teacher speaking on what she learned in teacher education courses:

> I only learned how to teach white kids. I didn't learn one thing about teaching Native kids. It *is* different, you know. But I don't think they even thought about that.

Clearly, in some sense, these educators feel themselves to be victimized by the institutions that seek to educate them. They believe their voices to be unheard, their concerns unheeded. The intent of the ongoing research described herein is to collect those voices and concerns in order to assist those of us in teacher education to better address the needs of preservice and in-service teachers of color. It is my hope as well that the findings will provide insights into how to better prepare those from the larger culture to teach the increasingly diverse student bodies they are likely to face in the course of their careers.

The data were collected in twelve in-depth, two-hour ethnographic interviews with six African-American and six Native American teachers or former teachers (see page 51 of the Notes section for the open-ended interview schedule), supplemented by five shorter telephone interviews with black teachers, and a group meeting with Native Alaskan teachers.[5]

What do people of color have to say about their experiences as prepro-fessional and professional educators? Despite the diverse ethnicities and backgrounds represented in the sample, the teachers interviewed showed surprising consensus on several points:

1. Most of the black and Native teachers interviewed believe accounts of their own experiences are not validated in teacher education programs or in their subsequent teaching lives.

A Native teacher who graduated in 1985 said that at the university there was no communication between the other non-Native students and herself or between her instructors and herself, "except to tell me that I did something wrong. I never felt I could say anything." She added that her sister, whom she described as usually assertive, quit the university because "no one would listen to her." This teacher also complained about courses outside the education department, particularly about history courses which she believed presented a one-sided view of the world:

> Those history books just said, "The Russians set up camp in Ruby" [an Alaskan village]. Nowhere did they talk about how they killed Natives for sport or stole women from their families and forced them to get married. My own Aunt ——— was one of those women. They [the professors and students] just couldn't see the other side. Finally, in all my classes I just gave up and decided to learn what they said to learn, so I could get out. If they said 2 + 3 = 5, I learned that. If they said Christopher Columbus discovered America, I regurgitated it back to them.

Another Native teacher, who completed teacher education in 1973 but never entered the teaching profession, reported that during her teacher education she always thought she should "shut up and forget about it" when people said things she knew were wrong:

> But then I started saying, "How come we can't say anything?" Then, when I tried to talk, they always said I didn't make sense. I kept hearing, "Could you explain yourself more?"
>
> Later, I began to think I must be a radical or a racist or something because *they* always said, "Everything's great, why make a fuss." I'd say, *"No, it's not!"*

Students of color are doubly disadvantaged in trying to get their voices heard, particularly in the university classroom. First, the university does not as a rule value personal narratives as having a legitimate cognitive function. Discourse in the university setting is more valued if it reflects independence of context, analysis, and objectification of experience. Such a style is more associated with written text, and consequently an oral mode that calls upon the written for validation (that is, citing previously recorded research) is more valued.

Because these students' experiences have not, in general, been so codified, they typically have no written text available upon which to call. Furthermore, they are often members of cultural groups for which narrative is

the preferred means of information transfer.[6] Thus, students find themselves feeling, as one African-American said, that the university professors
and students "only want to go by research they've read that other white
people have written," and that "if you can't quote Vygotsky . . . , then you
don't have any validity to speak about your *own* kids." Cazden paraphrases
an Alaskan Tlingit Indian woman in graduate school at Harvard:

> When someone, even an undergraduate, raises a question that is
> based on what some authority says, Professor X says, "That's a great
> question!", expands on it, and incorporates it into her following com-
> ments. But when people like me talk from our personal experience,
> our ideas are not acknowledged. The professor may say, "Hmhm,"
> and then proceed as if we hadn't been heard.[7]

A second reason that the stories of students of color may go unheard or un-
validated is that, as some scholars suggest, true performance of narrative is
connected to such factors as similar background and a shared sense of
identity.[8] Therefore, narratives are most likely to be "heard" or considered
legitimate when they are shared among people who consider themselves in
some way comembers of a group.[9] To the extent that people of color (or
students in general, for that matter) are not considered comembers of the
university professor's group, it is unlikely that their personal narratives will
be valued. Additional evidence suggests that, indeed, teachers of color do
not feel that in the university or in their subsequent teaching lives their
own cultural groups are considered to be of equal status with the dominant
culture. This is further discussed with the next generalization gleaned
from the interviews.

2. *The teachers interviewed frequently encountered negative and/or stereotypical cultural and racial attitudes directed toward themselves and toward ethnic minority
children during their teacher education and subsequent teaching lives.*

Every one of the teachers interviewed related experiencing some form
of what they considered to be racial bias.[10] Three interviewees who left the
teaching profession entirely cite these experiences as their major reasons
for leaving:

A forty-one-year-old black man who completed his math/science education degree in 1969, spoke of leaving teaching after two years in a junior
high school in Alabama:

> I left teaching because I got totally dissatisfied with the system I was a
> part of. The staff was 98 percent white and 2 percent black. Near the
> end of the first year, I realized that I was the only staff member inter-

ested in helping *students* progress, not in just covering the course material. I found I had to teach reading before I could teach science. I started asking questions: "Why hadn't the faculty taught the basics?" Eventually, I started telling faculty they weren't doing their job.

The black kids were bussed as a result of desegregation. They got the kids there, all right, but nobody cared about them once they got there. Finally I left because it was too much to handle. I couldn't get through to the staff that they were hurting kids. People really didn't care about black kids, whether they learned or not. There was so much inequality. Black kids just weren't given the attention they needed.

The other teachers and the department head thought we [he and the other black science teacher] were rabble-rousers because we kept pushing them to really teach black kids. . . . In a way, I'm sorry I quit, but then I probably would have gotten fired anyway.

A Native woman who completed teacher education in 1973, decided not to enter teaching after graduation. To be sure, part of her decision was based on another job offer, but she declared that her primary reason for leaving was her experience in student teaching:

The teachers at ———— [a boarding school for Native students] had the attitude that the students were hard to teach. Some told me that they didn't think the [Native] kids knew *how* to think. One teacher told me he'd give me a million dollars *if* I could figure out how to teach these kids. Now I know that there is a way, I should go back and collect! It wasn't that the kids couldn't think, it was that [those teachers] couldn't teach. . . .

From student teaching, I realized what kind of treatment I'd get from the other teachers—they wouldn't even let me use the Xerox machine. I expected that if I went into teaching, the other teachers would all tell me everything I was doing wrong. It was just too discouraging.

She added that, based on her own experience and her children's experiences in village schools, she knew that the teachers always separated themselves from the village people. "I'd have to choose sides—either with the teachers or with the village—and I'd choose the village. It would be too hard being in the middle like that."

The third nonteaching education graduate, a black woman who completed college in 1964 but decided not to begin a teaching career, also

cites her student teaching experience as the reason she chose not to enter
the profession:

> The school in which I did my student teaching, ——— High School
> in Detroit, was in transition from middle-class Jewish to black. The
> school was tracked. The highest track was all white, the middle track
> was mixed, and the lowest track was all black. . . . There was no at-
> tempt to understand black children, to reach these children or to
> make positive educational experiences for them. They would just tol-
> erate them at best.
>
> My cooperating teacher was just ruinous for black kids. She was ru-
> inous for low-achieving black kids. She had no notion of how to build
> self-esteem, or even that she should. In her opinion, the bright kids
> deserved attention, and she was there to prove that the others
> couldn't learn.
>
> After that one semester of student teaching, I felt I just couldn't
> work in the public school system. The system was corrupt, and I'd be
> fighting and fussing the whole time. No, the system was murderous. It
> didn't exist to educate children. I realized it was bigger than me, and
> I had to leave.

Other interviewees encountered attitudes of bias that can be organized
into four categories: bias toward children of color by nonminority teachers; bias against the interviewee by parents and/or children in a predominantly white school; bias toward the interviewee by other teachers; and bias
toward the interviewee or stereotypic attitudes directed toward his or her
cultural group by the university curriculum, professors, or fellow students.
None of the interviewees reported experiencing bias in all four categories,
but all cited experience in at least one.

Several comments about negative attitudes expressed toward children
have been cited above. Another black teacher complained of a white
teacher who loudly chastised two Athabaskan Indian children in the hallway, referring to them as "wild Indians."

Four teachers commented that white children and/or parents sometimes questioned their authority. A Native junior high school teacher reported that during her first year of teaching some white children would ask
derisively, "Who hired you?" One black and two Native teachers said that
white parents were more likely to seek conferences with them than with
their white colleagues, were more likely to wish to observe their teaching
(in some instances, even when they did not have children in the interviewee's classroom!), and were more likely to complain about their teaching.

Five teachers felt discriminated against at one time or another by their white colleagues, ranging from stereotyping (one black teacher complained that during student teaching her cooperating teacher wanted to know if her family was on welfare) to feelings of isolation (a Native teacher reported that she hung around the teachers' lounge for weeks in a large predominantly white high school without getting to know even one other teacher).

Perhaps the most poignant story is from a young Native woman who was in her first year of teaching. She was the only Native teacher at an elementary school with a black woman principal. She said that some of the other teachers resented her because they perceived the African-American principal as providing her with preferential treatment:

> It's difficult being the only Native here. I was an aide here before I received my degree, and everyone was very nice. Now I get a lot of resentment from the staff. I think it's because they resent the fact that a Native was hired [in a tight job market]; they think it should have been a white person.
>
> They don't give my degree as much credibility. Two teachers set up a meeting with me after school and told me I wasn't doing my job. They said I was the principal's favorite so she's not telling me all the things I'm doing wrong. It's people like that who intimidate me. I went home feeling bad about myself, feeling so incompetent.
>
> I even think some teachers pick on my students because they're my kids. I feel so excluded. They don't share anything with me. I found my own material, developed my own style to show them I could do it.

Finally, six teachers cited the fourth kind of biased behavior in their experiences in the university during their teacher education. Negative attitudes in the university appear to be expressed in two ways: directly toward the student, and/or more generally toward the student's cultural group. This bias can be classified, according to Benokraitis and Feagin's scheme of discrimination, as "overt" (most blatant), "covert" (clandestine, maliciously motivated), and "subtle" (unequal treatment that is visible but so internalized as to be considered routine in bureaucratized settings).[11]

Two of the teachers reported overt discrimination from their professors, who implied they were not sufficiently competent to complete the university program. One black teacher was told, for example, "You're not really capable of doing this work. You're only here because somebody paid your way." Another black teacher talked about what she perceived as covert discrimination when, during her teacher education, a group of professors met (without her knowledge) to discuss how to get her to resign from the program.

The most common experience of bias at the university falls into the category of subtle discrimination. The interviewees refer to such discrimination when they complain of the lack of credence given to their words and opinions. In addition, Native interviewees particularly complained that some of their instructors exhibited what Mehrabian has labeled "low immediacy" behaviors when interacting with them: "colder" voice tone, less eye contact, and distanced body orientation.[12] One of these educators commented that such behavior "made me feel like I wasn't there." Another said that she felt like the professor wanted her to "just disappear."

Several interviewees criticized professors, students, and the curriculum for perpetuating stereotypes about people of color. This kind of discrimination is exemplified by the comments of a Native woman who objected when a fellow student declared in class that one could not expect Native children to speak in a classroom "because they're just not like that, they're very silent." The people from her region, she counters, "are *very* vocal, and children are taught to be vocal, too." She continued:

> I resented those kinds of stereotypes about Native children. I remember in a reading class there was a discussion. The generalization was made that Native children coming from a village are a lot slower than white children living in town, and that you've got to expect this and you've got to expect that. And really, when everybody knows the clout of teacher expectations, people who say that really burn me up. They develop a very narrow view, a stereotype of how a Native child is. They don't really look at that child as a person, but as a Native. That was one thing I struggled with as well, people supposing things about me before getting to know me.

Another Native teacher said that "reading all those studies about 'the plight of Native students' made me feel like part of a group of people who were failures and I was the one exception. Why do they do that? I guess that's one way for a dominant culture to maintain dominance—not to recognize any of the strengths of another group." (It is sobering to realize that most of what concerns these teachers was probably added to the curriculum in an attempt to address issues of cultural diversity.)

Several researchers have observed that there are large numbers of non-white teachers who are certified to teach but are not teaching.[13] Consequently, those who seek to increase the numbers of teachers of color cannot only recruit new minority students to teacher education programs; they must identify why teachers leave the profession. If these interviews are in any way representative of the larger population, in order to recruit and *retain* teachers of color, schools of education must find means to address what these teachers perceive as racial discrimination during teacher education and beyond.

It is not easy to fulfill such a charge, in part because racial discrimination in present-day America is less likely to be the overt, blatant bigotry of the past. In a review of the survey data on racial attitudes gathered from 1942 to 1983, for example, another group of researchers has documented that there have indeed been major changes in white stereotypes of blacks and in abstract principles applied to racial issues: in 1942 only 42 percent of those whites surveyed believed that blacks had the same intelligence as whites. By 1956 that percentage increased to 80 percent, where it remained until the study was conducted.[14] Again, in 1942 only 42 percent of whites surveyed thought blacks "should have as good a chance as white people to get any kind of job"; by 1972, 97 percent did so.[15]

However, despite change in the stated beliefs of the white population, recent studies depict their actions as reflecting other values. Researchers have found that the reactions of whites to people of color display subtle discriminatory behavior: less assistance, greater aggression, overt friendliness coupled with covert rejection, avoidance, and assessment inconsistent with actual work performance.[16] Furthermore, whites are seldom conscious of this "modern prejudice," even as they practice it. Pettigrew and Martin discuss the ramifications of modern prejudice for black professionals:

> Precisely because of their subtlety and indirectness, these modern forms of prejudice and avoidance are hard to eradicate. Often the black is the only person in a position to draw the conclusion that prejudice is operating in the work situation. Whites have usually observed only a subset of the incidents, any one of which can be explained away by a nonracial account. Consequently, many whites remain unconvinced of the reality of subtle prejudice and discrimination, and come to think of their black coworkers as "terribly touchy" and "overly sensitive" to the issue. For such reasons, the modern forms of prejudice frequently remain invisible even to its (sic) perpetrators.[17]

Furthermore, the issue is apparently not just one of biased expectations and evaluations. Some researchers have demonstrated that bias can actually *cause* lowered performance for those who are its victims, possibly as a result of unexpressed anger, alienation, low morale, and other mental and physical symptoms of stress.[18] It is easy to anticipate how such lowered performance can readily lead to even greater stereotyping and bias, thus increasing the minority person's sense of alienation and frustration. And in an age of proliferating competency examinations, perhaps actually lowering achievement potential as well.

3. The teachers interviewed report significant differences from their white colleagues in classroom pedagogy and discipline, saying that their teaching styles are most influenced by their own experiences as learners, their reflections about their students, and from the culture bearers in their community.

In an informal survey of a class of graduate students, fourteen of fifteen white teachers named external sources as having the most influence on their present teaching styles: either a role model (typically a childhood teacher or a cooperating teacher during student teaching) or an in-service education class (such as writing project). This is in line with other findings which suggest that the majority of teachers tend to model their teaching on methodological orientations taught in teacher education or on other practicing teachers they have encountered.[19]

This is in sharp contrast to the teachers of color interviewed. All but one of these teachers cited internal sources of knowledge as a primary basis for their own teaching: reflections on their own experiences as learners or their own ability to assess and create. When an external source was cited, it was typically a nonformally-educated culture bearer in the teacher's community. In response to questions about what influenced their teaching style most, teachers' statements reflect these perspectives:

I tried to remember how I learned. I teach the way I learned, not the way I was taught.

I created my teaching from my own personal concerns—what was important to improve the condition of black people.

I knew how to teach Native children because I went through the same frustrations they went through.

I brought to mind remnants from how I was taught—and then I did the opposite.

My own experiences as a student influenced me the most.

My own self-determination—my ability to monitor, adjust, make things interesting.

I knew my culture and that's what helped me to know how to teach. I spent time with community people, particularly my mom—and she brought to mind what I had learned.

My mother. I think about how she raised her children and try to treat my students like that. She has influenced my style the most, even though she never went to college.

The one teacher whose comments did not fit into this general pattern was a black man whose own education, from elementary school through college, was in all-black settings. He spoke of his black teachers as role models: "I learned to teach from them; sometimes you have to see a master at work. I taught science the way I was taught science."

With the exception of this one man, a primary reason for the lack of external models for those interviewed may be the perception of a significant difference between themselves and other teachers in what constitutes good teaching. To summarize their responses, the teachers interviewed believed that what they encountered in their own careers as students, preservice teachers, and in-service teachers, was not often good teaching in their estimation. By contrast, they declared that:

1. Good teachers care whether students learn. They challenge all students, even those who are less capable, and then help them to meet the challenge.
2. Good teachers are not time-bound to a curriculum and do not move on to new subject matter until all students grasp the current concept.
3. Good teachers are not bound to books and instructional materials, but connect all learning to "real life."
4. Good teachers push students to think, to make their own decisions.
5. Good teachers communicate with, observe, and get to know their students and the students' cultural background.

Black and Native teachers alike expressed similar beliefs. Interestingly, although the question was not framed in racial terms, when asked how their teaching differed from the other educators around them, almost all the teachers responded by contrasting their conception of good teaching with that of white teachers (probably because the teachers interviewed taught in predominantly white settings). In order to clarify the distinctions they made, the teachers often called upon their experiences as learners:

A black principal of eleven years who taught junior high science for four years:
White teachers follow the curriculum in books and don't make it relevant. They apply it to the future—to what they'll need in college. But many kids don't go on to college. How can they use it now?

A black teacher of twelve years: I think everybody should be challenged. We work hard, but it's not boring. When the other teachers get a child who's a little slower they just let them sit there. I refuse to let even one child vegetate in my room.

A Native woman who decided not to teach after becoming certified: In high school I had only one Native teacher who taught American History. She made us *think.* She let us do all the talking. She used to say, "If you don't talk, who's going to talk for you; if you don't think, who's going to think for you?" I was surprised she told us we had to think. No other teacher had ever said that to us.

A Native teacher who graduated in 1985 and taught for two years: The books were alien to me, so I figured they'd be alien to the kids. I taught differently from the white teachers. I put a lot of Alaska into it. I taught the books, but I always put it in the present tense—showed the kids how what we read about was connected to me and to them. . . . Some of the white teachers were very nice; it's just that they are so into the books, books, books.

A black woman who decided not to teach after becoming certified: I had a really second-rate education in junior high and high school. Most of my teachers were white. Their approach was to pat us on the back and tell us we were fine. Nothing was required. They just gave up on us. . . . Once I had a black teacher who was really tough—but I loved her because she *cared.* She even dared to flunk people. She made us do difficult tasks, made us think hard about what we were doing. The others thought we didn't need schooling because we'd never be anything anyway, so there was no need to worry about teaching.

A black retired mathematics teacher: You have to justify what you want kids to learn. You have to show them how they'll use it. I got interested in math because my grandfather used to be a carpenter. He'd show me how to do all the calculations to build things. I showed my students how each thing I asked them to learn was useful to real life. White teachers want to get through the book, but I think it's more important to *really* learn a *few* things than to *not* learn a *lot* of things.

A black teacher who taught for two years and left the profession in 1971: Other staff felt that the most important thing was to get through the book. We [he and a black coworker] didn't try to cover the book. The department head said you have to cover the material—*x* number of pages in the semester. We said, why leave a chapter until it's fully covered and everyone understands the basic concepts? She wanted us to move on, thought we weren't teaching properly. . . . I like to challenge kids. Sometimes you open up an area and kids get excited. I think you should let kids explore a topic. I'd stay on it for a week, ask them what they wanted to do with it, where they think we should go. . . . My [black] science teacher always asked questions. You had to *think* in his class. He was always asking questions. He wouldn't just give it to you, you had to think and be creative. That's how I teach.

A Native teacher of two years: If there's someone who doesn't understand what I'm teaching, I try to understand who they are.

A black elementary principal who taught for seven years: My philosophy is, if it's boring to me, it's boring for the kids. I tried to make things fun, but realistic, rooted in the kids' real lifestyle. Then I integrated skills into all of that. Minority teachers bring in realistic things, white teachers are more superficial, more book-oriented. Minority teachers expect kids to make their own decisions; white teachers tell kids everything to do. Minority teachers say, "What do *you* think you need to do?" The kids have to make the decision.

A black teacher who now works in an administrative central office position: With my black elementary teachers you had to talk just like in a Baptist church. You have to *talk* to the preacher. There's got to be a dialogue. If you don't feel comfortable with your students, you won't do this. My instructors [in a black college] knew what you knew because they talked to you. They *knew* the students. That's really the only way to teach. . . . Teaching is all about telling a story. You have to get to know kids so you'll know how to tell the story, you can't tell it just one way. You can tell if you're on the right track by watching the kids. If their facial expressions aren't right, change the story.

A black teacher of seven years: You have to know the kids. They teach me how to teach them. They may be from all kinds of backgrounds and cultures, but if you really listen to them, they'll tell you how to teach them.

A middle-aged Native teacher who has taught in a village for two years: They [white teachers in the school] keep waiting for some program on a white horse to ride in and save them. I focus on the kids, think about what I didn't know at their age and teach that.

A first-year Native teacher in a multicultural urban setting: I believe that
the curriculum guides aren't the Bible. I'm teaching kids, not books.
The teachers move through the books whether the kids get it or not,
so I end up getting minority kids who can't read. . . . I use the curriculum guide, but move beyond it. I make the story connect to the kids'
real lives.

*A Native teacher who taught in a village for three years and then moved into
bilingual education administration:* You have to have high expectations.
If you challenge kids, they'll do what you want. Tell them they can all
get As, then tell them how to do it. They'll work for you if you challenge them and help them get there.

In addition to these highly consistent statements about pedagogy, the
Native teachers also observed that their disciplinary styles were different
from those of dominant culture teachers. They told of getting into trouble
with their administrators for not forcefully demanding obedience from
their pupils. The teachers seem to believe that it is unnecessary and excep-
tionally rude to shout at students or to use other coercive means to control
behavior. They preferred to allow students to have opportunities to vent
frustrations or to disagree with stated rules. When it was necessary to
change behavior, they sought to do so by appealing to affiliation rather than
authority. "Our people don't act like that" was often the unstated message.

Given the teachers' perspective that their own ideas about teaching are
so different from what they consider to be the mainstream norm, it is not
surprising that most of those interviewed spoke of teacher education as
just something "to get through" rather than as something to learn from.
When the teachers spoke of learning anything during the experience, it
was likely to be subject area knowledge or the more technical or more superficial aspects of the profession, for example, writing lesson plans, giving
tests, learning the jargon, gaining an understanding of mainstream values,
learning "how to act like a teacher"—and, as one teacher put it, "learning
to bullshit." This lack of true involvement in the teacher education experience can only have been exacerbated by the final generalized factor to be
discussed.

*4. The teachers interviewed often felt isolated from instructors and other students
during their teacher training.*

Because of the communication difficulties between instructors and students, many of the students of color felt that they were not able to talk to
many of their white professors. The Native teachers, in particular, found
communication with professors and other students difficult. Four dropped

out of college (although they later returned), in part because they felt so isolated in the dormitories and in classrooms:

> You get awfully lonely when no one can or will communicate with you. A lot of Native students run home and never come back. Others turn to drugs and alcohol just to fill the emptiness. Many don't make it, but those that go through have to learn to find companionship.

Six of the interviewees found professors of color to provide that companionship, and in several instances, these individuals became the interviewees' only motivation to remain in school. These professors established what the students perceived to be a human and caring relationship in a generally indifferent environment, and also served as role models for what they might become:

> I had one Native teacher in college, and this is where I relaxed and where I didn't have to feel pushed. My colleague, a Native from Kiana, and I used to just sit in there and say, "Oh what a relief to come to this class where we're not being threatened by so many things—academically, by words, all those uppity words. Here we can really talk to the teacher and we're able to talk our own language and work toward something we enjoy."

> Professor ———, at the University, was a role model for me—just to see a Native teaching. I always looked forward to going to his classes. I never went up to him to talk, but just seeing him made me want to go on. There was one black professor who was also a friend. I could talk to that professor about my frustrations. That's the only way I made it through.

One teacher had been enrolled in a special field-delivered, village-based teacher education program in which there was strong focus on using the village as a source of knowledge and in which the professors established individual tutoring relationships with the students. She reported that these white male professors were primarily responsible for her completing the program:

> Those teachers were just bothersome. It seemed like they knew when I was on the verge of quitting and they just showed up at my door. They spent so many hours with me. I started thinking that if *they* thought I could do it, then I could do it. They really cared. I really finished for them—it's like I owed it to them.

It is clear that the interviewees' difficulties are complicated by issues of cultural background, class, and individual differences, but if we wish to address the problem, we must give credibility to these educators' *perceptions* of the problem.

How can teacher education programs be expected to do that? First, given these teachers' response to the presence of faculty of color (that is, a reduced sense of isolation and alienation, an increased comfort level, and a sense of having an ally and/or role model), we would do well to seek to diversify our faculties. Members of a diverse faculty can also assist each other in understanding the needs of—and avoiding unintentional slights or insults to—diverse students; no individual can be expected to understand the intricacies of every culture without the assistance of members from those cultures.

Until schools of education can reach that apparently elusive goal of an ethnically representative faculty, however, the results from one interview suggest that nonminority faculty can also serve to reduce the sense of isolation. A Native village woman found great support from her white male instructors who provided individual attention and encouragement. This suggests the establishment of special, institutionalized mentoring relationships between university professors and students of color, a relationship that has shown positive results in other settings.[20] Another means of reducing isolation might be organizing students into cohorts, teams, or support groups. Such a structure may also help to reduce the negative repercussions of what has been called "token"[21] or "solo"[22] status, a condition occurring when a single individual is viewed as a representative of a low status group, often accompanied by assumptions of incompetence by majority culture members.

But there are larger problems at issue here, dilemmas not only for people of color but for all of us in teacher education specifically and for society in general: How can we structure education to encourage the active participation of students of color, and, for that matter, of all students? How can we best prepare our "mainstream" students to teach in the pluralistic society to which they will matriculate? How can we improve the education of the "minority" children who are likely to soon comprise the majority of children in our public schools? How can we lessen the "modern prejudice" that pervades our society, alienating and disempowering large segments of our population? I believe a reconceptualization of how we structure teacher education may provide the beginnings of a solution for all these issues.

The interviews quoted herein contain a gold mine of knowledge about how to educate not only teachers but *children* of color. From the interviewees' own learning experiences and from their knowledge of their own cultural backgrounds, they have developed models for educating children of their own cultural groups. Yet, judging from their reports, often this knowledge is barred from teacher education classes and not even formally explored with other teachers of the same culture. In short, we are, by virtue of our own pedagogical practices, excluding a great source of knowledge from our education curricula.

What might be the result if we restructure education classes so that all students are not merely allowed but *encouraged* to bring in their prior knowledge, their past experience, their own stories? The idea is not new. John Dewey advocated such a stance in 1904. In an article on the relationship between theory and practice in teacher education, he asserts that the "greatest asset in the student's possession—the greatest, moreover that ever will be in his possession—[is] his own direct and personal experience."[23]

Dewey recommends that students be encouraged to bring their personal experiences to bear upon subject matter presented in the classroom. Doing otherwise, he warns, prevents teachers from developing and using their own independent intelligence and reinforces their "intellectual subserviency." Dewey further advises that failure to allow students to explore their past experiences in light of theoretical constructs will produce only a mindless imitation of others' practice rather than a reflection on teaching as an interactive process—and it will leave teachers prime targets for any educational publisher's grand, new, state-of-the-art magic potion.

This is indeed how the interviewees viewed the mind-sets of their white colleagues when, as one teacher put it, these teachers seemed to be too book- or curriculum-bound, or, worse, "waiting for some program to ride in on a white horse and save them." It is interesting to note that although most teacher educators would heartily agree with the conceptions of good teaching espoused by these teachers of color, the teachers did not perceive their teacher education to have been based on such conceptions. Rather, they perceive teacher educators to be much like the classroom teachers they describe: whereas the classroom teachers are book- and curriculum-bound, the teacher educators "have never really been out there," but only go by "what they learned from books," or "only want to go by research they've read that other white people have written." In teacher education, "if you can't quote Vygotsky" then your words are not valid. If these teachers' perceptions are accurate, then Dewey's admonitions are doubly important to take to heart: not only might we not be allowing students to bring their critical intelligence to bear upon the teaching task, but we as teacher educators may be modeling behavior that is just the opposite of that which we wish to engender.

It seems likely that restructuring classes so as to build upon students' past experiences would appear to assist all potential teachers. Some teachers may need assistance in bringing reflection and critical thinking to the teaching role, thereby gaining encouragement to look beyond the books, the curriculum, and the experts to get in touch with their own "independent intelligence." Other teachers, particularly teachers of color, who may already have plenty of practice bringing their critical intelligence to bear upon the teaching task,[24] need to feel that their experiences and words are validated.

But the benefits of "story sharing" go beyond developing individual competencies or a sense of well-being. It is insufficient to allow students merely to make connections to their own pasts without exploring those pasts through multicultural lenses. Without such critical examination, we risk narrowing the student's perceptions and reducing his or her ability to understand diversity—so it is vitally important that the connections be examined, that the education professor highlight the narratives of the students of color and ask them to serve as resources for bringing to the fore differences in worldview, learning style, social organization, language, and so forth.

This could be accomplished by having small, culturally diverse teams of students observe children in classrooms, interview parents, or, through some other activity, collect data in order to develop potential strategies for working with diverse groups of children. The students should be encouraged to look to the "expert" in their group, the student or students from the same cultural group as the children observed, for advice and guidance in completing their assignments.[25]

This structuring effort can have several benefits. The educational problem posed by the professor is the group's to solve, but when a student of color is acknowledged as a source of valuable information, the group becomes dependent on his/her contributions. This can help to dispel any notions held by students (and faculty) about minority incompetence. Furthermore, during the informal interactions of the team members, common interests may become evident and possibly promote more interaction outside of the classroom across ethnic lines.[26] The students of color may find their experiences both admissible and valued in the classroom, which, along with the increased opportunity for interaction, may help to reduce their feelings of isolation from the university and their white classmates and professors.

On the other hand, white students will be encouraged to search for solutions to educational problems rather than to depend on books and curriculum guides for answers. They will also gain valuable insight into people of color and ways of teaching diverse students, and learn ways to talk across differences in discourse styles and interactional patterns—lessons that will serve them well in their future teaching careers. In addition, all students will have gained a model for organizing their own classrooms. Several researchers have demonstrated that this structure is successful in encouraging full participation and student success in multicultural classrooms of younger students.[27]

Finally, organizing the university classroom so that all students' stories are heard and all opinions valued may make inroads into that persistent scourge of American society, racial prejudice and discrimination—"modern" or otherwise. As white students and faculty learn to listen to and respect the words of people of color, perhaps they will carry these new attitudes of openness and acceptance of difference to other aspects of their lives, and certainly to their future teaching. The interviews quoted herein are just an initial attempt to hear the voices of diversity represented in the field of education. They have much more to tell us.

NOTES

1. Notable among many articles are the following: J.C. Baratz, "Black Participation in the Teacher Pool," paper prepared for the Carnegie Forum's Task Force on Teaching as a Profession, November 1986; B. Bass de Martinez, "Political and Reform Agendas' Impact on the Supply of Black Teachers," *Journal of Teacher Education* 39, no. 1 (1988); P.A. Garcia, "The Impact of National Testing on Ethnic Minorities: With Proposed Solutions," *Journal of Negro Education* 55, no. 3 (1986); A.M. Garibaldi, *The Decline of Teacher Production in Louisiana (1976–83) and Attitudes Toward the Profession* (Atlanta: Southern Education Foundation, 1986); G. Sykes, "The Social Consequences of Standard Setting in the Professions," paper prepared for the Carnegie Forum's Task Force on Teaching as a Profession, November 1986; and B. Taylor, "Generating Reform in the Teaching Profession: What Are the Implications of the Holmes and Carnegie Reports for Black Educators and Black Children?" *Perspective*, newsletter of the American Educational Research Association's special interest group, Research Focus on Black Education (Spring 1986).
2. P.A. Graham, "Black Teachers: A Drastically Scarce Resource," *The Kappan* 68, no. 8 (1987).
3. D. Kauffman, "Wingspread Conference: Consensus Reached on Policy about Minorities in Teaching," *Briefs* 8, no. 7 (1987).
4. Graham, "Black Teachers," 599.
5. The interviewees were six Native Americans and six African-Americans, eleven women and one man, ranging in age from thirty-two to seventy-three, who completed teacher education programs between 1952 and 1987. As of this writing, three had never entered the teaching force; one other left after two years of teaching; two taught for several years and then became principals; one is presently in an administrative position but hopes to return to the classroom; one is on leave from a teaching position in order to pursue a graduate degree; three are presently classroom teachers; and one is retired. The interviews were taped, usually in the interviewer's or the interviewee's home.

There was no attempt to seek a random sample, as these interviews are a part of ongoing research that aims to interview all of the teachers of color in Fairbanks (a total of about forty individuals). Fairbanks is a predominantly white town of about eighty-five thousand. The meeting with Native teachers was held in a rural Athabaskan village. Six teachers and this researcher were in attendance.

The telephone calls to black teachers served primarily to help validate the findings from the interviews.

6. Shirley Brice Heath, *Ways with Words* (Cambridge: Cambridge University Press, 1983); T. Kochman, *Black and White Styles in Conflict* (Chicago: University of Chicago Press, 1981); Ron Scollon and Suzanne B.K. Scollon, *Narrative, Literacy, and Face in Interethnic Communication* (Norwood, NJ: Ablex, 1981); Geneva Smitherman, *Talkin and Testifyin: The Language of Black America* (Boston: Houghton Mifflin, 1977).

7. D. Hymes with C. Cazden, "Narrative Thinking and Storytelling Rights: A Folklorist's Clue to a Critique of Education," in D. Hymes, *Language in Education: Ethnolinguistic Essays* (Washington, DC: Center for Applied Linguistics, 1980).

8. Regarding this point, see Scollon and Scollon, *Narrative, Literacy, and Face;* and N. Wolfson, "A Feature of Performed Narratives: The Conversational Historical Present," *Language in Society* 7 (1978).

9. Hymes with Cazden, "Narrative Thinking and Storytelling Rights."

10. Because I had not found references in the literature to teachers' feelings of bias in the teacher education program, I was somewhat surprised at the intensity of these feelings expressed in the interviews. It may be that because the interviewer was herself black, and that care was taken to provide a comfortable, conversational setting, teachers felt free to talk about topics they might not otherwise have discussed.

11. N. Benokraitis and J.R. Feagin, *Modern Sexism: Blatant Sexism, Subtle, and Covert Discrimination* (Englewood Cliffs, NJ: Prentice Hall, 1986).

12. A. Mehrabian, "Relationship of Attitudes to Seated Posture, Orientation and Distance," *Social Psychology* 30 (1968).

13. See, for example, Garibaldi, *The Decline of Teacher Production;* and L. Darling-Hammond, K.J. Pittman, and K. Ottinger, "Career Choices for Minorities: Who Will Teach?" paper prepared for the National Education Association and Council of Chief State School Officers' Task Force on Minorities in Teaching, June 1987.

14. H. Schuman, C. Steeh, and L. Bobo, *Racial Attitudes in America: Trends and Interpretations* (Cambridge, MA: Harvard University Press, 1985).

15. T.G. Pettigrew and J. Martin, "Shaping the Organizational Context for Black American Inclusion," *Journal of Social Issues* 43, no. 1 (1987).

16. F. Crosby, S. Bromley, and L. Saxe, "Recent Unobtrusive Studies of Black and White Discrimination and Prejudice: A Literature Review," *Psychological Bulletin* 87 (1980); E. Donnerstein and M. Donnerstein, "Variables in Interracial Aggression: Potential in Group Censure," *Journal of Personality and Social Psychology* 27 (1973); Pettigrew and Martin, "Shaping the Organizational Context"; S. Weitz, "Attitude, Voice, and Behavior: A Repressed Affect Model of Interracial Interaction," *Journal of Personality and Social Psychology* 24 (1972): 14–21; L. Wispé and H. Freshly, "Race, Sex, and the Sympathetic Helping Be-

havior: The Broken Bag Caper," *Journal of Personality and Social Psychology* 17 (1971): 59–65.

17. Pettigrew and Martin, "Shaping the Organizational Context," 50.

18. D.E. Berlew and D.T. Hall, "Socialization of Managers: Effects of Expectations on Performance," in D.A. Kolb, I.M. Rubin, and J.M. McIntyre, eds., *Organizational Psychology: A Book of Readings,* 3d ed. (Englewood Cliffs, NJ: Prentice Hall, 1971); and C.O. Word, M.P. Zanna, and J. Cooper, "The Nonverbal Mediation of Self-Fulfilling Prophecies in Interracial Interaction," *Journal of Experimental Social Psychology* 10 (1974).

19. G. Griffin, "Clinical Preservice Teacher Education: Final Report of a Descriptive Study," report no. 9026 (Austin: R&D Center for Teacher Education, University of Texas at Austin, 1983); S. Hollingsworth, "Learning to Teach Reading" (PhD diss., University of Texas at Austin, 1986).

20. S. Merriam, "Mentors and Protégés: A Critical Review of the Literature," *Adult Education Quarterly* 33 (1983).

21. G.B. Northcroft, "Affirmative Action: The Impact of Legislated Equality" (PhD diss., Stanford University, 1982).

22. Pettigrew and Martin, "Shaping the Organizational Context."

23. John Dewey, "The Relation of Theory to Practice in Education" (1904), in *Teacher Education in America: A Documentary History,* ed. M.L. Borrowman (New York: Teachers College Press, 1965), 153.

24. It is possible that these minority teachers are not representative of younger graduates. Some of the interviewees expressed alarm at the possibility that younger people of color were emerging from teacher education with ideas very similar to those of white teachers.

25. I thank Dr. John Tippeconic for his insightful comment cautioning us to beware that the student of color not be viewed as an expert only on issues regarding ethnicity. It is the instructor's role to ensure that these students be heard on other issues as well.

26. Pettigrew and Martin, "Shaping the Organizational Context."

27. E.G. Cohen, "Expectation States and Interracial Interaction in School Settings," *Annual Review of Sociology* 8 (1982); E.G. Cohen, *Designing Groupwork: Strategies for the Heterogeneous Classroom* (New York: Teachers College Press, 1986); E. Aronson, J. Sikes, N. Blaney, and M. Snapp, *The Jigsaw Classroom* (Beverly Hills, CA: Sage, 1978).

INTERVIEW SCHEDULE

1. What is your present job? What makes it good? What makes it difficult?
2. Do you think your ideas about teaching are different from other educators around you? How so?
3. What made you decide to become a teacher?
4. What kind of place did you do your teacher training in? Was that a good experience? [Graduate education?]
5. Did you feel that what you were taught was relevant to you and the children you wanted to teach? [Graduate education?]
6. What do you think has influenced your teaching most? Did you have any role models that influenced your teaching?

7. What did you learn in teacher training that is useful to you now?
8. Were you taught anything you thought was just wrong?
9. What was the relationship between you and non-minority faculty and students?
10. What would have made your teacher training experience better? Different faculty? Different curriculum? Different structure?

4

From *Black Teachers on Teaching*

Michele Foster

During the summer of 1994, while browsing in the public library in Lawrence, Kansas, I read the following item in the 10–16 June 1994 issue of *The Call,* a Kansas City weekly black newspaper established in 1919:

> Mrs. Mary Ella Tymony, 99, formerly a teacher in Moberly, Mo., and in Kansas City died Sunday, June 5, at the Timberlake Nursing Care Center where she had been a patient for the last seven years. Mrs. Tymony was widely known in this area for her work in education and in civil rights. Mrs. Tymony was born in Huntsville, Mo., one of the seven children of the late Charley and Martha Smith Hicks. She lived in the Kansas City area over 50 years. She was a member of the Paseo Baptist Church and its Women's Missionary Union. She was a graduate of Lincoln University, Jefferson City, Mo. She received her Master's of Education Degree in Guidance from the University of Missouri at Columbia. She was the former Dean of Students at Lincoln University, she [sic] was a member of the National Education Association, the Missouri State Teachers Association, former member in Moberly, Mo., an active member of the NAACP and served as the Missouri State Conference Branch Treasurer for eight years. She was an educator with the Kansas City Missouri School District before retiring. Her final years of teaching were at the Western Baptist Bible College. She leaves Bernard C. DeCoteau of the Center; one stepdaughter, Audrey Wynn of Miami, Fla.; two nieces, Nellie Mae Tolson of Moberly Mo., Helen D. Collins of Rock Island, Ill., and other relatives.[1]

Except to friends and relatives, this obituary was probably of little interest. Although I was not personally acquainted with the woman whose life it memorialized, my eyes fastened on it. Having interviewed black teachers for a life history project, I had seen her name in archival sources.

Mary Ella Tymony taught in Moberly, a small northeast Missouri town approximately sixty-five miles from Jefferson City (the state capital) and twenty-five miles from Columbia (the site of the flagship campus of the University of Missouri). In 1959, five years after the *Brown v. Board of Education* decision, she was one of eight plaintiffs in the *Naomi Brooks et al. v. School District of the City of Moberly Missouri,* where all eleven black teachers had been dismissed.[2] There was much publicity around the case. In May 1956 the *Southern School News* reported the "facts." In November of the same year, the paper revisited the case in an article discussing the displacement of black teachers resulting from desegregation.[3] Having followed the newspaper accounts, I knew that none of the eleven teachers had been reinstated in Moberly. Mrs. Tymony eventually secured a position at the historically black Lincoln University in Jefferson City. The obituary made me wonder what more there was to her story beyond the facts of the lawsuit and what was reported in the newspaper.

At the age of ninety-nine, however, Mrs. Tymony died with her story. But her obituary inspired me to complete my oral history project, during the course of which I have discovered the stories of many previously unknown black teachers like Mary Ella Tymony. Despite their exclusion from history books, they are part of the long line of teachers who have taught black children for two hundred years.

In a lecture delivered at Harvard University in 1950, Margaret Mead noted that "Teachers who are members of any group who are in a minority in their particular community will have to add in their own words that they are Negro teachers . . . as the case may be, redefining themselves against an image of woman who for most of the country is white, middle-class, middle-aged, and of Protestant background."[4] This comment, delivered forty-seven years ago, succinctly captures the condition of black teachers today, whose numbers are in sharp decline. Mead's commentary also describes the treatment of black teachers in scholarly literature where they are not well represented. This is true even though during the three decades following emancipation and the first six decades of the twentieth century teaching, along with the ministry, was one of the few occupations open to college-educated blacks. "The only thing an educated Negro can do is teach or preach," people would say. One difference between teaching and preaching, of course, was that teaching was open to women on an equal basis. In fact, one of the primary leadership roles available to black women was as teachers in their communities. Throughout history black teachers were more likely to be employed in states where there were larger numbers of black pupils and where schools were segregated.

Census data from the middle of the nineteenth century through the early twentieth century illustrate these patterns. Between 1890 and 1910 the number of blacks who were employed as teachers rose from 15,100 to 66,236. In the census years of 1890, 1900, and 1910, black teachers represented about 44, 45, and 45 percent, respectively, of professional blacks. In 1910, 76 percent of black teachers employed were women. The 1850 census compares the number of black teachers in two cities and two states, Northern and Southern. In that year, there were fifteen black and mulatto teachers in Louisiana but none in Connecticut. In that same year in New York there were eight black and mulatto teachers and twelve in New Orleans.[5]

The importance to the black community of teaching as a profession can be seen in reference material and other literature about blacks. For example, of the 641 biographies of individual black women contained in the two-volume reference work *Black Women in America: An Historical Encyclopedia,* edited by Darlene Clark Hine, 113 entries (18 percent) are indexed under the term "educator." A close reading of this encyclopedia reveals a larger number of individuals who, though not classified as educators, were temporarily employed as teachers. Another encyclopedia, *Notable Black American Women,* lists 150 educators among its entries.[6] Also included among the listings in *The Dictionary of American Negro Biography* are numerous biographies of both male and female teachers.[7] Seventy-four of the 450 entries (16 percent) contained in a bibliography of black American autobiographies written through 1974 list teaching as a profession or occupation.[8] More than a dozen of the women interviewed as part of the black women's oral history project archived at Radcliffe University served as teachers at one time in their lives. Included among the forty-seven older Southern black women profiled in the book *Hope and Dignity* are seventeen teachers. Finally, material on black teachers is embedded in memoirs, studies of black education, and life history studies.[9]

Black Teachers in Historical Context

Prior to emancipation, blacks held in slavery were forbidden to learn to read. Despite these prohibitions and severe punishments, blacks valued literacy and many learned to read despite these restrictions.[10] Some were taught by sympathetic whites; others learned alongside their master's children. But a significant number were taught by free blacks or by slaves who were literate themselves. Well regarded and respected, these black teachers understood both the power and danger associated with literacy. Leroy Lovelace, a retired high school English teacher, underscores the power of education: "When a people can think critically, they can change things. They are less likely to be taken advantage of and more likely to be able to avoid the traps that others set for us. An uneducated people can be taken advantage of because of their ignorance or naiveté."

Leonard Collins, a young teacher, is even more adamant: "I want kids to examine their world critically, to question everything. As kids get older they automatically accept the American ideology. But I don't want kids to just be the future; I want them to change the future."

Quoting James Baldwin, Edouard Plummer, a New York junior high school teacher who has taught since the early sixties declares: "Teaching black children is a revolutionary act."

Throughout history, black teachers have been hired primarily to teach black students. Because larger numbers of blacks resided in the South, a policy of "separate but equal" schooling, and Southern laws mandating that black teachers could teach only in segregated schools, greater numbers of black teachers were employed in the seventeen Southern and border states. Of the 63,697 black teachers in the United States in 1940, 46,381 were employed in the south.

Northern communities did not have laws segregating black teachers in black schools. As more blacks migrated to Northern cities, the school systems adopted policies that resulted in the de facto segregation of black pupils and teachers. In cities such as Philadelphia, Boston, New York, and Chicago it was customary to assign black teachers to predominantly black schools or to restrict them to particular grades (usually elementary). In Philadelphia the practice of assigning black teachers to all-black schools began in the early twentieth century. It was done, according to the superintendent of schools, "in order to give employment to a group of deserving numbers of the colored race, who by industry and capacity have won their certificates to teach in the public schools of the city."[11] Whatever the reason, as their numbers increased, black teachers and black pupils became segregated in predominantly black schools. Maintaining two separate eligibility lists, one for black teachers and one for white teachers, was one method the school board used to create and maintain all-black schools. Between 1932 and 1948 the number of black teachers doubled, but the pattern of segregation was firmly established. Of 186 elementary schools, ten were all-black. Not until 1935 was the first black teacher appointed to a junior high school, and not until 1947 was the first black teacher assigned to a high school.

In May 1950, in response to charges of bias in hiring patterns, the president of the Philadelphia School Board proclaimed that the public schools were not discriminating against the black teachers, because in making assignments the district considered the sentiments of the community. He announced that any efforts to assign black teachers to predominantly white schools would be undertaken carefully and slowly.

In Chicago the unprecedented growth of the black population through migration and deteriorating race relations culminated in the July 1919 Chicago Race Riot.[12] The residential segregation patterns combined to create the conditions for the de facto segregation that came to characterize the Chicago public schools. In 1916, 91.3 percent of all black students attended integrated schools. Four years later, 40 percent of all black students attended segregated schools. By 1930, the number had risen to 82.4 percent. Changes in the staffing patterns of black teachers mirrored the enrollment patterns of black students. In 1917, 41 of approximately 8,000 teachers were black; in 1930, 308 of 13,000 teachers were black. In 1917, three-fifths of Chicago's black teachers worked in integrated schools; by 1930, less than one-third did.

In the 1930s black teachers were three times more likely to be working as substitutes than as permanent teachers, and although they constituted 3.5 percent of all elementary school teachers, black teachers made up less than .9 percent of the secondary school teachers.

As in Philadelphia the policies of the Chicago School Board, as well as the informal policies at the building level, reinforced the segregation of black teachers. Throughout the 1920s and 1930s the Chicago School Board assigned more black teachers to substitute positions rather than to regular positions, no longer appointed black teachers to mixed schools, and ceased advocating for black teachers who met with resistance from white pupils and parents. At the school level, principals had the final word on hiring, could request particular candidates, and could reject those sent by the board. According to a race relations report issued in the mid-1940s, the result was that approximately 90 percent of non-white teachers were teaching in schools whose student population was more than 95 percent black.

In Northern cities, unlike in most of the South, black teachers did not enjoy unrestricted job opportunities within the de facto segregated system. In twenty-six all-black schools in Chicago in 1930, only 34 percent of the faculty was black. In Philadelphia in the mid-1940s, thirty schools with student populations of at least 75 percent black had predominantly white faculties and 140 had not one black teacher. Thus the patterns of teacher employment that emerged in Chicago resembled those in Philadelphia. Black teachers were restricted to segregated black schools and rarely taught white students, but white teachers could teach black and white pupils. As the decade of the 1940s came to a close, the pattern of de facto segregation with black teachers clustered in predominantly black schools was firmly entrenched in Philadelphia, Chicago, New York, and other cities having large black student populations.

As the relationship between employing black teachers and creating more segregated schools tightened, it caught the attention of W. E. B. Du Bois. In a 1920s article entitled "The Tragedy of Jim Crow," in *Crisis,* he described the dilemma of having to attack segregated public schools while at the same time trying to honor and appreciate black teachers. Almost twenty years later, in an article entitled "Winds of Change," in the *Chicago Defender,* DuBois revisited this problem.[13]

This practice of assigning black teachers to predominantly black schools was firmly entrenched when Joelle Vanderall began teaching in Boston in 1952: "At the time I started teaching in Boston most black teachers were assigned to a narrow geographic strip from the South End into Roxbury, between Tremont Street and Washington. Those assigned to schools outside that area had a very hard time."

When Bobbie Duvon, a teacher in West Virginia, first applied to teach in Hartford, Connecticut, in the late 1940s she was unable to get a permanent position, so each fall she returned to West Virginia. She relocated to Hartford in the early 1950s but was only able to substitute in the public schools. According to census data, no black teachers were employed in Connecticut in 1950. When a principal of the school where Bobbie had been substituting told her to file an application for employment with the school board, Bobbie replied that she already had. . . . We all knew where that application had gone: it went in the wastebasket because of the color of my skin. This was in fifty-three when there weren't many black teachers in the city."

When I began teaching in the Boston public schools in the late 1960s I encountered the same problem. As a first-year teacher I was assigned only to substitute teach in predominantly black schools and when I finally did secure my own classroom I was assigned as a "provisional" or temporary teacher in predominantly black schools. It wasn't until 1974, the year Boston public schools were desegregated by court order, that I was offered a permanent teaching position.[14]

The primary reason that black teachers were prohibited from teaching white children was the widespread belief firmly entrenched since the nineteenth century that, like others of their race, black teachers were inferior to whites and not suitable to teach white pupils.

In both the North and the South, however, whites retained the prerogative to teach in black schools. In 1911, when Ruby Middleton Forsythe began school in Charleston, South Carolina, black teachers were not allowed to teach in the Charleston city schools. Miss Ruby recounts why her mother decided to send her to a private school run by a black teacher: "She said that with all the teachers being white in the public schools, they treated you just plain mean like in slavery days. I was a bit obstinate, and she knew that these white teachers weren't gonna be able to tell me, 'You do so and so, you got to do so and so,' and I would just do it. She thought that having white teachers treat black children like that was too much like slavery." It was not until 1917, after Septima Clark organized black students at Avery Normal School to go door to door in the black community collecting signatures on a petition, that black teachers were able to teach in the city of Charleston.

In the 1940s black teachers in the North were already segregated by custom; black teachers in the South, by law. But in West Coast cities, such as Portland, Sacramento, and Seattle, black teachers were appointed to teach in the public schools for the first time. Only in Los Angeles had black teachers been working prior to the early 1940s. When Josephine Cole, for example, was hired in San Francisco in 1944, she was the first black teacher hired since the 1870s, when black teachers had been needed to staff the Jim Crow schools. Except for a few black women who had tutored black children in their homes between 1900 and 1920, black teachers had difficulty obtaining employment in predominantly white school districts on the West Coast.[15]

Ethel Tanner, a successful principal in San Mateo, tells what happened when she was first hired in the district: "This was a lily-white town in 1960; they didn't have any black teachers. The school board didn't want to hire me, but there was a principal that wanted to. After battling the school board, he did. The summer before school started I was away visiting my brother. When I returned, my husband told me that there had been a lot of commotion over my hiring. People had called my house and yelled, 'Nigger, nigger, nigger,' over the telephone. A group held a community meeting in a local church to protest my hiring. Over several days, I learned what had gone on during my absence. The more I thought about it, the more I decided that I had a right to that job and I wasn't going to let a bunch of racists keep me from it."

Often, as was the case with the Pennsylvania Association of Teachers of Colored Children, black teachers promoted their own employment cause by arguing that many black children were being harmed in mixed schools populated by white teachers, principals, and students. These black teachers also claimed that separate black schools assisted in the development of racial pride. Some members of the black community, especially those who favored integration, condemned black teachers for their self-serving stance.

The black community agreed about the importance of schooling for

their children. Far from being of one mind over the means by which to secure the best educational opportunities, the black community has been
deeply divided over whether integrated or segregated schools would
achieve the best outcome. This was especially true because integrated
schools often meant the loss of jobs for black teachers. Black communities
across the United States have grappled with this dilemma since the early
nineteenth century.[16] Black leaders often weighed in on both sides of the
issue. Some believed that by insisting on black teachers the community was
acquiescing to segregation. But there was still considerable sentiment
within the black community for retaining black teachers to teach in black
schools.[17] Even though the hiring of black teachers resulted in strengthening the system of segregated schools, blacks fought for teachers of their
own race. And many newspaper editors, educators, preachers, and other
influential blacks publicly appealed for black teachers to staff black
schools. According to an Albany black Baptist preacher, they followed the
motto: "Colored schools, colored teachers; colored churches, colored
preachers."[18]

Twenty-two years after the historic *Brown v. Board of Education* decision,
which outlawed separate but equal schools, local school boards in Minneapolis, Indianapolis, Louisville, and Pittsburgh have requested an end to
desegregation plans. Federal courts have already set aside court orders that
require desegregation in St. Louis, Wilmington, and Kansas City. Some
blacks are also questioning whether the gains of desegregation outweigh
the liabilities. Attorney Ted Shaw, legal counsel for the NAACP Legal Defense Fund, has stated: "My sense is a lot of people are saying, 'We're tired of
chasing white folks. It's not worth the price we have to pay.' "[19]

Perhaps it was W. E. B. Du Bois, a pragmatist, who although he remained
steadfastly committed to a desegregated society throughout his lifetime,
best summarized the situation.

> and I know that race prejudice in the United States today is such that
> most Negroes cannot receive proper education in white institutions.
> . . . If the public schools of Atlanta, Nashville, New Orleans, and Jack-
> sonville were thrown open to all races today, the education that col-
> ored children would get in them would be worse than pitiable. And
> in the same way, there are many public school systems in the North
> where Negroes are admitted and tolerated, but they are not edu-
> cated; they are crucified. To sum up this: theoretically, the Negro
> needs neither separate nor mixed schools. What he needs is Educa-
> tion. What he must remember is that there is no magic either in
> mixed schools or segregated schools. A mixed school with poor un-
> sympathetic teachers, with hostile public opinion, and no teaching of

the truth concerning black folk is bad. A segregated school with ignorant placeholders, inadequate equipment, and poor salaries is
equally bad. Other things being equal, the mixed school is the
broader, more natural basis for the education of all youth. It gives
wider contacts; it inspires greater self-confidence; and suppresses the
inferiority complex. But other things seldom are equal, and in that
case, Sympathy, Knowledge, and the Truth outweigh all that the
mixed school can offer.[20]

Many of the Southern schools where black teachers taught were dilapi-
dated; supplies were limited, and books discarded from white schools were
sent to black schoolchildren. Bernadine Morris describes one such school
in Hampton, Virginia: "In one of the all-black schools where I taught whenever the temperature dropped down below thirty degrees or thirty-two degrees, we were cold. There were times when the principal had to move us
from one side of the building and double up classes because it was so cold.
How can you teach in a doubled-up situation?"

Etta Joan Marks, a soft-spoken teacher from Lindale, Texas, frowns as
she recalls the abysmal conditions she endured in segregated schools: "In
1961 or 1962, when our school burned down, we didn't have textbooks of
any kind. We held classes in the church. The white schools sent us their
used textbooks just before they were ready to put them in the trash. Pages
were torn out; they were old, worn, and so marked up that there wasn't any
space to write our names."

Everett Dawson Jr. echoes these sentiments. "When people talk about
separate but equal, I know what they were talking about. I know why they
said the schools were inherently unequal, because I experienced it as a student and a teacher. In the black schools we only got the books that white
kids had already used. They did not get books that we had used. In other
words, we got the hand-me-downs. To this day it bothers me that those conditions existed anywhere in this country."

Black communities have a long tradition of having organized private
schools for the benefit of their children. By teaching in private schools and
establishing their own schools, black teachers have played a critical role in
the creation of this educational infrastructure. Black teachers founded
Sunday schools in the North in the late eighteenth century and native
schools in the South prior to the end of the Civil War. They established several private schools in the South during the late nineteenth and early twentieth centuries. And they taught in schools established by black churches
and organizations. Ruby Middleton Forsythe taught at Holy Cross Faith
Memorial School, an Episcopal school, from 1938 until she retired in
1991. The school was founded in 1903 for the benefit of black children

who lived on the rice plantations on Pawley's Island. "At the time there wasn't a public school for black children, not until later on. Once the public schools opened, they weren't fulltime. They only went for six months, but this school went for nine." When the Episcopal Diocese terminated the funding, the parents elected to keep the school open. Miss Ruby believes she knows the reason: "Regardless of what white people think about this school, the community thinks the school serves a good purpose. The parents don't want me to close the school. That's the reason we get the support that we do."

What was the price of desegregation? One price was paid by black children themselves. Anna Julia Cooper, a famous black educator of the late nineteenth and twentieth centuries, said she was opposed to desegregation because she feared that black children would no longer be taught racial pride as they had been in segregated schools.[21]

Echoing these sentiments, Ruby Forsythe, an eighty-year-old teacher, discusses how integration has affected black pupils: "When the children were integrated into white schools, they lost something. Integration has helped in some ways, but it has hurt our black children in some ways. Now, instead of seeing black children winning prizes for their achievements, you see them all in special education classes. This has caused them to lose their pride, their self-esteem. They have been pushed back, as far as leadership is concerned. Instead of being taught to lead, they are being taught to follow."

Bernadine Morris agrees: "I think when they integrated the schools, instead of the black kids seeing themselves as people who could go in there and make progress, they got linked and then linked themselves to all the bad things that the kids were doing. I can only relate to when I was in a segregated school. You'd go to high school commencement and I could see these kids walking up there with these four-year scholarships to places like Fisk and Howard or A&T or wherever. Now when I go to a high school graduation, the only kids I see getting the scholarships are white kids."

Etta Joan Marks describes what happened to black pupils when they entered the desegregated schools in Lindale, Texas: "The teachers made it clear that blacks were not welcome. In the classroom, the white teachers would put the black kids on one side of the room and the white kids on the other side. This is so that they wouldn't touch or mingle."

Everett Dawson, who transferred to the desegregated school (after having taught in the segregated school) in the same community, was upset by the treatment of black kids: "I also saw a lot of young black brothers get into the classes of white instructors who went into the class saying—not saying—not saying very loudly but very clearly—'These black kids can't make it.' And this really bothered me."

Bernadine B. Morris, one of the first black teachers to integrate the schools in Hampton, describes the way some white teachers treated black children: "Several times I had students who were acting up in the cafeteria, doing childlike things. These teachers wanted to make a federal case of it. They would say something like, 'He's still talking when I told him not to talk.' Well, this is what children do. I would always intervene and tell the teachers that I would take care of the problem. I had to do this, otherwise the teachers would make a big case out of nothing and then the children would get into trouble, be suspended or expelled. We had several white teachers in that school who retired rather than work with black children, which was fine. I felt like if they didn't want to teach black kids then they ought to leave."

How did desegregation affect black teachers? Predicting what might happen to black teachers, one black pundit declared that integration would jeopardize black teachers' security and undermine their morale. Not only would their livelihood be threatened, but their intellectual competence would also be called into question. Part of the problem lay in the *Brown* decision, which rested on the assumption that a school with an all-black faculty did not provide an education equal to that provided by an all-white faculty even if the buildings and equipment were superior. Some black teachers were underprepared and unable to compete. But many black teachers, especially those in large cities, had more academic training and longer years of service in the public schools than white teachers, who generally had more employment opportunities.[22]

Other voices from the black community tried to assure black teachers that they would not be adversely affected. Two editorials in the *Journal of Negro Education,* one written in the spring of 1951 and the other in the spring of 1953, grappled with how black teachers would be affected by desegregation. The 1951 editorial argued that there were not enough white teachers to replace black teachers in desegregated schools. But the editor concluded that even if school desegregation resulted in the loss of all of the 75,000 black teachers it would be offset by the elimination of segregated schools. A 1955 editorial noting that desegregation had been accomplished in southern Illinois, Indiana, Arizona, New Mexico, and New Jersey without dire results for black teachers concluded:

From an analysis of all available data, it seems unquestionable that the future status of the Negro public school teacher, under desegregated public schools, should not cause concern. Tenure laws in the District of Columbia and *seven* of the states involved are such that some two-fifths of the Negro teachers will be protected in their present position. And the teacher supply and demand situation means that even without tenure laws, as far as the elementary school is concerned it will be practically impossible to replace Negro teachers with white. While the situation as to high school teachers is not so overwhelmingly convincing as in the case of elementary school teachers, even here, tenure laws, the supply and demand picture and expanding enrollments make it highly questionable as to whether more than a few, if any Negro high school teachers could be replaced by white, even if there was an inclination do to so.[23]

Popular magazines such as *Ebony* also tried to reassure the black community that black teachers would not unfairly bear the brunt of desegregation. The November 1955 issue of *Ebony* acknowledged that 125 black Oklahoma teachers had lost their positions because of desegregation and that Oklahoma black leaders were predicting the loss of another 300 in the state. On a more hopeful note, *Ebony* listed several reasons why the South could not afford to relinquish its black teachers.[24] In other issues *Ebony* carried articles featuring black teachers in Phoenix who were teaching in white classes after the city integrated its schools.[25] Despite these reassurances, it became apparent in the school districts that immediately desegregated that black teachers would pay some of the costs of the *Brown* decision.

As the school year opened in 1956, black leaders in Oklahoma, a state that desegregated almost immediately, were contemplating the dismissal of eighty-six black teachers the previous July and considering whether federal lawsuits were warranted. Both the NAACP and the Oklahoma Association of Negro Teachers believed that some of the dismissals were the result of racial discrimination. Nonetheless, the NAACP decided against filing suit until more evidence could be gathered to substantiate claims of discrimination.[26] Similar dismissals were reported in other border states (West Virginia, Kentucky, Texas, and Missouri).[27]

Not all black teachers lost their positions. Some were transferred to newly desegregated schools, not always with favorable outcomes. The case of Leslie R. Austin, a black teacher assigned to a desegregated high school in Lincoln County, Oklahoma, is one example. When the Wellston (Oklahoma) schools became one of the first districts to desegregate in 1955, it closed the all-black Dunbar School and transferred its ninety students to an all-white school. Four of the five black teachers were dismissed; only Austin, who had served as principal, was hired to teach in the desegregated school. Though he was considered "an excellent teacher," he was dismissed after three years. (When white parents objected to his disciplining their children, the discipline of his classes was assigned to white teachers, and Austin was subsequently dismissed for failing to maintain a disciplined classroom environment.) Although the Wellston public schools claimed that his dismissal was not the result of discrimination, the town's segregationists had vowed to "'get rid' of the Negro teacher" during the school board election, and many of the community's black residents believed Austin's firing was racially motivated.[28]

Some of the black teachers I interviewed described the harm done to black teachers as a result of desegregation. Etta Joan Marks describes what happened to the black teachers in Lindale, Texas: "There were only two black teachers in the school, my cousin and myself. Neither one of us had a class because the townspeople didn't want us teaching their lily-white kids. In spite of all the problems I encountered, I was more fortunate than many black teachers. Most of those that worked with me in the segregated school didn't have jobs. They lost their positions and had to look for new ones in other communities. Only four of the twelve black teachers were retained in the system. Besides my cousin and I, only two other teachers—the homemaking teacher and her husband, the principal—were reassigned."

Since many school districts employed various delaying tactics to avoid desegregating their schools for almost fourteen years, it took more than twenty years before a complete picture of the negative effects on black teachers could be ascertained. The first eleven years of desegregation were later found to have had devastating effects on the number of black teachers in the seventeen Southern and border states. In that period alone, more than 30,000 black teachers lost their jobs.[29] Attempting to explain the reasons for this wholesale dismissal of black teachers, a task force of the National Education Association reasoned:

> It is clear that in the past, Negro teachers were employed specifically and exclusively for the purpose of teaching Negro pupils in segregated schools. Segregated schools required segregated facilities. Since Negro teachers were employed to teach Negro pupils, there were relatively few positions for Negro teachers in a school system with few classes for Negroes. In a system with no classes for Negroes, there were simply no positions for Negro teachers. It has been, and still is, widely assumed by many school board members that Negroes, both students and teachers, are intellectually inferior. From this specious premise, it follows that "quality education" can be obtained only when schools, even after being integrated, remain in spirit and often in name "white schools." White schools are viewed as having no place for Negro teachers.[30]

Another hidden cost of desegregation was the loss of community. Bernadine B. Morris discusses one way this happened: "Busing at that time meant closing the schools in black neighborhoods and sending the black kids to the white areas. They closed all the black schools. Greenbriar School where I once worked is now a recreation center. Murrow Peak, a school that the black community fought to have built for twenty years, was closed even though it was fairly new. Then integration came. Now Murrow Peak is a police academy. These schools no longer exist because they were located in black neighborhoods. They built new schools in predominantly white neighborhoods rather than keep those in the black community. The idea was to get the schools out of black neighborhoods—and they did a good job of it."

Etta Joan Marks compares the treatment of black students in segregated and desegregated schools: "I've taught in a segregated school and a desegregated school in the same town. If I had to compare the experiences, I would say that in the black schools teachers had to do a lot more work, but our kids were appreciated more. In the white school we get more materials, we have more to work with, but we—blacks—aren't appreciated as much."

Everett Dawson sighed: "I got disillusioned with integration because I could not get to my people and tell them all the things that they needed to know."

A dispirited Bernadine B. Morris observes: "It saddens me that so many of our black kids today are doing so poorly, even after integration. It saddens me that integration didn't turn out to be everything we had hoped for."

As early as the middle of the nineteenth century, black teachers had organized for their own benefit. The Association of Colored Teachers was in operation in New York as early as 1841. This group had its own publications: the *New York Journal of Education* and the *Weekly Messenger*. The group held meetings devoted to their problems and the promotion of education for New York's black pupils.[31] Another organization was the American Teachers Association of Teachers in Colored Schools, the American Teachers Association with associated state chapters continued until 1965 when it was merged with the National Education Association. Bernadine Morris discusses some of their activities: "In both North Carolina and Virginia I also got involved in the Teachers Association. We had our own black teachers associations. Black and white teachers held separate yearly conventions on the same weekend, usually in the fall. In North Carolina, black teachers met in Raleigh. In Virginia, we met in Richmond. The white teachers met in a downtown hotel. But because we couldn't go into the hotels, we would gather at Virginia Union University. There were sessions and workshops on various topics: how to work with slow children or how to work with advanced students, all the newest trends. Professors, principals, and master teachers lectured, presented workshops, and conducted the sessions."

Unprotected by tenure, subject to dismissal by white-run school boards, and fearful for their physical safety, many black teachers, especially those in the South, refrained from political action. Yet other black teachers actively participated in black teachers' associations to secure equal pay. Long before the *Brown v. the Board of Education* case was filed, black teachers had begun challenging the dual pay scales in Southern states. Between 1900 and 1930 discrepancies between black and white teachers' salaries had gradually decreased in thirteen Southern states. In 1900, black teachers earned 45 percent of the salaries of their counterparts; by 1930, black teachers earned 69 percent of their white counterparts' salaries.[32]

When Thurgood Marshall set up his law practice in Baltimore in 1934, he set out to organize black teachers throughout the state of Maryland and attempted to secure plaintiffs to fight for salary equalization. In 1931–32, black teachers in Maryland were earning $1,211 per year while white teachers earned $1,589.[33] Even worse, black elementary school teachers were earning $339 less than white janitors. Because Maryland's black teachers were covered by tenure laws, they were less vulnerable to being fired than were teachers in other states. Even so, many of the black teachers in Maryland were fearful of losing their jobs, so Marshall raised money for a trust fund to aid teachers in case they were dismissed once the cases were filed. Three years later, Marshall expanded the salary equalization cases to North Carolina and Virginia. In 1939 Marshall won equal pay concessions from nine Maryland county school boards.

In Virginia, where black teachers were not protected by tenure laws, Marshall had more difficulty securing plaintiffs. He filed a case on behalf of Melvin O. Alston, a city high school teacher who was earning $921 per year, $279 less than white high school teachers in the same school district. When the Norfolk School Board refused to renew the plaintiff's contract, Marshall jointly filed the suit on behalf of the Norfolk Teachers Association and Alston to prevent the firing of other teachers. The plaintiffs lost the case, but the decision was overturned by the Fourth Circuit Court of Appeals in Richmond. When the Supreme Court refused to hear the case, under the law at least, black teachers were entitled to equal pay.

In spite of the Alston case, it was several years before many school districts in Virginia and other Southern states complied with the law. The South Carolina State Legislature refused to appropriate the funds necessary to equalize the salaries of black teachers, and black teachers had to bring suit. In the 1944–45 school year, black teachers in South Carolina earned only 57.8 percent as much as white teachers. In 1945 Judge Waring ordered the Columbia and Charleston (South Carolina) public schools to pay black teachers salaries equal to those of white teachers.[34] By 1947 most of the South Carolina city schools districts were paying black and white teachers equal salaries, but in rural areas black teachers were still receiving unequal pay.[35] It wasn't until 1952, two years before the *Brown* decision, that the salaries of black and white teachers were equalized in Summerton County, South Carolina—the county of *Briggs v. Elliot,* one of the suits consolidated into the *Brown* case.

During the 1944–45 school year black teachers in Louisiana had earned approximately 50 percent of what white teachers earned.[36] It was not until 1948, after an eight-year struggle, that black teachers represented by Thurgood Marshall won a decision ordering the Louisiana State Board of Education to pay equal salaries to black and white teachers.[37] In the mid-forties, white teachers in Alabama earned 67.4 percent more than black teachers. Ruby Gainer, the president of the Jefferson County (Alabama) Teachers Association, filed a suit that initiated the struggle to equalize teachers' salaries in Alabama.[38]

It was ordinary black teachers like Alston and Gainer who, often in conjunction with their local teachers organizations, played critical roles in these struggles over salary equalization. In 1933, for instance, North Carolina black teachers received an announcement informing them of a mass meeting. One purpose of the meeting, to be held in Raleigh on October 29 in conjunction with a statewide meeting of the NAACP, was to protest unequal salaries.[39] The teachers were asked to attend the meeting and to encourage other teachers to attend. Although 2,005 blacks attended the Raleigh meeting, it is unclear how many of those in attendance were teachers.[40]

A retired North Carolina teacher recalls the importance of black teachers' organizations in equalizing salaries: "Through the leadership of the North Carolina Teachers' Association—that was the black teachers of North Carolina who had banded together in an association (now it's part of the North Carolina Association of Educators)—we organized and were able to bring enough pressure to get the salaries equalized. This happened around 1945 or 1946."

The writings of black teachers reveal that many teachers considered their pupils apt and intelligent learners, that they were committed and related well to students, and that they did not always try to imbue them with traits like tractability that so often characterized the teaching of white Northern schoolmistresses. This was often true despite class differences between the teachers and their students.[41]

In a letter printed in *The Liberator* in 1862, Charlotte Fortune, a black teacher, described her pupils in the Reconstruction era:

> It is very pleasant to see how bright, how eager to learn many of the
> children are. Some of them make wonderful improvement in a short
> time. It is a great happiness, a great privilege to be allowed to teach

them. Every day I enjoy it more and more. . . . They are certainly not the stupid degrading people that many in the North believe them to be.[42]

Another black teacher, Lucy Laney Craft, in a speech given at the turn of the century, criticized teachers who were ineffective with black pupils and called on black teachers to undertake their education:

> There's plenty of work for all who have the proper conception of the teacher's office. . . . But the educated Negro woman must teach the "Black Babies." But alas! These dull teachers, like many modern pedagogues and school keepers, failed to know their pupils—to find out their real needs, and hence had no cause to study methods of better and best development of the boys and girls under their care.[43]

One of the most insightful accounts about black pupils was written by Sara Stanley, who described the visit a government official paid to her classroom. The official was trying to convince her black pupils that whites were superior to them because of their education, but he was startled when the pupils insisted that if whites were better than they were, it was only because whites were richer and had stolen their money from black people:

> "Now, children," said he, "you don't think white people are any better than you because they have straight hair and white faces?"
>
> "No, sir," cried the children with intuitive comprehension of the great words uttered by Paul on Mars's hill.
>
> "No, they are not better, but they are different; they possess great power; they formed this great government; they control this vast country; they invent telegraphs and steamboats; they construct railroads and war steamers. Now, what makes them different from you?"
>
> The answer, "Education," seemed inevitable; but, instead a chorus of little voices instantly responded, "MONEY."
>
> "Yes," said the speaker, "but what enabled them to obtain it? *How* did they get that money?"
>
> A simultaneous shout burst forth, "Got it off us; stole it off we all."

This teacher, admiring her pupils for their childlike honesty and sagacious insight, concluded the article by writing, "A different answer might have been returned, but hardly a truer one as applied to the people of the South."[44]

The teachers interviewed for this book echo the views of turn-of-the-century schoolmistresses. Mabel Bettie Moss, a teacher in Philadelphia, complains: "Most teachers don't appreciate black children and their strengths. Black kids are creative, inquisitive, and bright. That's the best word to describe them. . . . in so many instances school is just so boring and unrelated to their everyday lives. Occasionally when I have gone into other teachers' rooms, and seen what is going on, I have realized how awful it would be to have to be a student in that classroom. Too many teachers make learning so boring."

A novice male elementary teacher, Leonard Collins, agrees on the importance of making school relevant to his pupils' lives: "I put Africans within the context of everything that I teach. I do this with other cultures as well. For example, when I taught about the transcontinental railroad, I showed my class how Asians were exploited, how they were denigrated during this whole process. I try to show what role each group has played throughout history. I do this in anything that I teach but especially in social studies. By simply presenting the perspectives of people of color, I believe I am making a contribution. The only thing I can do is teach my kids to question authority, question what the teacher says, not to be submissive."

In segregated schools where black and white teachers made up the faculties, some black teachers complained of low expectations for and prejudice against black students. A history of Chicago public schools noted that too often white teachers made few academic demands of black students. One black teacher commented that the black students who came to her class were often lacking in grade-level skill: "The worst cases I had came from children who had been pampered by white teachers."[45]

A retired Chicago high school teacher, Leroy Lovelace, reports: "Teachers have to realize that black students—or all students, but I'm talking about black students now—are very clever, especially with white teachers. Too many black students have learned to play the game, to play on a teacher's sympathy in order to get away with doing nothing. Teachers have to demand from black urban students the same as they would demand from privileged white students, and they have to be consistent. Urban black students can do the work, and in the hands of skilled teachers they will do it. They may have to work harder to achieve success. All students can con teachers if the teachers let themselves be conned. But it's often easier for black students to con white teachers because the students know that the teachers will pity them, feel sorry for them, and make excuses that these students can't do this, can't do that or that there's a problem at home. It particularly disturbs me when I see black teachers letting black students get away with doing nothing. Black teachers who do this tell themselves they are doing this sympathetically, but I don't accept that. I believe that black teachers are doing it because we've become middle-class—and now I am speaking of black folks including black teachers. Once black folks were poorer than Job's turkey and now that we have joined the white folks talking about 'They can't do it.'—you'd be surprised how many black teachers do that."

Not all black teachers are sympathetic to their young scholars. Color distinctions between light-skinned black teachers and their dark-complexioned pupils were sometimes enacted in the classroom with teachers favoring lighter pupils over darker ones. *The Chicago Defender* editor, Robert Abbott, himself a dark-complexioned man, complained,

> The pure-blooded, black children are seldom if ever the recipients of kindly counsel or special favors or justifiable considerations. We can neither, nor appreciate Race teachers who manifest no interest in, no sympathy and no consideration for those children of ours who show no sign of racial admixture. We resent it and decry it the more when Race teachers, who should be the last ones to exhibit aversion to their kind, practice the most objectionable form of partiality on the basis of color.

One black parent whose child was failing in school denounced her black teachers, "You colored teachers just don't like Mattie Lou cause she's black and ain't got good hair."[46]

Millicent Byard Gray is familiar with the attitudes about color that often permeate the black community: "The teachers at Lincoln High School were black but for the most part they were light-skinned. There was a lot of color consciousness in my community and in my school. I'm the brown-skinned child, one of the darkest children in my family. Even as child, I was serious. The neighbors used to comment, 'That little dark one—she's too serious; we need to watch her—she doesn't laugh when the rest of them laugh.' In those days people equated being dark skinned with being evil. I always resented that."

These teachers agonize over the disintegration of urban and rural black communities, the rampant materialism of the society, and the devastating effect these conditions have had on the pupils they teach. Joelle Vanderall describes her school community: "Many of my students come from neighborhoods that are devastated, communities in which drugs are rampant, where people haven't got the money they need to survive and they see no way out. Before, black people had more stability, jobs, and some hope. But now welfare has created a permanent class of expendable people without hope who can always be used as scapegoats by the politicians and the larger society."

A Philadelphia teacher, Mabel Bettie Moss, discusses the changes she has witnessed in the community surrounding her school: "I have been teaching in this community—in the same school—since 1961, and I can really see the negative effect that drugs have had on the community. The way things are going, it's only going to get worse. In the late eighties, we had a drug house right across from our school. With the grip that crack cocaine has on our community, a lot of the mothers are simply unable to cope. Crack cocaine is so cheap, and it grabs them so fast. In this community, more and more grandmothers are raising their grandchildren, and although many of them do a fantastic job, others are simply too worn out to raise another generation. One little girl in my class last year is being raised by her grandmother, a sickly woman, who has six children under twelve in her home, from three different daughters, all victims of crack cocaine."

A Southern teacher, Bernadine Morris, who earlier in her career taught in rural communities and once lived in a "teacherage" (a boarding house for teachers), remembers how living and participating in the daily life of the community cemented relationships between parents and teachers: "In Warrenton, teachers were respected by children and their families. I remember several Christmases, when even though the families didn't have money to go out and buy the teacher a gift, the children would come to school with gifts, something that their families had raised. If you'd go to the home, the parents would often invite you back to dinner. They would notify you if their children were involved in various church activities and invite you to come and see. The supportive relationships between black teachers and parents aren't like they used to be. And as a result children, black children, are suffering."

A Washington, D.C., high school teacher, Lerone Swift, places some of the blame for the disintegration of the community at the feet of the black middle class. He blames them for turning their backs on poor blacks: "middle-class parents have abandoned the school system that benefited them, that provided them with the opportunity to advance and become successful in society."

Whereas in 1974, historically black colleges, which had prepared the majority of black teachers, graduated approximately nine thousand teachers, ten years later they were graduating only half as many. By the end of the 1980s, a number of policy analysts were examining the reasons for the shortage and projected shortages of black teachers, whose numbers were in sharp decline. Black college students were no longer choosing teaching as a career. Some of the other reasons for this decline include the increased reliance on standardized tests for acceptance into and graduation from teacher training programs; the lower number of black students enrolling in and completing four-year colleges; and the expanded occupational choices available to black college graduates.[47] Because the number of black teachers had become so small and was projected to remain insignificant, some referred to them as an "endangered species." According to the 1990 census black teachers represented only 8 percent of all teachers.[48] Their numbers were declining at exactly the same time that black students comprised the majority in many urban school districts. To offset this imbalance, numerous programs were being developed and launched to recruit more black teachers into the profession. But the predictions for increasing the number of black teachers were bleak.

Black teachers' unique historical experiences are either completely overlooked or amalgamated with those of white teachers. In those few instances where black teachers are visible, their cultural representations are biased by society's overarching racism. For the most part, these cultural representations continue to render black teachers invisible as teachers of students of their own or of other ethnic backgrounds, while casting white female teachers as heroic figures. It is perhaps emblematic of this phenomenon that two of the most recent books about effective teachers of black and Latino students in New York and in California are *Small Victories* and *My Posse Don't Do Homework*,[49] the latter currently appearing as a movie entitled *Dangerous Minds*. Both books depict white, not black, female teachers negotiating the difficult terrain of urban classrooms.

The public rarely reads about black teachers like Mamie Williams, an exemplary teacher who taught in the segregated schools of Topeka, Kansas:

> Mamie Williams became a master teacher. A forceful taskmaster and disciplinarian, she was no ogre. Her classroom was never a place for rote learning, and she readily acknowledged that "children with their sincerity and candor can teach adults something new every day." She was a great one for mottos. One of her favorites was: "Life is infinitely rich in fine and adequate compensations. Never a door is shut but several windows are opened." Mamie Williams was a window-opener. She designed several projects of the kind she had heard about at Columbia. One of the most popular was a communal lesson in self-government: the whole school was organized like a state, with a constitution, by-laws, officers, and a legislative council. There were campaign speeches and elections, rousing inauguration ceremonies, and regular legislative reports to be filed and posted on the bulletin board in every classroom. She organized a "Little Theater," a project for which her pupils dramatized stories they had read together in class. One time, she turned her classroom into an art gallery; those who liked to draw contributed their work, the others brought in what

they liked from magazines and other sources, and every one was excited and stimulated and learned how widely human notions of beauty can vary.[50]

The shrinking numbers of black teachers have compelled me to publish contemporary accounts by black teachers, who talk about the racism in segregated and desegregated schools, the repeated cycles of attempted and aborted reform efforts, and the different perceptions of black and white teachers about the ability and needs of black students, parents, and communities. Much of what these teachers say is controversial. Nonetheless, it is my hope that these accounts will provide a voice for an historically marginalized group, that in the process they will enhance our capacity to understand the experiences of black teachers, and that they will assist contemporary and future African-Americanists, historians, and sociologists in reaching a more complete understanding of education, schooling, teaching, and learning in the United States.

NOTES

1. *The Call,* June 10–16, 1994, 2, 15–16.
2. *Naomi Brooks et al. v. School District of City of Moberly, Missouri etc., et al.,* U.S. Court of Appeals, Eighth Circuit (June 17, 1959), 267F.2d 733, in *Race Relations Law Reporter,* vol. 4, pp. 613–18.
3. "Missouri's Teacher Tenure Hearings Expected to Develop 'Case History,' " *Southern School News* 2 (May 1956): 8; "462 Negro Teachers Out, Many Land in New Jobs," *Southern School News* 3, no. 5 (November 1956): 1–2.
4. Margaret Mead, *The School in American Culture* (Cambridge, MA: Harvard University Press, 1950).
5. *Negro Population in United States, 1790–1915* (New York: Arno Press, 1968), 511.
6. Jessie Carney Smith, ed., *Notable Black Women* (Detroit: Gale Press, 1992).
7. Yraford W. Logan and Michael R. Winston, eds., *Dictionary of American Negro Biography* (New York: W.W. Norton, 1982).
8. Russell Brigano, *Black Americans in Autobiography* (Durham, NC: Duke University Press, 1974).
9. Some of the books or articles in which black teachers have been portrayed include: Houston Baker, "What Charles Knew," in *An Apple for My Teacher: 12 Authors Tell about Teachers Who Made a Difference,* ed. L. Rubin Jr. (Chapel Hill, NC: Algonquin Books, 1987); Bob Blauner, *Black Lives, White Lives: Three Decades of Race Relations in America* (Berkeley: University of California Press, 1989); J.L. Chestnut and Julia Cass, *Black in Selma: The Uncommon Life of J. L. Chestnut, Jr.* (New York: Farrar, Straus and Giroux, 1990); Patricia Hill Collins, *Black Feminist Thought: Knowledge, Consciousness and the Politics of Empowerment* (Boston: Unwin Hyman, 1990); Evelyn Fairbanks, *Days of Rondo* (St. Paul: Minnesota Historical Society Press, 1990); Mamie Fields with Karen

Fields, *Lemon Swamp: A Carolina Memoir* (New York: The Free Press, 1985); Walt Harrington, *Crossings: A White Man's Journey into Black America* (New York: HarperCollins, 1992); bell hooks, *Talking Back: Thinking Feminist, Thinking Black* (Boston: South End Press, 1989); Clara B. Kennan, "The First Negro Teacher in Little Rock," *Black Women in United States History*, ed. Darlene Clark Hine (Brooklyn, NY: Carlson Publishing, 1990), 773–83; Richard Kluger, *Simple Justice* (New York: Vintage, 1975); Sara Lawrence Lightfoot, *Balm in Gilead: Journey of a Healer* (Reading, MA: Addison-Wesley, 1988).

10. For a discussion on the value and appreciation of literacy, see Frederick Douglass, *Narrative of the Life of Frederick Douglass, an American Slave, Written by Himself*, ed. Benjamin Quarles (Cambridge, MA: Belknap Press, 1960). Other accounts of the desire for literacy can be found in numerous slave narratives; for examples see Thomas L. Webber, *Deep Like the Rivers: Education in the Slave Quarter Community, 1831–1865* (New York: W.W. Norton, 1978), 131–38.

11. The information about Philadelphia is drawn from V.P. Franklin, *The Education of Black Philadelphia: The Social and Educational History of a Minority Community, 1900–1950* (Philadelphia: University of Pennsylvania Press, 1980).

12. The information about Chicago is drawn from Michael W. Homel, *Down from Equality: Black Chicago and the Public Schools, 1920–1941* (Urbana: University of Illinois Press, 1984).

13. W.E.B. Du Bois, "Winds of Change," *Chicago Defender*, October 13, 1944, 13.

14. In 1963 thirteen schools in Boston were at least 90 percent black. Two years later the number of predominantly black schools had increased. A study conducted by the Massachusetts State Department of Education found that half of the black students (10,400) attended twenty-eight schools that were at least 80 percent black. Sixteen schools located in the black community were over 96 percent black. Six years later in 1971, 62 percent of the black students attended schools that were at least 70 percent black while 84 percent of the white students attended schools that were at least 80 percent white. Between 1965 and 1971 the number of schools that had more than 50 percent black student enrollment rose from forty-six to sixty-seven. See J. Anthony Lukas, *Common Ground: A Turbulent Decade in the Lives of Three American Families* (New York: Knopf, 1985), 126, 130, 132, 216.

15. Albert S. Brossard, *Black San Francisco: The Struggle for Racial Equality in the West, 1900–1954* (Lawrence: University of Kansas, 1993), 43, 280; "School Teachers: Many Cities Appoint Negro Instructors for the First Time to Meet Schoolmarm Shortage," *Ebony*, September 1948, 36–40.

16. Homel, *Down from Equality*, 2; James O. Horton and Lois E. Horton, *Black Bostonians: Family Life and Community Struggle in the Antebellum North* (New York: Holmes and Meier, 1979), 70–76; David Tyack, *The One Best System: A History of American Urban Education* (Cambridge, MA: Harvard University Press, 1974), 112–13; "Segregated Education: Two Views, 1850," in *A Documentary History of the Negro People in the United States*, vol. 1, ed. Herbert Aptheker (1951; New York: Carol Publishing Group, 1990), 297–99.

17. Horton and Horton, *Black Bostonians;* "Segregated Education"; Leonard P. Curry, *The Free Black in Urban America, 1800–1850: The Shadow of a Dream* (Chicago: University of Chicago Press, 1981), 169; Howard N. Rabinowitz, "Half a Loaf: The Shift from White to Black Teachers in the Negro Schools of the Urban South, 1865–1890," *Journal of Southern History* 40, no. 44 (November

1974): 578–79; Carlton Mabee, *Black Education in New York State: From Colonial to Modern Times* (Syracuse, NY: Syracuse University Press, 1979).

18. Mabee, *Black Education in New York State*, 99.

19. James S. Kunen, "The End of Integration," *Time*, April 29, 1996, 43, 45.

20. W.E.B. Du Bois, "Does the Negro Need Separate Schools?" *Journal of Negro Education* 4 (July 1935): 328–35.

21. Darlene Clark Hine, Elsa Barkley Brown, and Rosalyn Terborg-Penn, eds., *Black Women in America: An Historical Encyclopedia* (Bloomington: University of Indiana Press, 1993), 27.

22. Nick Aaron Ford, "Consider the Negro Teacher," in *A Documentary History of the Negro People in the United States*, vol. 6, *From the Korean War to the Emergence of Martin Luther King, Jr.*, ed. Herbert Aptheker (1951; New York: Carol Publishing Group, 1990), 387–91; "A Teacher Looks at Integration," in *A Documentary History of the Negro People*, 218–24.

23. Charles H. Thompson's editorial comment in *The Journal of Negro Education* 22, no. 2 (Spring 1953).

24. "Is There Hope for Negro Teachers? South Must Face Fact That to Scuttle Negro Educators Is to Wreck Its Schools," *Ebony*, November 1955, 35–39.

25. "Phoenix Keeps Its Negro Teachers: Colored Educators Teach White Classes in a City That Voluntarily Integrated Its Schools," *Ebony*, November 1956, 97–100.

26. "Negro Teachers Losing Position," *Pittsburgh Courier*, September 10, 1956, 16.

27. "462 Negro Teachers Out," *Southern School News*.

28. "Faculty Integration Receives Setback with Disclosure of Teacher Firing," *Southern School News* 5 (May 1959): 10.

29. "Impact of the 1954 *Brown v. Topeka Board of Education* Decision on Black Educators," *Negro Educational Review* 30, no. 4 (October 1979): 217–32.

30. National Education Association, "Task Force Survey of Displacement in Seventeen Southern States," Washington, DC, 1965.

31. Their petition was signed by sixteen African-American teachers. "Call to Negro Teachers' Meeting, 1841," in *A Documentary History of the Negro People in the United States*, vol. 1, *From Colonial Times through the Civil War*, ed. Herbert Aptheker (1951; New York: Citadel Press, 1979), 211–12.

32. Leander L. Boykin, "The Status and Trend of Differentials Between White and Negro Teacher's Salaries in the Southern States, 1900–1946," *Journal of Negro Education* 18 (Winter 1949): 40–42.

33. Ibid., 42.

34. Kluger, *Simple Justice*, 185, 191, 197–99, 214–16, 297, 303, 532.

35. Ibid., 16.

36. Boykin, "The Status and Trend of Differentials," 46.

37. "Louisiana Teachers Win Long Fight for Equal Pay," *Pittsburgh Courier*, August 7, 1948, 4.

38. Boykin, "The Status and Trend of Differentials," 47; "Noted Educator Ruby Gainer Resigns After Famed 49-Year Career," *Jet Magazine*, September 10, 1984, 26.

39. "Black Teachers in the South: Negro Teachers' Salary," in *A Documentary History of the Negro People in the United States*, vol. 4, *From the New Deal to the End of World War II*, ed. Herbert Aptheker (1951; New York: Citadel Press, 1979), 37–39.

40. George W. Streator, "The Colored South Speaks for Itself," in *From Colonial Times through the Civil War,* 40–45.

41. Jacqueline Jones, *Soldiers of Light and Love: Black Women, Work, and the Family from Slavery to the Present* (New York: Basic Books, 1985), 138; see also chap. 5.

42. Bert James Lowenberg and Ruth Bogin, eds., *Black Women in Nineteenth Century America: Their Words, Their Thoughts, Their Feelings* (University Park: Pennsylvania State University Press, 1976), 294–95.

43. Ibid., 297.

44. Ellen Nickenzie Lawsen with Marlene D. Merrill, *The Three Sarahs: Documents of Antebellum College Women* (New York: Edwin Mellen Press, 1984), 61.

45. Homel, *Down from Equality,* 110.

46. Ibid., 111.

47. Michele Foster, "African-American Teachers and Culturally Relevant Pedagogy," in *Handbook of Research on Multicultural Education,* ed. James Banks (New York: Macmillan Press, 1995), 2132–82.

48. Census of Population and Housing 1990: Equal Employment Opportunity (EEO) File on CD-Rom (Machine Readable Data Files/Prepared by the Bureau of the Census; Washington, DC: The Bureau [Publisher and Distributor], 1992).

49. Samuel G. Freedmen, *Small Victories: The Real World of a Teacher, Her Students and Their High School* (New York: Harper & Row, 1990); Louanne Johnson, *My Posse Don't Do Homework* (New York: St. Martin's Press, 1995).

50. Kluger, *Simple Justice,* 378.

5

From *Working*

Studs Terkel

Rose Hoffman, Public School Teacher

I'm a teacher. It's a profession. I loved and still love. It's been my ambition since I was eight years old. I have been teaching since 1937. Dedication was the thing in my day. I adored teaching. I used to think that teachers had golden toilets. (Laughs.) They didn't do anything we common people did.

She teaches third grade at a school in a changing neighborhood. It is her second school in thirty-three years. She has been at this one for twenty years. "I have a self-contained group. You keep them all day."

Oh, I have seen a great change since January 6, 1937. (Laughs.) It was the Depression, and there was something so wonderful about these dedicated people. The teachers, the children, we were all in the same position. We worked our way out of it, worked hard. I was called a Jewish Polack. (Laughs.) My husband tells me I wash floors on my knees like a Polack. (Laughs.) I was assigned to a fourth grade class. The students were Polish primarily. We had two colored families, but they were sweet. We had a smattering of ethnic groups in those times—people who worked themselves out of the Depression by hard work.

I was the teacher and they were my students. They weren't my equal. I loved them. There isn't one child that had me that can't say they didn't respect me. But I wasn't on an intimate basis. I don't want to know what's happened in the family, if there's divorce, a broken home. I don't look at the record and find out how many divorces in the family. I'm not a doctor. I don't believe you should study the family's background. I'm not interested in the gory details. I don't care if their father had twenty wives, if their mother is sleeping around. It's none of my business.

A little girl in my class tells me, "My mom's getting married. She's marrying a hippie. I don't like him." I don't want to hear it. It is not my nature to pry. Even a child deserves a certain type of privacy in their personal life. I don't see where that has anything to do with what a child studies. I came from a broken home. My mother died, I was eight years old. Isn't that a broken home? I did all right.

I have eight-year-olds. Thirty-one in the class and there's about twenty-three Spanish. I have maybe two Appalachians. The twenty-three Puerto Ricans are getting some type of help. The two little Appalachians, they never have the special attention these other children get. Their names aren't Spanish. My heart breaks for them.

They have these Spanish workers that are supposed to help the Puerto Rican children in their TESL program.[1] I'm shocked that English is the second language. When my parents came over I didn't learn Jewish as a first language at the taxpayers' expense. The Polish didn't learn Polish as a first language. But now they've got these Spanish-speaking children learning that at our expense. To me, this is a sin. As long as they're in this country, English should be the first language. This is my pet peeve. One of these teachers had this thick Spanish accent. So they picked up this accent too. He pronounces dog "dock." That's horrid.

The language! I could never use some of the words I hear. Up to five years ago I could never spell a four-letter word. Now I can say them without any embarrassment. The kids come right out and say it: "Teacher, he said a bad word." I said, "What's the word?" He said, "Jagoff." I said, that's not a bad word. And they all started to laugh. I said, "Jagoff means get out of here." They laughed. I came home and asked my husband, "What's jagoff?" So he explained the gory details to me. I didn't know it before. These children know everything. It's shocking to me because I think that anyone that uses that language doesn't know any better. They don't have command of any language. (Sighs.) But maybe I'm wrong, because brilliant people use it nowadays, too. I must be square.

There's a saying: Spanish people don't look you straight in the eye because of their religious background. It isn't respectful. I don't believe that. These children, they look you straight in the eye when they use those words. I have never learned how to use these four-letter words until I came into contact with them. I never could even swear. Now I'm brazen. I had a fight with my husband one day. You know what I said to him? "Fuck you." (Laughs.) And I never talked that way. (Laughs.) I hear it all the time from the students. They use it the way we use "eat" and "talk." They don't say "pennies," they say, "f-pennies." Every word. It's a very descriptive adjective.

They knew the words in the old days, I'm sure. But they knew there was a time and place for it. I have never had this happen to me, but I was told by some teachers that the children swear at them. A child has never done that to me.

I loved the Polish people. They were hard-working. If they didn't have money, they helped out by doing housework, baby-sitting for ten cents an hour. No work was beneath them. But here, these people—the parents— came to school in the morning. This is a social outpost for them. They watch their kids eat free breakfasts and lunches. There isn't any shame, there isn't any pride. These Polish people I knew, there was pride. You didn't dare do anything like that. You wouldn't think of it.

I see these parents here all the time. A father brings his kids to school and he hangs around in the hall. I think it's dangerous to have all these adults in the school. You get all these characters. I'm afraid to stay in my room unless I lock the door.

We see them at recess. They're there at lunch time. These people, they have a resentment that everything is coming to them. Whereas the Polish people worked their way out of the Depression. They loved property. They loved houses. My father loved his little house and if anyone would step on the grass, he would kill them. (Laughs.) He'd say, "Get out of here! This is mine!" (Softly.) There was a great pride. These people, they have no pride in anything, they destroy. Really, I don't understand them.

They take the shades. They take the poles. Steal everything. Every window is broken in our school. Years ago, no one would ever break windows. These kids, if they're angry with you, they'll do terrible things. (Sighs.) Yes, the neighborhood is changing and the type of child has been changing, too. They're even spoiling a nice little Jewish boy who's there.

There were middle- and upper-class people in this neighborhood when I first came. They were very nice people and their children were wonderful. There was an honor system. You'd say, "I'm going to the office for a moment. You may whisper." And they would obey. I was really thrilled. I don't dare do that now. I don't even go to the toilet. (Laughs.) I'm a strong teacher, but I'm afraid to leave them.

In the old days, kids would sit in their seats. If I had to leave the room for a few minutes, I'd say, "Will you please be good?" And they were. These kids today will swear, "We'll be good, we'll be good." I don't know what it is, their training or their ethnic background—or maybe it goes back to history. The poor Spanish were so taken they had to lie and steal to survive. I tell them, "You don't have to lie and cheat here. Everyone is equal." But their background . . .

The first contingent of Puerto Ricans that came in were delightful. They were really lovely kids. I adore some of them. I don't care what ethnic group you belong to, if you're a low-down person, I don't like you.

Today they have these multiple chairs instead of the pedestals, seats that were attached. The kids slide all over the room. Anything to make life more difficult. (Laughs.) If I didn't laugh at these things, I couldn't last. Whereas it was a pleasure to teach a motivated child, how do you motivate *these* children? By food? By bringing cookies to school? Believe me, these children aren't lacking in anything. If I ask for change for a dollar, I can get it. They have more money . . . We have seventeen that get free lunches, and they all have this money for goodies.

I've always been a strong disciplinarian, but I don't give these kids assignments over their head. They know exactly what they do. Habit. This is very boring, very monotonous, but habit is a great thing for these children. I don't tell them the reason for things. I give them the rote method, how to do it. After that, reasoning comes. Each one has to go to the board and show me that they really know. Because I don't trust the papers. They cheat and copy. I don't know how they do it. I walk up and down and watch them. I tell you, it's a way of life. (Laughs.)

At nine o'clock, as soon as the children come in, we have a salute to the flag. I'm watching them. We sing "My Country 'Tis of Thee." And then we sing a parody I found of "My Country 'Tis of Thee."

> To serve my country is to banish selfishness
> And bring world peace
> I love every girl and boy
> New friendships I'll enjoy
> The Golden Rule employ
> Till wars shall cease.

And then we sing "The Star-Spangled Banner." I watch them. It's a dignified exercise. These children love the idea of habit. Something schmaltzy, something wonderful.

I start with arithmetic. I have tables-fun on the board—multiplication. Everything has to be fun, fun, fun, play, play, play. You don't say tables, you say tables-fun. Everything to motivate. See how fast they can do it. It's a catchy thing. When they're doing it, I mark the papers. I'm very fast. God has been good to me. While I'm doing that, I take attendance. That is a must. All this happens before nine fifteen, nine twenty.

The next thing I do is get milk money. That's four cents. I have change. I'm very fast. Buy the milk for recess and we have cookies that I bring. To motivate them, to bribe them. (Laughs.) I also buy Kleenex for them, because they'll wipe their nose . . . (Laughs.) By nine forty, which is the next period, I try to finish the marking. Two of the children go to a TESL program. (Sighs.)

Then I have a penmanship lesson on the board. There it is in my beautiful handwriting. I had a Palmer Method diploma. On Mondays I write beautifully, "If we go to an assembly, we do not whistle or talk, because good manners are important. If our manners are good, you'll be very happy and make everyone happy, too." On Friday we give them a test. They adore it. Habit, they love habit.

They drink their milk. I have to take them to toilet recess. I have to watch them. No one goes unless they're supervised. We watch them outside. If there's too much monkey business, I have to go in and stop them. When they raise their hands in class, I let them go, even if they're lying. I tell them, "If you're lying and get in trouble, you won't be able to go again." So I hope they tell me the truth every once in a while.

About eleven o'clock, I give them an English workbook. I pass the free lunch tickets out about a quarter to twelve. Sometime during the day I give them stretching exercises. Sideways, then up and down, and we put our hands on our hips and heads up and so on. I'm good at it. I'm better than the kids.

I have reading groups. One is advanced, one is the middle, and one is the lowest. At a quarter to two we have our spelling—two words a day. Six words a week, really. If I did any more, it's lost. I tried other ways, they did everything wrong. I didn't scold them. I researched my soul. What am I doing wrong? I found out two words a day is just right. Spelling is a big deal. We break the words. We give them sentences. I try to make it last till two o'clock. Fifteen, twenty minutes, that's their attention span. Some days it's great. Some days I can't get them to do anything.

I take them to the toilet again because they're getting restless. Again you watch them. From a quarter after to about two thirty we read together. I give them music, too. That's up to me, up to my throat. They love music. I have it two, three times a week. At two thirty, if they're good, I give them art. I make beautiful Valentines. We show them how to decorate it. And that's the day. If they're not good—if they scream and yell and run around—I don't give them art. I give them work. If they're not nice to me, I'm not going to be nice to them. I'm not going to reward them.

Three fifteen, they go home. You walk them all the way down to the door. You watch them all the way. (Laughs.) I go home. I'm never tired. I go shopping. I give every store on my way home a break. At twelve o'clock I go shopping, too. I have to get away from the other teachers. They're always talking shop.

I don't take any work home with me. With these children, you show them their mistakes immediately. Otherwise they forget. When I'm home, I forget about school, absolutely, absolutely, absolutely. I have never thought of being a principal. I have fulfilled my goal.

As for retirement, yes and no. I'm not sixty-five yet. (Laughs.) I'm not tired. It's no effort for me. My day goes fast, especially when I go out the night before and have a wonderful time. I'm the original La Dolce Vita. If I have a good time, I can do anything. I can even come home at two, three in the morning and get up and go to work. I must have something on the outside to stimulate me.

There are some children I love. Some have looks and brains and personality. I try not to play favorites. I give each one a chance to be monitor. I tell them I'm their school mother. When I scold them, it doesn't mean I hate them. I love them, that's why I scold them. I say to them, "Doesn't your mother scold you?"

These children baffle me. With the type of students we had before, college was a necessary thing, a must. They automatically went because their parents went. The worship of learning was a great thing. But these children, I don't know . . . I tell them, "Mrs. Hoffman is here, everybody works." Mr. Hoffman teases me: "Ah, ah, here comes Mrs. Hoffman, everybody works." Working is a blessing. The greatest punishment I can give these children is not to do anything. If they're bad, you just sit there and we fold our hands. I watch them. They don't want a teacher, they want a watcher. I say, "Mrs. Hoffman is too dumb to do teaching and watching. If you want me to be a teacher, I'll be glad to be a teacher. If you want me to be a watcher, I'll have to watch you."

The younger teachers have a more—what is their word?—relaxed attitude. It's noisy and it's freedom, where they walk around and do everything. I never learned to teach under conditions like that. The first rule of education for me was discipline. Discipline is the keynote to learning. Discipline has been the great factor in my life. I discipline myself to do everything—getting up in the morning, walking, dancing, exercise. If you won't have discipline, you won't have a nation. We can't have permissiveness. When someone comes in and says, "Oh, your room is so quiet," I know I've been successful.

There is one little girl who stands out in my mind in all the years I've been teaching. She has become tall and lovely. Pam. She was not too bright, but she was sweet. She was never any trouble. She was special. I see her every once in a while. She's a checker at Treasure Island.[2] She gives no trouble today, either. She has the same smile for everyone.

Pat Zimmerman,
Alternative School Teacher

He is "headmaster" and administrator of the Southern School in Uptown.[3] *It's an alternative school. It began in 1969. "I knew the kids were getting in trouble around here. I simply felt I could teach them and make their troubles less. Someone offered me a storefront church which was used only on Sundays. Someone gave us desks and a couple of tables. I scrounged up some textbooks, and we began—even though there was no income for a while. There was none of the planning and campaigning that many free schools have for months . . . It began with about eight kids.*

"It's changed in its four years. We're much more diverse now. No more than fifty percent are poor Southern whites. The others are Chicago kids—blacks, Puerto Ricans, and a couple of Indians. Mike Mayer teaches a class of boys between the ages of eight and sixteen. Jean Fisher and Mary Ryan have a class of girls between the ages of seven and fifteen. I have a class of boys between the ages of twelve and seventeen. There are three classrooms, a large recreation room, and a TV area. We're up for accreditation in May."

He is thirty-one from South Carolina, of a working-class family. He "drifted until '67. Suddenly I had the urge. At one time, I'd have said I had the calling. I started teaching . . ."

I'm a strict kind of teacher. When I say something to one student in a very quiet voice all the way across the room, I want it quiet enough to reach him. I don't have to tell them to shut up very much. It's self-enforced.[4] I make a lot of demands on my students and I get honestly angry if they don't live up to their possibilities. The importance is not whether a teacher is strict. Is it for the kid's benefit or is it to make his teaching role easier and not get involved? My idea of being a teacher is influenced by my idea of being a particular person. I'm dealing with a particular kid.

I don't have any idea what any of them will end up being. So I'm an unsettled teacher in a classroom. A certain tenseness, nervousness about me because I don't like facing a lot of kids who have the cards stacked against them. They catch on and have some hope and that helps a little.

It isn't the kind of free school you read about. We're involved in picking up basic skills that others have neglected to teach the kids. Some of them have feelings of rage, undefined, and they're acting it out in school— dangerously. We try to calm them down.

In a neighborhood like ours it's very dangerous. It's low income and there are many ethnic groups. This community has experienced its war on poverty and hasn't changed. The kids now don't believe in politics. They don't believe things will get better for them. There's a feeling of hopelessness and despair.

They're from ages six to seventeen. The age difference doesn't really . . . Certainly a fifteen-year-old kid is not going to see an eight-year-old as his equal. But kids do throw off the age barrier and relate to each other as human beings. Because they see us doing the same with them.

The person's who's sixteen realizes he has a lot of catching up to do, work. He knows I'm not gonna embarrass him. Other kids are having the same problems. I discourage competition in the classroom. The only one I accept is the student's competition with himself. He has to compete against where he is, against where he wants to be, and against where he has been. I think every kid understands that. They don't have to prove anything to me. Each kid has to prove to himself that he's worthwhile. There's no cheating here. There's no reason for it.

We're not trying to jive 'em into learning. We lay out powerful materials in front of them, and tell 'em they're perfectly capable of doing it—and not to make any excuses about it. We use newspapers, too, and catchy urban stuff—but more as diversions. If you con someone into learning, you really believe they're not capable of it. So we're straightforward. Our learning materials are very hard. That's tough.

I have some that may end up in college, but I don't push them. I sent a boy to Latin School.[5] He got a scholarship. He was so unhappy there he did everything he could until I took him back. I thought he would have everything to make him happy. Bright, colorful people who smelled of the security of success, friendly teachers, a magnificent building, all the books he could read. But he was missing something—friendship.

I don't think they want to be doctors or lawyers. It's not because they don't know. It's that they have no expectations. Some have vague feelings of wanting to be teachers. They aren't interested in professional roles. See? They just want the security of working—a steady job. Something their parents haven't had in Chicago. These kids are living out their parents' hopes. It's popular today to look at success of minority groups in terms of upward mobility. I don't know that upward mobile groups are so happy.

The majority of our parents are on welfare. When they screw up, they get ashamed and hide from us. The family's falling apart and we've known them for a long time. They can't face the fact. They know it doesn't have to be as bad as it gets sometimes. They know what they're capable of.

We only get to know the families if they want to know us. If a kid doesn't want us involved, we trust that that's the best thing for him, that somehow he needs us all to himself, not to share with his family. If there's a real problem between the kid and his family, the greatest respect we can show him is not to get involved. To give the kid a chance to pull himself out by himself. We trust the kid enough to be an autonomous individual. Hopefully, if he feels better about himself, the family will pick up on that. Very often the kids become effective—quote—therapists—unquote—in the family situation. One kid has carried the major load in helping his father get through some difficulties.

I try to be fairly aware of their feelings. Sometimes I feel guilty that I identify too much. I always let them know when they touch on my feelings, and what those feelings are like. I think children are unaware of what adult's feelings are like. Some of these kids that I've taught for a while—I've had some for four years—who are sixteen and seventeen, are getting a taste of those feelings. On the other hand, adolescents have new feelings, different from the ones I had when I was their age. So they're willing to share my feelings as an adult, because they know that I know they have new kinds of feelings. Maybe that's the pain—trying to share it with them. They're reaching across and trying to touch something they've never experienced before—adulthood. In a specific situation of urban life—poverty.

In my school the teachers have the decision about who they want to take or not. No administrator does that. He decides what he wants to teach and how he teaches it. My only requirement, as an administrator, is that he teaches well.

Our classes are segregated by sex. It's easier for them to study. They don't have to play out the traditional sexual roles demanded of them in the neighborhood. They're not secure in being men, so they play at being rough around their women. They have to be. The girls overact and become overseductive and overteasing. We give them a chance to have one place in their lives where they can put aside these roles. Our students have a chance to become more natural in their sex roles as they get away from the defenses that their parents have felt.

We spend so many hours here. Our lives, fortunately or unfortunately. It's very hard for us to get away from it. My work is everything to me. I find myself trying to get an hour or two of personal life now and then—in vain. I'd rather die for my work life than for my personal life. I guess you can't really separate them. The school's not an institution. We have a building, that's where the school exists. But it also exists when we leave.

We often work after six. The people we work for—the National Institute of Mental Health—once wanted us to do an honest time sheet. After they saw our honest time sheet they said, "Just please put in eight hours a day on the time sheet." (Laughs.) Weekends? What weekends? (Laughs.) I work Saturday morning, writing letters, administrative details. I usually work Sunday afternoons and Sunday evenings.

My first year I taught at an all-black school on the South Side. I worked with a very strong woman teacher who was well liked by the students. I picked up a lot of her strength. My second year I was on my own and very unhappy. The students were holding back and I was holding back I couldn't get involved in their lives and they couldn't in mine. We were playing roles. It was like a polite dance. I liked them, they liked me. We both knew there was a great deal missing.

I have to have complete freedom in what I'm going to teach, and what words I use in the classroom. If I want to cuss at them for something, I cuss at 'em. A certain kind of cussing is an emotional release. If I want to discuss intimate matters with them, I want to be free to do so without justifying it to an administrator. I want to go to the parent's house and scream and yell at 'em if I feel that's gonna shape the kid up.

If I see the day's gonna be a rotten day because everybody's in a lousy mood, I want the freedom to pick up and go someplace and not pretend it's going to be an okay day. I don't tell them, "Let's be happy today, have fun." Sometimes I say the opposite. (Laughs.) I say, "I'm very unhappy today and we're not gonna have fun, we're gonna work." They pull me out of it. And when they're in a lousy mood, they don't hide it. They certainly let me know it.

We hosted a free school from Minneapolis. I thought the students were unhappy because they didn't have a whole lot of direction. There was a great deal of liberty that I don't think the kids wanted. The teachers seemed more interested in theory than in the actual work of teaching. It was incredibly well funded with a staff of twenty-five to 180 kids. There wasn't much I could say to them. In these situations adults are robbing adolescents of their childhood. Children deserve a chance to be irresponsible, to learn from mistakes. You lose your childhood soon enough in a low-income neighborhood.

I don't think these kids are capable of being adults—or want to. In some free schools adults are ready to give away their adulthood and take away from students their childhood. It's fraudulent and becomes chaos. They're forcing a young person to be older than he really is. The freedom of our school is bounded by two obligations: learning and no violence against another person, physical or emotional. That includes me too.

Our school has sixty-eight students and we're still too big. I wanted to set the limit at fifty. But I'm too tenderhearted. (laughs.) If someone knocks on our door long enough, they can get it open. I make a distinction between people who deserve to be cared about and some who have completely given up. They don't deserve the attention because they take too much away from the others, who somehow want to pull some worth out of their lives.

The self-destructive ones deserve someone to completely mother and father them. If someone is willing to commit his or her life to that one person, okay. But not in a classroom with other people who want to care as a group. You see a kid who's been fine for six months just suddenly collapse, and there's no way . . . What happens is the other kids spend an awful lot of time ignoring the fact that it's happening. They expend a lot of energy protecting themselves emotionally—from it catching on to them. A teacher goes through an awful lot of anguish watching someone they care about give up.

I was very upset yesterday. A kid collapsed in October and was sent away for criminal activities. He reappeared on a furlough, begging to come back when he gets out. Though I care about him very much—I don't know. It's like a ping-pong game. I haven't decided.

Grades? I give grades, but they aren't entered on anything. I simply keep them in mind as a trend . . . Kids like grades, 'cause they like to know where they are right now. Records? No. They have enough records. They have police records, social history records, welfare records. (Laughs.) I should have to keep records?

I think the parents are glad we're around. We take a great deal of pressure off them. We give them a chance to get on with other things in their lives. We've had a lot of families move back South. A great deal of our neighborhood has gone under the bulldozer of urban renewal. Families who haven't done so well after eight, nine years have now decided they'll give the South another try. Kids are getting in neighborhood trouble. City life may be just a bit too hard.

We're really content when our students get a full-time, good paying job. We're always around for him to learn if he wants to. He's still interested in learning about himself. He realizes his life doesn't end when he gets a job. Or when he gets married, his life doesn't end. He doesn't end up in heaven or hell because he got married.

From what I've read about concentration camps, there's a similarity in feeling to ghetto areas. The walls aren't built, they're there. How your life can become concentrated. Rather than escape from it, I've tried to do what some survivors did—find meaning in it to share with other people. Not in any martyr kind of a way, because I can always leave. But it's something beautiful to me. Being able to be hurt by things and then understanding how it happened and explaining to others who have been hurt by the same things.

I run into people who say how much they admire what I do. It's embarrassing. I don't make any judgments about my work, whether it's great or worthless. It's just what I do best. It's the only job I want to do. I work hard because I have to. I get tired. At four I feel as though I'm ready to die. (Laughs.) I don't feel bad about it. This is my life. I just *am*.

NOTES

1. Teaching English as a Second Language.
2. A "super" supermarket in the community.
3. A Chicago area in which many of the Southern white *émigrés* live; furnished flats in most instances.
4. When I was there last year for a commencement talk, the parents, many of them wives of *émigré* black lung miners, were attentive. The students were excited and voluble, what with soda pop and cake. A casual look from Pat, momentary silence—in fact, profound attention—and the ceremonies began. Later, I found out that the whispers and giggles concerned me. They were anticipating my surprise and speechlessness at the presentation of their gift—a railroad man's gold watch, inscribed.
5. A posh private school—upper-middle-class.

II

Combating Racism
and Homophobia

6

The Making of a Revolution

Judith Rényi

We want all of our children to graduate from high school. We want our schools to consider the possibility that they are poorly organized to achieve this aim. But the question of who decides what is taught in school and the basis on which school values are determined is widely disputed. Many Americans believe that we already basically know what we want our children to know, we just have to devise better methods and structures for making sure all our children learn those things. New voices have been raised, however, that say some of the things worth knowing have never been taught in school. These are things relating to what children know already, and especially children of minorities and the poor, who have been less successfully schooled in the past than the middle class. These voices say that we will never achieve the goal of school success for everyone until and unless the knowledge the children bring with them is respected, and indeed taught to develop, in school. These voices have joined a national debate that has angered and even outraged many Americans of all colors and classes.

The anger and outrage, audible on all sides of the arguments about what to teach in our schools, comes from a recognition that the determination to help all children graduate from high school has crept up on us without having caused any major changes in what we teach. Many Americans believe that what we teach should not change, but simply be offered more strongly and cohesively so that more Americans can learn to participate in what makes us great as a nation. But many Americans, and particularly Americans of color who are distressed at their children's continuing school failure, believe that that failure has to do in part with school teachings that leave them out or despise them. These critics say that schools will never reduce the drop-out rate until they teach a curriculum more inclusive of all Americans. In order to achieve the goal of school completion for all, a curriculum revolution must take place that respects the children and their knowledge and includes that knowledge in the content of school. Yes, the multicultural-education advocates say, school needs to teach a stronger, more cohesive curriculum, but that should not mean just more of the same. They say it should mean a transformed curriculum that encourages new faces to fill our senior-year classes—faces that have only sporadically appeared there in the past.

Traditionalists worry that the advocated multicultural education changes would weaken our national integrity, damage the world's most successful democracy, and fragment our polity into contentious forces splitting off in many different directions. Multicultural education, they believe, would destroy the unity of belief and loyalty to the nation that should be the primary teachings of the public schools. Multicultural education would allow each group of people, defined by ethnicity, to go its own way, neglecting in the process our national unity of purpose and democratic ideals.

Curiously, this message, advocated in national policies, has stressed primarily the economic purposes of schooling and has only begun to mention the necessity of an educated populace to participatory democracy in reaction to perceived threats to that purpose from multicultural education. Advocates of multicultural education seem to pose such a threat when, in their most radical moments, they announce that education and the content of school curricula are fundamentally racist and must be changed completely to teach each ethnic group to take pride in its ethnicity and learn in school about its ethnic heritage at the expense of learning about a more general American culture. What has been taught in school until now, say such writers, is that white Anglo-Saxon culture is the equivalent of American culture, and they reject that as no longer acceptable for children of other ethnicities. There can be no unity of belief and loyalty in the United States, they claim, as long as the content of school remains primarily a content that leaves out and disrespects the cultures of its minorities.

The charge of racism does not sit well with education leaders of any kind in this country. Our national habit has been to think our public schools have offered the best opportunity to shape a liberal democracy in the history of the world, and hence our public schools are fundamentally the seat of liberal reform—the ills of society, its inequities, its poverty, would all disappear from the democracy if only we could find ways to educate all Americans equally.[1] An educated populace, in Thomas Jefferson's terms, would become a populace capable of carrying on the work of the democracy. An educated populace, in Lyndon Johnson's terms, would also overcome economic inequities and provide equal opportunities for economic success to all citizens. If only we could ensure that all children graduate from a good high school, our country would become a stronger democracy and an even greater economic success, for each of its citizens and for the nation as a whole.

Many multicultural-education advocates, however, believe that a stronger democracy and equal economic opportunity will never be achieved as long as school disregards alternative ways of knowing, believing, and feeling. Ways of knowing, they say, are intimately bound up in culture: how people use language, how they come to understand who they are, how they got to be that way, and how they characteristically shape their visions of the world. Those ways of knowing differ from ethnicity to ethnicity. Anglo-Saxon ways of knowing are only one set, which happen to conflict with other ways of knowing peculiar to African-Americans or Native Americans or other ethnic groups. To continue to impose Anglo-Saxon knowledge and ways of knowing on all of these Americans would be to assume that Anglo-Saxon ways are better than other ways, to disrespect other ways, and hence to be racist.

Those who oppose such ideas countercharge that to define knowledge by ethnicity is itself a racist notion, one which assumes that knowledge is inherent in race and ethnicity instead of being universally available to all. Multicultural education ignores what we all as human beings and as Americans hold in common, in favor of highlighting differences. American public schooling should have as its primary focus the teaching of what we share, not what divides us. The forging of a single nation out of the world's most diverse population must require that public schools take us as we come in all our multifariousness and make of us a single people. Certainly, we need to be sensitive to the need to include more knowledge about the histories of minorities and women than schools taught in the past, but that should not alter our fundamental purpose of teaching how eventually we all come to be Americans and to share a common democratic purpose.

Both sides of this debate have clashed over a profoundly important question having to do with who we are as Americans, what we hold in common, and the extent to which public school is the crucible in which that commonality is forged. The major differences between those who hold opposing positions in this debate arise over a question of ownership of the curriculum and therefore over the stories we choose to tell our children about America and Americans.

This debate has arisen because we have actually begun to realize the dream of educating all Americans. This nation has a tremendous success story to tell about education. In 1820, 70 percent of American workers were farmers or farm laborers. By 1870, 50 percent worked on farms and 10 percent held white-collar jobs, while the rest worked in factories and mines, on railroads, and in other industries. By 1960 less than 10 percent worked on farms, while 40 percent held white-collar jobs,[2] and today, less than 3 percent of Americans designate themselves farmers. In 1870, when the vast majority of America labored in factories and on farms, only a total of some 80,000 adolescents were enrolled in 500 high-school academies nationally, and most of these private schools could be found in the Northeast. In 1870, 16,000 students received diplomas—only 2 percent of the population of seventeen-year-olds. Of these, most continued on to college. High school, just 120 years ago, was not an end in itself but academic preparation for college and a professional life. Only forty years later, in 1910, 1.1 million Americans were enrolled in high schools; of these students 90 percent were in some 10,000 public high schools, all of which had come into being in that forty-year period. Some 15 percent of children aged fourteen to seventeen were enrolled, most no longer headed for college. These schools were an end in themselves, providing the foundation for children destined to go into the working world only after an extended education.

By the end of World War I, most states had enacted compulsory school attendance laws, and school enrollments vastly increased. But those laws could not indefinitely hold the children of the poor, whose work was needed in the grocery store and steam laundry as well as on the farm and in the mills to supplement the family income. The 85 percent of young Americans who did not enroll in high school in 1910 had to make their way in the economy through work, not education. That 85 percent included European immigrants of all kinds—Italians, Slavs, Jews, and Scandinavians as well as newly annexed Mexicans in the Southwest and West, Native Americans, Chinese, Japanese, and the vast majority of whites of English, Irish, and German descent as well. In 1910, although high-school populations had grown hugely compared to the previous generation, it was normal to work. It was abnormal to go to high school.

High-school attendance in this century has very much to do with the kind of work and the amount of leisure available to children. When child labor laws were enforced early in the twentieth century, it became less possible to supplement family income with their labor. High-school enrollments exploded between 1900 and the 1920s as a result. These years also saw the beginnings of the Great Migration of blacks from the farms of the South to the industrial cities of the North. But the black population that moved north found itself trapped in cities whose manufacturing base was already faltering. Jobs for unskilled labor were declining in Chicago, Philadelphia, and Milwaukee as early as the 1920s. The Great Depression ruined marginal family farming as well as manufacturing industries in large parts of the country, sending new waves of unemployed whites as well as blacks out on the road in search of work. High-school enrollments continued to grow, ironically benefiting from the bleak work prospects of young, unskilled laborers. They stayed on in school for want of anyplace better to go.

While high-school attendance continued to grow steadily throughout the 1930s, significantly fewer than the majority earned a diploma. The great change to high school completion by the majority of teenagers occurred after World War II. Prosperity did it—a prosperity that created a booming economy, plenty of jobs, and the high wages that enabled most Americans of all races and income levels to keep their children out of the labor force until their late teens. While ideas of whom to educate had been evolving since the major growth of public schools at the turn of the century, revolutionary changes began only after World War II. Millions of G.I.'s returned from war to a country that wanted to build a strong peacetime economy but worried how to convert its immense war industry to peaceful purposes without suffering the catastrophic joblessness that had prevailed in the decade before the war. The solution was the G.I. Bill: the United States sent its young returning soldiers to college.

Until the late 1940s only a tiny minority of the nation had gone to college. The G.I. Bill taught the nation to believe in higher education for the majority. Ordinary men who would never have imagined that a college education was either possible or necessary found themselves capable of further study. The war had matured them, shown them a larger world that they would never have discovered in their home towns, and enlarged their visions of their own abilities. A nation of white men was transformed from the breadlines, soup kitchens, and despair of the 1930s to the corporate offices, confidence, and belief in progress of the expansive 1950s. The women who had riveted warships and conducted the business of the country during the war returned home, donned their aprons, and started producing the baby boom that, throughout the 1950s and 1960s, so increased the numbers of children that they threatened to burst the seams of the nation's public schools.

The industries that had vanished in the dust of the Depression and left a populace unhoused and unable to find work never reappeared. In their place came a new postwar economic expansion that could afford new jobs only for a more highly educated populace, one ready to expand America's power to world-wide cultural and economic leadership. American mass marketing, mass entertainment, communications, and advertising turned us into a consumer economy at home and an expansive economy abroad. We were ready to Americanize the world, and we went to school to prepare ourselves to do so.

Children of the 1950s and 1960s in turn grew up in households that expected from the start to send them to college. White America built and bought suburban homes, commuted to the cities to work, and enjoyed a prosperity and belief in America's greatness unprecedented in the history of the world. It all seemed normal, despite the too-recent memory of the ills of the 1930s. That had been an aberration, it seemed, in the strong America that could provide economic well-being for everyone. We were all going to enter the middle class. School meanwhile reinforced this image of the greatness of America, its political and ideological triumph, and its moral righteousness in an otherwise benighted world.

By 1957, the changes wrought by World War II and the G.I. Bill, domestic prosperity and the end of the industrial era, found 90 percent of adolescents aged fourteen to seventeen enrolled in high school. Many stayed longer because compulsory education laws in many states now kept children in school longer than in 1910. But 62 percent of those enrolled graduated. In 1940, 15 percent of the eighteen- to twenty-one-year-old population had gone to college. In 1959 that proportion doubled, largely due to the G.I. Bill; in 1960, 35.5 percent of the population eighteen to twenty-one went to college.[3] The high-school diploma had been, from 1900 to 1940, a final certification before work for almost all of the middle class. By the 1960s it was beginning to look as if even that was not enough. Most now began to assume that the majority of the population would go on, if not to college, at least to some form of postsecondary instruction in preparation for a career.

But what is true for the population at large is not true for specific minority groups. People of color did not partake fully of the prosperity that suburban white America was beginning to enjoy. We revolutionized who went to school and for how long for the white populace, but we had to go to court to do so for the black populace, not just once, but again and again in the 1950s and early 1960s, until we had learned to revolutionize our thinking about all Americans and put them all in school. In 1954, the Supreme Court dismantled separate schools for black Americans. After *Brown* v. *Board of Education*, public school meant public schools for all, white and black alike. Yet nearly forty years later, the full impact of that decision has not been realized.

While graduation rates have slowly but steadily improved for all minorities, large numbers of Hispanic, some African-American, and many Native American children have been left behind. With an overall urban school drop-out rate of one-third, as many as 45 percent of Native Americans drop out before earning the diploma. Such minority groups, moreover, disproportionately find themselves in classes for low achievers. One-fourth of all Native Americans and one-third of Native American boys are in special education classes. Those few Native Americans who make it to postsecondary education tend to be women in their thirties, who earn their diplomas through the General Education Development (GED) program. According to 1990 census data, however, 26 percent of all American nineteen-year-olds had not completed high school.[4] Belated attention to minority school completion rates did not occur until the 1960s. In studying differential school success for white and black populations, we learned that such success had more to do with the economic success of the population as a whole in a particular school building than with personal attributes of race or class of individual students. The 1965 Coleman report, *Equality of Educational Opportunity,* told the Congress of the United States that the nation's schools were still segregated, that they closely resembled each other in terms of how they were organized and what they taught, and that the ways in which they differed (e.g., library collections, teaching staff, spending) had little impact on differences of student performance. What made a difference for any one child was the extent to which that child attended school alongside others who were affluent. A black child—even a poor black child—in a middle-class school had a greater chance of academic success than a rich white child in a school largely filled with children of the poor.[5]

By the mid-1960s the War on Poverty was in full swing. It sought to address the economic woes of the inhabitants of cities, who were overwhelmingly poor and often black, left behind by white flight. The schools became the focus for social policies that sought to remedy the wrongs left unresolved by the courts. As a nation, we had already decided that everyone should finish high school. But not everyone conformed to the image of the white middle-class Americans for whom academic study was designed. Head Start would help prepare children suffering the deprivations— particularly the cultural deprivations—of poverty to enter school with the kind of knowledge white middle-class children got at home. Readiness for school meant knowing the names of colors and numbers before first grade and interacting with adults in ways acceptable to the norms of school. The poverty programs of the 1960s for the first time provided federal tax dollars to schools to serve the poor. The Elementary and Secondary Education Act of 1965 and its various programs provided money to states and districts based on poverty formulas that put extra resources into schools to compensate for children's deprivations. These programs defined the problem of lack of student success as lack of children's knowledge, for which school could compensate. The education revolution was in full swing; everyone would go to school, but school would not change its habits to accommodate everyone. The burden of change rested on the *children's* need to change to fit in.

Despite the War on Poverty, even despite the gains made for children in Head Start and its successes in remediating math and reading, poverty persisted and got worse. By the early 1980s the Secretary of Education, Terrell Bell, announced that ours was "a nation at risk" because our public schools had lost their capacity to produce a well-educated populace. Bell's report heralded a decade of changes. He told us that all our schools were failing, that even in white suburbia the best that could be said of schools was that they had declined from striving for excellence to being content to wallow in mediocrity. We asked too little of our students and we got what we deserved. We needed to strengthen our standards everywhere, get rid of the free-for-all education of the sixties that had produced the shopping-mall high school, and get back to basics. The states responded with a will. State legislatures launched new testing programs meant to shake up lackadaisical districts and improve their results. Getting those reading and math scores up was the new battle cry heard in state after state. Publishing all the districts' scores side by side allowed us to embarrass those districts that failed to do a good job. The districts responded in many places by throwing away electives and making sure all the teachers taught the standardized curriculum the state was going to test. "Drill the skill" was the order of the day as teachers prepared their charges for the tests.

But these national responses to the call for improving our schools continued to disregard the nature of the target population of schoolchildren. In the period 1971–80, 78.6 percent more immigrants entered the United States than had entered in the period 1950–60. From 1900 to 1980 the white population dropped from 87.7 percent to 83.1 percent of the total, while citizens of other races increased from 12.3 percent to 16.9 percent, exclusive of the 8.1 million Hispanics who were designated "white" in 1980.[6] Twice as many different nationalities resided in the United States by 1980 as had in 1920, partly as a legacy of the changes in the Immigration and Nationality Act of 1965 that equalized ceilings for countries in Europe with those of countries from other continents. Nearly three times as many immigrants entered the United States in 1980–89 as had entered in 1951–60. In the earlier period, 48 percent of the immigrants were of European extraction. In the last decade only 10 percent came from Europe, while nearly 80 percent came from Latin and Central America and Asia.[7]

This new diversity was more equally distributed across the United States than ever before.[8] Not just port cities, but the whole of the interior of the country began to see new faces in neighborhoods, at work, and in classrooms. Just as the U.S. population became more diverse than ever before in its history, the national call for school reform resulted in curricula more restrictive than they had been in the 1960s and 1970s, demanding more testing, more standardization, more containment, and less diversity in what was taught. The diverse population did not in this case cause the restrictive school reforms, but the effect of such reforms was to fall on a more diverse population than ever before.

Despite the increase in testing and standardization, the children of the poor went on failing disproportionately, even when the state tests were so easy as to be laughable measures of knowledge. The same districts that were at the bottom in the seventies stayed at the bottom in the eighties; the children of the poor and the children of minorities kept dropping out. Research showed they started giving up in third grade, were mental dropouts by seventh, and left at the first legal opportunity to do so in tenth. The racial differentials in high-school graduation rates persisted. According to the Children's Defense Fund only 58.4 percent of black eighteen- and nineteen-year-olds and 52.4 percent of Latinos of that age have diplomas. By the ages of twenty and twenty-one the gap narrows significantly for whites (85.2 percent with diplomas) and blacks (81.5 percent) but stubbornly remains at 54.9 percent for Latinos ("An Advocate's Guide to Improving Education," September, 1990).[9]

Throughout the 1980s substantial gains were, however, made. The Scholastic Aptitude Test (SAT) scores of black children rose steadily in math and English, and their drop-out rates fell.[10] Minority college participation rates also showed major gains.[11] Improved family income, raised expectations for college attendance, and possibly affirmative action seem to have increased the proportion of Americans who were ready and able to go on to higher education in the last decade.

Many teenage dropouts find an alternative way of earning the diploma later in life: in 1989, 81.1 percent of nineteen-year-olds, 86.5 percent of twenty-four-year-olds, and 86.9 percent of twenty-nine-year-olds had completed high school.[12] For members of the working poor who cannot afford to stay in school until their late teens, it has been common practice to drop out before receiving a diploma and then to return to earn an equivalency diploma if and when it becomes economically important to do so.

Despite the very high number of GED equivalent diplomas earned by older adults, we prefer to educate all Americans in their teen years. Fifteen percent of our children still drop out of school.[13] Why can't they, like the rest of the population, succeed just as well in school as we and our ancestors did? Why should there be any need for special changes in our successful formula, our tried-and-true method of Americanizing everyone?

There are two differences between this last 15 percent of schoolchildren today and the immigrants and the poor of the past. First, in the past we did not in fact ever expect the poor to finish school. We expected them to drop out, to go to work, and to succeed economically so that, perhaps, their children or grandchildren would have the leisure to afford to finish school. Immigrants were once content to postpone for a future generation what they did not expect for themselves. But now we are looking at the first generation of the poor who are expected to finish school whether or not doing so is economically viable for them. They are being asked to believe that school itself is the route to the middle class. Although this can be true, it has more often been the case that the capacity to go to school for twelve years was the *result* of having middle-class means. We now seek to educate the poor through the end of high school for the first time in our history— the first such attempt by any nation in the world.

The second difference between the poor of today and those of the past is that the poor Italians and Irish and Jews and even Scandinavians of the past were "voluntary immigrants," to use the phrase of anthropologist John Ogbu: people who chose to come to America to seek their fortunes or escape the ills of their homelands, although they might suffer both racial and other forms of discrimination when they came. Americans of African descent never chose to come here. Native Americans never chose to be Americans. Many Hispanics were incorporated into an America that annexed formerly Mexican territories.

More important to their perception of school than their involuntary origins, perhaps, is the fact that generations of these groups have earned diplomas without it making a difference to their social or economic status. Furthermore, many members of these groups perceive the educational opportunities available to them as below par in comparison to what is available to other Americans. A Gallup poll in 1991 reported that 83 percent of American whites believe that blacks and other minorities have the same educational opportunities as whites. Only 38 percent of blacks believe these opportunities are equal.[14] Such differences in perception signify a serious rift, matched by the differentials in drop-out rates between whites and blacks, differences in achievement, and ultimately, differences in hope for the future.

If the political leaders of this country and the population as a whole genuinely want all children to graduate from high school, then we must all of us take a very careful look at what divides us racially and ethnically in our perceptions of the current state of education and in the remedies needed to achieve our goals.

At present, the division seems to run along the following lines. Those who are successful and empowered seek to reinvigorate the common core of learning that has served them well for 150 years; they believe in the American dream of individual effort and hard work paying off with academic and economic success. Those for whom such effort, work, and achievement have not resulted in economic success, even after generations have gone by, take issue with the common core of learning because they see it as one of the ways in which white America excludes them from the promise of education. They seek to bring collective pressure to bear on changing the common core of learning, believing that success will come only from group solidarity. They feel the myth of individual success will not apply to them as long as racism obliterates the unique merits in individuals by lumping them together in ethnically stigmatized groups.

In all the raging debate about the schools, we have heard much about race and ethnicity and little about class, yet class also persists in defining much of what school is about. Multicultural educators, angry with school ways, often ascribe to racism school's will to make children learn middle-class manners and morals, sit still, dutifully complete mindless tasks, follow orders, and restrict expansive habits. Such teachings originated, however, in classism. Confusions of this kind occur when, as often happens, the poor who are the targets of school reprimands happen also mainly to be black or other minorities.

This becomes an important issue to keep in mind if we remember that the purpose of the revolution in schooling is to reach the remaining one-fifth of our population, the children of the poor, and to help them find a way to stay in school until graduation. While much of the contention over how to go about doing that has to do with cultural differences deriving from ethnicity, some of the difficulties children experience in school also have to do with class issues. Our intention, as a nation, is to educate a social class that has never in history been educated before. I believe that in order to do this, assumptions about schooling and the links between education and middleclass ways need to be reexamined very carefully.

Education in the world has undergone two major changes in the past two millennia. In the first phase, literacy and numeracy were necessary for two purposes: to conduct the administration of wealth and power, and to preserve and transmit sacred texts. Educated clerks and accountants have always been needed to carry out the first purpose and priests to carry out the second. In ancient China as well as Sumer and Mexico, writing developed and was transmitted to new generations in order to count and record food stores and other forms of excess wealth and to preserve stories about the divine origins of the kingship and the people. Not until the last few hundred years have the ranks of the literate and numerate increased significantly from a relatively small coterie.

In the Western world, the second phase of education occurred in the sixteenth century, when the Reformation and the invention of moveable type put sacred texts in the hands of massive numbers of people. Literacy and numeracy expanded well beyond the relatively few merchants and priests who had needed them until then. Protestantism brought to Christianity a will for each soul to interpret sacred texts for himself. The Renaissance also introduced to large numbers of people the possibility of reading secular texts. The middle class began to grow, partly defined by its economic place and partly by its literacy. But the texts at the center of their education continued to consist primarily of the sacred texts of the priestly class and the high-culture texts of the wealthy and powerful.

The third phase is upon us here and now in democratic America. Literacy and numeracy and the texts on which we center their acquisition should be available to all, we say. Yet the texts we use in teaching literacy and numeracy still seem to be partly descended from the priestly and royal purposes of ancient days and partly from the creations of the literate middle classes of the past few hundred years. Because of this history, the texts of school seem to concentrate on matters alien to the poor—to fail to give them voice. If we are seriously going to try to educate this last 20 percent, we need to consider how we are going to assist them in finding their voice so that they too can contribute to the dialogue through which educated people interact with each other across the ages. The revolution that wants all children to be successfully schooled suggests that the poor must enter that conversation and thereby make a new literacy and vision for us all.

In order to enter that conversation all students will need access to a powerful liberal education, but for most of this nation's history, high school curricula have not been studied by the majority of Americans. The common core that has been available to the poor as well as almost everyone else has been the elementary curriculum. As we shall see, that curriculum has never sought to develop intellectual capacities beyond minimal skills and has never contained very much of what we commonly call the Western liberal tradition.

As high schools developed at the end of the nineteenth century, a debate arose as to whether the most recent immigrants should be allowed to attend at all. The huge waves of new, diverse students threatened to overwhelm the schools. The response was a compromise: a two-track system developed in the early twentieth century that reserved the liberal arts for the elites and invented a new set of subjects called the "mechanical and manual arts" for the laboring masses. What little of history, mathematics beyond mere numeracy, science, second languages, and literature had until then existed in the common schools was removed from them, delayed until high school, and offered only in the academic track. Until World War II that content remained out of reach of 85 percent of American students. What was left in the elementary education that most Americans received bore little intellectual resemblance to what was taught in high school. That split in content between elementary and secondary curricula continues to this day. In elementary school, children read what educators and editors compose for basal reading series; they hit ninth grade and get Shakespeare for the first time. Youngsters fool around with arithmetic worksheets for eight years, reach ninth grade, and face algebra. Ninth grade is generally perceived to be a terrible year for school failure, and no wonder. Little in the first eight years of schooling prepares students for the shock of the academic high-school curriculum.

Our common school heritage, in this century as in the last, is the culture taught in the lower grades. In 1870 only 2 percent of seventeen-year-olds graduated from public and private high schools combined; 6.4 percent in 1900. Most of these were girls headed for brief teaching careers of their own. In 1898, 95 percent of all school enrollments were in elementary schools, with an average stay in school of five years. In 1920, nearly two-thirds of the relevant age group were enrolled in high schools, but only 16.8 percent graduated. Compulsory education laws by 1930 raised those figures to 73.1 percent enrolled and less than one-third graduated, and by 1940, 79.4 percent enrolled and slightly over one-half graduated. Meanwhile, for African-Americans, who embraced schooling wholeheartedly after emancipation, larger percentages (18.7 percent) attended public schools in St. Louis than whites (12.9 percent) in 1890; in 1897, 86 percent of six- to thirteen-year-old black children attended school in Philadelphia. Black literacy rose from 42.9 percent in 1890 to 90 percent in 1940, accompanied by a vastly increased high-school attendance rate.[15] By 1960, 99.5 percent of all seven- to thirteen-year-olds were enrolled in school. What they learned there, however, perpetuated the distinctions between the economic classes.

Since the early nineteenth century, highbrow subjects have been ridiculed as unsuitable for the masses, abstract studies that working people don't need.[16] Vocational education tracks satisfied the desire for a high-school education without having to offer academic subjects to the poor and people of color. Tracking into remediation and into vocational-technical programs has disproportionately kept these groups out of the academic subjects, even if they enroll in high school and even when they earn the diploma.

On all sides of the contentious and acrimonious debate over multicultural education, deeply held beliefs—for some, beliefs on which successful lives have been built—are being challenged. Because the poor of today are disproportionately people of color, what used to be a class issue has become a race issue. Race issues surface in public schools today as never before because race issues no longer focus merely on access to the school building; they now focus on access to the school curriculum.

The question before us, therefore, is one of rethinking the curriculum for everyone—how to offer a more substantive and valuable liberal education in all the grades of school and for all the students. The task before us is the invention, for the first time, of a common core of learning that will reach all of the students and engage them all in the conversation of the educated. This is an exciting venture, and perhaps the most important revolution in the history of literacy. It goes beyond questions of economic purposes for school, even beyond national or patriotic purposes. It goes to the heart of questions having to do with civilized humanity and what it means to invite all people of all races and economic circumstances to participate in civilization.

NOTES

1. See Richard H. de Lone, *Small Futures: Children, Inequality, and the Limits of Liberal Reform* (New York: Harcourt Brace Jovanovich, 1979).
2. Martin Trow, "The Second Transformation of American Secondary Education," in *Power and Ideology in Education*, ed. Jerome Karabel and A.H. Halsey (New York: Oxford University Press, 1977), 106.
3. Ibid., 107, 109.
4. Debra Viadero, "Dropout Rates for 5 States," *Education Week*, September 23, 1992, 24.
5. See Frederick Mosteller and Daniel P. Moynihan, eds. *On Equality of Educational Opportunity: Papers Deriving from the Harvard University Faculty Seminar on the Coleman Report* (New York: Random House, 1972) for analyses of the Coleman report, including Christopher S. Jencks, "The Coleman Report and the Conventional Wisdom," 69.
6. James A. Banks, *Multiethnic Education* (Needham Heights, MA: Allyn and Bacon, 1988), 11–12.
7. U.S. Bureau of the Census, *Statistical Abstract of the United States: 1991*, 111th ed. (Washington, DC, 1991).
8. Lawrence H. Fuchs, *The American Kaleidoscope: Race, Ethnicity, and the Civic Culture* (Hanover, NH: University Press of New England, 1990), 278, 283, 292–93.
9. I am convinced the large differential for Latinos is attributable to new immigrants being included with native-born Americans of Hispanic descent in these figures.
10. Russell Edgerton, "A Long, Deep View of Minority Achievement," *AAHE Bulletin*, April 1991, 3–7, 30.
11. Pew Higher Education Research Program, *Policy Perspectives* 4, no. 2 (March 1992), C.
12. Michael W. Kirst, "The Need to Broaden Our Perspective Concerning America's Educational Attainment," *Phi Delta Kappan*, October 1991, 118–20.
13. The Children's Defense Fund report issued in 1991 gives this statistic, pointing out that the current profile differs from the stereotype. The majority of the poor live outside of central cities; most are not on welfare, most are not black, and two of five live in two-parent households. The persistence of the stereotype, however, imagines the poor as black, welfare-dependent, inner-city dwellers and illegal immigrants. Such stereotypes inform much of the

corresponding school mythologies to be discussed in this book. On the Children's Defense Fund report, see *Education Week,* June 12, 1991, 4.

14. Stanley M. Elam, Lowell C. Rose, and Alec M. Gallup, "The 23rd Annual Gallup Poll of the Public's Attitudes toward the Public Schools," *Phi Delta Kappan,* September 1991, 47.

15. All statistics in this passage are from David B. Tyack, *The One Best System: A History of American Urban Education* (Cambridge, MA: Harvard University Press, 1974), 57–58, 66, 183, 122–23, 222.

16. David Nasaw, *Schooled to Order: A Social History of Public Schooling in the United States* (New York: Oxford University Press, 1979), 127.

7

We Make Each Other Racial: The Madison High World as Perceived by the "American" Student

Laurie Olsen

The discussion in Lisa Stern's sixth-period world history class began neutrally with students being asked to do a "quick write" introductory writing exercise using the prompt: "If it were up to you, what would you learn in high school that would be useful to you? What would you be studying?" They were then asked to share what they had written.

There were few affirmative answers about what might be useful to learn in school. Their responses were instead couched in accusations about what they are not getting and why. The discussion exploded into a general frenzy of voices. "Why do we have to learn the same thing over and over? Why do we learn about the past?" The anger was initially expressed as resentment that some students get what others do not.

> TONY (WHITE): If there's ethnic studies for one group, it has to be for all of us. It's not fair if the other guys get it and we don't! They think their culture is so important, well so is ours!

> MARVIN (LATINO): Yeah, but there is no ethnic studies here anyway, what are you talking about? No one cares at this school. They don't teach us nothing. Particularly us Latins.

> TONY, PERSISTING: Well, what if you wanted to learn about a different culture? It shouldn't just be Raza studies for the Latins. How come we don't have it for everyone? How come we can't study about white culture, too?

At this point, a student attempted to assert a class alliance, heading off the threatened racial split in the group and emphasizing how they are all treated alike.

ALFRED (WHITE): Knock it off, you know we don't get any kind of real studies at all because the school's too poor.

JEFF (WHITE): It wouldn't happen even if we tried. No one tries. No one comes together.

VIVIEN (FILIPINA): You said it, no one tries.

MS. STERN: You all sound so discouraged!

CLASS: YES

ALFRED: This school doesn't even have any money to spend on us.

TONY: We're getting NOTHING!

JENNIFER (WHITE): School isn't what kids want. If it was up to us, we'd never come up with a high school like this as what we want. We have to read *Lord of the Flies,* and the teachers don't explain it to us. They don't care if we understand it or not. They're just putting in their time. It's all a game. We're supposed to just put in our time, too—seat time. To grind us down. To learn that it's all about sitting still and taking it.

JEFF: A lot of stuff is just never even taught to us. And when we do read stuff, you don't get to discuss it. We don't get what other schools have. I know kids who go to other schools and they look down on us. We're the lowest. And we're supposed to think we're getting an education.

MARVIN: We come for the diploma. We want a diploma.

VIVIEN: To be able to say I finished high school. That's what keeps me coming. It seems like it's important, you know, to say that I walked across the stage, but then I think, say it to who? What does it matter?

MARVIN: We have to try to better ourselves. But we don't learn the stuff that helps to better ourselves. The students over in Oakland care. They had a walkout for ethnic studies. Here, no one cares. Our teachers are being laid off. The district don't care about us or what we think. All they do is get you down.

LORA (AFGHAN): They should be encouraging us! All they care about is getting us out of their hair.

And in this moment of solidarity, the villains become not just the teachers or the administrators or the district, but the newcomer students who are viewed as perpetuating the belief that school is about getting ahead.

VIVIEN: So for us, school is just, you come to classes and you just sit there. And if you sit there long enough, after four years they give you a diploma. After a while you figure it out—you don't get anything and you don't give anything. The only ones who don't get it are the ESL kids. People tell us, we should be more like them, we should try hard, we should study as hard as they do. I get so mad! They are so blind! They still believe. But sooner or later, they'll get it, too. We just don't matter.

The world inhabited by the "American" student at Madison High is every bit as intensely involved with "finding one's place" as the immigrant world; however, the arenas are not about being American, they are about "race" and class. The maps these students drew for Stern's social studies assignment were almost wholly racialized maps: almost every social group was labeled either by a racial identifier or the category "mixed race." There were two exceptions, which were labeled by school activities ("band kids" and "basketball players"), and a single undifferentiated group of "ESLers," a label referring to newcomers by their programmatic placement in English-as-a-second-language classes.

The descriptions they created for the school overall were largely American ethnic and racial categories, attended by great detail about the behaviors, activities, and common interests that mark these categories or distinguish sub-groups. For example, groups were referred to as "white skaters," "white smokers," or "white social outcasts." Many groups are also labeled by their geographic turf on the campus.

Here is a collection of the descriptions used to label the maps of the "American" students:

There are two categories of "the White race" students:

By A Hall and sometimes by E Hall or the Portables are the white skaters who hang out in the sun. They are largely excluded by the

PLAYING FIELDS

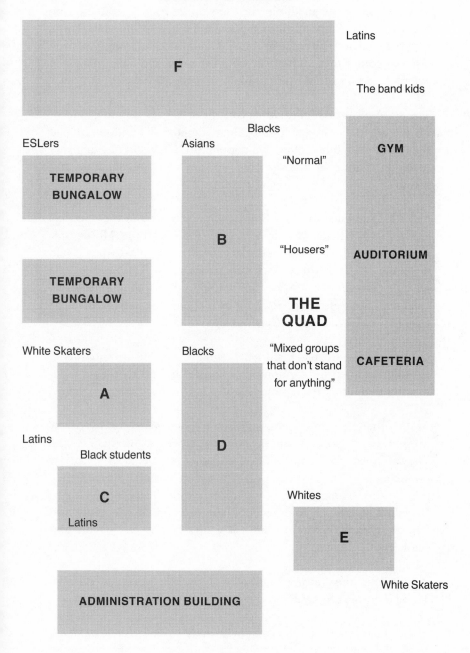

school. They dress alike; they don't care what others think. They aren't exclusive or anything; they are pretty friendly. But no one really pays much attention to them. They listen to the same music (heavy metal and "alternative" music), and they hang where no one else will bother them. They stay out of the way, and hang in a place where the administrators are unlikely to come after them.

The smokers [who] hang out across the street are another kind of white student, bound together by their addiction. They don't hide it, they like the visibility. They don't apologize. They don't belong very easily on campus in other groups, so they hang out separate and distinct.

Mexicans stay far from the administration, close to the street so they can see their friends who drive by and stop for awhile. Mostly they hang out outside of C Hall at the street end or just inside the C Hall, down the hall from where black students hang out. The Latinos dress alike. It's just their style. They are considered very cool. Others feel excluded, not welcomed. Some of us feel nervous walking through C Hall. It's a lot of the East Gardens kids.

In the middle are black students, a big group of around twenty (mostly freshmen and sophomores) who kid around a lot. They seem to know each other from junior high.

At the other end are Filipinos and some other mixed Asians. Nicely dressed, baggy pants, beanies. These are "housers," they can dance. They are relaxed. They don't exclude other people. They are pretty popular.

D Hall is where the cheerleaders hang out. These are white and female. These are another kind of whites besides the skaters and smokers.

B Hall is for the "normal" kids who study. You know, just normal. There is nothing to say about them.

In the Quad at the center of campus is where blacks practice dancing. Nerdy kids hang close to the cafeteria, studying. It's a place of mixed races, who are pretty accepting. There aren't quarrels in the Quad area. There is a definite Asian group, but they are pretty accepting of others and friendly. People in the Quad are just normal people. They don't have a title or a place or one race. They don't stand out for anything.

Hardly anyone hangs out near F Hall—It's a place for loners.

Near the basketball courts, kids who want to play go. This is a mixed-race group behind the gym. It is mostly guys, but some girls come to watch them play. When administrators aren't around, they play craps.

The quiet band kids are near the band room.

These descriptions are rich in aspects of youth culture that are deemed important: the kind of music people listen to, how friendly or unfriendly the group is thought to be, how they dress, how they are thought of by others in terms of being popular or cool. And almost all have racial labels. The one group that is identified by where they live are the Latinos, who would have been enrolled in Washington High if it were still open. They are markedly not part of the "community" of Madison High. What is unclear is whether they themselves have taken on the badge of their East Garden neighborhood as a key identifier, or whether it has been a label given to them by those who consider them outsiders.

The Quad is the one area of campus identified as the turf of mixed groups. It is interesting that the words attached to these groups are terms such as "normal," "accepting," "don't stand out," and "don't stand for anything." In fact, the Quad is a rather large area and quite crowded. Architecturally, it is the heart of the campus. It is widely acknowledged as an area of social mixing between the groups. And yet it commanded very little attention as students got into discussions about their maps and became engaged in describing the social world of the school. It is not that they deny that mixing across races occurs, or that there are some social arenas of the school life that are pretty "accepting and friendly." Rather, what holds their attention, what they feel is salient to talk about describing the dimensions of social life, are the separations, the differences of race and ethnicity.

Learning To Be Friendly, Carefully

The sixth-period "regular" class argued at length about whether the campus is primarily a mixed-race campus of friendship groups, with a few groups who keep to themselves or whether it is a wholly racialized campus of separate groups who stay separate, with a few kids who mix. There was enormous tension in the discussion, and clearly heavy investment in how students might choose to view their school's social climate. Is it divided by race? Is it a mixed campus? Is it happily diverse? Is it tense and hostile? Is it all of these things?

Some students spoke of their fear of walking past or through the turf of other racial groups, an issue that came up in the descriptions they gave of certain areas of their maps. Some mentioned being hurt when rejected or put down by people or groups of races other than their own whom they tried to befriend. Others insisted that their friends were of all races and they get along great. It was a heated and tense discussion. Apparently, there were high stakes in the social representation of their world.

After a lot of discussion, the consensus seemed to be that the social life of the school was about groups isolating themselves by race. The students viewed the sharpest conflicts as between the Mexicans and blacks, with heavy rivalry between the groups expressed primarily through verbal exchanges and occasional fights. C Hall was identified as the tensest locale on campus, and in fact, a stabbing occured there early one morning as school was just starting because of a conflict between rival gangs. Most agreed that the sharpest separations occurred between freshmen and sophomores who are new to the school and are still finding their way. The longer people are in the school, the more they claimed to have found a way to live comfortably in and with the divisions, to be more skillful when walking through the turf of other groups, and to make friends across ethnic lines. As one student said: "It's a matter of getting comfortable with it all, and then learning the skills of how to be friendly, carefully."

> There is a lot of teasing here about being a wannabee. People don't want others to think bad about them for not being where they belong. They don't want people to think they are rejecting their people by choosing to be with others.

How complicated the rules of interaction are at this school! By the time students are juniors and seniors, they have begun to master the art of being friendly with people of racial groups different than theirs without appearing too eager as "wannabees" and without appearing to reject their own racial identity.

Most of the social maps drawn by the "American" classes simply did not have any mention of the newcomer groups on campus. Only two had any mention, and they both put "ESL kids" on their maps as a single undifferentiated category. Absent are the national or language identities. The only notice is of a group in terms of its programmatic place in the school, defined by its lack of English. When the absence of the immigrant students was mentioned to the "regular" history class and comparisons made between the immigrant maps and their maps, the sixth-period students acknowledged that immigrants were indeed present in the school and should be on the map. "We just didn't think of them," the group said in defense of their social map. Then they proceeded to add to their map the descriptions: "ESLers hang out over by the edge of campus near the Newcomer School." The category they used was a single "ESL" label, echoing the basic truth that newcomers are seen primarily in terms of their lack of English-speaking ability. One student said, "By E Hall is where ESL kids sit and talk. They don't connect to anyone else. It's their differences that bond them." And another added, "They hold on to their language. They don't even try to speak English."

As a follow-up to the social-map unit, Stern had her classes continue to focus on aspects of the social experience at Madison High. Among the assignment were small group-class projects, created to examine what it is like being a white student at Madison and what it is like being an immigrant student at Madison. A third was assigned the task of probing interracial or interreligious dating.

Stern was particularly interested in having a group of white students explore their own experiences and those of their white friends in attending a school in which they have become a numerical minority. Her concern stemmed from knowing the increasing activity of white hate groups in the community and their recruitment efforts at Madison High. From class discussions and student journal entries, when she had done a social studies unit on historical scapegoating and prejudice in which she had the class analyze hate materials, she knew there was an undercurrent of fear and anger among many white students in the school.

> It seems like my white students think they have no culture at all, and
> it feeds a kind of targetless anger against things like Black History
> Month. I can't teach a curriculum that includes black history and
> Raza issues without somehow finding a way to address its impacts on
> the white kids.

She wanted to provide an opportunity, a safe and sanctioned opportunity, for white students to reflect and speak about their feelings. This new unit was a way to try to address that undercurrent. The assignment read:

EURO-AMERICANS/CAUCASIANS/WHITES
Your group, a group of white students, is charged with finding out what some of the racial attitudes of white students are at Madison. Each of you will interview about five students and you will pool your

information to make general conclusions based on what you found. You should try to determine several issues that you think white students are concerned about, and create questions to get good responses. For example, you might want to ask white students how they feel about being called names that are related to the fact they are white. Because you, too, are white (or look white to others), chances are they will be a bit more comfortable opening up to you. Do not put words in their mouths. Let their answers be entirely theirs. A second aspect of the project will give you an opportunity to reflect on your own feelings.

QUESTIONS TO THINK ABOUT IN FORMULATING YOUR INTERVIEW QUESTIONS:

- What are the feelings of white students about being in a diverse school?
- What kinds of problems do they face as a result?
- What advantages do they see in the diversity?
- What general social issues do they feel threaten them as whites?
- Do they think the school is racially harmonious?

It was, as Stern suspected it might be, controversial. One Latina asked, "Isn't that racism, Ms. Stern, to put people in a working group just because of their skin color?" But the white students wanted to do the project. And they defended with anger what they perceived as their right to be in an all-white assignment group. "You all get to have your clubs—the Black Student Club, and La Raza. We never get a club. For once, let us have a group."

The white students worked hard, as one student wrote in her evaluation of the unit: "We worked harder than we have ever worked on a social studies project. This just seemed so important. It was our one chance to let other people know what it is like for us. We wanted it to be good."

One strong pattern that emerged was the development of their own racial consciousness among white students.[1] In the midst of the intense racial sorting of the student body, white identity has losts its transparency for white students. They no longer are able to see themselves as raceless (a privilege associated with racial domination), but are awkwardly, painfully, and sometimes with great resistance developing a recognition of race for themselves. They are seeing themselves from the outside as a racialized person, as "white," "honkies," "crackers," or "oppressors"—the words others apply to them. A junior tried to explain this process:

You know everything was fine before I came to Madison. In elementary school up to middle school, we were just all friends pretty much.

Then you get to middle school and high school and WHAM, it's like you're white you belong over here, and you're black and you are supposed to act a certain way. Here, I'm a white kid. You know, it's something everyone says about other people—a way you describe people. You're white, like it's a big important thing about you. And you can't tell like if it's an okay thing and like they are just describing you, or like are they saying you're some kind of honky or bad person.

In the midst of this process, there is a crisis of identity among some of the white students at Madison. On arrival at Madison, they seem to find that for the first time in their lives they do not represent the majority. Despite the whirling demographic changes occurring in their communities, most residential areas are relatively separated by skin color. Students attend elementary schools in their residential neighborhoods, but as adolescents are combined into larger consolidated secondary schools; the multicultural reality of the city becomes apparent to them. School is the major public institution and public space where young people find themselves actually confronting this reality. As they move from elementary to middle school to high school, the white students see their numbers dwindle as the dominant group in their schools. This is not only their own experience as they move through school, but a perspective they have about the difference between things now and the way things "used to be" in the community before their time. Even though white students are still the majority among the academic classes of the Madison school system, many expressed anxiety or resentment at the increasing numbers of immigrants and Asians they perceive as pushing them out of their place in the academic hierarchy. The language used in Stern's sixth-period history class when students were explaining why they think immigrants come to the United States reflects the language they use in talking about being pushed out by Asians in their academic classes. It is almost evocative of the ways they talk about immigrants in general. Here is an example:

They come to take our jobs, and they are willing to break their backs for shit pay, and we can't compete.

These Chinese kids come over here and all they do is work and work and work and work, and all you have to do is look in the AP [Advanced Placement] classes and you'll see they are filling them up. No one else can compete anymore.

They just want to take over.

Many of the students at Madison are working class, who look beyond their high school years with an apparent kind of cynicism, knowing they have little capital in the world and what little they have stems from being white and English speaking and native U.S.-born. Although some white students sit back in silence, giving no hint of their opinions, others express enormous anger over affirmative action and regularly voice their feeling of being discriminated against. They rail against the existence of ethnic clubs in a school where ethnicity is the major basis of club organizations on campus, and insist they should be allowed to have a European American club, but have little interest in actually organizing one. Only rarely a voice speaks up in support of changes needed to address inequities and discrimination against students of color.

"She's Black and I'm White, and That's That."

Every one of the white students interviewed for this study is acutely aware of their white identity within the social world of Madison. But when they leave school, most move back to worlds beyond the school, where they believe their whiteness has no particular meaning. To them, school is the site, the place, the world that racializes them. School is the place they feel put down for being white, or excluded for being white. And school is the place they associate with being taught the lessons of racialism.

Several girls gathered to talk about the transition from elementary school to middle school, and the lessons of racialization. One spoke in tears about her best friend Rose in elementary school.

> We were so glad we were going to go to the same middle school. But something happened there. She's black and I'm white, and we just started having different friends. We'd still get together sometimes after school, but not at school. I don't how it happened, and we never talked about it. But she ended up with all black friends and I ended up with all white friends. And I missed her, but never said anything. Now we're both at Madison. You know, I see her pass by sometimes in the Quad, but we never stop to talk, and it feels kind of awkward. I used to cry about it, but now I'm used to it. It's just how the world is. She's black and I'm white, and that's that.

In Lisa Stern's social studies class, white students were outspoken about their discomforts. Jeff writes in his final paper on the unit on white experience, echoing what I heard over and over from white students about how localized at school the experiences of whiteness have become for them:

I don't like to talk about racism, and don't like that Ms. Stern is making us to find out about things like races at Madison. I never think of myself as white any place but at school. I don't like racism but there is nothing I can do, it is everywhere. We just have to learn to put up with different skin colors and cultures. These folks aren't gonna disappear. I'm proud to be a Euro-American even when dummys try to discriminate against me. I mean, what do they want me to do, change colors? People at Madison think in terms of race all the time. But out in the world, I never have to think of myself as white—only here.

Jennifer, as a white cheerleader, is safely ensconced in one of the few social settings of the school in which white students still predominate. After asking twenty white students what it was like being white students at Madison High Jennifer explained:

I liked the chance to talk to white students and find out exactly how they feel about being white in a diverse school. I mean, we talk to each other all the time, and people make remarks or comments sometimes, but we don't really talk about this. We don't think of ourselves as white until someone makes us think of ourselves as white. I was shocked! And I was surprised at how honest people were when I interviewed them. It turns out that inside, all of us at school know we are white and feel that it is this big thing. But we never talk about it to each other. When I interviewed them, none of them liked the idea of an unqualified black getting a job over a qualified white. But when asked how they felt in a school with lots of races and cultures, there were a lot of different and mixed feelings. It boggles my mind how differently people feel about the same situation! It really disturbed me that kids in this school would join the KKK. I thought the KKK only existed in the South in the 1800s, not here in Bayview now, not in my school. When I dug deeper into these kid's thoughts, I found out their parents were also racist. But it's like, you know, if they [the blacks] are gonna make a big deal about us being white, okay, we will too. I think a big part of the whole problem is how kids are raised and their upbringing. It's our parents. I wonder if things will ever change. I don't even think assemblies or anything about racism make any difference. It's all in how we see each other. We make each other racial.

As the white students' projects evolved, many of their comments in small groups focused on defending the right of white people to feel angry for the position they are thrust into. Here are some excerpts from these conversations:

As long as there is special treatment for some races, there will be angry people who don't get special treatment and it will cause major problems. You can't stop anger from people who don't get fair treatment. JESSE, A WHITE STUDENT TALKING ABOUT AFFIRMATIVE ACTION

Very few whites are really racist here. But most of us are upset about the way whites are constantly stereotyped. We feel like we are being forced to pay for the sins or mistreating that were invoked by whites a great many years ago (none of the kids here were even related to anyone who was around when there were slaves; our families came to the United States after slavery was over). And we are always getting threatened by other races. They have too many things to help minorities, like affirmative action. And they deserve them, but so do we. How come we don't get any help. LISA, WHITE

Education doesn't help one bit when certain races pass along a 200-year old hate. Most of the reasons why people hate each other is because lots of whites just hate blacks because they are black, and there are lots of blacks who just hate whites because they are white. It doesn't make sense, maybe, but hate is strong. There is a lot of tension that most people pretend not to see so they can figure there isn't a problem. They are living in a fantasy world. Things have been done to me because I'm white, and I have gotten to the point where if someone pissed me off really mad, I would have the guts to blow their brains out. I'm sick of it. Sick, sick, sick. Yes, I'm white. And I'm proud of it. MIKE, WHITE

For these students, trying to define areas of commonality and similarity and to dispute the notion that they have privilege is complex. They see a kind of class commonality, and do not see racial privilege. They have no historical perspective to help them, and little current information that might mitigate their stances that "racism was back then, this is now and we're in the same boat." Much of the conversation revolved around "being in the same boat as they are," claiming similar class positions, or feeling discriminated against, and disputing the existence of white privilege. Here's an example taken from a comment of a white boy who is a junior. "My old man doesn't have the money to send me to college either, so how come I can't get any help and a black kid can."

Few of the white students feel they are getting much help in "getting ahead." In particular, they talk about not getting help to go to college, not being able to get into college, and not being eligible for financial aid. Most are struggling. A class solidarity with students of color at Madison seems obvious to them. Their privileges as whites are invisible. The majority of their references to race were about black-white relations. Interestingly, most of the discussion about getting help, about being in the same boat, about comparisons to other groups who "get help" is in reference to blacks. The complaints, the anger, the hurt of white students is aimed at black students when it comes to "getting help." They simply believe that blacks are getting something that whites are not, and it is not fair. Their anger at immigrants has a different tint.

The comparison to "Latins" was rare. In fact, despite the large numbers of Latinos in the school and community, somehow Latinos seem irrelevant in the analysis and comments. The comparison to "Chinese" or "Asians" was often in terms of anger at being pushed out, but not felt as unfair. There may be resentment that these groups "work so hard," but their rewards were generally viewed as earned privilege, reasonable rewards. These groups were viewed as doing so well academically because they work so hard. The bitterness is expressed in terms of "they want to be better than us."

"It's Racial, Pure and Simple. There are Some Kids Who May Mix Here, But Mostly You Stay with Your Own Kind."

One's social capital at Madison in the world inhabited by "Americans" is measured and conferred in terms of one's identity. Crossing the line socially and one's style (dress and behavior) are heavily monitored by the students. It is not that students do not cross lines to have friends of different racial groups or even to date. In fact, there are plenty of mixed-race friendship groups. The campus is dotted with such groups. But unless these friendships are rooted in activities such as the band or sports teams, such mixing becomes noticed, commented on, and tempered by a lively discourse among peers and between students and their parents. The formal activities appear to provide a rationale or reasonableness about the mixed-race associations—but cross-friendships outside of the context of such formal activity seems somewhat in need of explanation or defense. Students talk pretty unanimously of the tension with regards to who your friends are, how you dress, and the racial appropriateness of those choices.

It is most often the peer reactions that dominate their concerns. For students of color, there is little that is as hurtful or as threatening to their sense of identity as being labeled "white-washed." "White-washed" is used a lot in passing conversation. One Latina explains: "If you don't speak your own language, you are white-washed—you have forgotten who you are."

"White-washed" refers to talking white, acting white, wishing you were white, getting good grades or "being in good" with the teachers. Move-

ment toward white behavior or white groupings on the parts of many students is carefully monitored by others and viewed as clearly objectionable,
disloyal, and forgetting who you are. It is not universally true that all students engage in this kind of monitoring. But it does appear to be the norm.
Those students who "mix" or "don't care how others want them to act
"tend to be defensive about their positions and often cite being put down
by others.

For students of color who are more culturally identified with another
nonwhite group, the monitoring term is the label "wannabees."
"Wannabees" is regularly used and sometimes refers to specific subgroups
of students, e.g., "those girls who smoke cigarettes and hang out near C
Hall are a bunch of Latin wannabees." These words have power. Apparently, no one wants to be labeled either white-washed or wannabee, for
they connote lack of authenticity. Underneath these terms lies a host of issues such as loyalty, resistance to white cultural domination, and fear. This
seems to be particularly true for Latino and black students. For example,
Trina, a Latina senior who has a mixed group of friends, explains: "My sister hangs around *cholas*—you know, wannabee *chola* types. She's said stuff
to me like, you're a white-washed Mexican, just look at your friends. I want
to smack her."

Aisha, a black student, said:

> Either you're a black person and you're hard, or you're white-
> washed. I've been called white-washed because I don't hang around
> just with black kids. Some of the black girls here don't like the way I
> do my hair (straightened). I'm supposed to have hair up to here with
> tons of grease in my hair and talk like I'm from the ghetto. I wasn't
> brought up like that, but there are a lot of people here who think
> that's how I ought to be.

Developing armor against the hurt of these charges becomes an important survival tactic for students who chose to still cross the lines. Sandy, a
senior who has been buffeted back and forth through periods of sticking
with black students and periods of venturing out into mixed groups, explains it in the following way:

> There is a lot of shit talking, but as you get older if you're a stronger
> person you can get over it. People say "You're not really black." Well,
> guess what, I'm always going to be black; my skin is black. The world
> treats me like I'm black. But since I don't act "black," then they say
> I'm not. I'm blacker than half the people at this school. I know more
> stuff about my history than they do. But they say, you don't have hair

up to here and you don't have five earrings in your ear and lip gloss all over your face, so you're not really black. I try to shrug it off, but it gets to me. I get it from both sides.

And Andrea adds:

Me and my sister are two different people. My sister is really into the black thing. She's a sophomore and younger than me. We walk down the hall together. I keep to myself. I won't say anything to anybody unless they say something to me. But Stephanie is out there. If someone looks at me wrong, she'll go up to them and say. "What the fuck are you looking [at]? Don't touch up my sister." I'm older and she is younger, but she's like out to protect me. She's the one where if any shit even threatens to come on, she's the first one to say, "Don't mess with her because I'll kick your ass." She's out there. And I'm more the white sister, the one that will keep to herself and not start shit with anybody. She's more defiant, more extreme, more black.

Patty, also African American, has a Latino boyfriend. They don't hang around with anyone else at school. She says, "I hear this all the time. You don't have a black boyfriend, you're not a black." For white students, the charge of being a wannabee is the strongest epithet. It is akin to saying "go back to your own kind."

And yet, for many of the students, hanging out with kids they identify as of their own culture, as sharing the experience of skin color, also has deep positive meaning. Their choice to be together is a choice of preference— of friendship that often has a history in their community and in elementary school, a choice for the ease and recognition that comes from sharing a code and culture. There is comfort from shared experience, a protected shelter against the racism and prejudices of others, as well as pride and loyalty. Raul, a tenth-grade student expresses some of this:

It's racial, pure and simple. There are some kids who mix here, but mostly you stay with your own kind. It's important to know who you are and be true to who you are. Some kids are wannabees, looking somewhere else instead of standing by who they are. Me, I'm proud to be Latin. I feel good to be with my Latin brothers.

And thus, the social life of the school is created around racialized groupings and maintained through an active system of monitoring. "Finding your place" and "staying within your own group" is generally viewed by students as a positive value. It is about loyalty to one's people and knowing who you are. The students who are the proponents of these values contrast them with "losing who you are," a process they define as living in a racist society that would deny them that identification. They view their strong group identification as resistance to forces that would make them invisible or denigrate them. Time and again, in discussing these racially defined social groupings, students would become defensive. Robert, a black junior, explained:

It's not about not liking other people. It has nothing to do with who you are, it's about who I am. We gotta know who we are and feel pride in that. I'm black, and that's me, and I don't kid myself about it and I won't let nobody keep me from myself. I'm black because I claim it!

And yet, they construct narrow boundaries for themselves and others, limiting the multicultural possibilities inherent in a campus and community that is so diverse. The friendships lost, the cross-cultural understanding and learning that might have been gained, the connections that might have been possible are foreclosed. The many students at Madison who are biracial or multiracial cannot embrace their full humanness, but rather are pushed to choose one part of their being for their social identity—or find it chosen for them.

"There Is What We All Say, That No One Is Prejudiced and We All Get Along—and Then There Is What We Do."

For the students presenting their maps and discussing these social issues in Stern's classes, each discussion eventually focused on the different versions of the social maps and on the seemingly crucial issue: "How separate are we?" This led to an examination of how students learn to perceive and find their way around a diverse and complex social environment.

The class puzzled about the kind of survival and coping skills they had to develop to make their way through the subtle divisions of the campus:

People getting along here depends on everyone pretending they're okay with each other. It's death for it to get around that you're prejudiced against another group, or that you're not willing to be with your people. You got to find a way to be with your own people, but not let it seem like you're doing it because you don't like any one else.

Everybody at this school seems to talk to everybody. We don't hang out a lot with each other, but we talk to each other. You talk to everybody but you hang around with your race. If you look once, you can see everyone talking to each other. But if you look again, you see that they walk in and out the door with their own race—people the same as them.

I knew we had all kinds at our school, but when I really started looking when we did our map, I was surprised. I didn't realize the number of groups that are out there. It was pretty overwhelming. I think most of the time I try not to notice too much, and I stay in my own part of the school.

The "trying not to notice," the "staying in my own part of the school," and the "surprise" students report when studying how divided the social maps were posed a crucial contrast to the depth of understanding they in fact all seemed to have exhibited about the actual divisions on campus. What is allowed to be noticed and remarked on, what is safe to perceive and articulate, does not seem to match the actual experiences of most students. The social-map activity began with brain-storming in the classroom when students were first handed the physical map of the campus. Most groups immediately filled in the maps and had to be admonished to take the time to "look around" and check their initial perceptions. They knew well what the divisions were on their campus. Yet, the students profferred "surprise" at what they found. I began to understand the complexity of a social world in which what students experience and what they are safe in articulating are quite different.

In the course of the discussion, students developed a theory that the more diversity there is, the safer students are because of two reasons— there is not any one dominant group that can get away with "getting down" on others very easily. For example:

[If there was] a huge amount of Latins at this school and a small amount of white kids, then the Latins would feel superior to the whites and the Latin kids would more likely make sure it was true and they wouldn't let the whites get in their way. It would lead to more hate and fighting. A huge amount of whites, and it would be just the opposite.

The other aspect of the theory is that with so much diversity, with so few of "your own kind," you just have to learn to watch your own back and not ruffle anyone's feathers. Either way, they agree that a lot of diversity pushes kids to keep a lid on acting out their prejudices. This is what it means, they say, to learn to live in a diverse society. They also noted that the larger the group, the more likely it is to act exclusive. This is how they explained that the three groups they view as being most exclusive are blacks, Latins, and ESL students. These three groups seem to them to have the numbers that allow for exclusivity. The newcomer students would, more than likely, be startled and surprised if they could hear this explanation of their social separation. The social predicament for students becomes having to hang out with others like themselves, but appearing to do so for reasons other than not liking other groups.

This student-developed theory of intergroup relations sharply contrasts with the faculty's view, which generally posits that intergroup relations became more volatile and dangerous with the increasing diversity of the student body.

The formal discussion only continued for two class periods. But the issue remained alive in the class for many weeks. Students in Stern's classes regularly write in reflective journals about things that arise for them from their work in the class. Students wrote a lot about additional thoughts on the mapping project. A tenth grader, an African American student (who wants to be a sociologist), wrote:

The thing that has been most disappointing to me as I did this research is that I found more groups consisting of all one race than those groups that have more than one race. Does this mean that most people like to hang with others of the same race? Before doing this research I believed what we all say, that Madison is a great diverse place and we're all mixed. I didn't think I would find many groups of just one race in areas like "territories." But I found that some races do have their own areas to be away from the others and it really bothers me. Why do the Mexicans have to hang in C Hall, and why do the whites hang in A Hall, and why do blacks hang in B Hall? This feeling that they have to have their own area and give people who don't belong there bad looks causes problems. Tension will start building up, and it also causes a problem for those who are outside of these groups because they feel uncomfortable to walk past them. If we all keep pretending we don't notice it, we just keep our discomfort inside and things stay calm. But it makes you kind of crazy.

Jennifer, on completing her social mapping project, was deeply disturbed by what she found:

Maybe it is better if we keep believing we are all mixed. Maybe it is better to just not see what I saw when I did my social map. There is what we all say—that no one is prejudiced and we all get along—and

then there is what we do, and that shows how separate we keep ourselves by race . . . I think we have to try hard to not see that because it
hurts. I think down deep we all really know what's up—that we're a
divided school.

Another student, a white eleventh grader, wrote:

Before I did this project I didn't think that many groups of people
hung out with their race. I just thought people hang out with their
friends. I just thought our school was filled with different races and
we [are] all mixed, and people had all kinds of friends. At first when
I started looking around at the groups for this project, I noticed that
some were the same ethnicity. Then I noticed that almost all were the
same ethnicity. It's not like we choose to be with our own race, but
that's who we are comfortable with and have things in common with,
and then other kids see us and they don't approach us so it gets more
and more rigid. Other people don't come up to us, and so we stay one
race. It made me really uncomfortable to see how separate we are.

The separateness of racial and ethnic groups is usually peaceful at Madison High, at least on the surface. Most, who remain in their own groups,
are careful not to get in the way of other groups. And those who choose to
"mix" do so in their own section of the school or keep it relatively quiet.
The system is kept in place not by open hostilities or threats or the physical
protection of turf through intimidation. It appears to operate more as a social system of pressures on individuals to place themselves and to stay
placed. But sometimes, the underlying tensions explode.

Madison sits in the neighborhood where the headquarters of the Ku
Klux Klan for the entire country is housed. Nearby high schools have had
some incidents with literature from the Klan, graffiti on lockers, etc. The
little post office on the corner near the school is the mailing address for
the South County John Birch Society. Although there have been no incidents directly attributable to these organizations, the presence of white resistance to the demographic changes in the community is evident among
some of the white students at the school. The presence of white hate responses appear to be generally confined to occasional comments made by
a few individuals. There have been bottles thrown at the buses of immigrants arriving at or going home from the Newcomer School as they pass
by Madison High, reportedly by white students. But on one occasion it was
Mexican Americans aiming at Afghan immigrants.

The "recently arrived" versus the "been here for a while" immigrants
versus the native borns is a tension described by students in each of these

groups. All of this is couched in terms of intense competition, a sense of eroding opportunities, and of being crowded and invaded by others who have an unfair advantage. Many native U.S.-born students feel that "immigrants are given everything"; many Latinos feel that newly arrived immigrants are pulling them down.

In Stern's sixth-period class, some of this resentment was voiced in the context of broader working-class anger, a sense of resignation, abandonment, and lack of future resulting in anger at those who believe in the American dream (as they believe the recent immigrants do). The anger and sense of being abandoned was very close to the surface in the discussion. Students cited the budget cuts in the district, the growing class sizes, and the lack of counselors as evidence that they do not really matter to the adults in the community. They talked about the bad reputation that Madison has as the "lowest" high school in the district. Some spoke of an assembly on colleges where a counselor reportedly told them even if they get all As, it would not mean anything in terms of getting into college because they will be competing against students from "good" schools.

Student anger gets acted out in two direct ways: noncooperation with school personnel and rage at the newcomer students who "still have dreams," and who view schools in terms of freedom and mobility. The noncooperation shows up in the slouched, passive postures of students sitting in classes with little response to their teachers. It also appears in the minimal amount of effort put into homework. The rage is evident in different ways. As one boy in this class said:

> Sometimes I see them [immigrants] with their backpacks and their books, studying so hard and I want to knock them in the face. What makes them think that studying so hard is going to do them a damn bit of good. They try so hard it makes me sick. School hasn't done a thing for any of us.

As "Americans" look across at the newcomers in their midst, the anger is partially about immigrant groups who achieve success in the school, and part of their anger is aimed at newcomers for reinforcing the ideology that acedemic achievement is a product of individual motivation and effort. That ideology is fundamentally the dominant view that teachers project, and "American" students view their newcomer peers as collaborators with teachers in perpetuating a belief that pins the academic failures of students back on themselves.

The rage at newcomers for "still believing" is one of the dynamics that serves to wear down immigrant students. They feel the resentment against them and many come to understand that holding to a belief in hard work and making it in the school stands in the way of being accepted by their American peers. From their early perceptions that "they think we came here to be better in school than they are," to the social exclusion from the social maps of the school as long as they continue to "hang out" with others of their own language and national group, to the daily brushes with the anger of established resident students, immigrants learn that the choice is between continuing to live at the margins of the map or becoming more like "Americans." And becoming more like "Americans" may mean changing their relationship to the academic system of the school, an academic system that is to an extent racially arranged. In making the transition to life at Madison High, newcomers face tremendous pressures not only related to the language they speak or the racial identity they adopt, but also in the relationship between those choices and academic success. It is easier for students who are Asian or white to find their way into the higher tracks of the school. It is harder for newcomers who become Americanized as Latinos or blacks to make their way out of the lower tracks to which they are relegated.

Academic achievement is not just a product of intelligence, self-perception, and effort. There is an institutional reality that provides groups of students with different resources, different encouragement, different curriculum. And it results in tracking some groups of students into futures with far more opportunity than others. From the moment kindergarteners enter school, the expectations of their teachers and the degree of effort and resources available to them make an enormous difference in their attachment to school and what they learn. Students who are in classes where a teacher speaks their language are far more likely to learn social studies, science, and other subjects than students who cannot comprehend what their teachers or texts say. In this country, in far too many schools, resources and expectations are meted out differently to children of color and white children, and differently to poor children and middle-class children. By the time they arrive in high school, students already have a well-developed sense of whether they are "smart" or not, whether teachers will like them and encourage them or not, whether they like school or not. But high schools also play a role in the continued tracking. Madison High, like most high schools, has three academic tracks: college preparatory, regular, and skills (for "remedial" students). Ninth-grade English teachers determine which social studies track a tenth-grade student will be put in. Once in a track, the curriculum students receive is different, leading to different futures.

Of the thirty-two Latinas (immigrant and U.S.-born) who spoke about wanting to go to college, twenty-nine told of seeking advice from a school counselor. When they expressed interest in college, they reported being told versions of "you aren't college material," "you don't have the credits," "you better consider the community colleges," "you don't have a prayer of getting into a four-year-college," or "don't bother." In fact, some of the young women do not have the required courses they should have had by this point because of lack of information. All, however, were hungry for help in planning for future higher education. Six of them spoke of individual teachers who were actively encouraging them to go to college, and trying to fill in and provide some college information because they believed the students could do it. At Madison High, where counselors' time is tremendously scarce and generally devoted to those who are obviously on the college-bound track, individual teacher advocacy is the essential avenue to college information for language-minority students or those who are not already into college-bound tracks. A severe fiscal crisis in Bayview schools resulted in cutting almost all counseling from Madison High, to a .7 position for the whole 1,800 student body. Here, the presence of the few young teachers committed to immigrant and LEP students makes a difference. One of these teachers spoke triumphantly:

> Hah! I was so happy when Gloria got into CSU. I'd worked with her for hours on the applications and financial aid forms, and encouraging her and encouraging her and encouraging. And then, you should have seen the counselor's face when I waltzed in and told her that Gloria had gotten into Cal State. She nearly fell through the floor. She had told Gloria she didn't even think she would make it through high school. I said, she made it through, no thanks to you!

During one late afternoon session with Lisa Stern and Rebecca Garrison, two teachers who see themselves as active advocates on behalf of immigrant students, the two spoke at length about the intertwined phenomena of race, ethnicity, social class, and academic level. They also spoke of the silence about this relationship among the faculty. Stern said:

> It's like you're fighting against this enormous monolith. The teachers protect it like crazy, the students keep it going. You know you see this tracking going on, and people don't see anything wrong with it, or they just want to keep it the way it is. How can you justify that? It's beyond me.

Students in the "high" college-preparatory classes and students in the "low skills" classes (classes for students who need basic skills and are considered "remedial") feel a sharp sense of identity tied to those placements, according to Garrison. The sharp boundaries are both academic and social.

They are really their own group. Every time you try to move one of the skills kids into regular or college-prep classes, they won't do it. It's hard enough convincing them they can do the work academically, but there is something else more powerful that holds them back. They believe they belong there. They've been convinced. And they believe they belong with the other kids who are there. They feel like they'd be so socially isolated if they were moved out. They want to stay with their friends. They want to stay where they think they belong. Last semester I moved Trina, a really bright African American girl into a college-prep math class. Her grades were high; she really could do the work, but she couldn't take it in other ways. She came back to me and begged me to put her back in the skills class. She said, I hated it there, we don't speak the same language.

It is not that there are no African American students in the college-preparatory classes, although their numbers and proportions are distinctly less than in the skills classes. African Americans comprise 16 percent of the school, but only 7 percent of those completing the A-F requirements that prepare them for college, and only 5 percent of those in chemistry and physics (laboratory sciences required for admission to many four-year colleges and universities).[2] But there are other distinctions that mark the divide. As Garrison describes:

In the college-prep classes, the African American kids group by themselves. I think that is true of all levels, but actually at the college-prep level there is less friendliness. It is a very competitive and clique-y track. The atmosphere in skills classes is really a lot friendlier. Kids are more accepting and curious about each other. If you come into skills classes, you find friends really fast. And the discussions are great. There is a relaxation about skills classes. Everyone knows they are at the bottom together. There is no competition. But at the college-prep level, it's competition for the top. It gets fierce sometimes.

Garrison and Stern ponder what holds students together at the skills level:

I think about these things every day now that I'm teaching a skills class. It's really interesting to watch them willfully accept it all. Even if I grab a kid and say, "You, you have potential" or "You're really smart, you could do the work in college prep," they don't want to see themselves any place but where they are. There is a sense of alienation they share. They identify ambition and behaviors of ambition as a sellout.

They don't want to fail, but there are certain things they know they'd have to do to be successful and they reject them. I think on some level it's fear and distrust. Fear of trying again and being put down—fear that if they let themselves believe the door is open and it just gets slammed in their faces again, it'll be unbearable. They reinforce each other. And it's a powerful bond. And its scary to realize the terrible power that teachers have to create in students a certainty that they belong at the bottom.

For the black and Latino immigrant students to break through these patterns requires enormous resolve and a willingness to pay high prices to jump from the skills track into the college-preparatory track.

Juanita Sanchez is one of these students. She came to my attention as one of the seniors in the Madison High School yearbook class that I sometimes observed. She went often to Ms. Stern, the yearbook sponsor, for advice and the two spent a great deal of time trying to steer through the mazes of college applications, interviews, financial aid forms, and Scholastic Aptitude Tests (SATs), which are required for college admission. After witnessing one of these episodes, I asked Juanita to tell her story.

Juanita spoke of a childhood of changing schools and being bounced between homes, each with different cultural influences, different messages about who she was and what she could accomplish, and different lessons about independence, attractiveness, and her class and educational future. She was born in Mexico and came to Bayview with her Mexican parents when she was young. Though moving often between living with one of her divorced parents, by middle school she found some stability living with her grandparents. Juanita began to closely identify with the Latino neighborhood in which her grandmother lived.

> I was going to the same school for a long time. We lived in an apartment where I had a lot of friends. Our neighborhood was full of kids. Everybody was Hispanic. There was hardly anyone white. A few Filipino, but mostly Hispanic. And we fit in finally. My sister looks white but she is still Mexican inside. We were home. We were with other Hispanics and we had someone to take care of us.

These were the middle school years. Juanita felt at home and proud as a Latina. But this changed when she entered Madison High and was placed in classes and tracks with few Mexican Americans, and her neighborhood friends were separated from her at school.

> I was so scared to be a freshman that someone would throw me in a garbage can or something. And I wasn't in classes with other Latinos.

I couldn't figure out why. My friends were in the skills classes. They were smart, but somehow, that's where they were.

In eighth grade, Juanita had taken placement tests and was told she should be placed in sophomore English and history classes. At first, she was sure it was a mistake. The freshmen year was hard. Mexicans at Madison High, according to Juanita, "were at the bottom." She missed her friends and was uncomfortable in the classes where there were few Latinos.

I started to cut [school] a lot with my friends. It was the only way I could see them. And I had to reassure them that I was still their friend even though I was in higher classes. Heck, I had to reassure me! I didn't want them to think I was stuck up. And I couldn't see them after school. I have the strict Mexican way, which means you can't have boyfriends until you're eighteen, you can't wear makeup—you know. It was strict Mexican ways for my grandfather. I wanted to go places with my friends and my grandfather was like, you can't. He's the kind of person that everything has got to come from the past. You can't move on. He was back in Mexico in his head. And he tried to keep us in Mexico, too. That just doesn't work here.

Juanita started to forget about school, and just "hang" with her friends. Her grades dropped and by sophomore year, she was back in "general track" classes with her friends. She recalls her dad as the only one who would encourage her to pay attention to her studies. He would say, "Keep your head up high and be proud of yourself. Your sister is beautiful and she will have many men falling for her, but you're smart, you're intelligent." Juanita looks back on that and thinks perhaps that is what saved her, because she took it to heart that her survival would rest on being able to "make something of myself."

I knew I wouldn't have men to take care of me so easy, so I would need to take care of myself. And I wanted to prove to my family that I was worthy. So I was in a war with myself. No one except me and my dad cared about being smart. All my friends hated school. But I knew there was no future for me if I didn't make it on being smart. I wasn't pretty, and I saw what being a weak woman did to my mother. But I was Mexican and didn't like the loneliness of being the only one of my friends to do well in school. And I didn't like the way I got looked at by teachers who kept thinking I couldn't be able to do the work in the hard classes.

Juanita tried to turn over a new leaf in her sophomore year. Ms. Stern was her history teacher and Juanita loved that class. For the first time she felt a teacher believed in her. That same year she met her boyfriend, and credits him and Ms. Stern for her staying in school. The older she got, the more her grandfather wanted her to stay home. He did not know she already had a boyfriend and was very concerned that she might become involved with boys. Juanita had to sneak to see Miguel, but she felt he was her lifeline. He was a senior, and although he encouraged her, he was not around school after that year. Ms. Stern had Juanita rescheduled into college-preparatory classes for the second half of her sophomore year. The racial dynamics of school achievement became even more difficult for Juanita after that.

> I was in honors classes with a bunch of Chinese people and a bunch of white people and one black girl. Ms. Stern scheduled me into the honors classes. She says, "You're too smart. I'm going to put you in higher classes than they schedule you for. You can write very well, you speak well and have a good vocabulary; you work hard and you have a lot of important things to say." I was all worried. "I'm not going to know anybody." But she kept saying, you'll make friends. She was wrong.

Juanita recalls that on the first day of her new classes, she was asked to check her schedule card in each class to be sure she belonged there. "It's like they believe you can't do it. It was awful. I started to doubt myself again. It gets me mad [that] I let it get to me, but it did."

Despite an ideology among most teachers that achievement is a product of effort, the disproportionately large number of Latinos that fail in the school ends up confirming their suspicions that it must be, in the words of one teacher, "a cultural thing." A host of damaging mistruths and stereotypes flow from that: Latinos do not value education, Latinos do not work hard, Latinos do not aspire to be much. And those who fight against it, like Juanita, have to stand up to expectations that she does not belong. She described the situation: "It's like, are you sure you are supposed to be in this class?" She felt as though students and teachers alike were looking at her as if she was in the wrong place.

> And they would be like, you got Latin blood in you, don't you? Like I was a weirdo or like they had never seen any Latin person in their classes and they couldn't believe it. And one day in Ms. Kramer's class we had to write a composition on a role model. And one Chinese girl

next to me goes, can I read your paper? I go, sure. So she reads it and her eyes were getting real big. I go, what's wrong. And she says, you're smart I thought you were going to be a dumb person in this class. That did it, and I got all hot and said really loud, "You're very ignorant. You're the one that's supposed to be smart and you should know its not just one type of person that is smart. Anybody can do honors classes if they apply themselves. They've just got to want to learn. It's not about nationality. The Mexicans in low classes just don't try. They get sick of trying and getting put down again. They just look around and say I'm gonna get a diploma and cross that stage and get a job and get married and have a family, and they don't see why they should try. But they're smart and don't you ever again think Mexicans aren't smart.

It was hard for Juanita, but she began to love going to classes despite the social isolation. She could not believe how much she was learning. She worked harder than she ever had before and felt very excited. She said: "I learned every day something new. It was like, oooh, I can't miss a day." Juanita still has some Mexican friends from her middle-school days, but mostly her friends now are Filipinos. She explains: "At school, I hang out with Filipinos because it's more okay to be into school with them. You can carry your books and they don't hassle you about it. It's okay."

But the pain associated with separation from her Latino friends runs deep. As Juanita says: "I wasn't sure you can really be Latina and be in college prep. I guess I kind of crossed over into some other identity. But it burns inside me. I know all my friends could've done it, but they were pushed down."

Juanita was accepted to the University of California at Berkeley, but did not have the money to pay the tuition and support herself. She was surprised by the deluge of college catalogs that came to her unsolicited, "probably because of my high SAT scores." But without scholarships or grants, her plan is to get some kind of secretarial job and save money to go to college later. When Juanita told me this, she began to cry.

I keep getting this feeling that I'm going to work and I'm never going to go back to school. I was going to go to work and then go to school at night, and it's like, now that I don't have the money to go right now. I'm scared that what if I have to keep putting it off and putting it off til I'm thirty and still in the same job and nowhere to go. And that's what I'm really scared of. And sometimes I look at Mexican women who are all middle aged and have all these kids and I wonder if any of them thought once that they were going to make it. I wonder if any of them had a dream like me. And I wonder if I'm going to be like them, never having gotten to where I want to go.

Going to college requires a desire to do so, a belief that it is an appropriate goal, academic preparation adequate for gaining admission, and information about admissions processes. For Juanita, as for many students at Madison, none of these come easy. Because budget cuts in the district eliminated almost all counseling positions (leaving just a single part-time person for the entire student body of almost 1,800), counseling advice about colleges ends up being channeled through a few large assemblies, brief daily bulletin announcements of key deadlines, and the particular relationships students forge with teachers who will be their advocates. Most of the information and teacher support comes through the honors classes at the school. Students who are not in those classes do not realize there was information that might have helped them prepare for college until it is too late.

Juanita ended up in honors classes, and she benefited from the help of Ms. Stern to get through the array of applications, SAT tests, and procedures of college admissions. She had a father, a boyfriend, and a teacher who believed in her dream and supported her, and still she found it a massive struggle. Juanita had to struggle with the social isolation of being a Latina in an academic track where few Latinos end up, she had to face down the prejudices of teachers and students who believed that as a Latina she did not belong, and she had to combat her own self-doubts. And in the end, Juanita felt she had to cross into a world that left her community behind.

For Juanita, academic achievement and the pursuit of her academic dreams were never divorced from her view of the future as a Latina. Believing she did not have the sexual capital of good looks as defined by "white" standards, her expectation was that as a female, her only hope of making it would be through her "smarts." But she also often looked around at the Mexican women she knew, and feared and rejected their futures as her own. Looking around Madison High, she also felt that given the numbers and dispersion of Latinos in the various skill tracks of the curriculum, she would have to beat tremendous odds to make it. She knew, she witnessed, she felt the viciousness of a racialized system that pressured to keep her in her place as an undereducated Latina.

Her journey and the journey required of newcomers involves learning and then accepting or fighting their place in the racial order—to accept it has a high price, to fight it has a price as well. Madison High is highly racialized and students who do not fall into those racial categories and the academic placements, which are thought appropriate, remain at the social margins. Immigrant students in this scheme are denied the richness of their many national and language identities, existing solely as an undifferentiated ESL category on the maps drawn by the "American" students. And the newcomer immigrant students look across from a perspective of a world divided by nationalities and language groups, where "American" is synonymous with "white" and English speaking.

For newcomers, this process of confronting "America" and coming to understand what is required of them consumes them during the first few years. It is a complex process that begins with the disenchantment that learning English will be enough.

NOTES

1. This process of white consciousness is reflective of the larger societal trends described by Howard Winant:

> The shifts brought on by the civil rights movement and the reforms it engendered also had an impact on white racial identity, which was rendered much more problematic than in the days of segregation. Whites had to change their attitudes toward minorities, which meant they had to change their attitudes toward themselves. A desirable feature of this shift was the beginning of racial dualism in whites. On the negative side, whites were threatened by minority gains. They sense a loss of their majority status. They suddenly noticed an identity deficit. Formerly their whiteness since it constituted the norm was invisible, transparent, but not in a more racially conscious atmosphere, they felt more visible and more threatened.

Winant, *Racial Conditions: Politics, Theory, Comparisons* (Minneapolis: University of Minnesota Press, 1994), 166.

8

Explaining Racism to My Daughter

David Mura

This happened last year:

I am putting my daughter to bed. She's eight, in third grade, a child of a Japanese American father and a mother who is three-quarters WASP and one-quarter Austrian Hungarian Jewish. I'm asking Samantha about her new friends at school, her classmates. Among other things I inquire about their ethnic and racial backgrounds, about whether these matters affect the relationships in her class.

Samantha says she really doesn't think about such things. Certainly most of her friends don't think about them as much as she does.

She says she thinks my asking about whether people are Asian American or African American or white, is racist. She tells me racism is something from the old days, like the internment camps or segregation. It doesn't really affect her life.

She implies that we should be beyond thinking about people in groups.

My daughter's words here don't reflect all her views on this subject. She's contradicting herself (as we all do). I know she was bothered when people mistook her in second grade for another Asian American girl or when her classmates implied she had a connection to this girl simply because of their Asian faces. I know she's played the role of Confucius in a skit before her class—a role she chose—and when she performed she told them pointedly that "Confucius is not from my country." I know we've talked about the media presentations of Asians and Asian Americans, of the stereotypes that still permeate present day American media. Once, in first grade, she and her friend Diwa, a Filipino Thai American, proclaimed that since Disney was not producing any feature films about Asian Americans they were going to make their own Asian American video (this was before *Mulan*). When Samantha and Diwa were even younger and were watching the old Disney *Peter Pan* they both turned to each other and said, "My mother says that Native Americans are really not like this."

None of this, though, comes up in her mind in our conversation in the dark of her bedroom just before sleep.

In a way, my daughter is telling me that my preoccupation with race is itself racist. That I should move beyond worrying about these matters. That we should just deal with people as people, not as Asian American or African American or white or Bosnian or Tibetan or Swedish American.

What should I tell her? Do her words indicate I need to teach her a new and more complicated way of thinking about racism? Or do they indicate some generational shift, some way of perceiving the subject that she and her generation feel and I do not? Or is it both?

When my daughter calls me a racist, how should I respond?

We are told that certain Inuit tribes use two dozen words referring to the snow. The implication is that such precision is required for the survival of the tribe. They need to be able to pinpoint these features of their environment, the shifts in the weather. One word is simply not an adequate set of tools.

We can see that racism threatens both children of color and white children in America, though in different ways. We know that it forms a crucial part of the environment they must grow up in and live with. We know it affects many aspects of their lives—where they will live, whom they go to school with, how they will be educated, whom they will become friends with, whom they fall in love with, whom they will work with and for, where they will work, what their salaries will be. It may even, as certain statistics indicate, help determine their health and how long they will live.

And yet we have only one word to approach this subject with: Racism.

Perhaps because he is a writer, Tahar Ben Jelloun, in his book *Racism Explained to My Daughter,* realizes that understanding racism involves a construction of language; racism possesses its own dictionary. His dialogue with his daughter is filled with painstaking definitions. It starts with the overall term racism. From this a whole and necessary vocabulary unfolds: *different, foreigner, prejudice, impulse, discrimination, ghetto, melanin, sociocultural differences, blood types, genetics, scapegoat, extermination, genocide, ethnic groups, slavery, apartheid, colonialism.* Some of these terms indicate practices or beliefs; some are scientific, some are political. Some, like ghetto or apartheid or slavery, require historical background and bring up questions about economics.

"What is racism?" a child asks. Perhaps only in the face of such a simple inquiry do we realize how difficult the answer is. It's rare, though, that we're asked such a pointed question about the subject. More often the subject appears obliquely or without an open invitation. A racist slur someone made at school, an old movie or cartoon on television with blatant and historic stereotypes, a racist opinion voiced at a family gathering, a politician with whom we agree or disagree, a demonstration on the news, an act of racial violence or hatred—we and our children confront such triggers to speak about racism in our daily lives. Some of us may use these occasions to speak to our children, some let them pass. But rarely do we go into as full and open discussion as Tahar Ben Jelloun undertakes here with his daughter.

The fact is that there are few other such texts we can give to our children. This tells us something about the state of race relations in our culture and our present abilities and efforts to educate our children about this subject.

To be precise, my daughter did not call me a racist. She said that my way of speaking and thinking about people was racist. This was because I seemed to pay inordinate attention to the grouping of people by race and ethnicity. The implication was that I should look at them as individuals and not as members of a group.

I suspect that my daughter might agree with Ben Jelloun when he says, "I suggest you stop using the word 'race.' It's been so exploited by bad people that it's better to replace it with the word humanity. The human species is composed of various groups. But all men and all women on this planet have the same color blood in their veins, whether their skin is pink, white, black, brown, yellow or anything else."

Certainly Ben Jelloun is correct when he states that "The word 'race' has no scientific basis. It was used to exaggerate the effects of outward, physical appearance." "Race" is a fictional concept, a social not a natural construct.

And yet this fictional concept affects how people think and behave in the world. In that sense it is neither unreal nor non-existent. It is a very powerful social force. And this means that although we are all one species, although we all have the same color blood in our veins, we do not act and think alike. We do not possess the same experiences.

For some people in American society, the categories of race have caused a whole range of negative experiences. For other people the same categories have enabled them to escape from these experiences. For some people the categories of race have excluded them from certain privileges. For others the same categories have availed them of certain privileges. For all people the categories of race have meant their ancestors experienced different histories.

We cannot speak of these differences in experience, privileges, and histories without referring to racial categories and the way they are used in our society.

Simply to stop speaking of such categories does not destroy or erase the social practices based on them. It does not erase the fact that unemployment among blacks in America has historically been twice that for whites. It does not erase the fact that the students in mainly white suburban Winnetka benefit from an education that costs thousands of dollars more than the students in the mainly black south side of Chicago. It does not erase the fact that it is far easier for a young white male than a young black male to receive a loan, or hail a city taxi, or drive through a suburban white neighborhood unmolested by the police. For this reason I would not tell my daughter, as Ben Jelloun does, to stop using the word "race." Perhaps it is a flawed or inadequate lool, a word that has been much misused, but without it, we are forced into silence. And the real causes and conditions of racism would be left untouched.

So what do I do with my daughter's reactions? I have told her that it's been my experience that many white people, even well intentioned ones, have difficulty understanding my own experiences as a person of color in America or my views on race. This is not as true with the people of color I meet.

She says that it seems then that I am prejudiced against white people. I am categorizing people by race.

I tell her that in one sense she's correct. I know there are white people with whom I can trust discussing my most inner feelings about race, but I also know there are fewer of them than people of color. Therefore I tend, at least initially, to trust people of color in some ways more than I do whites. It is a prejudice.

My daughter senses here a double standard. In this, her thinking is not very different from many conservative thinkers.

Take the case of a white person who believes people of color are more likely to be criminals or to bring down property values and who therefore does not want to live in neighborhoods with a majority of people of color. Statistically the white person may be correct. And what if the white person says that he or she would accept people of color who have good middle class values, who share their socioeconomic status and who act like them? This isn't really prejudice, many would say; it's just common sense. Of course, I believe such thinking is racist. But if this person is prejudiced, my daughter might ask, are they any more prejudiced than me, given my admission of a racially based sense of trust? My daughter wants to live in a world where people are not judged by the color of their skin. She wants to live in a world where the terms "racism" and "race" no longer exist. She believes that the way to accomplish this is not to pay attention to or acknowledge differences in race. To do otherwise is to be prejudiced. This is the same argument many conservatives use against affirmative action. We should not, the argument goes, grant privileges or benefits to anyone because of their membership in a given race. This is discrimination.

Can I satisfactorily explain to my daughter that my distrust of white people is not the same as a white person's distrust of people of color? Can I explain to her the reasons behind affirmative action? That it is, in some cases, necessary and a good thing to group people by race in order to redress a social injustice? How am I to do this?

To start off, I need to help my daughter see that we are both individuals and members of groups. The two facts are not mutually exclusive. That is, if you look at a person as a member of a group, this does not mean you cannot look at him or her as an individual. Indeed the opposite is true: Without knowing about the group the individual belongs to, how can you adequately know who he or she is? The more you know about Asian Americans, their histories and cultures, the more you're able to realize that we are not all alike. It's only if you're ignorant of our background and our ethnic groups that this happens.

For a child, and perhaps for most of us, the difficult task here is to move beyond the limits of a focus on the individual. This is particularly hard for Americans to do, given our cultural and historical emphasis on the individual.

What does such a shift in perspective mean in talking about race with my daughter? I must enable her to see that the practice of racism in society involves more than the acts of deluded or frightened or insecure or hateful individuals. Instead racism is, at its base, a social, political, and economic system which works on a group as well as an individual level. In other words my daughter must understand that individual acts of racism affect the workings of the society as a whole, and that these individual acts must be connected systematically. In doing this I must enable my daughter to see that racism is a system of power as well as of beliefs and actions. More specifically it is a system through which the power and resources of a given society are distributed unequally and unjustly. This system of power can be supported by silence and non-action as well as by active participation.

The system of power must also be supported by a system of beliefs. Some of the beliefs supporting this system are recognized as racist. Others supporting the system are not.

Needless to say, to explain all this is not an easy task. The concepts here are difficult for an adult to grasp much less a nine-year-old.

It is no wonder then that Ben Jelloun's dialogue with his daughter falls short in this. Part of the problem is that despite all his useful definitions and explanations he tends to address racism primarily as a moral and psychological or at times a historical issue.

But racism is also a political issue. Ben Jelloun, I feel, slights the view of racism as a system of power.

In the past, white Americans used racial insults much more openly than they do now. Particularly after the civil rights movement in the 1950s and '60s such words became more and more taboo.

In 1999, in American public life, we believe those who use those racial insults to hurt others are racist. Most whites also believe what they regard as a simple corollary: If you know these terms are wrong and don't use them, then you are not racist. Such terms become a litmus test and are used by many whites to assuage their conscience, to assure themselves they are not racist.

In reality things are not so simple. For one thing there are those who know these words are wrong and still use them in situations where they think no one will criticize them. Often this takes place in private with other whites. People who listen to this use and say nothing do not necessarily believe they themselves are racist.

Indeed people who use these terms privately or even openly do not always think of themselves as racist. Marge Schott, the owner of the Cincinnati Reds baseball team, was caught speaking of some of her ball players as "million dollar niggers"; she used the terms "kike" and "Japs." Yet when she was confronted with evidence of her remarks, she replied that she was not a racist. Her mouth spoke these words and not her heart.

The truth is that any time someone is publicly accused of being a racist, that person will immediately get up and say they are not racist. Their friends will be interviewed and they will say that this person is not a racist, that he or she doesn't have a racist bone in his or her body. After all, to admit being friends with a racist is to appear to be racist oneself.

One reason for this behavior is that we have equated being racist with being evil. It is generally believed that those who are racists are particularly loathsome; the label associates them with historically recognized villains such as Hitler, slave owners, and the Ku Klux Klan. If people have the choice between admitting to being a racist and being evil and not being a racist and not being evil, most people will say that they are not racists.

Unfortunately the real state of race relations and the real presence of racism in our society is much more complicated than this. There are many more racists in our society than people who will admit to being racist. There are many more racists in our society than most white people will acknowledge. This silence, this denial, is one of the ways racism is allowed to flourish.

· · ·

For many whites, an exception such as Marge Schott only reinforces their sense of their own innocence. They regard racism as the acts of a few deluded individuals. One reason for this belief is their definition of racism. A large number see racism solely as the acts of individuals and do not believe that racism is systematically built into our society. In contrast many more people of color believe racism works systematically as well as through individuals. One reason for this discrepancy is that most whites believe that racial insults are the prime indicator and example of racism. The absence of these examples in their lives says to them racism has vanished or is a great deal less prevalent than in the past.

In contrast many people of color believe that racism possesses many more forms of social practice than racial insults. They realize this because these more complicated and less obvious forms of racist practice adversely affect their lives.

It is easy to see that a white person calling someone a "nigger" or a "gook" is a racist act. It is a lot harder to see how the disparities in income in this country between whites and African Americans are caused by racism. It is easy to see a cross burning on someone's lawn and to interpret it as a calling card for white supremacy. It is much more difficult to see the ways African Americans are consistently denied access to bank loans in ways whites are not. Nor are such "invisible" acts commonly regarded as supporting white supremacy. The individual racist act is easy to witness and admit. The workings of the racist system are not.

Successful African Americans understand the way white Americans view the world. This does not mean they agree with it but they must understand it to be successful. In contrast most successful white Americans do not understand the way African Americans view the world. One reason for this is that their success does not depend upon this knowledge. In fact in many ways their success depends on an ignorance of this knowledge. The difference in the situation of successful African Americans and successful white Americans reveals something about who holds power in our society, about whom the structures and means of power are meant to benefit, about who is supposed to have an easier way.

To see the workings of this system means most whites must find a different way of interpreting and describing what they see. They must also find a way to see things they do not see. They must move out of the familiarities of their normal lives and vision. Richard Wright once remarked that black and white Americans are engaged in a battle over the description of reality. Why is this so? One obvious reason is that their experiences are different and so they interpret the facts of the world around them differently. Another is that the portion of the America experience that blacks see is generally quite different than that witnessed by whites: When they describe

America, whites and people of color are often describing two different worlds.

One tale about race I discuss with my daughter is the case of Texaco. In this corporate version of the Rodney King video, executives of Texaco were caught on audiotape discussing practices of racial discrimination in the company and ways of covering up those practices in the face of a lawsuit. The existence of this tape produced a general public consensus: There were individuals who discriminated against African Americans at Texaco. Moreover this practice was so widespread it could be deemed as systematic within the company. And yet most discussions about Texaco did not truly examine how this system was allowed to flourish. People first focused on the open racial insults on the tape (whose context was revealed later to be somewhat ambiguous). They then focused on the admission that there was evidence that certain individuals did discriminate against African Americans. Yet the existence of discrimination at Texaco did not depend simply upon these individuals who acted in an obvious racist manner. It also depended upon those who knew about these practices and did nothing to stop them. It also depended upon those who did not know about these practices.

You can be sure that the vast majority of African Americans at Texaco knew these practices existed. Those who did not know were mainly white. At the same time whites in the company benefited from these practices and received advances in an unequal and unjust manner. Are those who did not know of these practices innocent of racism? Are those who knew about them and were silent innocent? I would argue, No.

If they had said something about these practices, if they had done the work needed to learn about these practices and protest them, then the racist system at Texaco could not have been implemented. The system *depended* upon their silence and ignorance.

You can view the case of Texaco as a microcosm of racism in the United States.

A vast majority of whites have chosen, consciously and unconsciously, to be silent about and to ignore racist practices of other whites or to be ignorant about such practices. At the same time they accept the benefits they receive as whites in this racist system. The system will not change until whites stop their silence and ignorance and stop their acceptance of unearned privilege and power.

Here is what I tell my daughter about the ways I regard people of color and whites: Because of systems like the one at Texaco, the reasons why a person of color distrusts whites are fundamentally different from the reasons of a white person who distrusts people of color. The white person benefits from a system that supports his distrust in a way that the person of color does not. For example, the white person's distrust of people of color helps maintain predominantly white middle class suburbs where the schools receive financial support superior to those schools attended by the more racially mixed populations of the inner cities. This white distrust also helps keep environmental dangers from their children which the children in inner cities are more often exposed to.

The distrust whites feel towards people of color does nothing to change this situation. To make these two distrusts equivalent forms of prejudice is to engage in a racist act. This camouflages and ignores obvious differences in the way whites and people of color are treated in this society and the powers and privileges they receive. And yet even as I make these arguments my doubts remain. Why do I feel that the attempt to help my daughter to understand all this cannot be changed simply by arguments or reason, statistics or facts?

At the age of five, in every picture of me, I've got a pair of six guns cinched about my waist. Or else I'm pointing them at the camera, my black cowboy hat pushed back, my mouth snarling with a bravado and toughness I evinced only as a pose or when alone, walking down the dark steps of our apartment building out to the street. At each step I'd wave to the fans at the rodeo, shouting "Howdy folks," the way I imagined Roy Rogers did stepping into the arena and onto Trigger, the Wonder Horse. Before I went on to collect baseball cards, I collected cowboy cards, with the heroes from various television series, wrapped up together with a slice of chewing gum for a nickel: *Have Gun Will Travel, Sugarfoot, Maverick, Gene Autry, the Lone Ranger, The Rebel,* classic American icons of the fifties.

In one of my poems, I picture myself riding in the back of our Bel-Air, shooting at the glass, bouncing up and down in gunfight delirium, wearing the black cowboy hat and cold cocked steely gaze of Paladin, who'd leave his calling card, "Have Gun, Will Travel," everywhere he went. When my friend the Japanese Canadian playwright Rick Shiomi read the poem, he remarked, "Do you remember what happened at the beginning of that show? This Chinese guy with a pig tail would come running into the hotel lobby, shouting, 'Teragram for Mista Paradin, teragram for Mista Paradin'?"

I don't remember this Chinese messenger at all. All I see is Richard Boone striding down the stairs, the epitome of cowboy cool, his pencil-thin mustache and tight glinting gaze.

How did I know I didn't want to be like this Chinese messenger? What did my disassociation from him, my erasure of his presence from my memory, say about the way I felt about myself, my own body, my identity as a

Japanese American? I grew up as someone who wanted to assimilate into the white majority, who thought it a compliment when a white person would say to me in high school, "I think of you, David, just like a white person." From early on I perceived that the world felt there was something wrong about the way I looked, who I was as a Japanese, an Asian, an alien who could never quite be considered American, no matter how much I tried to pretend otherwise.

So how did all this affect the way I looked at whites and blacks? I remember this experience when I went to see the film *Out of Africa* in the Ginza during a year-long visit in Japan during my early thirties. For months I'd been living in this environment where everybody looked like me, where I was in the visual majority, even if I wasn't Japanese. All this began to change the way I felt about myself, about my body and the way I looked. Very quickly I started asking all sorts of questions about what race had meant to my identity in America.

And then I was watching this movie where Meryl Streep plays the Danish author Isak Dinesen. Early in the movie she travels to her Kenyan plantation for the first time. When she approaches the plantation, it is late at night and a crowd of Kenyan servants come up and greet her. As I watched this scene, suddenly I realized I was bored with Meryl Streep's face. I was bored with the white face at the center of the film. I had seen the white bwana in Africa over and over in films since I was a child. I knew that story. What I was really interested in was what was happening in the minds of the Kenyans. Their interior life. And I realized that all my cultural training had been to place the white face automatically at the center and to place the black faces in the margins. Suddenly I felt I wasn't doing this anymore. I was withdrawing affection, attention, and curiosity from that white face, and giving it to the black faces.

In that moment I realized that was a part of the way racism works. It's not only a question of whether you blatantly discriminate against people or not. It involves what happens when you see a face. How do you react emotionally? How does your psychic energy react? Does it go out to that face? What sort of assumptions does your psyche make about how interesting that person is going to be? How curious you are? How much affection do you feel? So much of that just happens in an instant, subconsciously. What conditions that reaction? How are children taught to identify themselves? To identify others? How do these identifications prevent us from seeing each other clearly? How to we learn new ways of understanding each other across racial lines?

Another story I've told Samantha:

One night I was talking in a bar with four black male friends, three writers and a theater director. These were men who had won prizes for their work, one had written for *The Cosby Show,* another had written a bestselling novel; they were all college educated. At a certain point they began trading stories about how they had been picked up by the police for driving in a white neighborhood. I was struck by the fact that while the stories were laced at times with anger and a sense of humiliation, the dominant emotion was laughter. It was as if they were trading long familiar stories, filled with an absurd humor, stories which framed almost as initiations, something you could not escape if you were an African American male in America.

I grew up as a middle class Asian American. I lived in the white suburbs, places where my black artist friends could neither live nor drive. My experience had been totally different from my black male friends. If I felt a sense of alienation, a sense of being out of place, an odd anomaly and sexual misfit in my suburban high school, I never felt endangered by the police. I never heard from my father that it was hard for him to find a place in the suburbs where people like us could live (although such places did exist).

I have also talked to Samantha about standing outside a New York hotel with my best friend, Alexs, who's African American. After a few minutes, I decided no taxi was going to come down the street and I suggested to Alexs that we walk up to Broadway and catch one. He turned to me and said, "Okay, we can do that. But I stand here because I know I might get a taxi here. If I go up to Broadway the taxis won't stop for me."

I've explained to Sam that when Alexs stands in front of the hotel the drivers think he's staying there and is not someone who might rob them. If he stands like everyone else on Broadway, all the taxi drivers see is a black man with dreadlocks, which sets them worrying that he might be a criminal.

I also relate what Alexs later said about this incident. "Now I know how to dress, how to look safe. But sometimes you just say to yourself, fuck it. I'll look just like that brother over there who is going to take you down. And it's your job to figure out if I'm an outlaw. And that's why I stay home a lot. That's why I stay in my house a lot. That's why when the phone, when the doorbell rings, I don't feel that good. I'm not anxious to see who is at my front door. I am never anxious to see who's at my front door. I won't go to the front door."

Finally, I told Sam that if Alexs stands on Broadway in New York with me and tries to hail a cab that might be okay. I never seem to have trouble hailing cabs. And that's one difference between being an Asian American male and an African American male in this country. It's a difference I never understood much about growing up.

• • •

At the time Alexs and I first became friends I was engaged in a growing rift between me and several white friends, a group of fellow writers in the Twin Cities. The rift had started with an argument over *Miss Saigon* and my objections to the play, and to the fact that a white British actor, Jonathan Pryce, was given the role of a Eurasian without any Asian Americans even being allowed to try out for the part. This argument quickly spilled over into other racial issues. At the time I was identifying myself more and more as a Japanese American, an Asian American and a person of color, and I was shedding the desires for assimilation and whiteness that I had grown up with. As this happened and as I began speaking more and more about race in my public appearances as a writer, I noticed a curious phenomena: The things I had been saying which had caused difficulties with my white writer friends were the exact same things which seemed to cause people of color in my audiences to come up and talk to me after my appearances. It became clear to me that, in certain ways, I had to choose one group or the other.

I've written about this elsewhere, so I don't want to go into this here. What I do want to mention is that this was an incredibly painful process. I seemed to be having the same argument with almost every single white writer friend I had (they in turn had to have the argument only with me— I was the only writer of color in the group).

One day as I was talking to Alexs and he was advising me, I realized that he knew more about dealing with racism than I did. I also felt he understood me at that moment better than anyone I knew, including my wife, whom I knew loved me more than anyone else in the world and who is white.

At that moment I realized Alexs was psychologically more astute than I thought he was. Then I realized he was smarter than I thought he was. Then I realized I had not seen this before because of my own racism. I thought: If I'm a person of color and I'm doing this to someone who's black, my whole view of racism needs to change.

I had until this point thought of Alexs as a bit bristly, a bit too quick to anger, someone with a chip on his shoulder. But, as we became friends, as he felt he could trust me more and more to try to understand his experiences rather than deny them or his interpretation of them, my vision, my interpretation of his world, changed. I realized that at the times I thought he was being too quick to anger, he was actually being restrained. After all, judging whether someone is too angry or not depends on whether you see all the reasons they have to be angry. I realized I did not see many of the reasons for Alexs's anger, his history of dealing with racism. Indeed, my whole education and cultural training had led me *not* to see these things. I came to view those moments when Alexs did raise his voice a bit, did allow his emotions to show, as great acts not just of restraint, but of survival, of tremendous will power, of spirituality and forbearance. Obviously my judgment of his character changed.

This, I tell my daughter, is one of the reasons why I don't think it possible for most white people to judge the character of people of color. If they don't understand or see the world people of color live in, what experience they bring to the table, how can whites judge our actions at the table? How can they know why the person of color is reacting the way they do? How can they know the struggles we have gone through to get to the table?

In an article in *Vanity Fair* (May 1998), Fran Leibowitz likened the competition between blacks and whites to a race. The white person sees the black person line up at the starting line and says, okay, let's have a fair race. If I win I'm the better qualified. But what the white person doesn't realize, argues Leibowitz, is that the black person has run several miles already to get to the starting line. It's not a fair race at all.

What I have been saying here can be summed up in two basic sets of contradictions. They both involve what whites learn about race in our society.

Here is the first set of contradictory beliefs which exist within the psyche of most whites in this country:

1. I believe white culture, white mores, are superior, and, in the end, I care more about what happens to white people than to black people. I have been taught through the culture and through my education that white people are superior to black people and are basically more important to me.
2. I must judge people fairly and equally and not practice discrimination.

Now what happens when a white person with these contradictory beliefs interacts with a black person? This is what I believe occurs, and my belief is based on the fact that this is also the way I was taught to think of black people:

The white person constantly tries to keep the second tenet in mind—I judge people fairly, I'm not prejudiced. But so much of that white person's cultural education has taught him the opposite; therefore that training must be kept from the focus of his consciousness.

Of course this attempt is problematic. At some conscious or subconscious level, the white person is aware that he is trying to repress this first message. This makes the white person very self-conscious. He is afraid of his own psyche, he fears that the part which thinks whites are superior, will somehow slip out, and he knows this must not happen.

The more contact the white and black person have, the more frank they become with each other, the more likely this first message will slip out. That is one reason why whites avoid intimacy with blacks.

And what happens when this first message slips out, when the white person reveals the message of white superiority that he has learned through the culture? When he shows the part of his psyche that thinks whites are more knowing and more important? The black person gets angry. And in turn the white person gets defensive or denies what he has said. Or retreats or feigns ignorance about what has angered the black person. In most cases the white person leaves the room psychically and often physically and does not come back to the relationship. The black person's anger brings up too much tension, points too directly to the contradictions within the white person's psyche.

Now the white person may not even be aware that he has let slip these beliefs about the superiority and importance of whites. After all, this is the part of his psyche that the white person wants to hide in any encounter with a black person.

In contrast the black person cannot hide from the existence of such a belief in the psyche of whites. A whole history of encounters the black person has had with whites and white institutions only point to the existence of such a belief. Richard Wright referred to this when he said that blacks have a song which says I can't believe what you say, because I see what you do.

What if whites were not frightened off by this anger and, more importantly, by the revelations of their own psyche? Perhaps they might be are able to cross color lines and achieve a truthfulness and intimacy that most relationships between blacks and whites in this country lack.

Here is the second pair of contradictory beliefs which the white person must deal with:

1. I benefit from a system which gives me special privileges as a white person and denies them to black people. All whites participate on some level in this system.
2. This country is a democracy, people are supposed to be judged as individuals and, in general, there is equality, only a few whites are really racists.

Here again, if the white person does not want to think herself a racist, she will cling to the second statement as a general truth and try to block out, to push from his consciousness the first statement. Yet, somewhere deep down in their psyches, whites know this first statement is true.

The sociologist Andrew Hacker routinely asks his white students this question: Say you accidently turned into a black during an operation—your features changed to an African American—and you will live approximately another 50 years. How much will you seek in compensation? Most of his white students seemed to feel "it would not be out of place to ask for $50 million, or $1 million a year. And this calculation conveys, as well as anything, the value that white people place on their own skins. Indeed, to be white is to possess a gift whose value can be appreciated only after it is taken away." (*Two Nations,* Andrew Hacker, Charles Scribner's Sons, 1992)

Again, when she is dealing with blacks, the white person will constantly propound the second statement, and deny the existence of the first statement or argue that it is false. But to the black person, the first statement is an obvious truth. It's much easier to see when someone is privileged if you don't share in those privileges. If you enjoy those privileges, they just seem a natural way of life, something you were born with.

In his book, *Savage Inequalities* (HarperCollins, 1991), Jonathan Kozol writes: "Total yearly spending—local funds combined with state assistance and the small amount that comes from Washington—ranges today [in Illinois] from $2,100 on a child in the poorest district to above $10,000 in the richest. The system, writes John Coons, a professor of law at Berkeley University, 'bears the appearance of calculated unfairness.'

There is a belief advanced today, and in some cases by conservative black authors, that poor children and particularly black children should not be allowed to hear too much about these matters. If they learn how much less they are getting than rich children, we are told, this knowledge may induce them to regard themselves as 'victim,' and such 'victim-thinking,' it is argued, may then undermine their capability to profit from whatever opportunities may actually exist. But this is a matter of psychology—or strategy—and not reality. The matter, in any case, is academic since most adolescents in the poorest neighborhoods learn very soon that they are getting less than children in the wealthier school districts. They see suburban schools on television and they seem them when they travel for athletic competitions. It is a waste of time to worry whether we should tell them something they could tell us. About injustice, most poor children in America cannot be fooled."

Thus the two biggest psychological barriers to dealing with racism involve the denial of whites of their knowledge that the following statements contain an essential truth about their psyche and lives:

1. I believe white culture and whites are superior to and more important than blacks.
2. I benefit from a system which gives me special privileges as a white person and denies them to black people.

If you are white and can begin to investigate, even a little bit, how these two statements apply to you, and you continue in that investigation, you will know what you need to do to combat racism. You will figure out the next steps you need to take.

We have come to the point where people in our society recognize racist insults and blatant acts of discrimination as wrong. What then are the other ways through which racism works in our society?

Can there be unconscious acts of racism?

How does racism work on a group rather than individual level?

In what ways does racism work as a system of power and privilege?

What are the acts or beliefs that many people of color believe are racist and whites do not?

Why is there disagreement about which acts or beliefs may be labeled racist?

In what ways are a person's experience in our society determined by skin color?

How do these differences in experience affect the way a person looks at and interprets the world around them?

How do whites tend to view these differences in experience and interpretation?

How do African Americans? How do Asian Americans?

Can we make such generalizations? Do we need to?

How do Asian Americans fit into this picture of white-black relations? Obviously, that's a complicated question. Here's one way I've tried to explain this to my daughter:

In 1944, when my father was interned with other Japanese Americans at the internment camp in Jerome, Arkansas, he would sometimes be allowed a day pass to go to Little Rock to see a movie. At that time when he left the camp and stepped onto a local bus, the bus was segregated.

When I asked my father where he sat then, he said, "We sat in the front of the bus, where the whites sat." And at the lunch counter? "We sat where the whites sat." And at the movies? "We sat beneath the balcony, where the whites sat."

In certain ways this decision is quite understandable: You sit where the power is. You sit where your life is going to be more comfortable.

The Nisei (second generation Japanese American) journalist Bill Hosokawa wrote about this situation:

The evacuees who were sent to Arkansas had been astonished to find they were regarded as white by the whites and colored by the blacks. The whites insisted the Japanese Americans sit in front of the bus, drink from the white man's fountain and use the white man's rest rooms even though suspecting their loyalty to the nation. And the blacks embarrassed many a Nisei when they urged: "Us colored folks has got to stick together." If there was no middle ground in the South's polarized society of black and white, in the rest of the country after the war, a Nisei could live as a yellow-skinned American without upsetting too many people, and he also discovered it was not particularly difficult to be accepted into the white man's world. *(Nisei: The Quiet Americans)*

What we notice here is the embarrassment Hosokawa attributes to the Nisei when they are offered solidarity with the blacks. We also see that after the war the Nisei are interested in fitting into the white world and the black world seems to not exist for them.

The implications of a Japanese American on this segregated bus are quite telling. For one thing, when my father steps on that bus, his identity is created not simply by his relations with his own community or with the white community who have seen him as a threat to American security and a perpetual alien. His identity is also created by the matrix of black-white relations.

When he sits in the front half of the bus, the whites grant him status as an "honorary white," with certain of the privileges that come from being white. But they grant him this status on two conditions:

First, he must accept that he probably won't sit in the very front of the bus and he will absolutely never be able to drive the bus. He must also understand that his cultural heritage is something to be left behind; it means nothing here.

Secondly, he must pay no attention to the people at the back of the bus, he must claim no relationship to the people at the back of the bus, and he must absolutely never ever protest what is happening to the people at the back of the bus.

Now this bargain, this honorary white status, is often still offered to Asian Americans. When we accept this bargain, other people of color in the back of the bus see our acceptance for what it is: an acceptance of the racial status quo. And they are, appropriately, angry at us for supporting a racist system.

When Asians immigrate to America, as so many have done since the immigration laws changed in 1965, nothing in Asian culture prepares them for what it means to be an Asian American, to look they way they do and live in America. At the same time they soon realize that the further down they are on the economic ladder the more they are regarded as being like the "blacks" and they soon sense what that means. After all they are exposed to the same education and stereotyped media as whites. Of course, they are not told how Asians became the model minority at the exact time blacks began protesting for their civil rights. They often do not know that doors are opened for them through anti-discrimination laws created by the efforts of African Americans. Instead many Asian Americans discover that the further they move up the economic ladder the greater the opportunities to become "honorary whites."

I was no different than my father, I tell my daughter. For a long time I wanted to be an "honorary white." Then I saw I needed to fight that wish, the price of the ticket. And everything changed.

When my daughter read Ben Jelloun's essay, she told me she found parts interesting, such as the discussion of cloning or the history of the word "ghetto," but most of it already felt familiar to her.

Some of this I suppose is because she's only nine years old. She says she doesn't hear racist insults toward any groups at school. The school she goes to is very racially mixed and also includes students from recent immigrant groups. No one group really predominates. She knows there are other schools and areas where there are more racial tensions but for now it doesn't play a big role in her life. A friend who has an older son has told me that at Samantha's school, it is in the junior high, when boy-girl parties start to happen, that racial segregation starts to set in. When I told Samantha this it didn't really register; boy-girl parties seem a long way off to her in fourth grade.

Just after I finished this essay, she and I had another discussion that started because of the issue of redistricting and busing in the Minneapolis suburbs. She'd read a letter to the editor where a white woman argued that the residents of her suburb were unfairly being branded as racists. In the course of our talk Samantha—ever vigilant against unwarranted generalizations—accused me of saying that all the people in the suburbs were racists. "I know for a fact that that's not so," she said. "You can't say that. Do you know everyone that lives there? That's just the same as the people from the suburbs saying everyone who lives in the city is a gangbanger. It's not like everyone in the suburbs is racist and everyone in the city is for diversity and isn't prejudiced."

We finally settled upon the statement that perhaps there were more people in the suburbs who were racists than those in the suburbs believed. (After all, if the suburbs were so free of racism, wouldn't people of color be flocking there in droves?) I told Samantha that this issue in part depended

upon the way you define racism and I went over some points I've tried to
make here. I think the stories about myself, my friend Alexs or other
friends, stories she's heard before about people she knows, affected her.
But whenever I got into something abstract like the systematic nature of
racism, she tuned out. At one point she said, "How old were you when the
first man stepped on the moon?" As I'm wont to do I ignored this signal to
change the subject and plowed on stubbornly until she said again, "It must
have really interesting when the first man stepped on the moon." The discussion was over. She was bored. I'd gone on too long.

Part of me suspects that our conversation had as much to do with the
fact that she'd recently come home from a trip to Japan with her mother
and our discussion was simply a way of our re-connecting. And I realize that
she sometimes says things which she knows I'll counter, just to see what my
arguments are and to test her own sense of independence. In the end,
she'll need to discover or create a way of looking at these matters that's
hers and not mine, some new way not encapsulated either by my beliefs or
the more conservative beliefs she's exposed to at school and through the
media.

Still, I'm left with this question: When she's older, how much will she
read our conversations as Dad ranting and how much as necessary discussions over a crucial issue? I just hope it's some mixture of both.

9

Everyday Antiracism in Education

Mica Pollock

The world of K-12 education contains infinitely complex race questions—
and endlessly oversimplified race answers. In U.S. K-12 education, the
field in which I work as an anthropologist of education, "race groups" are
often portrayed as falsely static firmly bounded groups. They are portrayed
as "cultural" groups, if not explicitly "genetic" ones, with different ways of
behaving that directly cause racially inequitable outcomes like "achievement." Educators need tools for thinking and talking far more complexly
about racialized difference and racial inequality.

Race Wrestling

I have found that anthropology and its methodological tool, ethnography,
offer some key tools for moving dialogue in education beyond oversimplified notions of "racial" difference and oversimplified explanations for
racial inequality. For rather than simply asking respondents to restate
these commonsense notions, ethnography can show educators the ways
in which they and their students struggle daily *with* race. By focusing attention on *everyday struggles* over race categories and racial inequality,
ethnography can facilitate what I call "race wrestling": people struggling
self-consciously with normalized ideas about "racial" difference and about
how racial inequality is produced.

Anthropology, in its serious attention to the ongoing everyday activity of
ordinary people, also helps educators think about how their own ordinary
moves either reproduce or challenge structures of racial inequality. Educators need tools for analyzing the consequences of their everyday behaviors
because they are often unsure which ordinary moves, in an already racial-

ized world, are racist and which antiracist. Indeed, antiracist educators must constantly negotiate between two *antiracist* impulses in deciding their everyday behaviors toward students. Moment to moment, they must choose between the antiracist impulse to treat all people as human beings *rather* than "race" group members, and the antiracist impulse to recognize people's real experiences *as* race group members in order to assist them and treat them equitably.

The ethnographic question to ask about antiracism in education is thus not abstractly *whether* people should be treated or not treated as race group members in schools (this is the typical US debate about "race consciousness" vs "color blindness"), but rather concretely *when* and *how* it helps in real life in specific places to treat people as race group members, and when and how it harms. Static advice to "be colorblind" regarding one's students, or to "celebrate" their diversity, or to "recognize" their "identities," is not equally helpful in all situations. In daily life, *sometimes* being colorblind is quite harmful to young people; *sometimes* a "celebration" of diversity can be reductive and harmful; *sometimes* "recognizing" one aspect of an identity (a student's or one's own) detracts from a sense of common humanity.

Educators in the US and elsewhere are routinely given too-static, overarching, abstracted recommendations for dealing with race in school. Educators need instead to wrestle with their own daily *struggles over* race in educational settings, and to consider moment to moment decisions about how best to assist real children in real world situations.

Lessons for Antiracist Practice

Some lessons for everyday antiracist practice in education have emerged in a forthcoming collection of essays I am editing. (See the work of sociologist Michele Lamont for exploration of "everyday antiracism" in other realms.) These lessons engage, in part, Audrey Smedley's arguments about the key features of racism since race categories were developed to facilitate slavery and colonial expansion in the 15th century. Then and today, racism has been about building structures of unequal resource and power on oversimplified notions of human difference.

Today, racism still involves unequally measuring human worth, intelligence, and potential along static "racial" lines, and accepting the distribution of racially unequal opportunities, and the production of racially patterned disparities, as if these are normal.

Everyday antiracism in education thus requires that educators make strategic, self-conscious everyday moves to counter these ingrained tendencies. First, then, everyday antiracism in education involves *rejecting false notions of human difference,* and actively treating people as equally human, worthy, intelligent, and potentialed. In educational settings, antiracism particularly requires actively affirming that intelligence is equally distributed to human beings, and that no "race group" is more or less intelligent than any other. Antiracism in education also involves actively rejecting race categories' "genetic" reality. It involves learning, proactively, that "races" are not groups that are genetically different in any real way, but rather geographical groups that developed minor physical differences and have come over centuries of social practice to live very different lives. Everyday antiracism in education also involves challenging oversimplified notions of human diversity, and asserting that complex people do not always fit easily into single, simple boxes of "racial" (or "ethnic") identity or behavior.

Second, everyday antiracism in education involves *acknowledging and engaging lived experiences along racial lines,* even if the categories themselves have been built upon genetically insignificant differences. Over six centuries of American history, people have both been lumped into ranked "races" by others, and chosen race-group membership for themselves as a means for social empowerment. The Irish "became white" in the 19th century, and Jews "became white" in the 20th; "Asian-Americans" became "Asian-Americans" in the 1960s; then too emerged "Latinos" or "Hispanics." Today, we all make one another "racial" on a daily basis. Racialized "groups" in the US today bring very different experiences to the table, and they are shaped by very different experiences with educational resources, opportunity, and success. Everyday antiracism thus entails engaging one's own and others' experiences of this differential treatment—whether we have benefited from such differential treatment or been sabotaged by it.

Third, everyday antiracism in education also involves *capitalizing upon, building upon, and celebrating* those diversities that have developed over centuries and decades to sustain strength and foster enjoyment within racialized groups, long grouped involuntarily and destructively by external others and grouped proactively and positively by themselves. As Cornel West wrote in "Race-ing Justice, En-Gendering Power," being "black," for example, involves both the negative experience of responding constantly to denials of equal opportunity (typically, in history, at the hands of "whites") and the positive experience of enjoying a community that has bonded through expressive and political practices with one another even in the midst of such oppression. Antiracism thus requires *enjoying* and *sharing* difference in ways that assist individuals to feel respected, broadened, and challenged. It involves not just sharing and respecting "group" forms of expression, but also sharing and respecting the critical lenses that members of various "groups" bring to any table.

Fourth, everyday antiracism in education involves *equipping self and oth-*

ers to challenge racial inequality. Everyday antiracism particularly involves actively challenging the widespread tendency to see racial disparities in opportunity and outcome as "normal." Everyday antiracism in education involves clarifying any ways in which opportunities must still be equalized along racial lines, and then equipping people to actually equalize life chances and opportunities arbitrarily reduced along racial lines. Everyday antiracism in education also entails proactively reminding students of color laboring under false notions of racial "inability" that they are equally intelligent and potentialed. Everyday antiracism in education also entails reminding white students that they are not naturally superior, but rather privileged by an intricate system that they, too, can make more equitable for others.

These four paragraphs suggest seemingly contradictory things: rejecting false notions of human difference, engaging lived experiences shaped along racial lines, enjoying enjoyable versions of such difference, and constantly critiquing and challenging systems of racial inequality built upon these notions of difference. The four are actually not self-contradictory. Rather, they demonstrate that everyday antiracism requires doing each situationally on a daily basis. Antiracism requires *not* treating people as race group members when such treatment harms, and *treating* people as race group members when such treatment assists. Deciding which move to take when requires thinking hard about everyday life in educational settings as complex, conflict-ridden, and deeply consequential. Anthropology can assist educators and students to turn a critical analytic lens on their own everyday experiences in schools and districts to see how "racial" difference and racial inequality are being produced or dismantled in small bits.

10

Why Do Some People Hate Us?
Homophobia

Michael Thomas Ford

A s most of us are all too aware, there are some people who do not like gay people. We read about gay people being attacked by gay-bashers; we hear congresspeople on television talk about not giving "special rights" to gays; we hear people say that they want to beat up faggots or show dykes "how to do it right." This kind of behavior is homophobia, which is any kind of verbal or physical abuse aimed at gay people.

Homophobia can be as simple as referring to someone as a "faggot" in a conversation, or not giving someone a job because you think she's a lesbian. Or it can be something more visible, like beating up or killing someone because he's gay, or not letting a parent in a divorce case have visitation rights because she is a lesbian. Homophobia takes many forms, some of them very obvious and some of them completely invisible. Whatever form it takes, homophobia is painful and hurtful.

Unfortunately, homophobia is a big problem. We live in a country where everyone is supposed to be equal under the law. We don't like to think that people can do horrible things to us just because they don't like us. But the sad truth is that, all too often, they can. Hundreds of gay women and men are beaten up and killed every year, just because someone doesn't like them. More are injured in far less obvious ways. There are entire political campaigns backed by millions of dollars just to get laws passed that say that gay people cannot have equal protection and equal rights. There are whole organizations established to "warn" the American people about gays. The armed services has fought a long battle to keep gays out of the military despite years and years of evidence that gay people make just as good or even better soldiers than straight people. Whether we like it or not, whether it's fair or not, homophobia is everywhere, and we have to

© 1996 by Michael Thomas Ford. This piece originally appeared in *The World Out There: Becoming Part of the Lesbian and Gay Community* (New York: The New Press, 1996), 52–61.

learn how to deal with it. We also have to learn how not to let homophobia prevent us from living proudly and happily as gay people.

The word *homophobia* says it all. *Phobia* means "a fear of." Homophobia is the fear of homosexuals. It is a *fear,* not an anger or a hatred. The anger and hatred come because people are afraid, but it all starts with a fear.

It sounds silly, someone being afraid of homosexuals. But think about it. Whenever you see someone talking negatively about gay people, what are they usually doing? They're shouting. Their faces are red and angry, their mouths are open, and their fingers are pointing and shaking. Sometimes they're waving signs or clenching their fists. Whatever they're doing, they always look afraid. They look as though they're trying to protect themselves from something that can hurt them.

But have you ever thought about *why* these people are afraid of gays? After all, there has to be some really good reason why they're all so angry at us, right? Wrong. In fact, some of the most homophobic people in the world have never even met a gay person, at least as far as they know. Their homophobia is based entirely on some strange concept of what they *think* homosexuals are.

So, what do they think we are? Well, most of them aren't even sure. Some of them just say we're perverts who go against God's teachings. Some of them say we're the cause of AIDS, without really knowing anything about how AIDS is caused or how it's spread. Some of them say we're these really scary people who want to take over the world and make everyone just like us.

Many times the issue comes down to children. For some reason, homophobic people are convinced that all gay people want to molest children or else "make" children gay. They think that just by being around us or just by knowing about us that all children will want to be gay too, just like they might want to be firemen or astronauts if they visit a firehouse or space center.

The truth is that about 98 percent of all child molesters are heterosexual men. Tell that to a homophobe and he'll probably argue back and forth all night about it; but the truth is that gay people very, very seldom molest children. The few who do have psychological problems that have nothing to do with being gay, just as heterosexual child molesters have psychological problems that have nothing to do with being straight.

What people are really afraid of when it comes to children, and even when it comes to themselves, is that being around gay people or even just knowing that gay people exist will give other people the message that it's OK to be gay. They are afraid that seeing that there are happy gay people will make young people understand that what they might be feeling is perfectly acceptable and normal. They're afraid that seeing gay people will give young people the courage to express themselves as gays if that's what they are. They think that if they "protect" children from gays, that children will grow up straight because they won't know that gays even exist.

But why are people afraid of homosexuality at all? That's where it gets interesting, because it's almost all about sex. When most people say that homosexuality is disgusting, what are they really saying? Usually they're saying that homosexual sex is disgusting. After all, to most people, what makes us gay is the fact that we are attracted to people of the same sex. That's it. That's all they "know" about being gay.

People seem to think that people are gay because they like the kind of sex that gay people have. In fact, some religious groups say that it's fine for a person to be homosexual and to have homosexual thoughts, as long as he or she doesn't actually act on those feelings and have sex with someone of the same sex. In other words, if a man who is gay marries a woman, he can have all the gay thoughts he wants to as long as he doesn't actually have sex with another man. According to these people, it's the physical sex that makes us gay.

The reality is that gay people like gay sex because they like the people they're having it with. You want to make love with a person because you're attracted to that person. When you analyze it, people pretty much have the same kind of sex whether they're gay or straight. So to say that someone decides to be lesbian or gay because she or he really loves to have lesbian or gay sex is pretty funny. Would anyone really go through all of the things gay people have to go through in this world just to have a certain kind of sex?

When it comes right down to it, most people are afraid of gay people because they don't want to think that they themselves might be in any way gay. This doesn't mean that all homophobic men are really gay, or that all homophobic women are really lesbians, although a surprising number of them are. What it means is that homophobic people are afraid of the *possibility* that they could be gay.

Yet, knowing that homophobia is caused by fear and ignorance doesn't make it any easier to feel better when someone calls us names just to be mean, or when they hurt us physically. But it does help us to understand why people act the ways they do, and understanding is the first step toward change. By understanding why people are afraid of us, we can begin to try and change the way people see us and the way we see ourselves.

Dealing with Homophobia

Why should we be concerned about homophobia? After all, unless we are actually the victims of it, it's a lot easier to ignore it and keep ourselves safely away from it.

But there are important reasons why all of us have to be aware of homo-phobia and know how to confront it. The most obvious reason is because homophobia can lead to violence. Many gay people have been beaten up or killed because we are gay or because someone thinks that we are gay. In the past few years alone, a lesbian woman and her gay male roommate were burned to death when gay-bashers threw a homemade bomb through the window of their home, two lesbians in Tennessee have repeatedly had peo-ple shoot at their home and threaten to kill them for being gays, and a young Navy seaman was beaten and kicked to death by several of his own shipmates because he was gay.

As gay people become more and more visible, and gay issues are more in the news, violence against homosexuals increases. People want us to stay silent and hidden, because that way they can pretend that we really don't exist. As more and more gay people stand up for their rights, it makes everyone realize just how many of us there are, and this makes them upset. People who are homophobic often look for people on whom to vent their anger and frustration, and too often their victims are simply in the wrong place at the wrong time.

Some states and cities have laws that make it illegal to hurt people who are gay. These are called "hate crime" laws, because the crimes are commit-ted simply out of hate and not for any other motivation, such as robbery or gang fighting. But these laws are often hard to enforce, because the people who commit hate crimes certainly aren't going to admit that they attacked or killed someone just because she is a lesbian, or just because he was com-ing out of a gay bar. It takes a lot of time to prove that a crime was motivated by hate, and most police departments are not willing to take the time.

And while some law enforcement people are helpful and compassion-ate regarding gay-bashings, many others are not. Many victims of hate crimes report being further teased or ridiculed by the police when they try to report the crimes. This makes it difficult for gay people to report these crimes against them. If someone feels that she or he is going to be ridiculed for being gay, especially for being attacked for being gay, the chances are that a crime will go unreported. No one wants to report what is already a traumatic and sometimes embarrassing incident if the people he is report-ing it to make him feel even worse. And even if a hate crime is reported and the criminal is caught, that doesn't ease the mental and physical pain of being attacked simply for being gay. For some people, it seems easier just to remain silent.

Gay-bashing is a very visible form of homophobia. But not all homopho-bia is so obvious. While the effects of gay-bashing can be seen in the bruises and cuts on a person's body, other scars from homophobia are less visible. All over the country, people are voting on laws that will, for example, give gay people equal protection and equal rights in matters of housing, jobs, adoption, health benefits. While these issues seem perfectly reasonable to us, many homophobic people want these laws overturned or rejected. Many even want there to be laws saying that gay people *can't* have equal rights. The most visible example of this is the ongoing campaign in Colorado, where homophobic groups have been campaigning fiercely and using all kinds of lies, distortions, and fear tactics to make people vote for laws making it illegal to give equal rights to gay people. But thanks to efforts by local gay groups, these laws have not been voted in. Still, it gets harder and harder each year to fight against the hatred and the fear caused by homophobia.

It's very easy for most of us to think that this doesn't affect us. After all, we might think, how many gay people really want to adopt children? And how many gay people really want to be in the military? The answer is that enough do so that it should matter to all of us. If even one person wants to adopt a child and is told no, that's enough reason for all of us to care. And the reason it's enough is because when we let people tell us we aren't worth fighting for, it lets them keep believing that we aren't people who deserve equal rights and equal respect. If we let people take away or deny us even the smallest right, then we let them tell us that we aren't worth enough as people to have that right. But if we stand up and say, "No, we deserve the right to adopt children," or, "We have every right to defend our country," then we make the people who say we can't do those things see that we will not be treated badly, that we respect ourselves and other gay people enough to demand that we be treated fairly. Besides legal rights and the threat of physical abuse, one of the biggest reasons homophobia is an important issue is because it prevents people from accepting themselves. Gay people often have trouble accepting themselves because they know there are people who will not like them simply because they're lesbian, bisexual, transgendered, or gay. If someone grows up hearing nothing but horrible things about homosexuals, that person is going to have very negative feelings about gay people. The chances are that person will also grow up to be homophobic. If that person is gay herself, then she is going to have an incredibly bad self-image, because she will have been taught to hate what she herself is, and it will be very hard for her to accept herself as a gay person. But if she sees that there are millions of gay women and men who demand equal rights and equal respect, then perhaps she will start to see that what she has been taught is wrong, that she is a person who has a lot to offer the world and who deserves happiness.

Even gay people can be homophobic. How? We can be homophobic by hating ourselves, by being ashamed of who we are and not wanting anyone to know us. We can be homophobic by refusing to admit our own gayness and refusing to let ourselves be happy the way we are. We can be homophobic by letting other people get away with saying horrible things about gay people, or by not informing ourselves about gay issues. We can be homophobic by saying things that are unkind about other gay people, such as belittling people for acting "too gay" or for being "too out" about who they are. Whenever we say that certain kinds of gay people don't belong in our community just because they aren't like us or because we are embarrassed by them, we are being homophobic.

How do we fight homophobia? Luckily, there are many ways. Fighting homophobia can mean stopping our friends when they start to say negative things about gays or start telling jokes about us. It can mean giving friends or family members a book about gay people so that they can start to educate themselves. It can mean joining or supporting a group that actively fights homophobia, such as the Lesbian and Gay Anti-Violence Project, which monitors anti-gay attacks and police response to them, or the Gay and Lesbian Alliance Against Discrimination (GLAAD), which monitors the media for anti-gay movies, television programs, radio shows, and print references. Another excellent way to fight homophobia is to make yourself heard. This means calling or writing letters to companies who support gay-positive television programs, advertising campaigns, or causes. This is a tool used very effectively by anti-gay forces, who have successfully prevented a number of gay-positive television programs and advertising campaigns from appearing by threatening to boycott the companies who advertise on the shows. By applying consumer pressure, people can greatly influence how a company spends its advertising dollars. If a company thinks that they will lose sales by offending a group of people, more often than not they will do what that group wants them to.

For example, when the television show *Roseanne* aired an episode in which Roseanne and a lesbian character kiss, many advertisers were besieged with telephone calls from anti-gay people demanding that they not buy commercial time during the program. The same happened when NBC aired *Serving in Silence: The Margarethe Commermeyer Story.* Some companies did pull their commercials; others did not. Interestingly, those companies that did air commercials reported that they received many angry letters and telephone calls, but very few supportive ones from gays and lesbians.

One way to make a positive difference is to write or call companies that do sponsor gay-positive television programs or movies and thank them for their support. If companies think that they are earning the trust of a group of people who can potentially spend money on their products, they are going to continue to be supportive. However, if they think that the community doesn't care, they probably won't bother. Conversely, if you write to companies that sponsor or support anti-gay programs, and let them know that you will be taking your business elsewhere because of their actions, you may help convince them to alter their spending patterns.

All of these things can go a long way toward fighting homophobia. They may also be more than you can do right now. Many of us feel that we can't tell our families about ourselves yet, and don't feel comfortable joining a gay group. There's nothing wrong with that. That's just the reality of homophobia.

One thing we can *all* do to fight homophobia, no matter where we live or who we are, is start to think of ourselves, and all gay people, as worthy of respect. If every gay person in the world really believed that she or he deserved equal rights and equal respect, then we would have an unbeatably strong family that would make amazing changes. But as long as we hide and let other people treat us badly, we will not be able to fight effectively for our rights.

How do you do this? There are many things you can do. You can educate yourself about gay issues. Find out if your state or city has laws protecting the rights of gay people. Find out if your city has hate crime laws that punish people who attack gays. Find out if gay people in your state can adopt children. How do you find out? Go to the library and ask how to look up information on state and local laws, or call a local lesbian and gay community center. Many centers are meeting places for political action groups.

If there are presidential, congressional, or local political elections coming up, find out what the candidates think about these issues. Read newspapers and listen to the evening news to see what the candidates running for office think, not just about gay issues but about all kinds of issues. Because the more you know now, the better prepared you will be to really start making a difference in the way things work.

Another thing you can do is to remember that no matter what anyone may say or do to you, you are a valuable person. The way homophobia gets to us is by making us feel ashamed, embarrassed, or angry about being gay. It's very easy to be intimidated by homophobia. We start to think that people are picking on us because something *is* wrong with us. The truth is, there's something wrong with them. If someone feels the need to tease or hurt someone else just for being different, that person is sick.

But if you are the victim of homophobia, then what do you do? First, don't let yourself react to someone who taunts you, because that is exactly what she wants you to do. Walk away if you can, because words only mean what you think they mean. But if the abuse becomes physical, then you have several options, none of which is easy. You can always fight back. But remember—physical violence almost always leads to more and more violence, and it doesn't solve the problem, at least not in the long run.

However, one positive option is to take self-defense classes. Self-defense, including the martial arts, is not fighting. It is a way to avoid fighting by making it impossible for people to attack you. You learn to block attacks and how to disarm punches, kicks, and other blows your attacker may try to use against you. Martial arts are based on spiritual principles about nonviolence, and they are excellent ways both to exercise and to learn self-control and self-protection. Many gyms, YMCAs, YWCAs, and community centers teach self-defense classes, and there are many private schools teaching all kinds of martial arts and self-defense techniques. These are good classes for *anyone* to take, and knowing a few smart moves could easily prevent an attack.

TEN THINGS YOU CAN DO TO FIGHT HOMOPHOBIA

1. **KEEP INFORMED** on gay issues
2. **FIND OUT** what your local school's position is on teaching about gay issues and gay people; join the school board
3. **SUPPORT AND CAMPAIGN** for gay-positive political leaders
4. **ORGANIZE** a gay neighborhood watch or patrol to discourage anti-gay activities
5. **DON'T BUY** records or books by anti-gay artists
6. **ASK** television producers to include positive gay characters on their shows
7. **DON'T PATRONIZE** stores or restaurants with anti-gay policies
8. **VOLUNTEER** at a gay anti-violence project
9. **SUPPORT** gay rights organizations by volunteering or making a donation
10. **PATRONIZE** credit card companies and long-distance telephone services that donate to gay causes

If you are the victim of a serious gay-bashing incident, where you or someone else is hurt badly, then you should report it to the police. If you are afraid to go to the police, then I suggest you call a local lesbian and gay community services center or one of the groups listed in the resource section of this book. Groups such as the Lesbian and Gay Anti-Violence Project in New York City can help you and tell you where you can report the crime to people who will listen to you and be respectful and helpful. If you don't have such a group in your area, then you should tell a trusted friend or someone who can help you go to the police.

If you are the victim of gay-bashing, and you feel that there is not a single person around you that you can tell about it, call one of the hotlines set up for gay people. These are anonymous, and the people who answer the phones are there to help you and listen to you. As painful as it may be to talk about, keeping it inside will only make it worse.

Homophobia can be very, very scary. It can be so scary that we start to think that we will never let ourselves be active gay people because someone might hurt us. That's what homophobes want us to think. They want us to be so scared that we shut up. They want us to be so scared that we stay invisible. They want us to be afraid of them.

We can beat homophobes and homophobia by standing up to that fear. Yes, it's OK to be afraid. Sometimes it's even OK to run away. But every time we stand up to an incidence of homophobia—every time we refuse to laugh at a homophobic joke, refuse to eat at a restaurant that won't hire gay people, are kind to someone who has experienced homophobia—we make the power of homophobia that much weaker.

11

Some Reflections on Teaching
for Social Justice

Herbert Kohl

The idea that you have to advocate teaching for social justice is a sad statement about the state of moral sensibility in our schools and society. I remember one of my elementary school students who was involved in a civil rights demonstration saying, "You know, Mr. Kohl, you can get arrested for stirring up justice." You can also be fired as a teacher for stirring up ideas and provoking conversations that challenge privilege and try to make issues of democracy and equity work in the everyday life of the classroom. The problem is that many people do not believe that justice is a value worth fighting for. Sadly, this applies as much to children as it does to adults. One cannot simply assume that because an action or sentiment is just, fair, or compassionate that it will be popular or embraced. At this moment in our history, there are many sanctions for the idea that self-interest overrides communal sanity and compassion. The enemy of teaching for social justice is "The Real World," which is characterized as hard, competitive, and unrelenting in its pursuit of personal gain and perpetuation of bias and institutional and economic inequities.

So what are social justice teachers—that is one who cares about nurturing all children and is enraged at the prospects of any of her or his students dying young, being hungry, or living meaningless and despairing lives—to do in the classroom so that they go against the grain and work in the service of their students?

I have several suggestions, some pedagogical and some personal. First of all, don't teach against your conscience or align yourself with texts, people, and rules that hurt children. Resist in as creative a way as you can, through humor, developing and using alternatives, and organizing for social and educational change with others who feel as you do. Don't become isolated or alone in your efforts. Reach out to other teachers, to community leaders, church people, parents. Try to survive, but don't make your survival in a particular job the overriding determinant of what you will or won't do. Find a school where you can do your work, risk getting fired and stand up for the quality of your work. Don't quit in the face of opposition: make people work hard if they intend to fire you for teaching equity and justice.

However, in order to do this you must hone your craft as a teacher. I remember trying to jump into struggles for social justice when I first began teaching. During one of my earliest efforts someone in the community asked: "So, what's going on in your classroom that's different than what you're fighting against? Can your students read and do math?" I had to pause and examine my work, which was full of passion and effort but deficient in craft. I needed the time to learn how to teach well before extending myself with the authority and confidence that might lead to sustained change. This is essential for caring teachers—you have to get it right for your own students before presuming to take on larger systems, no matter how terrible they are. As educators we need to root our struggles for social justice in the work we do on an everyday level in a particular community with a particular group of students.

I believe there is no single way to teach well, no single technique or curriculum that leads to success. Consequently, a third piece of advice I would give teachers is to look around at everything other people say is effective with children. Pick and choose, retool and restructure the best of what you find, make it your own, and most of all watch your students and see what works. Listen to them, observe how they learn, and then, based on your experience and their responses, figure out how to practice social justice in your classroom as you discuss and analyze it.

Teaching is fundamentally a moral craft and makes the same demands on our sensibilities, values, and energies that any moral calling does. That means, in a society where there is too much institutionalized inequity and daily suffering, you have to understand the importance of being part of larger struggles. It is not enough to teach well and create a social justice classroom separate from the larger community. You have to be a community activist as well, a good parent, a decent citizen, an active community member. Is all of this possible? Probably not—certainly it isn't easy and often demands sacrifices. Believing that all children can learn can be a blessing in your own classroom and unleash your creativity. It can transform angry and resistant students into challenging, creative, funny, loving learners. It can also get you in trouble with your supervisors for creating new expectations for other teachers who might be failing or unwilling to put the energy and love into their work that you somehow call up. And at the end of the day it might also make you sad because there is so much more that needs to be done, so many students who don't even have the advantage of a decent classroom and a caring teacher.

This leads to my final suggestion. Protect and nurture yourself, have some fun in your life, learn new things that only obliquely relate to issues of social justice. Walk, play ball or chess, swim, fall in love and give yourself in love with joy and fullness to someone else. Don't forget how to laugh or feel good about the world. Sing with others, tell stories and listen to other people's stories, have fun so that you can work hard and work hard so that you and your students and their parents can have fun without looking over their shoulders. This is not a question of selfishness but one of survival. Don't turn teaching for social justice into a grim responsibility but take it for the moral and social necessity that it is. And don't be afraid to struggle for what you believe.

III

Advocates for Equity:
A Range of Perspectives

12

Growing Up Poor

Robert Coles

To grow up poor is to begin to know, even in the first decade of life, what that adjectival word means, what its implications portend for the years ahead. Here is a young American, Jimmie, from Boston, who has figured out already at only ten, what *is,* what *will be,* in his life:

> You've got to be careful, my dad says, and my mom says "Amen," when he tells us that. He means you can't waste what you have, or else you'll be down to nothing—so you don't throw something out if you can eat it, and you don't leave soap in the water, or you'll have less and less to use. Sure, if you've got all you want, and if you want more, you can go to the store and buy all your heart tells you to buy, then you're "sitting pretty," dad says. But if "every penny counts," then you'd better remember [that], and when I'm all grown up, and out of school, I'll still remember, like my mom and dad—what can happen when there's no money to buy the food and pay the bills. "Find yourself a good job," dad tells us, my sister and my brothers, but don't be taking anything for granted, or you'll fall "flat on your face," that's his "philosophy," he says.

A pause, as a lad named Jimmie tries to become the man he hopes to be, named Jim:

> When I'm all grown up, I'll use my dad's name [Jim], and I'll try to get a job, and I'll try to save, so there'll be some "spare cash." If you've got some "spare cash," my folks say, you're living on "easy street," but if you're strapped and no money is anywhere—then anything can come at you, around the corner, and boy, you're walking on thin ice,

and you can just go under, fast, and that's it! "Plan in advance and hope for the best, but don't expect it," that's what "big Jim" says, and that's what I'll tell my kids when I'm older than I am now.

So it goes: parents teach children a felt jeopardy, vulnerability, and soon enough, those boys and girls are quite aware of their uncertain, if not grim prospects—to the point that they foresee clouds on the horizon, not only for themselves but for their own children. Not that those who grow up under modest circumstances, or indeed, amidst an obvious and unrelenting poverty, are necessarily without hope and ambition: many children born to parents struggling hard, against high odds, to make a go of it, nevertheless find their way to strong convictions about the desirable, and too, the possible. In the words of the youth just quoted:

You can have a lot of trouble, and you're on the ropes, and you can be facing a knockout, but that doesn't mean you should give up. My uncle was on the boxing team [in high school] and he said, "If you're down that doesn't mean you're out," and my dad will say that a lot. He'll be sitting and trying to figure out "if we'll make it or we'll go to the poorhouse," but he always says: "Don't know where the poorhouse is, and no one I know has ever seen one, or been to one!" Maybe when I'm older I'll have enough money so I never think of a poorhouse, or talk about it to anyone.

Ironically, a family's poverty has enabled a son to think of the long run, to achieve a kind of distance on things—his dad's money problems, and his own ambitions as a boy who looks ahead, figures out what he wants from life. I came to know this boy, Jimmie, well enough, long enough, to understand from him (and his sister and one of his brothers, and his mom and dad) that a setback in life need not be regarded only as something that went wrong, badly awry—so the boy who spoke of his future life was able to point out clearly, in a forceful but polite reprimand for those who would gladly, even eagerly offer him compassion:

Don't be ashamed, my folks tell us—it's no crime to be poor, so long as you keep working! Then [if someone does so] you should be proud of yourself. The worst thing is if you start feeling sorry for yourself—that means you've become a loser! I hear kids say, if you grow up and make a ton of dough, then you win, and if you grow up and you're poor, then you've lost. So, we argue, oh boy, *do* we! I'll say: "Hey you guys, you're *all* poor; everyone in this neighborhood, he's poor, she's poor, we're all poor." No one's walking around this street with wads of dough and a big bank book! But that doesn't mean you can count us out; and besides, some people with a lot of money are crooks—look at the news in the papers and the TV! If you feel sorry for yourself, you've lost; but if you can look yourself in the mirror, my dad says, you're on your way, because you can own your life, even if you have a lot of bills to pay, and you can't find the money to pay off what everyone wants from you (something for the food, something for the clothes, something for the rent). It's murder, all right, this life, but you shouldn't let yourself slip or fall!

In strongly vivid, compelling and colloquial language a child echoes a family's jeopardy, but also its willfulness, the latter (again, the irony) an occasional consequence of the former: his parents have told him candidly of their precarious financial situation, but they have also told him of their determination to persist, if not prevail—the fight they have in them no matter the strenuous odds they must daily face. To be sure, some parents have good reason to feel almost overwhelmed by poverty, to the point that they and their children have seemingly (and sadly) lost the kind of fighting spirit Jimmie has chosen to articulate with his friends, and in conversation with others, such as his teacher, and me, a doctor who sometimes worked at the school he attended. But some of us who want to know about the Jimmies of this world, want to understand the considerable hardships many poor families must endure, ought be mindful of the resourcefulness, the tenacity of mind and heart, that people who are hard-pressed, even down-and-out, socially and economically, can nevertheless muster—parents and children, both.

Poverty is, possibly, a hazard, a burden, a tough, demanding, exhausting ordeal, but poverty is also, now and then, a distinct challenge to those who experience it, and even a spur to those who feel hemmed in, or without much they wish they had, or know full well they need, yet who manage steadfastly to hold on tightly to their self-respect, their pride. The point, of course, is not to put on a pedestal those who often pay dearly in their minds for the tough life they have to endure—while at the same time, though, we can properly make allowance for the universal truth that suffering (illnesses, accidents, injuries, bad luck of various kinds) may also prompt those hurt, slapped down by fate and circumstance, to dig in, to summon all the strength and purpose they can find in their heads, in their bodies. In Ralph Ellison's novel, in Raymond Carver's stories and poems, or those of Richard Ford, even in Zora Neale Hurston's fictional account of harsh poverty as experienced by migrant farm families, one meets people of pluck and passion as well as travail—their eyes, after all, *are* "watching God." There is to such individuals, as the poet and physician William Carlos Williams kept reminding us, based on his own firsthand acquaintance with working poor people of Paterson, New Jersey (where America's first factory was built), a *mulish* or stubbornly enduring side to their life, no matter the aches and worries that keep being experienced.

The challenge for *us* is to keep in mind what happens to the minds of *others* lest we be blind and deaf to how they must make do, and what they have to say, amidst the hard-fought lives that are theirs by dint of daily poverty. I have already referred to vulnerability and marginality as two aspects of poverty—both of them, not rarely, appreciated quite readily by children who have to live under such conditions. But let me move from social description to psychological experience. Here is Jimmie's sister, Sally, two years his senior, at thirteen on the edge of adolescence, speaking not of the future, as her brother was sometimes wont to do, but of the past—remembering, in fact, her own childhood as an elementary school girl who learned how to read and write and count, but who also learned how to read the world's values, take them in, realize their significance, and who learned how to write to herself, in a diary she kept, and not least, who learned how much she counted, in her parents' estimation, and how little she counted to others, or so it sometimes seemed to her:

I don't know how I became me, but I remember being in the second grade and the teacher was always upset with us, and she said we had to learn how to *behave,* and *dress right,* or we'd never get anywhere. Where is that "anywhere," I used to wonder to myself? Where she lives I suppose! Miss Carroll, she was totally full of herself, that's what my best friend Alice and I thought. I can remember a few kids, even back then, who were so stuck on themselves, and the teacher, that Miss Carroll, was stuck on them. Even so, Alice and me, we figured we'd rather live just where we do, right here in our own broken-down building [they lived in an apartment house that badly needed repairs] than be with those big-shot kids, so uppity their noses touch the clouds, and they're always sniffing at somebody, saying she's not so good, too bad!

Now [in junior high school], it's worse. The kids who have it made (their parents drive them to school in fancy cars) sit together when they can, especially in the cafeteria, and us, we come by bus and streetcar, and we hang together. My mom says, "That's life"; she says people stick with their own kind, that's how it goes, and you learn that when you grow up, and you leave your own because you go out in the world, to school where the kids are coming from all different places, and they have their different ideas, and some are "loaded," you just know.

I'll admit, it's hard; you see people, they've got fancy clothes—when you go downtown to the stores—and you think: some people have the luck and I'm not one of them. Mom says to forget that, but it's hard to stop your mind from "running all over the map"—you have these thoughts and you have to try and try to forget them. What thoughts? [I had asked.] Well, sometimes it's questions that I have, that I ask myself. I used to ask them when I was little, in the first grade, and now I'm still asking them, and I am in the seventh grade. I mean: why did it happen that some have everything that their heart wants and some don't know if there's the next meal around the corner, or a flat nothing will be there to eat, whether their stomach is growling or not? (I've heard my mom and dad talk like that, but they tell me to forget what they say and "get on with it.")

Another question I'll hear myself asking is—it's also one of the big ones: will good luck come and say hello to me, like it does to some people, or will I just be out of it all the time—you know, looking for a good deal, a good job, a good guy (who's nice, and *he* has a good deal, a good job) or will it be Mr. Nobody (who's going nowhere) who wants to take me with him?

I shouldn't have said that [she paused, then turned on herself with a scowl on her face]. I'm not being nice to all of us folks who live on his street when I get the idea in my head that nothing is green on this side of the fence, but on the other, you have heaven all over the place! Mom says, some people have their heaven, but we've got to make our own, right here, the best we can, and not be thinking, always, of what's out there, who's got it better than us—because that's not what the Lord wants heaven to be, a place where you're everyday thinking of others, "comparing, comparing, comparing," she says, my mom to us, when we say, "if only I could have this." *"If only,"* mom will give it right back to us: *"if only* we could pay attention to who *we* are, and what *we* can do with the time the good Lord has given to us!"

I'll always remember when I asked if there's some way people having trouble can get out of it, and people looking for jobs that pay good can find them—and dad said: "Look" (he always starts that way!), "there are those who have a lot, and those who have a little, and we belong to the second, those kind of folks, but even so, bad can come to people who have a lot; they can get sick and die, like everyone else, or they can be mean to each other and selfish, just like bad can hit us (more than it hits them, who've got oodles of cash in their wallets and pocket books). One thing you should never lose sight of, *never ever:* that there's equality in this life. The sun shines on all of us, and the rain pours, the same way, down hard, and even if you've got a solid, expensive roof over your head, you have to go outside. Time belongs to no one—you can't buy it, you can only live during it (sure some people can spend their time buying, but that's *their* waste, you see!)." Dad tells us, when he says good night, that you can be *down* but not *out,* and you can be way up there, and take a big fall, and then you're really, really *out,* because the longer, the steeper the fall, the harder it is. So, we should stop comparing and comparing—just find our dream, wherever it takes you, and try to build it, the best you can.

So it went for Sally—a girl growing up poor, whose parents had grown up poor, but a girl who owned her very own outlook on life, her very own notions of what is desirable, possible. Yes, at times those notions, part of a broader, overall outlook, had their downside, even as she struggled long and hard to be upbeat, to try earnestly (as her mom often put it, drawing on the old and familiar lyrics of a song) to see the "sunny side of the street." Indeed, to grow up poor (for Sally and her brother Jimmie, for their parents, too, their kinfolk, their neighbors near and far) could sometimes mean to scan that other side of the street, to feel envy for it, to be rivalrous or competitive with it, to long for what it has to offer, to hope against hope that somehow, in some way, things would get much better, money would be more available, good food and shelter more reliable—and such being the case, life would be more predictable and kindly, less harsh and precarious. Still, as Sally knows in essence to remind not only herself but a listener who converses with her, perspective matters, puts the precarious in a larger framework of understanding, supplies a certain "sense of things"—that phrase Sally has acquired from her mom and dad, and she uses it as she tells how it is, living in a given place:

> If you are upset, and if you feel it would be better if you had more (a beautiful dress and some really snazzy shoes), then what you need is to get a "sense of things"—that means you have to keep being yourself, and stop trying to be someone else. Even rich people aren't satisfied with their eyes—they want and they want and they want. So you can be greedy (with all you've got not enough for you) and you can live right here, where we do, and if you're "level-headed," dad says, and you have "a good sense of things"—why, that will keep you in harness, and you won't lose your head and go running in every which way, so you get confused and lost.

The longer I have listened to poor children across this nation, and abroad, the more sharply I hear their self-consciousness conveyed—their intention, really, that I hear in no uncertain terms what they have come to figure out in their brains, feel strongly in their hearts. These are young people who know how close to the edge their parents, and they as boys and girls with them, live each day. These are children who sometimes long to live elsewhere, have a different kind of life, more secure and providing materially. These are children who now and then want what others may assume naturally to be theirs—want higher hopes and expectations not only felt but grounded in an observable, everyday existence. These are children already aware of what words like "loss" and "race" can come to mean—thus does a social and an economic background shape ideas, ideals, wishes and worries. These are children who have learned certain decisive social lessons, and don't forget them later, no matter the personal and professional breakthroughs they achieve.

Such children, of course, have their frailties and fears to confront—constant companions, alas, on a particular life's journey. Yet, such children can also be savvy in so many respects, alert in the face of any number of difficulties put in their way by events and individuals.

13

"... As Soon As She Opened Her Mouth!": Issues of Language, Literacy, and Power

Victoria Purcell-Gates

A warm afternoon in a midwestern U.S. city: A fourth-grade teacher grinned up at me knowingly as she condemned a young mother: "I knew she was ignorant just as soon as she opened her mouth!" This teacher was referring to the fact that Jenny, the mother of Donny, one of her students, spoke in a southern mountain dialect, a dialect that is often used to characterize poor whites known variously as "hillbillies," "hicks," or "ridgerunners." As this teacher demonstrated, this dialect is strongly associated with low levels of education and literacy as well as a number of social ills and dysfunctions. And sure enough, Donny, the child of parents who could neither read nor write anything except for their names, was failing to become literate in school as well.

A warm afternoon in a rural village in El Salvador: A 66-year-old Salvadoran campesina (peasant), Maria Jesus, explained to my co-researcher why, when she was young, children in her village did not go to school: "All five student that were there [school] didn't learn anything. So there was no reason to go. And it was too far from where we lived. It was really far, we had to cross the trails, and there was a ravine that got so full in the winter, we couldn't get through."

Researchers around the world have been focused on this problem: the cavernous and uncrossable ravine that seems to lie between children of poverty (and the adults they grow up to be) from marginalized, or low-status, groups and their full potentials as literate beings. Overall, the best we have been able to do is to describe the situation over and over again, using different measures, different definitions of literacy, different theoretical lenses, different methodologies. Again and again we conclude that in developed countries and in third-world countries, learners from impoverished and low-status groups fail to develop as fully and productively literate as compared to learners from sociocultural groups that hold sociopolitical power and favor. Further, this reality continues despite what appears to be clear identification of the problem, and billions of dollars spent by national governments and international agencies. It is this relationship between class and power, language and literacy that I write about here. I have pursued this topic in a number of research projects, and I'll draw a few examples from these.

Some children bring "literacy knowledge" to school with them. Does this mean that they already knew how to read? How to write? No, such literacy knowledge refers to the concepts children acquire during their preschool years, during the years preceding the beginning of formal literacy instruction, in kindergarten and first grade, in reading, writing and printed language.

Let me give you some examples: A little girl about two years old was sitting with her mother in the parents/children room at church one Sunday. Bored with the actual church service, this little girl asked her mother to read to her. Her mother, trying to focus on the service, put her off for as long as she could. "Read!" commanded the child, "read!" Her mother, silently following along in her Bible, said, "I AM reading." "No!" said the two-year-old. Reaching up with her hand, she opened her mother's mouth and began to move her lips up and down.

Another example: A four-year-old boy was experimenting with paper and pencil one day during a quiet time at home. Suddenly he rushed up to his mother, holding out a piece of paper with some scribbles on it. "Mommy!" he cried. "What did I write? What did I write?" "I don't know sweetie. What did you write?" answered his mother. "I don't know! I can't read!" he cried.

Both of these children have acquired some basic, crucial, concepts about reading and about written language. And they learned these concepts not by being formally taught, but by being there and part of the action when important people in their lives were reading and writing for their own purposes. The little girl had figured out that "reading" meant that activity which happened when her mother would read aloud to her, something that inevitably meant her mouth was open and her lips moving. Silent reading was not known to this child yet, since she had not observed it (or did not know that she had). The little boy also knew some important things about reading/writing and written language. He knew that people wrote by making marks on a piece of paper. He also knew that one could read what someone had written. Through experimentation, he realized that he had "written" something. He also knew enough at this point to know that while he may have written something, he did not know how to read it!

These examples probably seem very familiar to all of you who have had young children. In fact, young children behaving in this way, and doing things like pointing to an exit sign in a store and asking "What does that say?" or writing the first letter of their names in crayon on the living room wall, seem part of the natural way of children. All children do these things, don't they?

In fact, all children do not behave in ways that let us know that they have learned and are learning about written language when they are very young. That is because not all children learn about written language to the same extent during their pre-formal instruction years. To learn about written language, to learn that "print says." To learn that written stories sound different from the way people talk, to learn that letters make words and words make sentences, and that when you read you must begin at the left and move your eyes across to the right and then go back to the left again, to learn that letters stand for individual sounds—to learn all of these basic concepts requires extensive experience with people using print, with people reading and writing around you and to you and for you and allowing you to try your hand at reading and writing.

The degree to which you do not experience these extensive uses of print in your young life is the degree to which you do not know/understand the concepts that are so crucial to making sense out of beginning reading and writing instruction in school.

Social Class and Emergent Literacy Knowledge

To explore this relationship between experience with print and emergent literacy knowledge and a possible link to social class membership, I conducted, along with Karin Dahl, a two-year study of kindergarten and first-grade children (Purcell-Gates & Dahl, 1991). We began by measuring the emergent literacy knowledge held by these children from economically stressed homes. We found that, across the board, these children had less knowledge of written language and how reading and writing work than children from more middle-class homes.

We then followed them through their first two years of school, documenting their literacy instruction and the ways in which they made sense of it. We found that by the end of first grade, those children who began kindergarten with more knowledge of written language, and especially more knowledge of the functions of print in the real world—what we called The Big Picture—were the most active learners and the most successful readers at the end of first grade.

What does this suggest? It suggests, among other things, that children who *experience* other people in their lives reading and writing for many different reasons in the years before they begin school are better equipped conceptually to make sense of—to learn from—the beginning reading and writing instruction in their schools. It also suggests that, as a group, children from homes of poverty experience fewer instances of people reading and writing for a broad number of purposes than do children from mainstream homes. To the extent that parental education—which is going to affect the frequency and the types of reading and writing people do—is related to poverty, this makes some sense.

I followed up on this two-year study with, first, a single case study (Purcell-Gates, 1995) and then a larger study of twenty families with young children from low-income homes to document how much people read and wrote in these homes and what kinds of things they read and wrote (Purcell-Gates, 1996). Looking at the larger study first, I documented that, yes, overall there were relatively few instances of reading and writing in these homes; but there was a range from almost no uses of print to print use that looked just like the middle-class homes described by others (Taylor, 1985). Further, by measuring the emergent literacy knowledge of the young children in the homes, I found clear relationships between both frequency of reading and writing events in the homes and children's conceptual knowledge of written language and between the kinds of reading and writing events and children's emergent literacy knowledge. The more parents read and wrote beyond simple clauses like you find on cereal boxes and coupons, and the more they involved their young children in reading and writing events: pointing out letters, sounds, words, and reading to their children, or involving their children in reading events that focused on things of interest to the children, the more those children knew The Big Picture. They knew different concepts of print, the alphabetic nature of our print system, and that letters stand for sounds.

Conversely, looking at the case study of Donny and his mother, Jenny, the parent and child with which I began this paper, I documented the degree to which the almost total lack of reading and writing events in the home can present a serious challenge to young children's ability to learn from school instruction on reading and writing. In Donny's home, because neither parent could read nor write, the children grew up understanding that life did not include print. In fact, they did not understand that print existed as a meaningful semiotic system; it did not "mean," did not function in their lives. And they lived full and interesting lives without it. This was, I believe, a key insight I came to as I worked with and collected data from this family over two years. Donny, the little school-aged boy of the family, did not, could not make sense of the beginning literacy instruction he received in school. Without an understanding that written language *communicates*—that it *means,* he had no idea what to do when he was "taught" to "sound out" words, to match beginning letter sounds, to fill in blanks using words he was supposed to have learned.

Language, Literacy, and Power

At this point I want to stop and caution you about where you may think I am going with this. It is true that I have been busy documenting knowledge—specifically, knowledge of written language—that children from homes of poverty lack, or hold to lesser degrees, than children from more middle-class homes. I have also been documenting the degree to which this knowledge and lack of it affects their ability to learn to read and write in school. However, I want to state *unequivocally* that this is not a deficit theory, nor is it placing the blame on the children, their parents, or their homes. This is where the "Power" part of my title comes in.

What I have been describing, and what I have been documenting, is *experience,* I have been documenting the ways in which experience—in this case, experience with written language use—varies across homes. What I am saying is that children come to school with different experiences. The experiences they have as young children are culturally driven. Within this, I see literacy use as cultural practice. It is cultural practice because reading and writing are woven into the everyday experiences of people, and these everyday activities, attitudes, and beliefs help to define and distinguish among cultural groups.

The implications of this stance of cultural *difference* instead of *deficit* for educators is profound. Let me try to make this point with an illustration—an example—of cultural difference that could affect education. Let's imagine an educational situation in which experience is significant but not as politically charged as that of literacy. Let's think about driver's education, for example. Let's say that a young man enrolls in a driver's education course along with twenty other young people. However, this young man has just arrived from the desert of Palestine or from a rural village in Afghanistan. The other twenty enrollees are from either the United States or another western country where almost everyone drives and rides in automobiles. Let's also assume that this young immigrant speaks, reads, and writes English. The driver's ed instructor comes to understand that this man, Phil, does not have a clue about cars. He does not understand how they run, the purposes for which they are used, the ways in which drivers drive, steer, brake, push the gas pedal, or stay on the right side of the road. All of the written materials, the drivers manuals, the ways in which the instructor instructs the class, depend on this background knowledge, this previous experience with car use. For example, "Put your key in the ignition, and turn it to start the car." Phil thinks, "Key"? "Ignition"? "Start"?

Are we going to interpret this as a flaw, a deficit, in Phil? Or are we going to interpret it as a lack of crucial experience, a difference in the experiential backgrounds between Phil and the other members of the drivers education class?

It does make a difference how we interpret this. If we assume that Phil's problem is due to a deficit, it is easier to write him off, tell him he cannot learn to drive, or put him in a remedial drivers ed class that gives the same classroom instruction at a slower pace, but still without giving him experience with cars. However, if we assume—rightly, I believe—that Phil's difficulties stem from a lack of actual experience with cars, and recognize the importance and role of that experience in learning to drive, we can set about providing that experience with cars that Phil—through no inherent fault of his own, or of the culture in which he grew up—has not had up to this point. We can give Phil lots of experiences with riding in cars, with observing other people driving cars, with exploring cars and how they work, with observing how important cars are to this culture in which he now lives.

Can we look at differences among children in the amount and type of written language experiences they have had before schooling in the same way, without assigning inherent deficit, or inability to learn, to children who do not have as much literary knowledge as other children? I believe so; I believe that if we claim to allow equal access to educational opportunity to all children in our schools then we must. But I also know that whether we interpret differences among children—or adults—as *deficit* or *difference* depends primarily on our preconceptions, attitudes toward, and stereotypes we hold toward the individual children's communities and cultures. If the child's family is poor, his parents undereducated, his dialect nonstandard, then we are much more likely to interpret experiential difference as a deficit in the child, in the parents, in the home, in the sociocultural community within which this child has grown up. And when we do this, we play God, conferring or denying educational opportunity to individual, socioculturally different, children. And we do not have the right to do this.

This was the second key insight I came to as a result of my two-year ethnography of Donny's family. While documenting the effect of growing up in a nonliterate family on Donny's conceptual knowledge of written language and the problems this posed for his learning to read and write in school, I had to ask what the school was doing about this. How were they

dealing with this experiential difference so that his learning could pro-
ceed? Nothing. Absolutely nothing. Not only were they failing to address
this experiential difference—much like our pretend driver's ed instructor
would have addressed Phil's inexperience with cars—they were also seemingly unconcerned about his failure to learn.

How could this be? Having seen two of my own children through elementary schools and having garnered a wealth of experience with schools
in general, I knew that teachers, specialists, and administrators would have
created quite a big fuss if any middle-class child finished first grade knowing how to read only one word. Parents would be called and consulted, assuming they hadn't already been haunting the school corridors, testing
would have been recommended and carried out, the instruction and
teaching would have been questioned and examined, and elaborate educational plans drawn up to remediate this issue would have been drawn up.

But no notice was taken of Donny's failure to learn—except by his
mother. Oh yes, Jenny knew that Donny wasn't learning. She recognized a
very familiar and ominous pattern. Donny was not learning to read and
write just as she and Donny's father had not learned to read and write. "I
don't want what happened to us to happen to my son," she told me. "It's
hard not knowing how to read! I know!" She worried that they would just
pass him along until he eventually dropped out of school, just as she and
her husband had both done in their seventh-grade years.

Jenny was down at her son's school constantly. She would go down to
tell them that neither she nor his dad could read so please don't send notes
home, but to call if they needed to talk to her. She would go down to try
to tell them that Donny did not know enough about reading to be passed
on to second grade. She would go down to complain that even though
the teacher had told her that she would retain him in second grade, that
he had been passed on to third—just as had happened to her and her
husband.

As if she had never appeared before them, the teachers and the principal continued to send written notes home, never to call, and to complain officially
that the parents never responded to messages.

As if she had never appeared before them, they passed Donny to second
grade, dismissing her concerns about his failure to learn.

As if she had never appeared before them, they passed him on to third grade.
They passed him on to third grade until, someone—a real person in their
eyes—called to express concern and support for the idea that he be retained in second grade. You see, when Donny was passed on to third grade,
I had been working with him and his family for a year. Jenny called to tell
me what had happened. So I called the school office to request the right
to attend a conference with the principal that Jenny believed she had

arranged. As a result of this phone call, the school secretary took note of the fact that Dr. Purcell-Gates was also concerned about the failure of the school to retain Donny in second grade, as was promised by his second-grade teacher. An hour after this call, the secretary called me back and informed me that the principal would see to it that Donny was moved to a second-grade classroom if I believed that was best. An actual meeting with the principal of this school was never conducted.

Why wasn't Jenny listened to? Why wasn't she taken seriously? Jenny's concerns aside, any examination of assessment and classroom evidence revealed clear evidence of Donny's failure to learn. Why wasn't this taken seriously?

Jenny and Donny belonged to a social underclass. They were members of a cultural group referred to as "urban Appalachian," "Poor Whites" from the mountains or hills, "hillbillies," "white trash." Donny's failure to learn was not considered worthy of attention, and Jenny's inability to get herself heard was intimately related to this fact. Jenny wasn't taken seriously as a rightfully concerned mother because it is a deeply held belief, or stereotype, of the middle class that poor urban Appalachians are unfit as parents (Starnes, 1990). This stereotype prevented school personnel from interpreting her complaints and concerns in the same way they would interpret complaints and concerns from a middle-class mother. Donny's failure to learn *anything* was not noted because this was the expected pattern. Nothing to get excited about. What do you expect from these people? Happens all the time! That someone would care about this family was somewhat unsettling to the school.

Now, while this study is often cited as noteworthy because it focuses on poor whites instead of poor people of color, I want to suggest that this marginalization and denial of educational opportunity is not restricted to this urban Appalachian population. Rather, I see this study and the struggles and dreams it reveals as an up-close *example* of the devastation wrought by issues of class and power in all of our schools and in all of the countries of the world where clear underclass populations exist in illiterate or low literate and impoverished conditions. I am saying that insofar as the lower classes, the socially low-status peoples of this country fail to learn to read and write commensurate with their middle-class peers, there is not much difference between the United States of America and third-world countries. The issues are the same.

First, socially and politically marginalized people are held in disdain by those who hold the power. While they may be pitied and while many well-meaning middle-class people may volunteer clothes and money to help stave off the most devastating effects of poverty, there is always a generalized belief that they cannot learn as well as those in power—the middle/

upper classes. It is believed that they "just don't have it" as far as intelligence and/or the will to learn, to achieve, to move out of their impoverished conditions go. This disdain, this general stance of diminished expectations exerts a powerful and insidious effect on the education offered to marginalized people. I've referred to the effects on the education of Donny, and my book, *Other People's Words,* details this and describes similar effects on the education of Donny's mother and father (Purcell-Gates, 1995). In El Salvador, where I studied the literacy education of impoverished peasants (Purcell-Gates & Waterman, 2000), there was no real effort to offer schooling at all for the campesinos in the rural areas. Most of the patched-together schools with their seriously undertrained teachers were the result of volunteer operations run by various church organizations or social/political action groups. Yet meaningful and effective education is being offered to the middle and upper classes in the cities.

Second, language always seems to play a central role in this class-related denial of educational opportunity. This is undoubtedly because the language one speaks is the clearest and most stable marker of class membership, as George Bernard Shaw's *Pygmalion* demonstrated so entertainingly for us many years ago. While in some third-world countries, this means a completely different language spoken by the marginalized, in most, including the United States, it also means socially marked different dialects. I say socially marked because dialects of those in power do not elicit the same knee-jerk disdain and assumptions of deficit as do the dialects of the sociopolitically marginalized. For example, the Boston dialect of the Kennedys or the southern dialect of Jimmy Carter are never pointed to as evidence of cognitive and linguistic deficit. But let a poor, urban Appalachian woman speak for only a few minutes and powerful attitudes of prejudice and assumptions of inferiority are elicited. The vignette at the start of the article occurred when I was visiting Donny's classroom a year after the end of the study to observe his functioning. I introduced myself to his teacher and explained my interest in Donny. She conveyed her opinion of him and his school ability mainly through eye rolls, shrugs, and knowing grins. When I told her that I felt he had made great strides given the nonliteracy of his parents, she volunteered that she had met his mother, Jenny, and then added, "As soon as she opened her mouth, I *knew* she was ignorant!"

"As soon as she opened her mouth!" I knew exactly what this teacher meant. Jenny's dialect marked her immediately, within this context of a city where urban Appalachians make up the poorest and least successfully educated minority population, as unworthy, stupid, and of no real concern to teachers like her.

I have seen this same attitude and dismissal on Native American reservations in this country, in Israel toward the Palestinians, in England toward the lower classes and the immigrants, and in El Salvador toward the campesinos.

With these sociopolitically driven attitudes toward the language that people speak, think with, and learn with, is it any wonder that there is a class difference in learning and achievement? Particularly for literacy development, one of the first basic, driving concepts and experiences needs to be the realization that the *printed word codes language.* The negative attitude toward the spoken language of urban Appalachians is so strong in the cities that teachers regularly insist that students not speak or read orally unless they drop their dialect and use "standard English."

If you are forbidden to use your language to learn to read and write, if you are forced to speak differently when reading and writing, then you are in effect being closed off, or at least seriously impeded from accessing the world of print. Jenny described it powerfully for me one day when, after realizing that her words could be written down and read, she exclaimed, "I never read my *own* words before! I only copied other people words! I never knew that I could write my own!" It took me an incredible amount of effort to get little Donny to just try to encode his own words and to stop only copying from books. But when he finally did, he began his journey toward the world of the literate where he now resides, a real reader and member of the literate community.

What Schools and Teachers Can Do

There are several moves that schools and teachers can make to help erase the entrenched class differences in literacy achievement. These suggestions are made assuming that the sociopolitical world remains as it is, with some groups in power and other groups marginalized. My ultimate wish would be to erase this imbalance of power. However, until that occurs, I believe that we must not allow one more day to pass implicitly cooperating in the denial of educational achievement to significant portions of our citizens and fellow human beings. The recommendations I am going to make are not untried. They draw on my own work as a teacher and teacher of teachers, on the work of educators such as Marva Collins, the Black Panthers in the '60s and '70s who ran successful programs in the inner cities, the teachers described by Lisa Delpit who saw to it that their poor, African American children learned to read and write and to function successfully, the teachers in the illegal slave schools in this country before emancipation who brought precious literacy to children and adults held in bondage, and the public school teachers struggling and succeeding to educate poor minority children within the public schools today.

First, and most obvious, teachers and schools must accept, believe, and act upon the belief that *children of poverty are learners, have been learning since birth, are ready to learn at anytime, and will learn.* This crucial beginning stance on the part of teachers will help to ensure that any failure in the achievement of these children will lead to an examination of their instruction and not to a shrugging off of their futures. It will lead us to examine ourselves and ask ourselves what is wrong with the way we are teaching these children? What do they need to learn? There is no one answer to this; it depends on the children, their cultures, their previous experiences, their dispositions, and so on. In the case of young Donny, I, as his teacher, after assessing the lack of experience he had had with literacy in his life, needed to provide him with multitudes of experiences with people reading and writing, show him how he could connect with the world of print through his language and his thoughts, and explicitly point out to him the ways in which print coded the world he knew as well as "other people's worlds." I did the same for Jenny, working with her to make the connection between her words and other people's words.

On the wider level of the classroom, I observed a teacher for one year in an inner-city school serving African American children living in a large housing project. This African American teacher absolutely refused to accept poverty and its many consequences as excuses for her first-graders to fail to achieve. I watched her as day after day she exhorted, insisted, directed, ordered, and led her charges in learning to read and write. She never doubted for a minute that they could learn, and she never for a minute assumed that they could learn without her. It was sometimes hard for me, as a white middle-class person, to watch.

One scene stands out in my mind: a little girl who often came to school hungry, tired, and stressed. This one morning she kept falling asleep on her desk as the class was reading from their reading books together. Miss M. (the teacher) sharply told her to stay awake and follow along, but when her eyes closed and her head hit the desk for the third time, Miss M. insisted that she stand while she joined the other children in the oral reading. *"No one* in this class is going to sleep when they're supposed to be learning to read!" declared this teacher. And learn to read they did. The class mean on the California Achievement Test at the beginning of the year was in the 30th percentile, after a year of kindergarten, significantly below average and absolutely typical for a low-SES population. At the end of this first-grade year, the class mean was at the 55th percentile, well within the national average, with a good number of children above average and the lowest scoring child at the beginning of the year, reading at mid-first grade level. This achievement would not have happened without this teacher and her absolute belief that, yes, life was hard for these kids, but they *were* learners, they would learn, and it was her job to see that they did, in ways that worked for them.

Secondly, and as part of this stance of accepting the children as learners, it is necessary to accept their language as that with which they learn, and use that language to help them begin their education. It is the need to conceptually separate the process of learning to read and write from the sociopolitical issues surrounding language use. Nonstandard, socially marked dialects do prevent people from succeeding in the middle-class world, but they do not prevent people from learning to read and write. If we insist that learners learn a different way of talking and communicating before, or as a condition of, learning to read and write, we leave them irrevocably behind. No one "talks" like written language. Everyone uses fragmented syntax, different pronunciation patterns, and different types of vocabulary words when they talk as compared to when they read and write. The belief that educated people talk in complete, standard, syntactically integrated sentences is just wrong and ill informed. The concept of "sentence" as well as of "word" is a written language one. The "sound" system taught through phonics instruction never matches *anyone's* spoken language. The difference is that people with social and political capital get away with their "deviations," learn to adjust their language to the oral or written context, and are never made to believe that the way they talk is responsible for any failure to learn to read and write.

People without this social/political capital are told, as Jenny was, that they cannot learn to read because of the way they talk. "That's why it was hard for me to sound my words out," Jenny echoed her teachers. "Because I talk different; 'cause I'm, you know, countrified. And my words don't come out the way they're supposed to." When Jenny was shown that her knowledge of language could help her learn to read, that she did not have to say words the way the phonics system described the pronunciations, that what she had to do was to "sound out" to her dialect, then she could get a toehold on this process of learning to read. Miss M. never told the children in her first-grade class that they talked wrong. She did point out for them how the written language they were learning to read and write said things differently when syntax and vocabulary were involved. And she completely accepted their pronunciations of vowel and consonant sounds when they were learning to "sound out." I saw the same teacher attitudes and behaviors with the same successful results in literacy classes in El Salvador.

Third, we must realize that speakers will use the appropriate oral language register (or "type" or form) to fit the social context they find themselves in, if they know it. Similarly, writers will use the appropriate written register to fit the social context they are writing in, if they know it. In other words, when opening a book, a reader will call upon—"activate"—his knowledge of written language rather than oral language because a book is a written-language context. Knowing standard oral registers will not, by itself, help readers and writers with written registers. Readers must be familiar with written narrative language, for example, in order to read and write it easily and accurately. They must know the vocabulary choices that occur more frequently in written narrative (e.g., *entrance* as compared to *door*); they must be familiar with the syntactic constructions that mark written narrative from oral (e.g., *"Begone!" said the furious queen, throwing the mirror after the fleeing princess.* as compared to *The queen was really mad and threw the mirror at her and went like "Go away!"* which would be much more typical if one were relating the same information orally.) But because readers employ a "nonstandard" mode in oral discussion, it does not follow that they cannot learn other modes for written communication.

Origin of Language Knowledge

None of us is born knowing how to talk appropriately in church, in court, in school, in a group of friends, and so on. Similarly, none of us is born knowing how to write a personal letter, a story, a science report, an excuse note, and so on. We all have learned whatever we know about different language variants or registers by being with people who are using them. However, while we are absorbing language knowledge as it is being used, most of us also have benefited from being given explicit language knowledge by people who have it. Examples of explicit explanation of language conventions include such information as: "We don't use that word in church!" "When you meet Mr. Rogers, be sure to look him in the eye and say, 'Pleased to meet you, sir.' " "When you write a letter, always begin with 'Dear So and So' and put a comma after that before you go down to the next line and begin your first sentence." "An argumentative essay usually begins with your claim, then has about three to five paragraphs providing facts or opinions that support your claim, and ends with a concluding paragraph where you restate your claim and your reasons that support it."

These two sources of language knowledge—experience of language in use and explicit explanation of the language features that distinguish different types, or registers, of language—must inform the curricular decisions teachers make as they teach children to read and write. The children need to experience the many different types of written language in use, listening to it, observing its formation by the teacher, and then reading and writing themselves. In the process, the children need clear and unambiguous information about how language shifts and changes to accomplish different social and learning goals—how to form and how to read the different types of written language found in stories, poems, reports, personal narratives, information texts, and so on. Insuring these children the opportunity to learn about written language forms is essential to ensuring that they grow and develop as readers and writers.

Beyond "Linguicism"

Some people refer to the prejudicial stereotyping involved in blaming nonstandard speakers' oral dialects for their academic failures as "linguicism." I agree that the negative attitudes toward nonstandard dialects and the resulting misguided instructional attempts to change people's speech are based on misinformation and ethnocentricity just as are the other "isms" like racism, sexism, and ageism. And, like the other "isms," linguicism, especially as it impacts literacy development and educational achievement, is responsible for insidious social and political marginalization, resulting in blighted lives and unfulfilled opportunities for legions of people.

My greatest hope is that we can begin to move away from these old, uninformed notions about language and literacy. We must begin to comprehend and deal with the real issues involved in the failure of the schools to teach, to their fullest potential, the millions of children and adults from minority and low-socioeconomic communities.

REFERENCES

Purcell-Gates, V. and K. Dahl. 1991. Low-SES children's success and failure at early literacy learning in skills-based classrooms. *JRB: A Journal of Literacy* 23, 235–53.
———. 1995. *Other people's words: The cycle of low literacy.* Cambridge, MA: Harvard University Press.
———. 1996. Stories, coupons, and the TV guide: Relationships between home literacy experiences and emergent literacy knowledge. *Reading Research Quarterly* 31, 406–28.
——— and R. Waterman. 2000. Now we read, we see, we speak: Portrait of literacy development in a Freirean-based adult class. Mahwah, NJ: Lawrence Erlbaum Publishers.
Starnes, B. 1990. Appalachian students, parents, and culture as viewed by their teachers. *Urban Appalachian Advocate,* January, 1–4.
Taylor, D. 1985. Family literacy: Children learning to read and write. Exeter, NH: Heinemann.

14

Urban Pedagogy

William Ayers and Patricia Ford

Is there a distinctly urban pedagogy?

In the front row of a celebrity press conference announcing a major grant to the Chicago school reform effort sat five young men: Cornell Faust, Antwoine Conaway, Kelly Floyd, Derrhun Whitten, and Darnell Faust. Wearing starter jackets and gold chains with elaborate designs etched into their short-cropped hair, they draped their long bodies casually over the folding chairs. City kids. "I'll bet that's Farragut's fabulous five," whispered a reporter. "They're a cinch to be state basketball champs this year."

When the young men were introduced fifteen minutes later, and stood with awkward smiles and waves, there was an audible gasp throughout the auditorium, followed by sustained applause—these were state champions all right, 1994 Illinois state chess champions from Orr High School. Orr is a Chicago Public School, eighty-five percent low-income, ninety-five percent African-American. The chess team defeated New Trier High School from the wealthy gold coast suburbs to advance to the nationals, where they came in second by half a point to New York's famous Peter Stuyvesant High School. Something in the contrast between the stereotype of young black men and the actual accomplishment of these students made the applause warmer and more moving.

The chess program at Orr began in 1986 under the leadership of math teacher Tom Larson. "I love chess," Larson said, "And I believe in these kids. I thought chess could be a way to get them to sit still and begin using their thinking skills. So far it's worked." Larson is a big bearded man on a mission. "My job is to guide them to independence, to guide them through the process of maturing . . . I'm trying to build the dream. Faith, hope, and love."

Tom Larson has qualities all good teachers need: a passion for something (in his case, chess, but it could as easily be literature, music, art, politics, geometry, history, algebra, quilts, or quarks), and an unshakable belief in the capacities of his students. In other words, he loves the kids and he's engaged in life. He brings to his teaching a passion for the world and an abiding regard for his students. Faith, hope, and love.

The city is a place, a big and growing place. On September 20, 1994, the Chicago *Tribune* wire service reported that according to a World Bank Study, the world's big cities together are growing by a million people a week. Within a decade, the study predicts, more than half the earth's people will live in cities. It is a geographic location for billions.

But the city is more than geography. It is bright lights, big chances, a place for new experiences and bold experiments. It is also a metaphor for corruption and degeneracy. And increasingly it is a code for the poor, the nonwhite, the immigrant, the economically marginal. The city as seething.

The problem for teachers is to figure out what and how much to take into account when inventing teaching in city schools. There is the danger of not taking enough into account—poverty is significant for kids who are unable to acquire the basic sustenance for a healthy life; race matters in a society that structures rewards and privileges in part on the hierarchies of color and background. Hungry children can't learn; hurt children can't learn; frightened or distraught children can't learn; upset children can't learn. There is a lot that city teachers need to take into account.

On the other hand, there is the danger of taking too much into account or of making stereotypical generalizations about children and their families that can destroy teaching efforts. For example, when a group of new city teachers met for orientation with their principal, he was kind enough, and complimentary: "I'm so glad you will be with us for the coming year," he began. "You're just what we need—energetic, fresh, filled with youthful idealism." When anyone applauds youthful idealism, duck! He went on to explain to them that even though they thought these kids would become great students under their tutelage, they had to understand the real world. "These kids come from homes where there is too much noise and chaos," he explained. "Just learning to listen is hard enough. Don't expect them to be good readers."

In a single gesture, this principal lowered expectations, encouraged teachers to teach less, and reduced the power of the curriculum—all in a benevolent-sounding talk to new teachers about the "real" world of city kids. He based his advice on assumptions about families he didn't know in any sustained or personal or intimate way. And his beneficence would have a terrible impact on the kids.

For teachers "being nice" can lead to teaching less. "I don't ask much of April," says her teacher. "She's probably got a tough life." Probably? What's the evidence? Be careful. This is no help to April. Caring for kids' lives—*really* caring for them—involves understanding and nurturing them in the present, and also seeing to their futures. It involves knowing them well, knowing their strengths and capacities and abilities. Teachers need to know the world well enough to help kids envision and nurture a future, and they must know kids well enough to know what it will take to advance learning. Families can be important allies and informants in serious attempts to teach—and families must be approached with respect and a sense of solidarity if they are to be a source of knowledge and assistance. No teacher is truly student-centered who is not at the same time family-centered.

Doris Lessing grew up in rural Africa in a strict, highly regimented family. She was not a happy child, and yet by the age of twelve she knew "how to set a hen, look after chickens and rabbits, worm dogs and cats, pan for gold, take samples from reefs, cook, sew, use the milk separator and churn butter, go down a mine shaft in a bucket, make cream cheese and ginger beer, paint stencilled patterns on materials, make paper mache, walk on stilts . . . drive the car, shoot pigeons and guinea-fowl for the pot, preserve eggs—and a lot else . . ."

And so in spite of living in a society she describes as stingy and cold-hearted, and a family that was cruel and abusive, Lessing says of her long list of knowledge and experience at twelve, "That is real happiness, a child's happiness: being enabled to do and to make, above all to know you are contributing . . . you are valuable and valued."

This lesson from rural Africa has application to urban America. "Being enabled to do and to make"—to find opportunities in our schools for every youngster to create meaning, to construct projects, to invent products, to leave a mark. Every child needs something important to strive for, real work to do, something to belong to and care about. A good school—or a good classroom—provides multiple entry points for students to do and to make, and there is evidence of doing and making in the halls, on the walls, throughout the space.

"To know you are contributing . . . you are valuable and valued"—once again, the message that this place is incomplete without you, cannot function fully without your effort, is not whole until your piece is added.

An urban pedagogy must be built on the strengths of the city, the hope and the promise of city kids and families, on the capacities of city teachers. We must create an enjoyable teaching experience and a classroom life that teachers want to be a part of. The classroom cannot be a place where teachers bite their lips, hold their breath, and endure. Rather, urban classrooms must be places where teachers can pursue their ideas, explore their interests, follow their passions—and be engaged with students in living lives of purpose. This, as opposed to some phony stance of unquestioned authority, is the essence of teacher professionalism.

This is not simple. It requires attention, effort, intelligence. It takes enormous commitments of time and energy. And it takes focus—focus on the child first of all, focus on the student as a learner, focus on the strengths and assets youngsters bring with them to school, and focus on our shared world.

"What do you need to know and experience? Why?" These are good questions to invite into your school or classroom. Embedded in these questions are a wide range of other questions: "Who are you? What do you know? What is the nature of the society we share and the world we inhabit? What is required of each of us practically, politically, ethically, socially?" In order to answer—collectively or individually—the question "What do you need to know and experience?" we are pushed to focus on children as dynamic, diverse, unique, whole, and real. And we are pushed to know more about an infinitely interesting and ever expanding world. We cannot simply close our doors or put our heads in the sand—we must engage, interact, be involved.

Education is not a commodity, like a car, to be bought and sold. Education is never neutral; it is always toward something, toward some changed condition or situation, or toward maintaining things just as they are. Good city teachers start with the lived experiences of youngsters, with how they think of themselves and their lives, and take as a fundamental stance, "You can change your life." There are, of course, skills needed to change lives, and those skills include the capacity to read the word. But perhaps more fundamental, youngsters need sustained opportunities and open invitations to make sense of the fabric of their lives or, as Paulo Freire puts it, to read the *world*. Students don't simply learn to read and write as a repetitive, meaningless skill; they read and write to make sense of what's happening to them, to join with, participate, and overcome when necessary.

In a sense the basic curriculum becomes an engagement with the question of what ought to be. Education for a free people is education designed to understand the world as it is, honestly and fully, to act responsibly upon that world, and, where appropriate, to transform that world. This means that education for a free people is education that encourages people to be subjects, not objects, actors *in* history not victims *of* history. It is education that encourages people in the process of becoming more human, in the vocation of thoughtfulness and care. There is an urgency to this kind of teaching in our precious and precarious cities today.

And not just in our cities. The broad outlines of what is described here could productively inform teaching from the gold coast suburbs to the red hills of Georgia or the rich farmlands of the prairies. Every community faces problems of alienation, disconnection, meaninglessness; every young person deserves a chance to make and remake, to become valued and valuable. The city is the place where these contradictions appear with fire and intensity.

During the historic "Freedom Summer" of 1964, when volunteers poured into Mississippi to fight for civil rights, register voters, and participate in the movement, hundreds of "freedom schools" were organized to teach basic skills to the victims of racism so that they could register and vote, and in the process to transform the social order of the south. The schools were vital centers of learning, and explicitly political settings. As Charlie Cobb, an activist with the Student Nonviolent Coordinating Committee, wrote, the freedom schools would draw "the link between a rotting shack and a rotting America."

The curriculum of the "freedom schools" points, again, to the ways learning to read the word can link powerfully to reading the world. Teachers in these schools were advised that while every student would be different, all would likely bear the scars of a racist system—cynicism, distrust, lack of intellectual preparation. But students would have important strengths to build upon as well, notably experience and knowledge of how to survive under the intense pressure of poverty, discrimination, and injustice. As with many of our kids today, the scars of distrust and poor preparation are plainly visible, but so are the strengths of knowledge and experience concerning survival on some complex and sometimes mean streets. The curriculum of the freedom schools included a basic set of questions: 1) Why are we (teachers and students) in freedom schools? 2) What is the Freedom Movement? 3) What alternatives does the Freedom Movement offer us? Secondary questions included: 1) What does the majority culture have that we want? 2) What does the majority culture have that we don't want? 3) What do we have that we want to keep?

In the first unit teachers tell students that they are there to learn alongside their students, that they will investigate important questions together, and that they will help each other find their way. The initial investigation is into the state of their schools, and a comparison with what more privileged students enjoy. What kind of school do you attend? What is its physical condition? How old is it? Do you have a library? A science lab? What foreign languages are taught there? What do you learn about citizenship? How many graduates go on to higher education? And on and on.

Later questions include: What do people learn in school besides read-

ing, writing, and arithmetic? Do schools teach you things you think are un-
true? At one point teachers are encouraged to pass out copies of the
Pledge of Allegiance, and to engage students in a serious analysis of it.
Does America mean everything it says? How do you know? What is the evidence? Later the Bill of Rights is analyzed in the same withering detail.

Once again, there are lessons from the countryside that might expand
our sense of what city schools and urban pedagogy might be today. Think
of serious, engaging questions to focus your teaching: What are the unemployment trends in the neighborhood? How does it compare to twenty
years ago? What happened to make it so? What could change it?

The celebrated children's book author Maurice Sendak and the dark car-
toonist Art Speigelman highlight the inner life of children in a dialogue in
the *New Yorker* about art. When Speigelman says, "I wanna protect my kids!"
Sendak responds, "Art—you can't protect kids . . . they know everything!
I'll give you an example . . . My friend lost his wife recently, and right at the
funeral his little girl said, 'Why don't you marry miss so-and-so?' He looked
at her as if she were a witch. But she was just being a real kid, with desperate
day-to-day needs that had to be met no matter what. People say, 'Oh, Mr.
Sendak, I wish I were in touch with my childhood self, like you!' As if it were
all quaint and succulent, like Peter Pan . . . I say, 'You are in touch, lady—
you're mean to your kids, you treat your husband like shit, you lie, you're
selfish . . . That *is* your childhood self!' In reality, childhood is deep and
rich. It's vital, mysterious, and profound. I remember my own childhood
vividly . . . I knew terrible things . . . But I knew I mustn't let adults *know* I
knew . . . It would scare them."

We would do well to remember this: childhood is deep and rich, vital,
mysterious, and profound. What kids know can be scary, but denying them
voice, denying their experiences and their sense-making, will undermine
their capacities to learn, and withhold an education of value and power to
them. If we offer ourselves as teachers to the city's young, we will need to
step forward with appreciation, respect, and a little awe.

15

Segregated Housing and School Resegregation

Gary Orfield

People often visualize cities as if they are collections of stable neighborhoods, but American cities have always been in a state of constant change. Americans are a restless, mobile people. The average family moves every five or six years, and young families move even more often. The story of a family's development and success is often told in terms of a series of moves to better homes and neighborhoods. When the older population in a neighborhood is white and the newcomers are black or Latino, the continuing changes create segregated schools and undermine desegregation plans. All of the communities we have studied confronted policy and legal choices forced by community residential change, and many worried about the effect of school policies on their community's ability to hold its residents. Unfortunately, federal courts often fail to devise rules and policies that work effectively in coping with racial change. In fact, in its resegregation decisions, the Rehnquist Court has used these changes to justify dismantling desegregation, arguing that the spread of housing segregation shows it is futile or counterproductive. Understanding the paths toward viable, lasting school integration requires sorting out the links between schools and housing changes.

The Supreme Court made a good start in describing and beginning to correct the impact of residential apartheid on school segregation in the early 1970s. As the Court turned toward resegregation, however, it radically changed its understanding of housing segregation.

Even where extensive desegregation was achieved under an old court order, racial integration was threatened by the spread of minority segregation in city neighborhoods and the continuous construction of new all-white suburbs. Trying to deal with changing communities with a static desegregation plan was often an exercise in frustration. School district officials claimed that there was nothing they could do as segregation spread. Officials asked to be set free of desegregation requirements to reinstitute neighborhood schools. Civil rights groups, on the other hand, argued that school decisions on location, boundaries, transfers, and decisions of other public agencies compounded the segregation, and that courts should hold both school and housing officials responsible.

The Supreme Court entered the era of urban school desegregation with findings that policies affecting school and housing segregation were intimately interrelated. By the time of the resegregation decisions, however, the Court described housing segregation as something separate and mysterious—something that simply happened—and that local officials could do little about. Justice Sandra Day O'Connor described residential change as the result of white flight and "natural, if unfortunate, demographic forces" in 1995.[1]

Serious school segregation today is overwhelmingly caused not by the isolation of students within school districts but by the separation of overwhelmingly minority city systems from overwhelmingly white suburban districts. Three-fourths of the nation's residents and more than 80 percent of minority students live in metropolitan areas. In most states, the metropolitan communities are broken up into many school districts. Residential segregation produces concentration of the African American and Latino students in a small number of districts, thus maintaining segregated education even if authorities try to desegregate within each school district. As long as the spread of residential segregation continues, the schools will constantly face choices among further segregation, continually redrawing plans as the population changes and trying to desegregate with the suburbs.

Trying to cure school segregation without understanding the nature of housing segregation can easily compound the problems. Lasting school desegregation requires either stable integrated housing or a plan that copes effectively with the patterns of spreading housing segregation.

Judicial Theories About Housing

During the past two decades, the Supreme Court and many lower courts have taken spectacularly inconsistent positions on the question of why metropolitan areas are so segregated and whether the schools cause segregation or are simply victims of housing changes. As the Court changed through conservative appointments, the origin of housing segregation has been increasingly described as an innocent result of private choices. When an earlier Supreme Court decided that busing was needed to desegregate cities, it recognized that the violations had deep roots in both school and housing discrimination. When the Court later decided first to limit and then to terminate desegregation, however, it saw housing segregation differently. When it blocked suburban desegregation in the 1974 *Milliken* decision, the Court said housing segregation was something that happened for some unknowable reason. Later, when it approved school resegregation, the Court described residential segregation as a natural force that courts and school districts could do nothing about.

The changing conception of housing, often announced as fact, provided grounds for judicial acceptance of segregated education. The Supreme Court's failure to examine the housing underpinnings of metropolitan segregation in the 1974 *Milliken I* decision made desegregation almost impossible in the metropolitan North. Full and lasting desegregation had become unachievable within increasingly minority city boundaries. Suburbs were protected from desegregation by the courts ignoring the origin of their racially segregated housing patterns.

The *Milliken* decision, which blocked desegregation in the North, *Dowell* (1991), and *Pitts* (1992), permitted resegregation of Southern school districts and embraced changing views of housing segregation. The 1995 *Jenkins* decision said courts must not require policies designed to offset white flight by improving city schools to attract whites.

The great shift of constitutional priorities in *Milliken* from requiring actual desegregation to asserting the primary importance of suburban local control rested on a theory of suburban innocence. The Court ruled that, in order to win a remedy, civil rights groups needed to prove suburban guilt for discrimination or segregation. This meant that findings of guilt in the arena of housing discrimination would have been the only possible way to achieve total school desegregation. After all, many Detroit suburbs had such severe housing segregation that the school districts had virtually no black students to discriminate against. Thus, when the Court excluded all discussion of how the Detroit suburbs came to be among the nation's most rigidly segregated, it guaranteed segregation of Detroit's black students. The Court said that even though both the city and the state had intentionally segregated black students and the lower courts had found that desegregation without involving students in the suburbs to be unworkable, suburban schools could not be included unless there was proof that they discriminated.

By failing to examine housing, the Court gave neighborhoods that had successfully segregated their housing an exemption from school desegregation requirements. City neighborhoods that had not excluded blacks,

on the other hand, faced mandatory desegregation. Fragile, racially changing neighborhoods of the city were punished with a desegregation plan
that would almost certainly speed ghetto expansion. Under the plan, the
ghetto would expand because desegregation would be concentrated in
small areas in transition and all-white schools would be protected from desegregation. This effectively created refuges for whites fearful of minorities
moving into their schools.

The Detroit plan produced no significant lasting school desegregation
and undermined neighborhood integration. Detroit was the nation's second most segregated metropolitan area a generation after this "remedy."
The Detroit schools, 72 percent black the year of the *Milliken I* decision, became 89 percent black by 1986 and remained at that level in 1992. Eighty-
six percent of Detroit's black students were in intensely segregated schools
with less than 10 percent white students. Only half of one percent (.006)
were in majority-white schools.[2] The Detroit experience shows the high
stakes in correctly understanding and acting on housing issues.

Segregated urban school systems are built on a base of housing segregation. The vast differences between inner-city and suburban schools help
determine where white families with choices will live, as people moving to
a new metropolitan area will almost immediately discover from realtors
and relocation services. Such services usually show newcomers nothing in
central cities or racially changing suburbs. As minority suburbanization
grows, realtors also determine where African American and Latino families live. The struggle to integrate schools of urban areas has been an effort
to reverse some of the educational inequalities growing out of a comprehensive system of urban segregation in which schools, housing, and employment are racially separate. The system has grown out of public and
private forms of discrimination unchecked for many decades. Many effects
of that discrimination continue today.

The Supreme Court recognized the interaction of school and housing
decisions, in its first urban desegregation case, the 1971 *Swann* decision
that authorized busing: "The construction of new schools and the closing
of old ones are two of the most important functions of local school authorities," said the Court. "Over the long run, consequences of the choices will
be far-reaching. People gravitate toward school facilities, just as schools are
located in response to the needs of people. The location of schools may
thus influence the patterns of residential development of a metropolitan
area and have [an] important impact on composition of inner-city neighborhoods."[3]

The Court's first northern desegregation decision, *Keyes*, arose directly
out of issues related to neighborhood residential change. In Denver, resi-

dents of the integrated Park Hill neighborhood feared that school boundary changes would resegregate local schools. The residents then initiated
the lawsuit that led to a citywide desegregation order.

The ruling declared that Denver's practices had effectively labeled
schools by race, affecting the racial makeup of neighborhoods throughout
the city's housing market. The Court pointed to school sites and attendance boundaries that undermined integration. The complex interaction
between school and housing segregation was a key part of the Supreme
Court's reasoning for ordering citywide desegregation on the basis of
neighborhood level violations:

> First, it is obvious that a practice of concentrating Negroes in certain
> schools by structuring attendance zones . . . has the reciprocal effect
> of keeping other nearby schools predominantly white. Similarly, the
> practice of building a school . . . to a certain size and in a certain loca-
> tion, "with conscious knowledge that it would be a segregated
> school," . . . has a substantial reciprocal effect on the racial composi-
> tion of other nearby schools. So also, the use of mobile classrooms,
> the drafting of student transfer policies, the transportation of stu-
> dents, and the assignment of faculty and staff, on racially identifiable
> bases, have the clear effect of earmarking schools according to their
> racial composition, and this, in turn, together with the elements of
> student assignment and school construction, may have a profound
> reciprocal effect on the racial composition of residential neighbor-
> hoods . . . We recognized this in Swann. . . . [4]

Protecting the Suburbs

What the Supreme Court recognized in *Swann* and *Keyes,* it forgot in *Milliken,* one year later. Desegregation in Detroit and many other large cities
was made impossible. This decision ended the rapid growth of desegregated schooling for black students that had begun in the mid-1960s and
blocked efforts to desegregate the soaring Latino population, more than
85 percent of which was concentrated in metropolitan areas.

In *Milliken,* the Court faced an issue full of housing dimensions yet the
Court's majority opinion literally ignored housing evidence, although civil
rights attorney Nicholas Flannery in his oral argument before the Court
had presented the evidence and trial court findings on housing. He argued that "the segregated school practices, operated in lockstep with an
area-wide metropolitan policy of confining by housing discrimination . . .
black families to an identifiable core in Detroit. . . ." He cited eight wit-

nesses who testified about "the containment pattern, housing and schools, that was coming to characterize the metropolitan area" and noted that the lower courts had accepted the containment theory.[5]

Chief Justice Burger's opinion, however, asserted that "the case does not present any question concerning possible state housing violations."[6] Justice Potter Stewart, the decisive fifth vote on the case, wrote in a footnote that housing segregation was caused by "unknown or unknowable causes," asserting that "no record has been made in this case showing that the racial composition of the Detroit school population or that residential patterns within Detroit and in the surrounding areas were in any significant measure caused by governmental activity."[7]

The plaintiffs in *Milliken I* had asked the Supreme Court to send the case back to the lower courts because no specific remedy had been approved by the trial judge. Although the Court's majority said that the housing issues had not been raised, the Court asked neither for lower court examination of the housing issue nor for an actual plan from the lower courts before making its decision. Thus, the Supreme Court accepted metropolitan segregation without any effort to find out why the communities were segregated.

By the 1990s, the Court had created, with its theories of housing segregation, a twentieth-century equivalent of the theory of "racial instincts" that an earlier court used to justify *Plessy's* separate but equal doctrine. In *Plessy*, the Supreme Court had portrayed itself as helpless, explaining that "legislation is powerless to eradicate racial instincts . . . and the attempt to do so can only result in accentuating the difficulties of the present situation."[8] Under the contemporary version of that theory, if housing segregation happens because of some modern version of "racial instincts," then the courts can use similar logic to assert that it is best do nothing since attempts to desegregate schools will inevitably be undermined by the natural "demographic forces" that produce residential segregation.

Ignoring Urban History

Basic assumptions about urban change in many recent decisions are in conflict with research on federal housing policy and the findings of numerous courts about the intentional segregation of subsidized housing. A number of the decisions also require standards of proof for plaintiffs that are impossible.

Few aspects of urban history are clearer than the fact that governments at all levels fostered residential segregation for many years. In most cities it is easy to show that housing segregation was initiated and institutionalized with massive official support, that most minority neighborhoods segregated during the period of overt segregationist policies remain segregated today. Many millions of minority families still live in segregated housing markets, surveys show that this is not by choice.

Segregation has been spreading beyond the borders of older minority communities since World War II. The most recent federal studies of housing market and lending practices show that discrimination continues to be widespread. There is an unbroken pattern of ghetto expansion dating back to the period of overt discrimination, and segregated black communities now extend well into sections of some suburban rings. In many housing markets, most black families have been segregated for generations. The physical isolation of those in the core of the minority communities becomes more extreme as the borders of the ghetto expand and middle-class black families abandon the core.

It is easy to prove that a variety of types of discrimination existed in most housing markets and to show that the segregation they helped institutionalize still continues. Black fears of violence and intimidation in some white communities are still serious obstacles to housing choice. Whites and white realtors almost never look for housing in what are defined as minority communities, and real estate operations are often organized along racial lines. Minority brokers are seldom employed by white offices and rarely get listings in white areas unless racial transitions are well under way. Because most people shop for housing in areas where they have knowledge of housing or acquaintances, the fact that the history of segregation has given blacks and whites familiarity with separate sets of communities and fears about each other's neighborhoods tends to reinforces a self-perpetuating segregation. In these and many other ways, the history of housing discrimination continues to shape communities and, therefore, their schools.[9]

What civil rights lawyers have trouble proving are all the specific linkages between the past and present. Residential segregation was such a pervasive part of the American past that it is built into many institutions, fears, and expectations, but there is no way to prove scientifically just how much of contemporary segregation is directly linked to historic violations. Social science is not capable of accurately measuring the relative influence of the official and private elements of generations of discrimination on the patterns of segregation many years later. To measure the impact of official discrimination alone, it would be necessary to have some cases without private discrimination. To try to measure all the impacts over time, researchers would need to untangle all the beliefs and practices that grew out of the official discrimination and track the relative importance of those factors on contemporary practices. In order to make even very rough estimates of these relationships, it would have been necessary to initiate massive studies generations ago to provide baseline data, control groups, and other essential elements of social research. This, of course, was not done.

Although the courts often impose requirements of specific proof from civil rights lawyers, they often adopt their own theories about housing as if they were simply common sense. Courts also make findings about the causes of segregation on the basis of surveys of racial attitudes conducted for the local officials. Surveys cannot, by their nature, assess the two fundamental legal issues—the degree to which attitudes are a product of the history of discrimination and the degree to which opinions would change under a new policy. The first is a central question in judging the guilt of governmental agencies; the second is crucial for devising remedies that work.

Although surveys are often presented by school districts and accepted by courts as proving the existence of immutable natural private preferences that make lasting remedies impossible, survey data is incapable of proving such a claim. Even if one concedes the validity of fairness of the questions, attitudes could well be shaped by previous illegal housing segregation policies. What opinion surveys can never tell us is how people would respond if they confronted a new reality, if they actually were to live together peacefully in an integrated community and test their fears and stereotypes against that reality. If the Supreme Court had relied on an opinion poll at the time of the *Brown* decision, the fact that 81 percent of white Southerners believed the Court to be wrong would have been taken as a justification for inaction. We would have never known that forty years later, only 15 percent of white Southerners would hold that attitude after two decades of experiencing the nation's most integrated schools.[10]

Sometimes the courts' approach is not to look at any evidence at all but simply to announce that all historic housing violations prior to the 1968 federal fair housing law do not matter, because the law canceled the effects of generations of discrimination. It is as if a court concluded that the national debt had stopped growing because several times in the past fifteen years, Congress has adopted legislation promising to balance the budget. In fact, a finding that discrimination and the effects of past discrimination do not matter ignores the recent national research commissioned by the federal government. The research findings show serious discrimination in housing markets decades after 1968. They demonstrate that the government failed to enforce both the notoriously weak 1968 fair housing law and the 1988 amendments.[11]

The U.S. Civil Rights Commission pointed out in 1994 that HUD was far behind the congressional goal of handling fair housing complaints within

100 days. It had done very little to enforce the goal on a systematic basis. HUD rarely tested for discrimination and developed only about one broad case a year in the entire United States.[12]

Judicial Assumptions
That Minimize the Effects of Segregation

Because the levels of segregation remain high and studies show continued discrimination,[13] it is difficult to understand the basis for the court findings that the laws erased the impacts of the long history of state-supported residential apartheid. Though the attitudes, practices, and institutions that created and perpetuate residential segregation developed during that period of overt discrimination and many continue today, the courts often assume that at some point they became detached from their historic roots and became matters of private preference for segregation. A frequent assumption in court decisions is that discrimination existed until the point of a key court decision or passage of a civil rights law. This assumption, which contradicts studies on the implementation of civil rights decisions or laws, is almost always put forward without evidence.[14]

A less extreme version of this judicial approach claims that historic violations have diminishing effects with the passage of time. Thus, over a number of years, discrimination could be safely discounted. In his opinion in the 1995 *Jenkins* case, for example, Justice Clarence Thomas described the way in which "state-enforced segregation recedes farther into the past," as it is replaced by "massive demographic shifts" that are "beyond the practical ability of the federal courts to try to counteract."[15] Although Americans tend to see history as a story of social progress, there is no empirical basis for asserting that racial attitudes gradually improve. The historical record clearly shows, to the contrary, that attitudes and policies change in both directions. Discrimination and exclusion, for example, became more rigid after Reconstruction ended and *Plessy* legitimated segregation.[16] In contrast, the Supreme Court's 1973 *Keyes* decision rejected "any suggestion that remoteness in time has any relevance to the issue of intent."[17]

Some courts raise even more barriers to considering the housing issues. In *Swann*, the Supreme Court had noted that not too much should be put into one case, since a single case "can carry only a limited amount of baggage." This obscure phrase gave lower courts a plausible way to dispose of even extremely serious housing issues. A court can jettison serious housing evidence by claiming that the court will be overburdened by hearing and considering all the evidence on these relationships. Chief Justice Rehnquist employed the excess baggage theory in his decision reversing the Kansas City remedy in 1995.[18]

Plaintiffs sometimes seem inside of a housing maze with no exit: if they present limited evidence, it will be dismissed as failing to establish the required proof of continuing effects of past violations. But if they try to prove the entire intricate history of metropolitan discrimination in a housing market, the argument may be dismissed as presenting more than the courts can cope with.

Atlanta: Examples of Judicial Avoidance

The court decision in the 1979 metropolitan Atlanta desegregation case show how the manipulation of housing issues was used to preclude a remedy. District Judge William O'Kelley decided that the case was too complex for the court to handle, holding "there is just so much baggage a school case can carry."[19] He discarded thousands of pages of proof that the entire racial structure of the Atlanta area was built on many decades of explicit residential discrimination, expressed first in formal segregation laws, then in planned construction of racial borders, in formal agreements between the city's white and black leaders about segregated housing for blacks, and in the administration of many programs shaping housing, transportation, and neighborhood development.

The court, however, wished to avoid forcing what the judge saw as "drastic" change—"to change the residential patterns which exist it would be necessary to rip up the very fabric of society in a manner which is not within the province of the federal courts."[20] The court found eighteen ways in which government agencies had caused housing segregation, including racial zoning laws, segregated relocation from renewal lands, racial designation of schools, and overtly racial public housing site selection. Violations were found both within the city itself and the surrounding suburbs. The court concluded that metropolitan segregation was "caused in part by the intentional acts of government officials,"[21] but treated this as little more than an interesting historical observation. Because a fair housing act existed now, the court ruled, contemporary segregation should no longer be blamed on past discrimination.

Survey data provided by David Armor, the conservative social scientist and former Reagan administration official, was used by the court to claim that "why people live where they do can never be fully explained."[22] The judge spoke of the role of economics, personal preferences, and the "tipping phenomenon."[23] The judge did not consider the possibility that preferences and expectations were themselves vestiges of a history of segregation. Segregation was seen as a hopelessly complex natural force.

The court's Atlanta decision also rejected the linkage of housing and school issues. Since the school districts were not at fault for ghettos and segregated white areas produced by other policies, the court held, school officials should not have to desegregate. The court's approach made it impossible to obtain school desegregation based on intense housing violations. Intense housing segregation, on the other hand, made it impossible to prove, as *Milliken I* required, that all-white suburbs had engaged in school discrimination, since black families could not even live there. At the time of the decisions, metropolitan Atlanta remained one of the South's most segregated urban regions, with a pattern of pervasive educational inequality strongly related to race documented several years later.[24] The courts denied public responsibility for any of this.

When the metropolitan Atlanta case reached the Supreme Court, the Court took the unusual step of affirming the lower court's decision on schools in the Deep South's largest metropolis without even giving a hearing to the parties.[25]

Housing and the Resegregation Decisions of the 1990s

In its key decisions on resegregation, *Dowell* and *Pitts,* the Supreme Court revisited the housing issue but was divided. In the 1995 *Jenkins* decision the five-member majority adopted the entire conservative argument, claiming that school policies do not affect housing except when white flight from school desegregation occurs.

The 1992 *Pitts* decision found the Court's majority relying on a variety of techniques to minimize the accountability of public officials for housing segregation. They included switching the burden of proof, assuming that time cured the effects of past discrimination, and accepting the natural preferences theory of segregation. In *Jenkins* the court majority also adopted the white-flight theory.

The Complexity of the Problem

Some of the court decisions evade the issues. The problem that confronts any effort to demonstrate the precise nature of the school-housing relationship is that public and private discrimination, past and present, are woven inextricably together. A single example can illustrate the difficulties

of precise analysis. A black family has children in segregated schools because it never looked for housing in white areas—a seemingly clear-cut
case of private preference for which no government agency would take responsibility. If, however, the family did not look for housing in white neighborhoods because the wife's parents' house had been vandalized by white
neighbors and the police did nothing, causing the family to decide to
move back into the ghetto, the decision actually was a result of fears arising
from past government actions fostering discrimination. Similarly, if a family lacks the equity to buy a suburban house, this would seem like the most
obvious example of economic rather than racial discrimination. But if we
knew that the family did not have the wealth of similar white families because they were discriminated against under Federal Housing Authority
(FHA) redlining policies that kept them from owning a starter home years
ago, the cause would be a continuing effect of past discrimination. If we
knew that a community that would meet their needs had rejected a proposal to build affordable housing on racial grounds, another element of
official action would be implicated.

Multiplying the issues affecting a single family by hundreds of thousands in a large metropolitan housing, it becomes clear how impossible it is
to sort out all the "private" and "public" elements of housing segregation.
How much, for example, should the rejection of subsidized suburban
housing be attributed to racial fears and stereotypes and how much to economic exclusion? Considering how all these decisions shape minority communities over time and considering the reciprocal effects on white
experiences and attitudes, it is clear that past and present discrimination
are woven into the fabric of communities in ways that could never be precisely sorted out.

Given that reality, the real legal issue is what assumptions and standards
of proof the courts use to reach their conclusions. Those seemingly technical questions powerfully influence whether a community will have segregated schools. In the last two decades the courts have been imposing rules
and procedures that lead to conclusions that housing segregation simply
happened and that government agencies should not be held accountable.

The History of Housing Discrimination

Resegregation cases require courts to consider whether official actions
including the district's implementation of its desegregation plan and decisions of other local agencies contributed to the segregation of neighborhoods and schools. Approving a return to neighborhood schools is much
more difficult if the court recognizes that actions of the school board or

the public housing authority created more segregation or that school decisions helped spread residential segregation.

The new theories of suburban innocence and voluntary segregation, however, contrast with the findings of many urban historians. Research on the formation and expansion of residential segregation in major cities shows extensive official involvement on many levels. Even in recent times, courts found HUD and local authorities guilty of past and current discrimination.[26] Federal officials enforcing fair housing and fair lending policies freely concede that their efforts have been far too weak to end discrimination.[27] Segregation is related to regulations, laws, practices of officials, and lax enforcement of antidiscrimination laws.

Discrimination by public agencies dates from the black exodus from the rural South triggered by World War I and World War II labor shortages in the North. Public and private institutions worked together to confine blacks to overcrowded, overpriced, and deteriorating ghettos whose inferior city services included inferior segregated schools. Local actions included police toleration of white racial violence against blacks moving into white areas, use of zoning and planning powers to foster separation, planned segregation of subsidized housing, school siting and boundaries, and many administrative practices that fostered residential and school separation.

The first mass migration coincided with the rise of zoning and city planning. Leading cities of the southern and border states including St. Louis, Baltimore, and Atlanta, enacted zoning laws prescribing where blacks could live—official apartheid laws.[28] The Supreme Court struck down such laws, but some cities continued to enforce them.

Although outlawing racial zoning, the Supreme Court authorized court enforcement of private agreements to accomplish the same purpose.[29] In the 1920s, there were neighborhood organizing campaigns for restrictive covenants that attached racial exclusions to deeds on homes. The court enforced the covenants and the federal government, in its home mortgage programs, encouraged their use. After the Court upheld covenants in *Corrigan v. Buckley*,[30] they spread rapidly in areas with significant minority population.[31] Many black communities were almost totally cut off from significant growth by an iron curtain of legally enforceable covenants on all of their boundaries.[32] This created incredible housing demand, massive overuse, a "race tax" on housing prices, and deterioration of housing within the racial boundaries.

Black households confronted with artificially high housing costs and low wages because of job discrimination had no alternative but to double up in housing. Landlords profiting from the housing shortages had little incentive to maintain the property and the resulting decay contributed to the white stereotype that entry of black residents caused decay or "blight." Disinvestment was fostered by policies denying federally insured mortgages to buyers in inner cities and integrated areas. These housing discrimination policies were part of the vicious self-perpetuating cycles that grew up around the ghetto system. Those syndromes contributed to discrimination and flight from integrated neighborhoods long after fair housing laws were enacted.

Not until 1950 did the FHA stop requiring racial covenants in new developments.[33] By that time, the postwar suburban boom was set within a framework of segregation. Massive mortgage financing flowed to FHA and Veterans Administration (VA) buyers in white subdivisions and almost none to older communities or minority home seekers, even black veterans.[34] No significant FHA and VA financing was available to minority families until the late 1960s.

The entire system was one of government-sponsored segregation and a denial of even "separate but equal" opportunities for minority families. The lack of mortgage capital contributed powerfully to the decline of minority and integrated communities and the inability of minority families to enter the housing market under extraordinarily favorable post–World War II conditions that led to huge increases in the worth of the housing investments of millions of families who bought for low prices in new suburban developments and later sold for many times more.

It is not surprising that when urban renewal came along in the 1950s as a strategy to save the downtowns; most of the areas where "blight" was eliminated through "slum clearance" were those of minority communities.[35] With no fair housing rights and no serious plan for replacement housing, leveling black communities to produce new middle-class developments near downtown poured displaced black families into segregated housing markets. This rapidly resegregated neighborhoods and created new ghettos. Suburbs that had small minority pockets often used renewal dollars to level those communities and redevelop the land, sending the residents to live in new housing projects in the inner city. These programs produced a sudden expansion of ghetto communities, serious conflicts with working-class white areas, and reinforcement of stereotypes about the instability of residential and school integration. The new urban freeways built under the Interstate Highway Act in the 1950s and 1960s often resulted in the displacement of more minority communities in a similar manner. The rapid construction of high-rise segregated public housing projects in inner cities compounded the problem; projects were segregated because local politics blocked construction of lower-density subsidized housing in outlying white areas with excellent schools.[36] Subsidized housing site selection doomed generations of children to weak segregated schools.

When the federal approach shifted from building public housing projects to reliance on the private market and nonprofits for subsidized housing in the large programs of the early 1970s, the results once again
reinforced segregation and inner-city decay. The low-income homeowner-
ship program known as "Section 235," for example, provided subsidies
that allowed poor families to purchase small homes by virtually eliminating
down payments and subsidizing mortgage interest down to 1 percent.
Since the program pumped dollars into segregated markets without challenging their discriminating nature, it enabled many low-income white
families to obtain subsidies that they used to leave integrated areas and buy
small new homes in outlying white areas. Black buyers, however, tended to
end up in old homes in ghettos or racially changing areas. The program reinforced residential and school segregation and helped finance the resegregation of residentially integrated-city communities.[37] In some cities,
many black buyers were stuck with old homes with severe deficiencies. The
result was the abandonment of a number of black communities, particularly in inner cities, and hundreds of millions of dollars in losses for the
government.[38]

Section 8, the next HUD program, begun in 1974, was smaller but relied
even more on private developers and owners. Local agencies gave rent subsidy certificates to eligible tenants, and landlords rented to tenants who
passed their screening. Although there were "affirmative marketing" requirements about advertising, there was no significant outreach by owners
for minority tenants for most suburban sites, which filled up with whites.
The result was subsidized housing for white families in suburban school
districts and reinforcement of minority concentration.[39] President Reagan, in turn, drastically cut back those programs in the 1980s.[40] No significant new housing programs had been enacted by 1996.

Thus, federal subsidized housing programs, administered by local agencies or private owners, intensified residential and school separation decade after decade. One of the clearest patterns of official discrimination in
housing has been the selection of segregated housing sites and the assignment of tenants in ways that produced racially defined communities, often
served by segregated schools. Many cities went so far as to build schools for
projects. Others gerrymandered school attendance districts to keep the
project children out of white schools. A 1994 HUD report concludes that
the public housing tenants living in the "poorest tracts" are "almost exclusively (91 percent) African American."[41] Most white subsidized tenants
lived in low-poverty areas where the proportion of residents living in public
housing was one-fiftieth that of the poorest tracts.[42] Black public housing
tenants often attend inferior schools almost totally segregated by poverty
as well as race. A significant portion of the total black enrollment in some

central city school districts live in public and subsidized housing.[43] Norfolk, the first city to resegregate with federal court approval, created some
black schools almost totally populated by public housing project children.

Lower courts examining the history of public housing outside of school
cases have often found unambiguous discrimination, and they continue to
make such findings. In Chicago, where the city council vetoed housing
sites on racial grounds for decades, the district court found in 1969 that
the site selections and tenant assignments of the Chicago Housing Authority (CHA) were unconstitutional.[44] The court ruled that there was "uncon-
tradicted evidence . . . that the public housing system operated by CHA was
racially segregated, with four overwhelmingly white projects located in
white neighborhoods and with 99.5% of the remaining family units located in Negro neighborhoods.[45]

In Yonkers, where the Justice Department brought its first combined
lawsuit against both school and housing officials in the same community,
the court found that 97.7 percent of public housing for poor people was
located in the city's southwest quadrant where about 80 percent of black
residents lived. The court ruled that "the desire to preserve existing patterns of segregation has been a significant factor."[46] In other words, housing policy had influenced racial segregation in the city schools.

The Dallas Housing Authority was convicted of intentional segregation
in 1989.[47] A HUD-funded study of housing in metropolitan Dallas had earlier concluded that public housing had "obvious implications for segregation in public schools," since 97 percent of the units had been built in
all-black areas or areas in the path of transition that became virtually all minority.[48] The study found that the later HUD programs, such as Section 8,
also contributed to segregation of minorities and the resegregation of integrated neighborhoods, as did some of the city's land use and development
policies. "Racial isolation in the public schools," the report concluded, "is
directly related to the housing policies which the city of Dallas has pursued." The U.S. Justice Department later conceded HUD responsibility in
Dallas.[49] Nonetheless, the federal court in Dallas enforcing the school desegregation plan became one of the first to permit resegregation following
the Supreme Court's resegregation orders.

Subsidized housing is a small part of the housing market, though it provides homes for a substantial fraction of the low-income central city
African American families who are so highly segregated in schools. The
much broader effects of the history of housing discrimination are built
into a variety of institutions serving the white and minority housing markets. Sets of attitudes, practices, contacts, and business specialists grew up
around the color line. In the separate markets there were and are sales and
rental professionals often with offices located on opposite sides of the

color line who specialize in different white or minority areas. There are separate and unequal capital and mortgage finance markets, which, until recently, rarely provided conventional mortgage financing in minority communities.

Since all the minority demand for additional housing was concentrated by real estate practices in areas just outside the existing ghettos, great profits could be made by transferring a new area from the white to the black housing market. There were specialists in racial transition ("block busters" and "panic peddlers") who profited from the process of frightening whites into selling suddenly and cheaply and then jacking up the price for black buyers with few choices. Such racial changes tended to be fast and destructive, with entire streets posted with "for sale" signs. The fear of this process fed the tendencies of white discrimination and harassment of minority households. White fears of ghetto expansion and black fears of harassment both continue to reinforce segregation. Studies in metropolitan Chicago showed that large fractions of black families feared harassment if they moved to white areas. The key to residential stability was white beliefs about the future of the neighborhood.[50]

Housing and the Viability of School Desegregation

Though findings about housing often received little attention in school cases, they were fundamental to the effects of the decisions. In *Milliken I* and the resegregation cases, housing was treated as if it were unrelated to the effectiveness of school desegregation plans. This produced easily predictable failures like the Detroit central city plan.

Viable desegregation plans consider housing in formulating the school plan. Simply ordering school desegregation in the central city while ghettos and white suburbia continue their rapid expansion can be counterproductive. If white families, for example, face a choice between a central city area where all schools have 80 percent black "desegregated" enrollments and dozens of virtually all-white suburban districts, few will chose the city community. A desegregation plan that assumes a static racial boundary is assuming something that no American city possesses. A plan that combines immediately adjacent black and white neighborhoods, for example, when the white neighborhood is already experiencing rapid in-migration of African Americans or Latinos has almost no chance of producing lasting integration. School desegregation transfers in these areas may well further inflame explosive race relations. In such circumstances, choosing the shortest possible busing distances could accelerate resegregation. Some of the most notoriously difficult desegregation situations, such as the bitter confrontation at South Boston High School in the mid-1970s, had short busing times but brought together two groups of disadvantaged students across an explosive racial boundary.

Some of the plans with the least tension have involved long-distance transfers of minority students to suburban schools. A voluntary plan of this sort, METCO, has existed in metropolitan Boston for three decades with few serious problems.[51] Large city-suburban busing plans have been operating for a quarter century with high levels of desegregation and stability in a number of cities with countywide school systems. Many integrated magnet schools in minority areas have become very popular and receive willing white transferees. The ghettoization process arising from generations of discrimination is self-perpetuating.[52] Dual markets, mutual fears, unequal market knowledge, mortgage discrimination, and lack of positive models of successful integration made the momentum of past discrimination very powerful. Separate markets in which minority families were less likely to own a home than similar white families and where they usually had to invest in areas that produced smaller gains yield much less accumulated wealth to provide down payments on bigger homes and, therefore, fewer options.[53] Viable school desegregation plans must not be designed in ways that reinforce racial transition and fears; the best plans try to create stably integrated schools that can help support the development of stably integrated neighborhoods.

Fair Housing: The Federal Record

In theory, the federal government committed itself to the principle of fair housing in 1968, but the commitment was limited. In spite of language in the 1968 law that required all federal urban programs to be administered in order to foster fair housing, the 1970s and 1980s brought large additional federal investments in housing *segregation*.[54] The weakness of the 1968 law, which gave HUD no power to impose sanctions even in the face of clear violations, was criticized by HUD secretaries from both Republican and Democratic administrations, most of whom called for stronger enforcement tools. Only the Justice Department could pursue sanctions through lawsuits, and it brought only about twenty fair housing suits a year, though there were an estimated two million violations occurring annually.[55] Not until 1988 was the law strengthened. In early 1995, Roberta Achtenberg, HUD Assistant Secretary for Fair Housing, conceded that "the federal government, including HUD, has a long history of having precipitated and perpetuated housing discrimination." After detailing the ways in which various housing and urban development programs had increased segregation and damaged integrated and minority neighborhoods, she noted that "federal fair housing law has been weak and inadequate."[56]

During more than two-thirds of the time since fair housing became law, the federal government was dominated by conservative administrations deeply skeptical of efforts to remake the segregated housing patterns in the metropolitan areas of the United States. President Nixon and President Ford attacked strong efforts to integrate suburbia.[57] So did President Carter, during his presidential campaign, when he said that he saw "nothing wrong with ethnic purity being maintained" in urban neighborhoods. Carter said that he thought this was a "natural inclination."[58] Except for HUD Secretary George Romney's brief leadership (before he was fired by President Nixon), there was no serious effort to use federal housing and urban development tools to increase integrated housing in metropolitan areas until the administration of HUD Secretary Henry Cisneros, which began in 1993. Cisneros was hampered by severe cutbacks in the HUD budget and his major legislative initiative to subsidize suburban mobility by the poor was defeated in Congress.[59]

Federal and local housing subsidy programs normally fed money into a segregated housing market. HUD and local housing authorities usually did nothing to address the problems of limited knowledge and fear by tenants and discrimination by landlords.[60] When HUD succeeded in encouraging more subsidized housing in suburbia in response to the 1974 Housing and Community Development Act's requirement for "spatial deconcentration of the poor," there was no serious effort to make sure that minority families obtained access to that housing.[61] Whites rented subsidized suburban housing and minority households remained in the city—increasing school segregation.

There were alternatives. Experiments with housing counseling for subsidized tenants in Chicago and Louisville showed that if minority families were taken to look at housing outside of segregated and racially changing areas, a large fraction of low-income black households were prepared to consider moves even into virtually all-white areas. Moreover, the evidence shows that such moves were highly successful in terms of the children's education.[62] Such a model implemented in Louisville in the mid-1970s was described in research reports and policy debates a generation ago.

After it was directed by the federal district court in St. Louis in 1980 to submit a housing plan to support desegregated education in the St. Louis area, HUD was on official notice to examine the implications of its policies for school segregation. Following that order, HUD commissioned a study of the relationship between subsidized housing and school segregation in three other metropolitan areas. In each, there was a strong relationship between the location and tenancy of subsidized family housing and school segregation. A substantial share of the segregated minority students in city systems were living in locations determined by subsidized housing policies and practices. In each area studied, much of the busing required by school desegregation orders was attributable to the segregation of subsidized housing for low-income minority families.[63]

By the end of the Carter administration, the impact of the housing policies on school segregation had become clear to HUD officials. In its final days, the administration sponsored sessions on coordination of school and housing desegregation policies in various cities, including Denver. It issued a regulation requiring that housing decisions be taken in light of the implications for school segregation. This regulation was rescinded in the first days of the Reagan administration and was never put into operation. Regulations implementing the broad provisions of the 1968 fair housing law were never issued in the twenty years following its enactment.

Only in the Clinton administration did serious discussion of these issues resume, but by that time federal housing and urban programs had become so much smaller that their potential leverage was much weaker. President Clinton himself proposed massive additional cuts in HUD following the GOP congressional victory in 1994 and even considered dismantling the department.

When the courts announce that housing discrimination ended because the fair housing law was passed, they are assuming an enforcement record wholly at odds with what actually happened. In the years since fair housing has been enacted, there has been much larger federal involvement in subsidizing new housing segregation and resegregation than in ending housing discrimination.

Housing in School Cases:
Legal Fictions and Unequal Legal Resources

The federal courts are currently making important decisions on the basis of fundamentally inaccurate understandings of past and present housing discrimination. The errors can be partially explained by the fact that housing issues are presented in a skewed way in court proceedings. The school districts, which try to use housing as a justification for school segregation, often have the money to create what appears to be plausible evidence that local segregation is a product of choice by minority and white families, not discrimination. The plaintiffs usually lack the money to prove the history of housing discrimination. They cannot document the vicious cycles that led to those "choices." They often lack the expertise to attack the validity of flawed survey data assessing the issues of guilt and remedy. Some courts adopt as facts what are speculative interpretations of misleading data used for inappropriate purposes.

School districts typically try to convince the court that mandatory desegregation should end because it makes white flight worse and because it is futile in the face of natural private preferences that constantly expand segregation. A group of hired social science witnesses has testified in many cases that schools are not an important factor in housing decisions that families make, so school policies should not be held accountable for any of the segregation. In the *Pitts* case, for example, the DeKalb County school board hired the leading national experts who worked in judicial battles against desegregation and paid for original surveys in the county. In one year the board spent $441,000 in legal costs.[64]

During the 1980s, the experts testifying for school boards, and the Reagan administration Justice Department also received the only grants from the U.S. Commission on Civil Rights and the U.S. Department of Education for research on the issue of white flight, which the Reagan Justice Department used as a basic argument for dissolving desegregation orders. Professor Christine Rossell, a Boston University political scientist who testified and prepared reports for many school boards, received the only major U.S. Department of Education grant for desegregation research during the twelve years of the Reagan and Bush administrations. Her research was featured in many desegregation cases and in her book, *The Carrot or the Stick for School Desegregation Policy: Magnet Schools or Forced Busing*.[65] David Armor, the most active witness against desegregation, chaired the advisory committee for the U.S. Civil Rights Commission's white-flight study, the only other substantial federally funded work on school desegregation in the 1980s. Armor was active in many of the key cases discussed in this book including Oklahoma City, DeKalb County, Atlanta, Little Rock, Los Angeles, and Norfolk.

Civil rights groups never had sufficient funds to finance a major survey of housing attitudes. The evidence from academic research, however, shows that responses to questions about racial policies depend strongly on how the questions are posed and how the data is analyzed. After a survey was presented in the Kansas City case, for example, and an expert testified that schools were not important for housing choice, a rebuttal witness ran the data and found that if one looked at families with young children, schools were the families most important consideration.[66]

White Flight

In just two years from 1974 through 1976, the facts of white flight changed from an issue the civil rights forces used to try to obtain more far-reaching school desegregation orders to an issue opponents used to defeat desegregation. The decline of white students in city schools as white suburbanization continued had been going on for decades, and it created a central barrier to full desegregation. The policy shift that made white flight an argument against desegregation was the product of both the Supreme Court's *Milliken* decision blocking suburban desegregation and Professor James Coleman's 1975 research on white flight.[67] After *Milliken*, since the courts could not deal with long-term suburbanization trends by including suburban schools in the desegregation plan and the debate turned to the question of whether doing anything within single districts would produce so much white flight that the effort would be futile. In the 1983 Houston case, for example, the court of appeals concluded that school authorities "have no affirmative fourteenth amendment duty to respond to the private actions of those who vote with their feet."[68] Crossdistrict desegregation was rejected in Houston, even though the city had stopped expanding its school district as the city boundaries grew, the year of the *Brown* decision. (The city now has many school districts within its boundaries and a high level of segregation.)

Civil rights advocates had long been concerned with white suburbanization. By 1965, six years before the first busing decision, elementary school statistics showed that there the enrollment of whites in Washington, D.C., was only 9 percent; in Wilmington, Delaware, 31 percent; in St. Louis, 37 percent; in San Francisco, 43 percent; in Newark, 23 percent; in Philadelphia, 41 percent; in Detroit, 44 percent; and in Richmond, 35 percent.[69] As soon as the Supreme Court ordered urban desegregation, courts began to search for the way to desegregate cities with a heavily minority district. Thurgood Marshall, dissenting in the *Milliken* case, argued that a city-only plan would provide no remedy. On July 25, 1974, when the decision was announced, he said:

> The Detroit school system has in recent years increasingly become an all-Negro school system, with the greatest increase in the proportion of Negro students of any major northern city. Moreover, the result of a Detroit-only decree, the District Court found, would be to increase the flight of whites from the city. . . . Thus, even if a [racial balance] plan were adopted . . . such a system would, in short order, devolve into an all-Negro system.[70]

The fears of Justice Marshall were proven correct when Detroit continued to go through rapid racial change. It became a virtually all-black district despite extra money spent to upgrade the schools. Two decades after the Supreme Court's decision, Detroit Superintendent David L. Sneed would report that "the Detroit community has deteriorated dramatically; the concentration of poverty in the city has increased."[71] By 1990, metropolitan Detroit had the most intense residential segregation in the United States and its black students were more segregated than any other metropolitan area except Chicago.[72]

The grim aftermath of desegregation plans focused only on the central city in cities like Detroit, however, was often not interpreted as a confirmation of Justice Marshall's argument that metropolitan desegregation was indispensable. Often it was seen as proving that nothing could or should be done. Almost no attention was paid to the successful city-suburban desegregation plans in many metropolitan areas, most in Southern states with countywide school districts.

In the mid-1970s, housing evidence became a tool for limiting or reversing desegregation orders. Many courts witnessed statistical battles over possible relationships between desegregation and white enrollment loss. The national press gave massive publicity to Coleman's and Armor's claims about white flight and paid much less attention to those who argued that the trends showed the need for more far-reaching remedies.[73] Although there was an intense academic debate on the degree and duration of white flight, researchers agreed that white decline had existed before desegregation and occurred in cities where desegregation was never implemented. In fact, there has been a substantial decline in the percentage of white births in the country.[74] Some court decisions, however, blame all white enrollment decline on busing with no analysis of preexisting trends, birth rates, immigration, or experience of other cities where there has been no busing. School desegregation was not the sole cause of white enrollment decline, though almost all participants in the debate agree that there are some forms of desegregation plans (particularly mandatory plans busing many white students in heavily minority central cities) that accelerate the decline of white enrollment. On the other hand, the proportion of white students remains much more stable in a number of districts with countywide city-suburban mandatory desegregation. More than half of the nation's largest districts that have been *most* successful in holding their proportion of white students have countywide plans.

Two of the largest of the countywide districts, metropolitan Charlotte and metropolitan Raleigh, North Carolina, actually had a rising proportion of white students in recent years and were growing rapidly in the 1990s. The metropolitan Raleigh (Wake County) schools are as clear a

demonstration of the absence of a simple link between mandatory desegregation and white enrollment decline as could be found. The district has
large scale mandatory desegregation across city and suburban lines and
substantial growth in both the overall district and white enrollment, with
minority enrollment up 18 percent and white enrollment soaring 37 percent since 1976.[75]

Raleigh has flourished as a community. *Fortune* rated it top place to do
business, especially for knowledge-based industry; *Money* magazine rated it
the best place to live in 1995.[76] An early 1995 report found that the Raleigh-
area housing market led the nation in increased home value.[77] Its school
district is one of the nation's largest, substantially bigger, for example, than
those in San Francisco, Boston, Denver, or Atlanta.[78] The success of the metropolitan Raleigh plan does not mean that there is no white flight; it shows
that under some circumstances busing of many more students may be
linked to greater stability. The greater success of the metropolitan Raleigh
district was one reason why adjacent Durham recently voted to merge city
and suburban school systems. The Greater Raleigh Chamber of Commerce
was convinced that the areawide desegregation was one of the reasons for
the economic health of the community and passed a resolution expressing
its strong support for the continuation of desegregation in 1995. "On many
measures," the resolution said, "our public school system is equal to that of
any other urban area in the nation" and noted that only 5 to 7 percent of
local students went to private schools, many fewer than in other affluent
areas. The resolution hailed the decision to merge city and suburban
schools in 1974 and praised the foresight of leaders who "recognized that a
strong and prosperous inner-city with a quality school system was a vital element in the future economic growth and prosperity of the entire country."
The chamber praised local leaders for decisions "many of which were un-
popular in the short term, but which were critically important in the long
term." It called on the county to "steadfastly maintain its commitment to
racially balanced public schools."[79]

Among the many problems with white flight evidence being used in
courts now is that most of it is drawn from experience with the type of desegregation plans that have not been ordered for fifteen years. The claims
are also largely based on black-white relationships and the research rarely
considers the multiracial schools of many contemporary cities or the fact
that the most segregated minority is now Latino. Pure mandatory reassign-
ment plans have rarely been adopted in the past fifteen years. Recent plans
tend to provide new educational options and choice as major ingredients.

In a nation where more than a third of the states now have Latino students as their largest minority and Asian enrollments are soaring, using a
black-white model is senseless. White flight evidence also usually ignores

changing birth rates and immigration, whose effects are sometimes implicitly blamed by courts on desegregation orders.

The Supreme Court returned to the white-flight issue in the 1995 *Missouri v. Jenkins* decision, dealing with it in a variety of ways and reaching decisions that would tend to maximize flight and prohibit some important efforts to offset white decline. The majority opinion expressed the belief that the implementation of an earlier plan limited to the city district was probably the cause of white flight. In response to the requirement to desegregate and to long-term white suburbanization, and the concern about the effect of a mandatory plan under such circumstances, the Kansas City plan attempted to attract white private school and suburban parents into the city schools to offset the continuing residential changes. Justice Rehnquist ruled that this effort to "attract nonminority students not presently enrolled in the KCMSD" was not legal and should be stopped.[80] He said that the requirement was to desegregate the students within the school system, not to attract outsiders. Such a plan would have all schools about two-thirds black at the outset, stripped of some of their special resources, with lowered teacher salaries, and faced with continuing white decline from residential change, even if there were no white flight. The kind of plan suggested by the Court would make all schools largely black in a largely white metropolitan area and would make no effort to compete with private or suburban schools—providing all the ingredients for maximizing white flight.

What Is Known About Housing Segregation

Housing conclusions by courts often contradict established knowledge. The following generalizations would, we believe, be accepted by the great majority of scholars doing empirical work on the development of residential segregation. Though there are major disputes among researchers, generalizations of the sort often found in court decisions and politics are often clearly wrong about areas in which there is little or no scholarly debate. Widely accepted generalizations that simply express demographic facts or are uncontroversial include:

1. a history of overt housing segregation for black people, who have been more segregated than any other ethnic group since World War I; [81]
2. segregation in cities was and remains high a quarter century after fair housing laws were enacted; [82]
3. economic differences explain only a small fraction of the existing

segregation. Though incomes differ substantially by race, there is enough overlap of income and variation in housing prices within communities so that there would be no all-black or all-white census tracts in most sections of metropolitan areas if economics determined residence;[83]

ghettos and barrios are still spreading. Many governmental programs and decisions are related to the origin and spread of minority segregation;

4. massive discrimination continues in housing and home finance markets. Federally funded tests of housing sales and rental show persisting discrimination against black and Latino homeseekers.[84] The most recent national HUD study found that 53 percent of black renters and 46 percent of Hispanics confronted discrimination during a typical housing search. Among buyers, 59 percent of blacks and 56 percent of Latinos faced discrimination;[85]

5. subsidized housing has historically been openly segregated in many cities and has produced neighborhood schools extremely segregated by race, income, and a high level of joblessness of parents. Public housing still contributes strongly to school segregation;[86]

6. minority families prefer integrated communities by large majorities, but their ideal level of integration differs from that of white families;[87]

7. white attitudes toward residential integration have changed substantially in a favorable direction in the last generation even in highly segregated areas, but whites still prefer lower levels of integration than blacks;[88]

8. many long-term effects of prior housing discrimination continue;[89]

9. most suburban middle-class communities exclude subsidized housing, rental housing for families, and affordable housing through official decisions about housing and land use and develop new housing on the edge of suburbia, which is sold to an overwhelmingly white clientele. Schools are important in marketing this housing;[90]

10. major declines in white school enrollment have occurred in central cities and older suburbs with neighborhood schools as well as those with desegregation plans;[91]

11. some of the most rapidly growing school districts in the country have had mandatory city-suburban enrollment for years and have been among the nation's most successful in holding white students;

12. housing subsidies often help resegregate integrated neighborhoods and their schools. That pattern continued long after fair housing became law.[92]

Although many of these assertions are incompatible with conclusions reached by various courts in resegregation cases, they do not deny the presence of significant private prejudice and nongovernmental discrimination. Nor do they show the precise effects of past discrimination. They indicate only broad general patterns of relationships, patterns far more compatible with the Supreme Court's findings of pervasive housing-school interactions in the *Swann* and *Keyes* decisions than with the housing assumptions in the resegregation cases.

Is Segregation Natural and Immutable?

Though there are different ideal levels of integration for whites and blacks, the research on this issue falls far short of supporting the argument that there is an immutable structure of private racial preferences that courts and public officials cannot solve. There is good evidence, in fact, that these attitudes are not purely private, that they are subject to change, and that there is considerable evidence of substantial overlap between black and white preferences. In fact, residential integration has increased significantly in many smaller cities as has acceptance of fair housing in the last generation. The growth of integration occurred even as government policies continued to underwrite segregation. There are stable communities with levels of minority population assumed to be impossible under the preference theory.[93] Research from other areas of civil rights policy, such as school desegregation and attitudes toward election of black political leaders, shows that attitudes change with experience.

Survey research on preferences is often introduced in trials as definitive evidence that segregated housing results from the choices of buyers, not discrimination. This evidence is presented without recognition of two fundamental limitations of surveys: they cannot show the degree to which the attitudes expressed resulted from past discrimination and they cannot show the degree to which attitudes may change in the future. Attitudes, for example, may very well be products of the illegal practices of the past; if they are, they are not natural and private matters but vestiges of that past segregation. Judgments courts must make about legal responsibility are judgments about the continuing influence of past discrimination. Decisions they make about remedies involve estimating not what is practical now but what will happen if the court order alters the status quo in various ways. Survey data has often been used as proof for issues where it is not relevant and may be highly misleading.

In *Dowell v. Board of Education of Oklahoma City,* the Supreme Court made it clear that lower courts must determine whether spreading segregation is a "result of private decisionmaking and economics"[94] The courts normally see only a skewed reflection of knowledge from research because of unequal resources for litigation. Evidence is strong that blacks do not prefer segregation and they would be highly integrated if they lived in the same neighborhoods occupied by whites of similar income.[95]

Courts and local officials often speak of a "tipping point" in racial change, reflecting the belief that there is a certain percentage of black residents in a community that makes total racial transition inevitable and irreversible. Until recent decades, few residentially integrated neighborhoods had ever remained stable because of the block-by-block racial change process adopted by local realtors and property owners to manage increased black housing demand during the decades of overt segregationist policies.[96]

When Thomas Schelling devised the theory of the mathematical incompatibility of the preferences for racial composition of neighborhoods, it seemed to lend scientific status to the tipping point idea.[97] The centerpiece of this theory is that blacks prefer to live in neighborhoods that are 50 percent black and whites prefer to live in neighborhoods that are considerably less integrated, and a half-black neighborhood the theory predicts that interracial communities will continue to change until they are all minority, even though almost no one finds that outcome ideal. Surveys conducted in 1978 in the Detroit metropolitan area in which participants were asked about different racial mixes in a block have been widely cited to show that incompatible preferences do exist.[98]

Although differing preferences do present real difficulties for stable integration, there are a number of logical and empirical flaws in the argument presented in court. The first is that integration is increasing and there are substantial numbers of stable integrated communities. According to the preference theory, these things should not have happened. Attitudes are changing; for example, when white households were asked, "if black people came to live in great numbers in your neighborhood, would you move?" the percentage who responded "yes" declined consistently from 78 percent in 1963 to 32 percent in 1990.[99] Although people may prefer a particular racial mix, most say that racial composition is not high among their considerations in housing searches. The best-known surveys of incompatible preferences came from metropolitan Detroit, which had the most severe segregation among large urban communities in 1990. This means that the incompatibilities may be less in other cities. Attitudes changed substantially even among Detroit-area whites between 1976 and 1992.[100] Since white attitudes have been based primarily on experiences with white-black transitions, there may be less fear of change and greater possibility of stability in the emerging multiracial neighborhoods in many cities. The declining birth rate and out-migration of blacks from many metropolitan areas means much less population pressure on integrated areas than in the past. The decline in housing segregation means that black housing demand will not be so concentrated on a few areas. Many communities are also experimenting with ways to break the syndrome of racial change through direct intervention in the housing markets and effective responses to the feared symbols of neighborhood deterioration.

If courts rely heavily on the preference theory to justify returning to segregated schools, they will be limiting the rights of minority students on the basis of the following unsupported assumptions: that the attitudes are inherent, not the product of a history of ghetto creation and expansion under discriminatory policies; that school and housing desegregation would not improve attitudes and increase stable integration; and that the school districts' hired experts are presenting reliable and impartial evidence on attitudes.

In fact, racial preferences are related to a long history of destructive racial change *supported* by public policy and may prove as changeable as many other kinds of racial stereotypes and prejudices have in the last half century.

Toward a Legal Approach Reflecting Urban Reality

If the assumptions about housing in the resegregation decisions are highly questionable and there are serious effects of housing on school desegregation, it is important to consider under what conditions housing violations should lead to additional school desegregation requirements. In the Indianapolis decision ordering city-suburban desegregation, the United States Court of Appeals for the Seventh Circuit formulated standards to judge whether an interdistrict school remedy is an appropriate response to housing discrimination:

1. Discriminatory practices have caused segregative residential housing patterns and population shifts.
2. State action, at whatever level, by either direct or indirect action, initiated, supported, or contributed to these practices and the resulting housing patterns and population shifts.
3. Although the state action need not be the sole cause of these effects, it must have had a significant rather than a de minimis [minimal] effect.
4. Finally, an interdistrict remedy may be appropriate even though the state discriminatory housing practices have ceased if it is shown

that prior discriminatory practices have a continuing segregative effect on housing patterns (and, in turn, on school attendance patterns) . . . [101]

Applying the Indianapolis standards to the housing history of metropolitan America would, no doubt, produce many cases in which the courts would be obliged to consider expanding school desegregation.

The St. Louis case was another example of a potentially crucial development in the law linking housing and school segregation. In its 1980 decision ordering a new desegregation plan, the federal district court ordered the housing agencies to submit a plan to the court to change housing policies in ways that would support school integration. HUD and the local community development agency developed and submitted plans to the court, but because of the replacement of the judge and inaction by the parties, the court never acted on the plans.

Housing as a Path Toward a Solution?

The use of housing issues has evolved radically in school desegregation battles, yet another set of changes is needed if there is to be movement toward integrated neighborhoods with integrated schools rather than a surrender to segregation. Civil rights lawyers in the early years of urban desegregation plans routinely proved how residential segregation was imposed by public agencies as a basic part of winning a school desegregation order outside the South. It was easy to do in most cities because housing discrimination was not hidden until fair housing laws began to appear in the 1960s. In government-operated housing and housing with FHA and VA mortgages, discrimination was particularly blatant. Understanding housing history was a powerful tool for winning desegregation orders by proving intentional official segregation.

The Supreme Court's 5-4 decision in *Milliken I,* however, transformed housing issues from reasons for more desegregation to justifications for less or none. Based on a single district afflicted with spreading segregation (the typical American city profile), opponents argued that resegregation would be accelerated by desegregation and so nothing could be done about it. The white-flight arguments and incompatible preference arguments about the instability of interracial neighborhoods were, essentially, ways of arguing that housing made lasting school integration impossible and, therefore, the effort should be abandoned.

Opponents of school desegregation have been arguing two contradictory things about the relationship between schools and housing. In their white-flight claims, they assume that school desegregation plans have a powerful effect on housing choices, because whites flee the increased contact with minority students. On the other hand, in their theory that people have a natural preference for segregation that is reflected in the private market, they argue that the courts can ignore the interactions between schools and housing issues. Segregation is not a public problem requiring judicial intervention but the result of private natural preferences unconnected to a history of discrimination. Whites simply prefer far lower levels of contact with blacks than blacks do with whites. These contradictory arguments were adopted simultaneously by the Supreme Court majority in the 1995 *Missouri v. Jenkins* decision.

Both of these theories argue that there is a kind of vicious cycle perpetuating and spreading segregation. Both claim that it is results from white resistance to increased presence of blacks in situations where it is possible for whites to leave an interracial institution or community for a segregated white one.

These theories do not explain how it is possible to reconcile the insistence on white opposition to desegregation with the national surveys showing large increases in white acceptance of substantial levels of school and housing integration. One way is to assume that the statements mean nothing. Another, however, is to consider evidence that whites are prepared to accept integration but fear the spread of the ghetto. Much of this resistance may be resistance not to integration but to white fears of resegregation, a fear deeply rooted in many communities by generations of bitter experience.[102]

If the spread of segregated schools and the fear of resegregation compound problems of housing segregation by making whites fearful about moving their children into an area where they will be isolated in minority schools, successful plans for widespread stable integrated neighborhoods with integrated schools may help break this vicious cycle. In fact, there is considerable evidence that strong and extensive school desegregation policies can increase residential integration. A variety of housing policies can help develop better integrated neighborhoods with more integrated schools. Communities should consider the following options.

HOUSING COUNSELING

The Kentucky Human Rights Commission was the only civil rights agency in the country to take an early and strong initiative to use housing to help school desegregation. The Kentucky commission put up billboards that said "End Forced Busing"; the next line, however, read "Support Fair Housing." A commission staff member worked to decrease segregation by driving black recipients of rental subsidy certificates around to introduce them to housing options outside the ghetto. About half of these subsidy recipients decided to move to white areas. Under the Louisville school plan, they were immediately exempted from busing, since their moves increased integration. The housing plan allowed recipients of Section 8 housing subsidies to move anywhere in the metropolitan area. Before that time, one half of all black Section 8 families lived inside two school attendance zones in the city. After the plan, four in five were choosing housing outside of those two areas.[103]

EXEMPTION OF INTEGRATED COMMUNITIES FROM BUSING

Many skeptics about school desegregation plans argue that it would be better to deal with the root of school segregation—housing—than to try continually to treat the educational symptoms of residential apartheid. In some cities they point out the irony of busing children out of integrated neighborhoods. Residents who are living in integrated areas bitterly criticize plans that split up their neighborhoods and bus away children who could walk to an integrated school. There are now, however, plans that exempt integrated neighborhoods from busing in a number of cities, some of which show steady reductions of busing as the number of integrated communities increases. Such policies begin to turn vicious cycles into positive cycles of growing integration.

Such policies have been in place for years, for example, in St. Louis and Denver. In Louisville, neighborhoods with enough black residents to meet school desegregation standards regained neighborhood schools. The plan showed the possibility of positive initiatives at low cost. Between 1975 and 1982, the percentage of black students living in predominantly white suburbs nearly tripled.[104] The district was able to exempt thirty-two schools from busing by 1982. As fewer students required busing, the average hour time was cut in half, and the total number of students being bused fell from 18,000 to 11,000 while desegregation was maintained.[105] In Denver, fair housing groups worked with realtors to increase residential integration of Denver neighborhoods so that they could have integrated neighborhoods that would get back their neighborhood schools. This effort was successful in some communities.

GAUIREAUX: LESSONS OF A HOUSING REMEDY

The Chicago Housing Authority and HUD were found guilty of generations of intentional housing segregation in metropolitan Chicago in 1969. After the Supreme Court upheld the decision, the courts ordered a set of changes including a larger and more complex approach to the problem of the use of housing subsidy programs to intensify segregation. To help break the pattern of segregation and ghetto expansion in one of the nation's most segregated and resistant housing markets, black families from Chicago housing projects were given counseling about housing opportunities in white areas, escort service, and personal support after their moves. The program was designed to overcome their lack of knowledge about housing in white areas and their fears of violence and intimidation from whites.

Although it began slowly because of intense fear and the lack of experience among eligible households, interest mushroomed after the first groups moved successfully. Once the word got back about the experience of the early participants, thousands applied for the available slots each year. The plan permitted several thousand female-headed poor families to move out of city projects or off the waiting list to suburban private units with rent subsidy certificates.

The program moved children from segregated city schools with low achievement and graduation levels to vastly more competitive outlying suburban schools. The city children had surprisingly successful and positive experiences in the suburbs.[106] The same model has now been expanded under court order to several other cities and is a centerpiece of HUD Secretary Henry Cisneros' "Moving to Opportunity" program.[107] Although the programs have reached only a very small share of segregated minority families, they showed the possibility and potential effects of expanding housing choices for the poor.

SPECIAL MORTGAGE FINANCING FOR PRO-INTEGRATION MOVES

Ohio, the state of Washington, and Wisconsin all have policies providing financial incentives for families whose moves contribute to housing and school integration. Many states have special programs in which they offer a small number of first-time home buyers special low-cost financing to purchase homes. Since mortgage interest is by far the largest cost of owning the home, this is a powerful subsidy.

Civil rights organizations have persuaded these three states to set aside some subsidies for families whose moves increase integration. These subsidies reach relatively few people, but the program illustrates the possibility of using a number of relatively small programs in different ways to produce overall changes.

The legality of the Ohio plan, according to Ohio Attorney General Celebrezze, rested on supporting school desegregation.[108] In 1988, the state housing agency agreed to set aside 5 percent of its low-interest loans for families who move into neighborhoods in which their race is underrepresented in the schools.[109] Approximately 150 people participated in this program each year, half of whom are African American.[110]

The consent agreement settling the metropolitan Milwaukee school desegregation case clearly recognized the housing issue in one of the nation's most segregated areas. It provides state funds for a program to provide families with counseling and information about making moves that promote racial integration, as well as provide low-interest loans to people moving into areas where their racial group comprises less than 15 percent of the population. The state provided 15 percent of the state's low-income housing federal tax credits to encourage the development of new affordable integrated housing, and the state housing agency also committed itself to issuing $5 million in mortgage bonds for prointegration sales.[111]

Seattle, Washington, school officials won an agreement with the state housing officials in 1989 to provide up to a $2,000 tax credit to low- and moderate-income home buyers who bought homes in places that would aid school integration. The credits reduced average mortgage payments by 20 percent. The school superintendent noted that even fifty families making such moves would save annual busing costs exceeding the cost of the tax credit in the first year.[112] The policy was designed to reinforce the school district's new 1989 desegregation plan, which was supposed to reward integrated neighborhoods by giving them neighborhood schools.

STATE AND LOCAL POLICIES FOR SCATTERED SITE SUBSIDIZED HOUSING

Several highly urbanized states now have considerable experience in developing subsidized housing in normally closed suburban areas as a result of state court decisions or legislation limiting suburban land-use controls. The *Mt. Laurel* plan resulted from the New Jersey Supreme Court's 1983 ruling that exclusionary zoning regulations blocking low- and moderate-cost housing in many communities conflicted with the state constitution. Each New Jersey municipality was required to provide a "fair share" of low- and moderate-income housing based on an assessment of the needs of the state as a whole.[113] The remedy made it easy for developers to sue for and win exemption from zoning regulations in areas that had totally excluded subsidized housing.[114] The production of many thousands of units of housing under this remedy has shown its potential power. Relatively few of the outlying units, however, have gone to black families because there is an immense unmet need for subsidized housing for white suburbanites, and blacks are unlikely to hear about the units unless integration is a specific goal. This shows clearly the need for more tenant outreach and counseling and integration goals similar to what exists in Louisville and Chicago.

There are similar court orders or state laws in Massachusetts, Pennsylvania, and Connecticut. Local policy has instituted a requirement for affordable units in all major developments in Montgomery County, Maryland, one of the nation's richest suburbs. Clearly there are now ample models to show that such approaches are viable and compatible with both good design and excellent housing markets. If they could be carried out more broadly and tied to housing counseling for potential minority residents, they could have a significant positive effect on school desegregation.

SCHOOL CONSTRUCTION CHOICES AS
LEVERAGE FOR INTEGRATION

Many growing school districts have to make decisions on building schools, particularly in the Sunbelt and in the newer suburbs. Site decisions are crucial to housing markets and to school segregation. A school makes a new housing development much easier to market; school boards usually build wherever developers expand, regardless of the racial consequences. Experience in several communities has demonstrated that developers are willing to negotiate in order to obtain schools. Positive experiences show successes in some cases.[115]

Important experiments in Denver and Palm Beach County have begun to explore the possibilities of using school construction choices to spur residential integration and thus reduce the need for busing. During the 1980s, Denver began several creative efforts to deal with the housing issues underlying school segregation; it developed positive policies to integrate both newly developed and older communities to reduce busing and also moved toward scattered-site public housing. The city council adopted a strong scattered-site policy and built more than 800 units of scattered-site housing; a study by the *Rocky Mountain News* shows that its residents were much more likely than the residents of the old projects to finish high school.

The planned integration in a large new development of private housing on the last large vacant tract in the city is another important example of the use of leverage. A court order prohibiting the construction of new schools that would be segregated stirred fears that the lack of a local school would seriously damage marketing. The problem was solved by an agreement, approved by the board and the court, to design and market the new community for integration; it was implemented successfully according to research by the University of Colorado's urban affairs center.

The same issue arose on a larger scale and from a different source in

Palm Beach County, Florida, after the U.S. Education Department found evidence that new schools contributed to "the resegregation of the system as a whole, as well as the disparate treatment of black students." The Palm Beach school district negotiated agreements with various developers to aim for black households at a minimum of 10 percent of the total in developments that would receive neighborhood schools.[116] The experiment showed that many were willing to consider such agreements but it also demonstrated that without clear enforcement authority and sanctions, such agreements would have mixed results. Some developers reached the goal and their new neighborhoods opened with populations producing significantly integrated enrollments at the new schools; in other developments the marketing fell far short. A more targeted and closely monitored process, perhaps building the school only after there was evidence of success with the marketing, might be more effective. In 1995, the metropolitan Raleigh (Wake County) school board entered into its first agreement with a developer.

Ending Urban Apartheid

The school segregation that exists in any given community today shows the enduring effects of practices and expectations rooted in past discrimination in housing. It is, of course, affected by private prejudice and preferences, but those themselves may be products of a long history of discrimination. Contemporary policies also continue to produce segregation and undermine integrated communities and schools. The promise of fair housing has been addressed by only feeble enforcement efforts.

The best way to escape both the destructive trends of spreading segregation and the uncomfortable necessity of outside intervention in local policymaking is to adopt policies replacing the vicious cycles of ghetto expansion with policies fostering integration of neighborhoods and their schools. The Nixon administration examined such a policy and rejected it in an explicit play for white political support. The Carter administration, near the end of its term, was approaching such a policy, but the Reagan and Bush administrations abandoned the effort and worked to dismantle the tools. The Clinton administration reopened the idea of a major attack on housing segregation, but experienced substantial resistance in Congress. There is now ample experience from successful local experiments to provide a basis for mutually supportive school and housing integration policies to overcome the effects of generations of intentional segregation. To make such a policy politically viable, national leaders in and outside of government must systematically examine the results in communities that have provided leadership. Ironically, it may be that the most complex and wide-ranging planning of school and housing remedies would lead to the most natural, stable, and least coercive outcome.

If the courts choose, on the other hand, to use unsupported presumptions and burden shifts about housing issues to justify resegregation of schools, decades of commitment to the goals of *Brown* will give way to seemingly quiet acceptance of segregated schools serving segregated neighborhoods. Housing theories are being presented as key justifications for acceptance of a new *Plessy* in the metropolitan areas of the United States.

A much better path is to accept the unworkability of urban apartheid and to begin to put in place proven and new remedies that could lead toward a more integrated, fair, and workable urban society. In such communities solutions to school segregation issues often could be natural by-products of facing and resolving the deeper issue of racially defined housing, perpetuated through housing markets and housing policies.

NOTES

1. *Missouri v. Jenkins,* 63 U.S.L.W. 4486 (1955).
2. Computations from 1992–93 Common Core of Educational Statistics, U.S. Department of Education.
3. *Swann v. Charlotte-Mecklenburg Board of Education,* 402 U.S. 1 (1971).
4. *Keyes v. School District No. 1,* 413 U.S. 189 (1973).
5. Paul R. Dimond, *Beyond Busing: Inside the Challenge to Urban Segregation* (Ann Arbor: University of Michigan Press, 1985), 106–7.
6. Ibid., 111.
7. Ibid., 113.
8. *Plessy v. Ferguson,* 163 U.S. 537, 551 (1896).
9. Gary Orfield, "Ghettoization and Its Alternatives," in *The New Urban Reality,* ed. Paul Peterson (Washington, DC: Brookings Institution Press, 1985); Gary Orfield, "Federal Policy, Local Power, and Metropolitan Segregation," *Political Science Quarterly* 89 (Winter 1975): 777–802; Gary Orfield, "School Segregation and Housing Policy: The Role of Local and Federal Governments in Neighborhood Segregation," *Integrated Education,* 48–53.
10. Gallup poll in *USA Today,* May 16, 1994.
11. Beth J. Lief and Susan Goering, "The Implementation of the Federal Mandate for Fair Housing," in *Divided Neighborhoods: Changing Patterns of Racial Segregation,* ed. Gary Tobin (Newbury Park, CA: Sage Publications, 1987), 227–67. HUD's failure over twenty years to enforce civil rights requirements for subsidized housing was documented in the *Dallas Morning News'* Pulitzer Prize-winning series, "Separate and Unequal: Subsidized Housing in America," February 10–18, 1985; more recent shortcomings were documented in U.S. Commission on Civil Rights, *The Fair Housing Amendments Act of 1988— The Enforcement Report* (Washington, DC: GPO, 1994).

12. "Fair Housing Enforcement Needs Additional Improvement," *Civil Rights Update,* December 1994/January 1995, 3, 8.

13. John Yinger, *Housing Discrimination Study: Incidence of Discrimination and Variation in Discrimination Behavior,* report to U.S. Department of Housing and Urban Development, October 1991.

14. Studies of enforcement reflect complex political and institutional processes with very imperfect compliance. See, e.g., George R. Lanoue and Barbara A. Lee, *Academics in Court: The Consequences of Faculty Discrimination Litigation* (Ann Arbor: University of Michigan Press, 1987); Kenneth J. Meier and Joseph Stewart Jr., *The Politics of Hispanic Education* (Albany: State University of New York Press, 1991); Michael A. Rebell and Arthur R. Block, *Educational Policy Making and the Courts* (Chicago: University of Chicago Press, 1982); John B. Williams III, *Desegregating America's Colleges and Universities* (New York: Teachers College Press, 1988); Richard Neely, *How Courts Govern America* (New Haven, CT: Yale University Press, 1981); Donald L. Horowitz, *The Courts and Social Policy* (Washington, DC: Brookings Institution Press, 1977); Jeffrey A. Raffel, *The Politics of School Desegregation* (Philadelphia: Temple University Press, 1980).

15. *Missouri v. Jenkins,* 115 S. Ct. 2038 (1995).

16. C. Vann Woodward, *The Strange Career of Jim Crow* (New York: Oxford University Press, 1966).

17. *Keyes,* 413 U.S. 210 (1973).

18. *Missouri v. Jenkins,* 115 S. Ct. 2038.

19. *Armour v. Nix,* No. 16708, slip op. (N.D. Ga. 1979).

20. Ibid.

21. Ibid.

22. Ibid.

23. Ibid. The Court describes tipping as involving "elements of fear, personal prejudice, and other psychological and economic factors [which] may partly explain the evolution of transitional neighborhoods from totally white to almost totally black composition, leaving few integrated neighborhoods existing in the Atlanta area today."

24. Gary Orfield and Carole Ashkinaze, *The Closing Door: Conservative Policy and Black Opportunity* (Chicago: University of Chicago Press, 1991), chap. 5.

25. *Armour v. Nix,* 446 U.S. 930 (1980).

26. *Hills v. Gatreaux,* 425 U.S. 284 (1976).

27. HUD Assistant Secretary Roberta Achtenberg, address at the University of Pennsylvania Law School, March 24, 1995.

28. Clement E. Vose, *Caucasians Only: The Supreme Court, the NAACP, and the Restrictive Covenant Cases* (Berkeley: University of California Press, 1967), 3. Oklahoma City was one of the cities that originally set out racial zoning; see *Dowell,* 244 F. Supp. 971, 975 (1965).

29. *Corrigan v. Buckley,* 299 F.2d 899 (D.C. Cir.), appeal dismissed, 271 U.S. 323 (1926). In dismissing the case, Justice Sanford found the challenge "so insubstantial as to be plainly without color of merit and frivolous." Two decades would pass before the issue would come back to the Supreme Court (Vose, *Caucasians Only,* 18).

30. 271 U.S. 323.

31. *Shelley v. Kraemer,* 334 U.S. 1 (1948).

32. Gunnar Myrdal, *An American Dilemma,* vol. 2 (1946; New York: Harper Torchbooks, 1962), 623–24.

33. Charles Abrams, *Forbidden Neighbors* (New York: Harper and Row, 1955), 235.

34. Douglas Massey and Nancy Denton, *American Apartheid: Segregation and the Making of the Underclass* (Cambridge, MA: Harvard University Press, 1993).

35. U.S. National Commission on Urban Problems (Douglass Commission), *Building the American City: Report of the National Commission on Urban Problems to the Congress and to the President of the United States,* House Document 91–34 (Washington, DC: GPO, 1968), 163.

36. Orfield, "Ghettoization"; Orfield, "School Segregation," 48–53; Gary Orfield, "Federal Policy, Local Power, and Metropolitan Segregation," in *Political Power and the Urban Crisis,* ed. Alan Shank (Boston: Holbrook Press, 1976).

37. U.S. Commission on Civil Rights, *Home Ownership for Lower Income Families: A Report on the Racial and Ethnic Impact of the Section 235 Program* (Washington, DC: GPO, 1971).

38. Brian D. Boyer, *Cities Destroyed for Cash: The FHA Scandal at HUD* (Chicago: Follett Publishing, 1973); Leonard Downie Jr., *Mortgage on America* (New York: Praeger Publishers, 1973), chap. 3.

39. See statistics on Section 8 programs in Robert Gray and Steven Tursky, "Local and Racial/Ethnic Occupancy Patterns for HUD-Subsidized Family Housing in Ten Metropolitan Areas," in *Housing Desegregation and Federal Policy,* ed. John Goering (Chapel Hill: University of North Carolina Press, 1986), 235–52.

40. The number of authorized additional subsidized housing units was cut nearly in half in the first year of the Reagan administration. See John William Ellwood, ed., *Reductions in U.S. Domestic Spending* (New Brunswick, NJ: Transaction Books, 1982), 268.

41. John Goering, Ali Kamely, and Todd Richardson, *The Location and Racial Composition of Public Housing in the United States* (Washington, DC: U.S. Department of Housing and Urban Development, December 1994), 2.

42. ibid.

43. Gary Orfield, "Housing and School Integration in Three Metropolitan Areas: A Policy Analyses of Denver, Columbus, and Phoenix," submitted to U.S. Department of Housing and Urban Development, HUD Order No. 50007-80, February 17, 1981.

44. *Gautreaux v. Chicago Housing Authority,* 480 F.2d 210 (7th Cir.), cert. denied, 414 U.S. 1144 (1974).

45. *Gautreaux v. Chicago Housing Authority,* 296 F. Supp. 907, summarized in *Hills v. Gautreaux,* 425 U.S. 284, 288 (1976).

46. It is worth noting that President Reagan actually took steps to further hinder integration when he rescinded a regulation requiring housing authorities to report racial statistics. See U.S. Department of Housing and Urban Development, Notice H81-12 (October 18, 1981).

47. *Walker v. U.S. Department of Housing and Urban Development,* 734 F. Supp. 1289 (N.D. Tex 1989).

48. Scott Cummings and Wayne Zatopek, "Federal Housing Policy and Racial Isolation in Public Schools: The Case of Dallas," in *Racial Isolation in the Public Schools: The Impact of Public and Private Housing Policies,* ed. Scott Cummings,

report to U.S. Department of Housing and Urban Development by Institute of Urban Studies, University of Texas at Arlington, 1980, 194–95.

49. "HUD's Responses to Plaintiffs' Requests for Admission," *Walker v. U.S. Department of Housing and Urban Development,* May 11, 1994, 1.

50. Richard P. Taub, D. Garth Taylor, and Jan D. Dunham, *Paths of Neighborhood Change: Race and Crime in Urban America* (Chicago: University of Chicago Press, 1984), *Chicagon Sun-Times* poll, 1983.

51. Orfield, "Ghettoization."

52. Ibid.

53. John F. Kain, "The Spatial Mismatch Hypothesis: Three Decades Later," *Housing Policy Debate* 3, no. 2 (1992): 371–460.

54. U.S. Commission on Civil Rights, *Home Ownership.*

55. During the Reagan years, the Justice Department began asking for more narrow remedies than had been requested earlier and used some of its scarce litigation resources to sue those trying to manage stable integration with racial quotas in their buildings, an enterprise supported by Jesse Jackson and part of a consent agreement with the NAACP, which the Justice Department intervened in a successful effort to overturn.

56. Address at University of Pennsylvania Law Review Forum, Philadelphia, February 24, 1995.

57. *Nixon: The Third Year of His Presidency* (Washington, DC: Congressional Quarterly Inc., 1972), 23.

58. Betty Glad, *Jimmy Carter: In Search of the Great White House* (New York: W. W. Norton, 1980).

59. "Outcry Stalls Housing in Baltimore Suburbs," *National Fair Housing Report* 4, no. 6 (November/December 1994): 6.

60. Daniel H. Weinberg, "Mobility and Housing Change: The Housing Allowance Demand Experiment," in *Residential Mobility and Public Policy,* ed. W. A. V. Clark and Eric G. Moore (Beverly Hills: Sage Publications, 1980), 168–93, shows limited mobility; U.S. Department of Housing and Urban Development, *Gautreaux Housing Development* (Washington, DC: GPO, 1979) documents fear and lack of knowledge as basic barriers to using Section 8 subsidies in suburbs for city black residents during the startup period of the Gautreaux program.

61. Richard Stuart Fleisher, "Subsidized Housing and Residential Segregation in American Cities: An Evaluation of the Site Selection and Occupancy of Federally Subsidized Housing" (PhD diss., University of Illinois at Urbana, 1979); Gray and Tursky, "Local and Racial/Ethnic Occupancy Patterns."

62. J. F. Rosenbaum, L. S. Rubionwitz, and M. J. Kulieke, *Low Income Black Children in White Suburban Schools* (Evanston, IL: Northwestern University Center for Urban Affairs and Policy Research, 1986).

63. Gary Orfield and Paul Fischer, *Housing and Social Integration in Three Metropolitan Areas: A Policy Analysis of Denver, Columbus, and Phoenix,* report to HUD, 1981.

64. Letter to author from Marcia W. Borowski, January 5, 1995; DeKalb County Public Schools, "Summary of DeKalb School's Legal Expenses Requested by F. Pauley."

65. Christine Rossell, *The Carrot or the Stick for School Desegregation Policy: Magnet Schools or Forced Busing* (Philadelphia: Temple University Press, 1990).

66. Testimony of D. Garth Taylor, Kansas City school desegregation trial, Federal District Court, Kansas City.

67. James S. Coleman, Sara D. Kelly, and John A. Moore, *Trends in School Integration, 1968–73* (Washington, DC: Urban Institute, 1975).

68. *Foss v. Houston Indep. Sch. Dist.*, 669 F.2d 218, 288, citing Supreme Court decision in *Pasadena City Bd. of Ed. v. Spangler,* 427 U.S. 424 (1976).

69. U.S. Commission on Civil Rights, *Racial Isolation in the Public Schools, Appendices,* 1967, 2–12.

70. Thurgood Marshall, "Nos. 73-434, 73-435, and 73-346, *Milliken v. Bradley,*" read in Court by Justice Marshall, typescript in Thurgood Marshall papers, Manuscript Division, Library of Congress.

71. Address of Superintendent David Sneed to Council of Urban Boards of Education Conference, New York, October 1, 1994.

72. Reynolds Farley, Carlotte Steeh, Maria Krysan, Tara Jackson, and Keith Reeves, "Stereotypes and Segregation: Neighborhoods in the Detroit Area," *American Journal of Sociology* 100, no. 3 (November 1994): 751; U.S. Department of Education data tapes, 1992–93.

73. An account of the controversy is given by Gary Orfield, "Research, Politics, and the Antibusing Debate," *Law and Contemporary Problems* 42 (Autumn 1978): 141–49.

74. U.S. vital statistics data from the 1960s through the 1980s show that non-whites consistently had larger families than whites and that whites were having children below the replacement level since the early 1970s. See *Statistical Abstract of the United States, 1992* (Washington, DC: GPO, 1992), 67. See also Ben J. Wattenberg, *The Birth Dearth* (New York: Pharos Books, 1989).

75. Enrollment data from districts; for overall projections see Charles D. Liner, "Update: School Enrollment Projections," *School Law Bulletin, University of North Carolina* 26, no. 1 (Winter 1955): 16–18.

76. *Boston Globe,* February 15, 1995, 1.

77. National Association of Realtors data for period between the last quarter of 1993 and the final quarter of 1994, in *Investor's Business Daily,* February 10, 1995, A17.

78. National Center for Education Statistics, *Characteristics of the 100 Largest Public Elementary and Secondary School Districts in the United States: 1991–92* (Washington, DC: GPO, 1994), 12.

79. Greater Raleigh Chamber of Commerce, Resolution Concerning the Wake County Public School System, May 24, 1995.

80. *Missouri v. Jenkins,* 115 S. Ct. 2038, 2051.

81. Charles Abrams, *The City Is the Frontier* (New York: Harper Colophon, 1967), chap. 5–8.

82. Robert D. Bullard, J. Eugene Grigsly III, and Charles Lee, eds., *Residential Apartheid: The American Legacy* (Los Angeles: UCLA CAAS, 1994).

83. Massey and Denton, *American Apartheid;* Kain, "The Spatial Mismatch Hypothesis."

84. Margery A. Turner, "Discrimination in Urban Housing Markets: Lessons from Fair Housing Adults," *Housing Policy Debate* 3, no. 2 (1992): 185–215; George Galster, "Racial Discrimination in Housing Markets in the 1980s: A Review of the Audit Evidence," *Journal of Planning Education and Research* 9 (1992): 165–75.

85. Turner, "Discrimination," 197.

86. Orfield, "Housing and School Integration"; Cummings and Zatopek, "Federal Housing Policy."

87. *USA Today* poll, *USA Today,* September 22, 1989. In a 1989 national poll, only 10 percent of blacks expressed a preference for a "mostly black" neighborhood, but 53 percent lived in one; Farley et al., "Stereotypes and Segregation," fn 72.

88. Farley et al., "Stereotypes and Segregation."

89. Kain, "The Spatial Mismatch Hypothesis"; Gary Tobin, ed., "The Costs of Housing Discrimination and Segregation: An Interdisciplinary Social Science Statement," in *Divided Neighborhoods* (see note 11), 268–80.

90. A 1995 study by the Federal Reserve Bank of Boston found that the forty communities in greater Boston with the highest housing price growth in the 1988 to 1994 period had the highest scores on standardized tests and the communities with the lowest scores had housing prices rising only one seventh as fast. Steve Bailey, "Top Schools, Pricey Homes Linked," *Boston Globe,* May 22, 1995.

91. Gary Orfield and Franklin Monfort, *Racial Change and Desegregation in Large School Districts: Trends through the 1986–87 School Year* (Alexandria, VA: National School Boards Association, 1988).

92. U.S. Commission on Civil Rights, *Home Ownership;* Fleisher, "Subsidized Housing"; Gray and Tursky, "Local and Racial/Ethnic Occupancy Patterns."

93. Taub, Taylor, and Dunham, *Paths of Neighborhood Change.*

94. *Dowell v. Bd. of Educ. of Oklahoma City,* 11 S. Ct. 630, 638 (1991). This was done against the strong dissent of Justice Marshall, who argued that illegal segregation should not be excused simply because it may be self-perpetuating.

95. George C. Galster, "Residential Segregation in American Cities: A Contrary Review," *Population Research and Policy Review* 7 (1988): 93, 95, cited in John Charles Boger, "Toward Ending Residential Segregation: A Fair Share Proposal for the Next Reconstruction," *North Carolina Law Review* 71 (June 1993): 1573.

96. Karl E. Taeuber and Alma F. Taeuber, *Negroes in Cities, Residential Segregation and Neighborhood Change* (New York: Atheneum, 1969), chap. 5.

97. Thomas Schelling, *Micromotives and Macrobehavior* (New York: W. W. Norton, 1978).

98. Reynolds Farley, Howard Schuman, Suzanne Bianchi, Diane Colasanto, and Shirley Hatchett, "Chocolate City, Vanilla Suburbs: Will the Trend Toward Racially Separate Communities Continue?" *Social Science Research* 7 (December 1978): 319–44.

99. Anthony Downs, "Policy Directions Concerning Racial Discrimination in U.S. Markets," *Housing Policy Debate* 3, no. 2 (1992): 697; Farley et al. shows that even in metropolitan Detroit white attitudes have improved significantly though black attitudes became less favorable.

100. Farley et al., "Stereotypes and Segregation," 750–80.

101. 637 F.2d 1101, 1109 (7th Cir. 1980), cited in Thomas M. Dee and Norella V. Huggins, "Models for Proving Liability of School and Housing Officials in School Desegregation Cases," *Urban Law Annual* 23 (1982): 111.

102. Taub, Taylor, and Dunham found that interracial neighborhoods in Chicago tended to stabilize when people believed that stability would not remain, not

when there were certain proportions or conditions. Commitment of powerful local institutions to maintaining integration played an important role.

103. Kentucky Commission on Human Rights, *School and Housing Desegregation Are
Working Together in Louisville and Jefferson County*, Staff Report 83–5, 1983, 5.

105. Some of this is attributable to declining birth rates, but it is worth noting that
white flight has not been a big problem in Louisville. In the decade from
1981–82 to 1991–92, black enrollment (as a percentage of the total) fluctu-
ated less than 2 percent, actually dropping in the final seven years of that
span. School system data printout supplied by the *Louisville Courier-Journal*.

106. James E. Rosenbaum, "Black Pioneers: Do Their Moves to the Suburbs Increase Economic Opportunity for Mothers and Children?" *Housing Policy Debate* 2, no. 4 (1991): 1179–214.

107. *National Fair Housing Advocate* 5, no. 1 (January/February 1995): 5.

108. Op. Ohio Att'y Gen. No. 87-095 (1987).

109. Zupanc, "Two Pro-Integrative Groups Get State Funds," *Sun Observer*, February 15, 1989.

110. Suja A. Thomas, "Efforts to Integrate Housing: The Legality of Mortgage-
Incentive Programs," *New York University Law Review*, June 1991.

111. Leadership Council for Metropolitan Open Communities, Recent Developments in Housing, October 1989, 3–4.

112. *Seattle Post-Intelligencer*, June 1, 1989.

113. The assessment is made by a state agency, the Council on Affordable Housing
(COAH).

115. *Palm Beach Sun-Sentinel*, 1994.

116. "Affordable Housing and Racial Balance," Palm Beach County School Board
Report, June 6, 1990; *Sun-Sentinel*, May 31, 1990.

16

What Alondra Learned

Peter Schrag

I

By the time she was a seventeen-year-old high school student, Alondra Jones was a fully qualified survivor. She was then staying with two room-mates in a publicly supported "transitional home" about a mile from her San Francisco school. In the prior eighteen months she'd lived with her cousin, who was her legal guardian, and the cousin's two teenage sons; she'd had to share a room with one of them. Before that she'd lived with her great-aunt, where she shared a room with the great-aunt's grandchil-dren, ages eighteen and sixteen. She had also lived for a month in Okla-homa with her grandmother and her father, and before that for another few months (in San Francisco) with her father and another cousin and her two minor children. Between her stay in Oklahoma and her stay with Cousin II, she said, "I went back and forth between my sister and my father's first wife." During part of that time she was out of school, once be-cause her father hadn't enrolled her and once because she had, as she said, "family responsibilities" taking care of her cousin's kids.[1]

Given that history, little should have fazed her. She's a smart, feisty, even flamboyant young woman. But after three years at Balboa High School, she'd discovered that she was getting the short end of the educational stick and was angry enough to sue as a plaintiff in the ACLU's adequacy case against the state. Balboa is a once-grand seventy-five-year-old Spanish-style building in San Francisco's Mission District that now houses roughly twelve hundred students, of whom about one-fourth are black, another fourth Latino, another fourth Filipino, 4 percent white, and the rest Chinese and Samoan. Its ranking on the state's test-based Academic Performance Index was near the very bottom, even in comparison to other high-poverty schools.[2]

Some of her complaints were common enough, not only in such urban schools but in many rural schools, and they came from other students as well. There were, as is often the case in schools serving poor students, not enough textbooks—because there was often only one set per teacher for several classes, no one could take a book home—and so teachers struggled to copy enough pages to hand out to their classes. (Lawrence Poon, another Balboa senior, said that during his three years there, he'd never had any books to take home for homework).[3] There were the strings of substitute teachers. There were the dirty and often inaccessible bathrooms, one with yellow caution tape across the door "that police use when somebody gets shot or killed," and ones that, when they were open, had "that smell, that horrible, horrible smell." The stalls, one visitor observed in the fall of 2000, "are covered with graffiti, the toilets and floors caked with scum, and the walls are smeared with crusty, hardened spitballs made from wads of toilet paper."[4] There were labs without equipment and classrooms where, at least in the first weeks of school, there weren't enough seats or desks for the forty or fifty students who had been assigned there. (At Mission High School in San Francisco, where Alondra Jones had gone in her freshman year, classrooms were, she said, sometimes jammed because when the roof leaked the whole third floor was flooded and "there would be different subjects taught in one classroom.") At Balboa, there were classrooms that were too hot in the fall and spring, especially on the sunny side of the building, and too cold in winter.

There were, of course, the mouse droppings—"we joke back and forth about who's seen the most rats at their schools"—and the bird "doodoo" in the gym where the birds had come in through the broken windows: "We used to try to hit the birds with a basketball. We made that a game in gym." The gym teachers tried to clean it up after the windows were repaired. "It's still bird stuff on the floor," she said. "But it's not like centimeters apart. . . . Now if you are in gym class and playing basketball, you can like avoid the spots by zigzagging."[5]

But that was just the beginning: There was the class called Modern World where the teacher got sick in the fall "and we had a bunch of substitutes instead. Sometimes they would stay just for one day, and sometimes they would stay for one week. . . . We'd get a new assignment from a new substitute . . . before we'd finished on a project from a substitute we'd had before the new one came. We had so many teachers that year that the report card didn't list a teacher's name—it just listed teacher F." There was the constant turnover of teachers, as in her Spanish class in eleventh grade, where the teacher left school in November and there was a different sub every day until finals. "We played games in class," she said, and the subs showed films. "We saw *Rush Hour, Entrapment, Amistad, Liar Liar,* and *Hal-*

loween. . . . People would just bring movies from their houses and we would watch them in class."

One of the substitutes, she said, caught her reading and told her to close the book and watch the movie. Finally, "one girl who'd transferred to our school . . . tried to teach class sometimes because she'd learned some things at the other school. But she's not a teacher and she didn't really know much more Spanish than we did. . . . [But] we still had to take a final exam at the end of the semester even though we hadn't had a teacher or learned any Spanish. Everybody failed the final. . . . I asked the assistant principal how I could get a grade after all we had was substitutes. . . . I told the assistant principal it would be okay if they tested on the movies we watched in class, but they shouldn't have tested us on the Spanish we didn't learn. The assistant principal just told me they had to give us a test."[6] The same thing happened to Lawrence Poon in two English classes in his sophomore year. (The previous year, he said, he also had a full semester of Spanish without a regular teacher.) And because Balboa, in a budget-cutting move, suddenly truncated its schedule from seven to six periods, Poon found it nearly impossible to take all the courses he needed to get into college. So he planned to take physics at a community college on his own.

But what most angered Alondra Jones was her discovery of what things were like on the other side of the tracks. A young, socially engaged social studies teacher named Shane Safir had taken her and some fifty other Balboa students on exchange visits—including a weekend retreat—to Marin Academy, an expensive private school just north of San Francisco, where the tuition is $21,000 a year, plus books and various other fees. Marin had a "director of diversity" named Lisa Arrastia who had a special interest in issues of educational equity and who, as part of a midwinter mini-course, had sponsored exchange visits with an inner-city Chicago high school whose "ultimate goal was to empower all students to affect change in the economic imbalances that maintain current inequities in the U.S. education system."

The Balboa exchanges were part of Safir's broader effort to raise the social awareness of her students. Safir took her students to the state capitol in Sacramento to lobby for better school conditions. She assigned them to read Jonathan Kozol's book *Savage Inequalities,* a polemic about urban schools, which Safir had bought with money from an outside grant she and another teacher had secured. She gave them Richard Wright's *Native Son* and Lorraine Hansberry's *Raisin in the Sun,* a perennial school favorite, described in one teacher trot as being about "unfulfilled dreams, human motivation, and racial prejudice . . . dreams that are shaped by society's superficial standards."[7] She talked to them about bipolar societies and social pyramids, and, most significantly, had them read parts of the Brazilian

educator Paolo Freire's *Pedagogy of the Oppressed*, a document of social reform widely quoted in the late 1960s and early 1970s about curricula and
materials that make "oppression and its causes objects of reflection by the
oppressed" in the hope that "from that reflection will come their necessary
engagement in the struggle for their liberation. And in the struggle this
pedagogy will be made and remade."[8] Freire, who died in 1997, saw education as the path to liberation; the book elaborated an ongoing dialectic
among an awareness of oppression, education, and liberation. Safir, who's
too young to recall the sixties, says she learned about the book when she
was training to be a teacher at Stanford in the 1990s.

But as the participants tell it, it was mainly from the visits to other
schools—both to Marin and to better San Francisco public schools—that
Alondra and her classmates got the message and outraged sense of injustice that came with it. "The really good thing about this experience," said a
student who'd gone on an earlier Marin visit, "was that we didn't know how
screwed we were getting; now we understand." Later, when the district cut
its mismanaged budget and Balboa faced staffing cuts—Shane Safir was
one of those whose jobs were threatened—they went to a school board
meeting to protest both the cuts and the general conditions and mistreat-
ment of the school, and were further insulted when Bill Rojas, then the superintendent, kept walking out to take phone calls as they were trying to
make their case. "He's a jerk," said one afterward. They tried hard not to
break down as they read their statements to the board.[9]

After she became a named plaintiff in the American Civil Liberties
Union's adequacy suit against the state of California, Alondra, giving a deposition, was asked by one of the state's lawyers why she'd done it.

"It's the unfair conditions," she answered, "the fact that we didn't
have . . . enough textbooks to take home to do like homework, whereas
Marin Academy does, and that's unfair to us." She had seen the new per-
forming arts center, the science and computer facilities, the multimedia
workrooms, the theaters, and all the rest. At Balboa, Safir said, "the science
labs are a joke," lacking enough materials to do more than one or two experiments a year.[10] Even the old art room had been closed down; teachers,
working in makeshift rooms, scratched to find enough materials for projects. Students had to share textbooks, and sometimes, as in chemistry, they
spent the whole period reading or copying notes from an overhead projector because the books couldn't go home. And since they didn't have books
at home, they never could look anything up when they did their homework. "Our chemistry class and the other period's chemistry class," said
Alondra Jones, "shared the same book, like my health ed class. And so
when I got the book to use—and chemistry, it was kind of like a capitalist

society; it was dog eat dog—I had my book. That was all I was worried about."[11]

Some of Alondra Jones's complaints, and those of some other students as well, were tinged with adolescent hyperbole. Some sounded like echoes from Kozol's book. Some probably stretched the length of time when their classrooms were without enough desks or chairs from days into weeks, enlarged mice into rats, and recalled rooms as being in even worse shape than they actually were.

Patricia Gray, the most recent in a series of principals at Balboa, said a lot of it was exaggerated: she'd never heard many of the complaints registered by students like Alondra Jones. The charges that there weren't enough books were mostly false, the bathrooms were cleaned daily, there weren't nearly as many substitutes in classes as the students said, and she rarely heard complaints about heat or cold. She also said that, as one of her first acts after she became principal, she wrote a "movie policy," banning all films not related to the courses in which they were shown. Gray also spoke proudly about a couple of recent graduates who'd gone to Berkeley and were doing well, and when she was asked whether Balboa students were receiving a good education, she said yes. But Alondra Jones was hardly the only one who complained about subs, toilets, filth, and lack of books. She had company among both teachers and other students.

What's certain is that when Patricia Gray was named principal in 1999, the place was in chaos—the school, in her words, "hadn't stabilized." In the three years before she came, teacher turnover at the school exceeded 100 percent, and although it was now lower than it had been before she arrived, it was still substantial. Nearly 40 percent of her staff lacked full regular teaching credentials. On orders from downtown, moreover, she had to "consolidate" classes to help solve a district budget problem, meaning that she lost seven of her sixty-six teachers.

With the exception of ninth-grade English and math classes, which were limited to twenty under state law, Gray said, the average Balboa class had thirty-four or thirty-five students. (At Marin Academy, the average class had fifteen students. For its 385 students, Marin had nearly as many teachers, forty-nine, as Balboa had for its 1,200.) It was tempting for her best teachers to leave, she said; the pay was higher in San Mateo, just south of San Francisco, and hers was a tough school in which to teach. In places such as the Bay Area and Los Angeles, high housing costs made it particularly tough to attract teachers to inner-city schools. Like a lot of others, she believed that there should be combat pay for schools like hers. "You don't treat cancer like you treat the common cold."[12]

Gray also acknowledged that for security reasons, as in hundreds of other schools, bathrooms were unlocked only during lunch and (appropriately enough) "passing periods," the five or six minutes when students change classes. Students who needed to go at other times had to find a security guard to let them in.[13]

But by themselves none of the specifics, from the strings of subs to the bird droppings, were really so significant. What mattered, as the ever-articulate Alondra Jones said in a deposition, was the cumulative message: it was an insult to students—they were, as someone at Balboa said, "throwaway kids"—and Alondra Jones was smart enough to get it:

> You know what, in all honesty, I'm going to break something down to you. It makes you feel less about yourself you know, like you sitting here in a class where you have to stand up because there's not enough chairs, and you see rats in the buildings, the bathrooms is nasty. . . . Like I said, I visited Marin Academy, and these students, if they want to sit on the floor, that's because they choose to. And that just makes me feel less about myself because it's like the state don't care about public schools. . . . It really makes me feel bad about myself.
>
> Probably you can't understand where I'm coming from. . . . And I'm not the only person who feels that. . . . And I already feel that way because I stay in a group home because of poverty. Why do I have to feel like that when I go to school?
>
> Also, like the standards, they set real low standards for us. They have to. If we don't—if our test scores are the lowest, the standards are not set as high. So set standards like private schools have. Set high standards that Lowell has. Set high standards that Marin Academy has. You know, set high standards for me.
>
> Don't sit there and expect me to fail and then pass me old used-up textbooks and expect me to achieve from that. I have achieved that because I can persevere, obviously. I've been through a lot so I can persevere.[14]

Some of that was probably acquired from adults—a mix of edpolicy talk and homeboy language. Some probably also reflected the feelings of adults, many of whom appeared to be just as depressed and demoralized by the circumstances in which they worked. But by the time she finished her little outburst she was in tears.[15] Patricia Gray would say that Alondra Jones's record at Balboa was "erratic." But she had indeed persevered; she was about to graduate, had been admitted to a number of universities, including the University of California, and was preparing to go to Howard University in Washington, D.C., to begin her freshman year.

II

Like Tolstoy's unhappy families, dysfunctional schools are sometimes unhappy in their own fashion, depending on place, circumstances, and culture. More often, however, their troubles are variations on common themes. The adequacy lawsuits filed since the late 1980s resonate with those themes and with iterations of the financial inadequacies, inequities, and mismanagement that plaintiffs, and many others, associate both with the current shortage of classroom resources and with the low performance of students in failing schools, and which contribute to their perpetuation. One of the difficulties those suits face is that between the time they're brought and the time they come to trial the specific complaints they allege—a shortage of books and leaky ceilings in school A, the lack of Advanced Placement courses and laboratory equipment in school B—are dealt with, often as a result of the suit, only to pop up in other schools. It's like "whack-a-mole," said Michael Jacobs, an attorney with the San Francisco firm of Morrison and Foerster, who is working on one major adequacy suit in California. The reference is to the old carnival game in which the player uses a mallet to hit a succession of moles that pop out of holes; each time one is whacked, another pops up. Unless there is systemic reform, the game would go on forever. The same problem, of course, confronts the parent, the reporter, and the official evaluation team. The specific conditions at any given school are addressed, sometimes in whole, more often just in part, only to be replaced by identical failures at another school or by different problems at the original school.[16] Whack-a-mole.

In Ohio, after a survey in 1993 of the condition of the state's school buildings, Superintendent of Public Instruction John Theodore Sanders declared some students were "making do in a decayed carcass from an era long passed"—"dirty, depressing places." Another official, Jack D. Hunter, supervisor of school facilities with the Ohio Department of Education, testified that some 75 percent of Ohio's public school facilities "have asbestos that should be abated . . . either immediately or near-term." In one school in Wayne County, three hundred students were hospitalized after breathing carbon monoxide fumes leaking out of defective heaters and furnaces. In another district students were "breathing coal dust which is emitted into the air and actually covers the students' desks after accumulating overnight. Band members are forced to use a former coal bin for practice sessions where there is no ventilation whatsoever, causing students to complain of headaches."[17]

It makes for a long list. In one Ohio school there were maggot infestations behind the particleboard that had been installed to cover the peeling plaster; at another, raw sewage backed up onto the school playing fields from the school's ancient sewer system. At Miller Junior High in Shawnee, the principal and custodians "deliberately knocked plaster off the ceilings so that the plaster would not fall on the students during the day." And at Straitsville Elementary School in Perry County, as former student Christopher Thompson recalled it, "plaster was falling off the walls and cockroaches crawled on the restroom floors." The building gave him a "dirty feeling"; he would not use the bathroom at school because of the cockroaches. Later, according to the Ohio Supreme Court, Chris Thompson "had to contend with a flooded library and gymnasium, a leaky roof where rainwater dripped from the ceiling like a 'waterfall,' an inadequate library, a dangerously warped gymnasium floor, poor shower facilities, and inadequate heating. In fact, due to construction and renovation of the heating system, when Chris attended high school, there was no heat from the beginning of the fall of 1992 until the end of November or beginning of December. Students had to wear coats and gloves to classes and were subjected to fumes from the kerosene heaters that were fired up when the building became very cold."[18]

It's mostly banal stuff. You can compile such lists anywhere you look—in New York City, in Los Angeles, in rural Alabama or North Carolina, in Philadelphia, in Chicago. Many of the situations are so familiar that they're hardly noticed anymore except by the people who are stuck in those schools: falling ceiling tiles, leaking roofs, insufficient lighting, cafeterias and hallways converted to classrooms and corridors into makeshift lunchrooms, filthy or nonfunctional toilets, windows that don't open or don't shut, buildings where teachers and children freeze in the winter and swelter in the spring and fall (and sometimes both, depending on what part of the building they're in) and, where schools run year-round, as they do in many urban districts, in the summer as well.

In New York in 1998, after the teachers' union sued the district over the dangerous conditions of the buildings its members were required to teach in, "the court [in the words of a subsequent complaint] ordered the parties to agree to a judgment providing for a safety plan. The plan adopted involved the extensive use of temporary scaffolding to safeguard people but did not involve the actual repair of defective conditions. As a result of this judgment close to one third of all school buildings in New York City at the time of trial had sidewalk shedding around their exteriors—simply to ensure minimal safety, not in preparation for remedial measures."[19] In San Francisco's Bryant School, said eleven-year-old Carlos Ramirez, his teacher, Lily Malabed, would spray her students with water when things got too hot. Once, he said, he fainted because the room was too hot. He also said he never ate the school food because "the lunches were green." He was talking not about the salads or the spinach but about the hot dogs.[20] "The roaches and mice are really distracting and discouraging to my students," said Cynthia Artiga-Faupusa, a teacher at San Francisco's Luther Burbank Middle School. "They complain and regularly ask me why they have to go to school in a ghetto."

Poor city kids get the highest doses, but they're not the only ones. Other locations also suffer from such conditions as: student allergic reactions traced to classroom mildew and spores, classrooms "not conducive to learning because students cannot hear over the noise of window air conditioner units," and "labs" where the failed plumbing has long been disconnected and where the wiring was obsolete a half century ago (and, needless to say, where there are no Internet connections for computers, much less decent art or music rooms). In a large Oakland high school, said a teacher, "the only thing that designates a room as a science room is a sink." In rural North Carolina there are high school biology classrooms that, as described by a teacher there, have "only one sink that is clogged, no fume hood and few electrical outlets," and in a large Los Angeles high school the budget for laboratory supplies and equipment for ninety science classes with some twenty-seven hundred students runs between $6,000 and $10,000, an average of less than $3.70 per year per student. In Richmond, California, a junior high school principal testified about roof leaks into classrooms and hallways "almost every time we had a good rain." In Baltimore, a 1992 master facilities plan rated only 16 percent of the city's school buildings as being in good physical condition; 20 percent were deemed to be in poor condition. In the rural South, schools built for blacks in the 1940s and 1950s, in the era of segregation, were barely adequate when they went up.[21]

In 1997, the New York City schools, which then generated thirty-five thousand repair requests annually and which had completed twelve thousand repair projects in the prior year, had an official backlog of nearly twenty thousand repair projects—roofs, walls, windows, furnaces, wiring, plumbing—that had not been completed. "In one of my schools," testified Kathleen Cashin, a New York district superintendent in Brooklyn, "the ceiling in the hallway where kids walk all the time just collapsed." In another, "every time it rained, the children had to be moved out of the classroom. The wall would just get moist and start leaking. The stairways are rippled, I mean it is just rippled. So if I go there wearing anything but sneakers you have to be very careful walking up and down the stairs. I don't know why it is rippled but it is rippled all over the place."[22] In the same year, the State Education Department reported that 420 New York City schools required major modernization; 56 percent needed extensive roof work, 86 percent needed plumbing repairs, 79 percent had problems with their heating/

ventilating/air-conditioning systems, and more than half were inaccessible
to the disabled:

> The situation in New York City is at the breaking point [said a report
> by the State Board of Regents]. Decades of neglect, deferred mainte-
> nance and mismanagement have resulted in overcrowded class-
> rooms, leaking roofs and flooded gymnasiums. Parts of roofs and
> walls are dangerously falling apart through lack of timely repair. Un-
> healthful environments exist for many teachers and students. Re-
> sources have been wasted by energy-inefficient buildings. Large
> numbers of students have been denied access to science laboratories,
> technology or other learning environments necessary to meet the
> high standards needed for success in today's world. Current spend-
> ing in New York City is not even able to stabilize existing buildings
> and prevent further deterioration.[23]

Nor was it just New York City:

> In the rest of the state, from small rural school districts to the big
> cities, the practices of deferring maintenance and minimizing main-
> tenance and capital budgets in favor of competing demands are
> showing a steady decline toward the catastrophic conditions that
> exist in our largest city.[24]

With the deferred maintenance came the special problems of overcrowding—thousands of classes where teachers and students scurry
around the halls to find enough chairs, or where they double up or sit on
desks or on the floor as they did at Balboa, or where closets that have been
converted into offices, or where two or three classes are held simultaneously in gyms or cafeterias with each trying to hear over the noise of the
others, or the occasional places where students eat lunch under awnings in
the rain because there's not enough space to eat inside. In one Paterson,
New Jersey, elementary school in the early 1990s, where remedial classes
were conducted in a converted rest room, the kids ate lunch in the boiler
room; in a school in East Orange, New Jersey, lunch was eaten in shifts in
the first-floor corridor; in Irvington, New Jersey, a coal bin had been converted into a classroom.[25]

In some middle and high schools, the remedies include "service
classes," periods in which students run errands and do odd jobs for teachers because all the real classes at a given time are too full. Still more common is the experience of Los Angeles high school junior Glauz Diego, who
spent three days trying to get a sixth-period class. "I first tried wood shop,

but it was too crowded. Next I tried chemistry, but it was too crowded also. I ended up with soccer. . . . It's easy to get a sport because the field is so big." His sister Cindy, trying to find a class, was told to take Advanced Placement Spanish even though she'd already taken it and gotten a top score on the AP test. At Crenshaw High in Los Angeles, D'Andre Lampkin, a tenth grader who, like his twin brother, wanted to enroll in algebra, was told there weren't enough teachers—the classes were full—and was put into a "math investigations" class instead. Leticia Paniagua, who wants to be a brain surgeon and, in addition to her required courses at Los Angeles's Fremont High, sought an elective that she thought would help her chances to get into college, was told there was no room in the journalism course she wanted, so she was put in a cosmetology class. At Fremont, a good proportion of students for whom there's no room in academic courses are dumped into such classes.[26]

Almost inevitably in such schools, even schools in rural districts, teachers like Michael Keim, who teaches social studies at Hoke County (North Carolina) High School, have to become "roamers," the flying Dutchmen of the education system, who go from room to room "with a limited amount of equipment traveling with them" because they have no room of their own. Roamers—in some places they're "rovers" or "travelers"—migrate from class to class, usually pushing a shopping cart or towing a roll-around suitcase stuffed with whatever minimal teaching materials they need: books, charts, videos, lesson plans, all of which have to be unpacked and packed again for the next class. Of course they can't hang anything permanently on classroom walls. And to do any preparation in school, the roamers have to beg space from other teachers because the teachers' lounge isn't big enough for more than two or three people; sometimes they work out of their cars. Given the nearly universal pecking order in schools, sometimes enforced by tradition, sometimes by union contract, it is of course the beginning teachers, people who most need support and stability, who draw the roaming honors.[27] In Los Angeles, there's also a district policy that calculates capacity with "the aim that teachers will travel." (It's probably fortunate that the term *roamer* isn't used there, given the name of the superintendent of the huge system, former Colorado governor Roy Romer.)

And then there are more familiar space stretchers: New York City, which has roughly 60 percent of the state's poor and 73 percent of its ethnic minority students, stuffs five more kids into each elementary school classroom than the state average, seven more into each high school classroom.[28] And in parts of the city, as in many of the high schools in Queens, some of which enroll half again as many students as they were designed for, and in some cases double the number—Cardozo High School,

Francis Lewis High School, Newtown High School, Richmond Hill High School, William Cullen Bryant High School, and several others—the solution is double "end-to-end" sessions: from 7:00 A.M. to noon, from noon to 5:00. To do that, one period (of seven) had to be eliminated, which means a lot of students (as in Los Angeles) can't take the courses they want. If they're on the morning shift, they can't participate in sports or other after-school activities unless they have the money to return to school; for many on the afternoon shift, such activities may not be possible at all because their classes run too late.

But the system also creates less obvious difficulties. Ninth- and tenth-grade classes are offered only on the late (less desirable) shift, upper-level courses only on the early shift. As a consequence, as John Lee, the district's superintendent for Queens high schools, pointed out, "the older students cannot take the lower-level remedial courses they may need, while academically gifted younger students cannot take the advanced courses that would challenge and enrich them." It also, of course, inhibits social interaction between younger and older students and makes it still harder to recruit new teachers, who because of the pecking order usually get the afternoon shift but who in many cases have children of their own who get out of school at 3:00.[29] Necessarily, they also get the younger and, in general, the more difficult students. In 1999, only 56 percent of the students who started ninth grade in Lee's district in 1996 were still in school and had reached their senior year.

Still, when it comes to devices to alleviate schoolhouse overcrowding, there's little to match the surrealism of Los Angeles's year-round "Concept 6" multitrack schools. In the City of Angels, a considerable number of schools are now under construction. But for the thirty years after 1970, the city opened no general high school, and very few schools of any kind, despite the district's booming population of children, in part because there was too little money or open land, in part because the people who voted were not the people with children, in part because state school bond allocation formulas had been stacked against the district, and in part because the district was notoriously mismanaged. (In perhaps the most egregious such case on record, Los Angeles was on the way to completing its new $200 million Belmont Learning Center when inspectors belatedly discovered that it was going up on a toxic site—an old oil field oozing with poisonous hydrogen sulfide and methane. There was at least a possibility that the place could blow up.)[30]

Ever since the passage of California's tax-cutting Proposition 13 in 1978, "deferred maintenance" in public facilities has been a mainstay of budget writers and policy analysts. More than 25 percent of the state's students are housed in portable classrooms, which now crowd schoolyards and playgrounds like so many migrant camps. Altogether, 1.3 million California students are on some sort of year-round schedule. But Concept 6 is in a class by itself.[31]

In Los Angeles, some 240 schools with 328,000 students, nearly half the district's enrollment, are on multitrack schedules, most of them following the Concept 6 calendar. Because their schools are the most crowded, nearly all the multitrack students are black or Latino. Among those schools is Fremont High in South Central Los Angeles, a sprawling place, now surrounded by an eight-foot spike-topped steel fence, with 4,800 students, 90 percent of whom are Latino, 10 percent black. (In 2001–2, according to official state figures, the school also had one Asian student and two non-Hispanic whites.) Under the criteria defined by Robert Balfanz of Johns Hopkins University, who studies the problem, any school where the ninth-grade class has shrunk by 50 percent or more by twelfth grade is a "dropout factory." Fremont, whose ninth grade class of 1,573 in 1998–99 had shrunk to 438 seniors in 2001–2, qualified handsomely. When one teacher complained about overcrowding in her classes, said a colleague, "She was told to wait a while and 'attrition will take care of it.' This confirms a sense among many teachers at Fremont, including myself, that the district builds an expectation of a high dropout rate into its planning, creating a self-fulfilling prophecy."[32] Fremont's academic achievement, like Balboa's, is stuck near the bottom among California schools, even those serving similar low-income and minority populations.

To find enough classroom space at Fremont, the system, using Concept 6, assigns its students to one of three tracks.[33] Only two tracks are on campus at any given time, each for a total of 163 days a year rather than the usual 180. The A and C tracks follow a vaguely normal school calendar: the A track begins in late August (the dates are for 2002–3) and runs through Christmas, then, after two months' break, runs again from early March to the end of June. The C track starts around July 1, runs to October 22, and then, after a break in November and December, runs again from early January through April 30. But to make things come out right, the B track is in school from July 1 to August 23, then off for two months, then back from October 23 to Christmas, then back from January 2 to March 5, then off another two months, then back from May 1 to June 27. These two-month chunks are called "mesters."

Since not all courses can be offered on all tracks, students who are (in more ways than one) on the wrong track may discover that a class they want, or may need for college admission, isn't offered on their track. Students on the B track (who are not in school in March and April) who want to take Advanced Placement exams may also learn too late that they have to take the AP tests in May, well before they finish the courses on which the tests are based. If they want help, they have to come back during their off-track time—provided they can find someone to give it. Sometimes they also have to take critical tests, including the state's exit exam, a day or two after they come back from one of those extended breaks. And because places like Fremont have only one counselor for every six hundred or seven hundred students, there's little chance that students will get much counseling help, especially on exotic matters like college admission. The B track students, meanwhile, can't commit to a vacation job for more than two months at a time. (For working parents of elementary school kids, of course, it's a special headache.) Off-track students who are on athletic teams or in activities like band or chorus have to come back during their break if they want to take part. At Jefferson High, another multitrack Los Angeles school, students who finished first-year French discovered that second-year French wasn't offered on their track the following year, so they took Spanish even though most already knew Spanish and even though the University of California then required two years or more of at least one foreign language.[34]

Teachers such as Steve Bachrach, who teaches at Jefferson High—and some students as well—say the 163-day year doesn't give them nearly enough time for adequate instruction in most courses, especially when "kids come in reading at a third-grade level."[35] That's often true even for good teachers with up-to-date materials, a combination that, in any case, isn't often found in urban schools. Margaret Roland, the principal at Fremont in 2001–2, responds that since the district adds a few minutes to each class period, students on multitrack schedules are getting the same number of minutes of instruction as those in other California schools, who go to school 180 days a year. But the seventeen lost days leave less time for homework, though that may not make much difference if there aren't enough books and materials for the kids to take home. One school administrator said that if the class doesn't cover all the required material in 163 days, it's the teacher's fault.[36]

But the multitrackers were still better off than the students at Fremont and other overcrowded Los Angeles schools who can't be accommodated even with the multitrack system at their home schools and are transported, often for as much as two hours each way, to other schools. The Fremont kids had to show up at school by 6:15 every morning for the bus ride through Los Angeles rush-hour traffic to a school on the other side of the city that had room. In order not to miss the bus back in the afternoon, they couldn't participate in sports or other extracurricular activities. Even so, they didn't get back to Fremont until 4:30. Not surprisingly, Fremont students struggled not to be bused despite Fremont's many problems. When she was asked about it in 2001, Roland, who'd never seen the other school—she didn't even know which school it was or where it was—said she didn't think busing kids affected their learning because "it's the travel time, not the instructional time they are missing." [37]

III

For the most part, the crucial gaps in the schools serving the nation's neediest kids—and, to repeat, many others as well—are hardly exotic or even colorful. They stem from the lack of good teachers, books, or materials, and often all three. Recent data, particularly an analysis of teacher qualifications in New York City schools generated by Hamilton Lankford, an economist at the State University of New York at Albany, puts those generalizations in the starkest terms. In a grim version of those macro images showing the perfect geometric patterns of insect eyes or leaves or flowers, Lankford traced the near-perfect association of weak teachers with low-income schools: the higher the poverty rate, as measured by free or reduced-price lunches, the lower the scores of the teachers on their own preprofessional examinations. [38]

In his massive analysis covering the 1997–8 school year, Lankford divided New York's schools into quintiles, ranking schools from those with the fewest students qualifying for free or reduced-priced lunches (quintile 1) to those with the most (quintile 5). He then calculated average teacher scores on a variety of required state teacher certification tests—the Liberal Arts and Sciences Test, the Elementary Content Specialty Test—and certain national teacher exams. Among the teachers in New York City's highest-poverty schools (quintile 5), 42 percent of elementary teachers had failed the Liberal Arts and Sciences Test at least once. In the schools with the fewest poverty-stricken kids, only 16 percent had ever failed. Among teachers outside New York City, the failure rate was under 7 percent. The same was true of the median scores on those tests: the first time that teachers in the highest-poverty schools took the arts and sciences test they got an average score of 225, barely above the 220 passing mark; for teachers in low-poverty schools, it was 247; for teachers outside New York, it was 257. Between them, going through the intermediate quintiles, there was an almost perfect curve, as if nature itself was at work.

Lankford found the same pattern in the state's test assessments of elementary school teaching skills and in its tests of high school teachers' subject matter knowledge. Among all of New York's high school math teachers, 47 percent failed the state's Math Content Specialty Test at least once. Outside New York, the failure rate was 21 percent. In the high-poverty schools, moreover, nearly 40 percent of teachers were working with a provisional credential or no teaching credential at all. In low-poverty schools, the number was under 20 percent. Outside New York City, it was 15 percent. Lankford also found that New York City teachers graduated from colleges with weaker academic profiles (in terms of SAT scores and high school grade point averages of entering students, and in ranking in college guides) than teachers outside the city. And some were—and are— truly awful. John Murphy, a former superintendent in two major school systems, called to testify by New York State in its attempt to show that New York City's schools passed constitutional muster, said that after a visit to one school, he changed his whole rating scheme:

> During my five days of observation, I visited 56 classrooms. Normally I rate teachers from below average, to average, to above average, and to excellent when I prepare reports. After this experience, I needed to create a new category—that is "terrible"! I visited a few classrooms where the children would have been better served if they did not come to school on that day.[39]

Making things still more complicated in New York were provisions in the United Federation of Teachers (UFT) contract that, in an effort to protect tenured teachers against capricious negative evaluations from principals who just didn't like them, not only made the evaluation process extremely complicated, as is the case in many other places, but also gave teachers who got unsatisfactory ratings the right to remain in the school for another three years. Combined with the fear that even an innocent transfer would leave a principal with a vacancy he or she couldn't fill, that put a powerful damper on any negative ratings.[40] It's not surprising, therefore, that while dedicated teachers struggle to make things work, some simply blow the job off. A teacher, observing some fisticuffs between two children on an Oakland, California, elementary school playground, called it to the attention of the teacher who was supposed to be supervising the playground, to which she replied, "I don't do fights."

The patterns appear to be similar elsewhere, though the system is not always as byzantine. A recent audit of Chicago's eighty-one worst-performing schools showed that more than one-fifth of their teachers were not certified, that some had no formal training at all, and that many had either failed or never taken the state's basic teacher test in reading and math. In another survey, one-third of the teachers in sixty-six South Chicago schools were found to lack certificates.[41] Teaching jobs in Baltimore are so unattractive that the district hires 62 percent of the people who apply. (In most districts in Maryland, the figure is about 10 percent.) In California, according to the Center for the Future of Teaching and Learning, an independent research organization, of forty-two thousand teachers, some 14 percent (in 2001) didn't have full credentials. Of first- and second-year teachers (in 2001), nearly half didn't have a credential. In 41 percent of the state's schools—mostly white, Asian, and middle-class—there were few or no uncredentialed teachers. But where over 90 percent of students were black and/or Latino, 26 percent of teachers were underqualified. In the lowest-performing schools, one of four teachers was underqualified.[42] (Nationally in 1999–2000, 19 percent of all secondary school classes were taught by people who had neither majored nor minored in college in the subject they were teaching; in high-poverty schools it was 34 percent. In math in high-poverty schools it was 40 percent.)[43]

In some places the numbers, already depressing, concealed even bleaker situations, not merely because a credential is only the crudest indicator of teaching ability (there are, of course, also people without credentials who are great teachers) but because all the turnover and all those subs weren't really measurable at all. Here's twelve-year-old Randell Hasty in 1999, at the time a seventh grader in rural North Carolina, answering a lawyer's questions. Lots of students can tell similar stories:

A. In the sixth grade, I had a substitute that stayed for nine weeks, and this year the substitute stayed for four weeks.

Q. Four weeks this year?

A. Yes, ma'am.

Q. This year in your math and science class, what kind of work did you do when your substitute teacher was there?

A. We read out of the book and answered questions.

Q. And then last year in the sixth grade, you said you had a substitute for nine weeks?

A. Yes, ma'am.

Q. What class was that in?

A. Math and science.

Q. At what point in the year did the substitute teacher come?

A. At the beginning of the year, and we had—we had seven teachers that year that weren't teachers. It was six substitutes and one teacher—two teachers.

Q. Is that in your math and science class?

A. Yes, ma'am.

Q. Had seven teachers in that one class?

A. Yes, ma'am.

Q. And you said you had two permanent teachers?

A. Yes, ma'am.

Q. Did you start with a permanent teacher?

A. Yes, ma'am.

Q. And what happened to her?

A. She left, and we got substitutes.

Q. Okay. And how many substitutes did you have?

A. We had five substitutes.

Q. And at what point in the year did you get another permanent teacher?

A. At the end of the year.

Q. What kind of work were you doing in that sixth grade math and science class when the substitutes were there?

A. We were reading out of the book.[44]

Another student in the same district told about the subs he'd had, including one eighth-grade social studies teacher who never assigned any reading except as punishment for classroom misbehavior. "That was her way of telling us to be quiet; if you don't be quiet, then you got to read two chapters tonight for homework."[45] At the start of the 1999–2000 school year, 27 of the 102 certified staff positions at Hoke County High School, chosen by a court as representative of a large class of North Carolina rural schools, were vacant; of nine mathematics teaching positions, five were vacant; of nine in English, seven were open. There were other vacancies in chemistry, general science, and foreign languages. Those vacancies were filled, sometimes for many months, by strings of substitutes who were not required to be certified, or to be college graduates, or to have any qualifications in the subjects they were teaching. (One math sub had not graduated from high school.) On average, students in such schools spent an average of eighteen days a year—10 percent of all class time—in classes taught by subs. Not surprisingly, a state study also found that teachers who came from the top ranks of their college classes were much more likely to leave the poor rural schools. Those who had the weakest records stayed. In its desperation, according to school administrators, the district "has tried to recruit teachers in unusual locales, including the checkout stand at a Wal-Mart."[46]

All that turnover and all the substitutes marching through those classrooms will never be counted in any set of official statistics. (And what is "a permanent teacher" who leaves at the beginning of the year?) At the same time many districts, and sometimes whole states, fudge the numbers they do report. Under the new federal No Child Left Behind Act (NCLB), which was a keystone of George W. Bush's 2000 election campaign and his first-year domestic agenda, all schools getting Title I funds, money earmarked for schools with high concentrations of students from low-income families, have until 2005–6 to get "highly qualified" teachers into their classrooms. That, for all its good intentions, is a little like King Canute commanding the waves to stop.

The Canute command quickly produced its own fudges. Responding to a U.S. Department of Education survey, the District of Columbia school district, one of the nation's most famously dysfunctional districts, reported that all its teachers were qualified.[47] Similarly, in 2002, New York City, after decades of hiring large proportions of underqualified teachers—and in the face of new federal and state regulations that prohibit the city from putting any uncertified new teacher into its worst schools and requires all New York City teachers to be certified by September 2003—suddenly claimed that because of higher pay and other reforms, 90 percent of its new hires were certified. But as Arthur Levine, the president of Columbia University's Teachers College, gently pointed out, the claim was "disingenuous."

New York had indeed raised beginning salaries. But it had also instituted what many, including Levine, regarded as a watered-down alternative certification program under which the city recruited people in mid-career, plus young college graduates, gave them a month of intensive education courses, and sent them—again—into the neediest schools. That may or may not be as good as the traditional route—in some instances, given the frailty of many traditional ed-school programs, it may even be better—but any celebration was obviously premature. As one measure of how incredible New York City's latter-day claims about its cadre of newly certified teachers really were, in 1998, 56 percent of its new hires were uncredentialed. In that same year, nearly 36 percent of Manhattan high school teachers had two years or less of experience. And so far no one knows how any group of new recruits will do or how long they'll stay. Of all the people who begin in the classroom in this country, more than a third quit before they finish five years. In urban areas, according to Stanford's Linda Darling-Hammond, the founding director of the Commission on Teaching and America's Future, it's half.[48] For Levine, it was yet another betrayal of poor and minority students, who, under one label or another, would still get a disproportionate share of unqualified and inexperienced teachers.[49]

There were similar reports from other cities that, under pressure from NCLB, were in theory to have only "highly qualified" teachers in the core subjects in all schools getting federal Title I funds. The federal deadline was 2005–6, but the law also prohibited districts from hiring new teachers who were not "highly qualified" by 2002–3.

Although the merits of the objective were beyond dispute, the "highly qualified" requirement, like some other parts of the law, was almost certainly beyond reach without massive infusions of money that neither the federal government nor the states were prepared to spend. Districts such as Chicago or Houston, using aggressive recruiting, signing bonuses, housing allowances, and other inducements, and (in Houston) hiring teachers from Puerto Rico, Spain, and even Russia—and sometimes bringing in retired military people or others looking for second careers—claimed to have found good applicants even for inner-city schools. Most have not, and there was doubt even about the claims of many that had. As soon as the law went into effect, both the states and the Department of Education began looking for what one teacher union official called "wiggle room" in the definition of "highly qualified" and a range of other provisions.

Probably the most blatant wiggle was California's, where the State Board of Education, in a sort of miraculous laying-on of hands, submitted data to comply with the new federal law that simply redefined things in such a way that its forty-thousand uncredentialed teachers were suddenly "highly qualified," among them thousands who had no credentials and had barely started in the classroom. That, said Rep. George Miller, one of NCLB's liberal co-sponsors, in a letter to the board, was an "audacious and truth-defying step." It showed, he said, "a lack of regard for students, parents, and taxpayers. . . . By declaring every teacher 'highly qualified,' the state has essentially abandoned any effort at reform. Instead, the board has in effect voted for inertia."[50] Even California officials acknowledged that the state had a horrendous "distribution" problem for which they had no ready solution. No one has ever tried to measure what such fudges do to the morale of able teachers who have the experience and qualifications that really deserve that distinction.

Nationally, in the mid-1990s, urban schools hired twice as many unqualified new teachers as other schools. In some schools, indeed, it was almost inevitable, since they refused to hire any new people until enrollment had "stabilized" two or three weeks after school started:

> And so [said a California teacher] for a whole month there are classrooms that have way too many children, and then at the end of that month's period, the district would say, okay, you have this many students, we can allocate you this many more teachers to make more classrooms. And then at that point the students who have now been in one classroom for a month . . . are then pulled out of that class and an overflow class is made for them, which a lot of times is at first run by a sub. Because at the moment the month ends and we're allocated a teacher, then we start the hiring process, so it might be a few more weeks before we have the permanent teacher hired. And a lot of times that sub is someone with an emergency credential or noncredentialed who hasn't been through an education program of any sort. And the teacher who is generally hired is usually a noncredentialed teacher because by September or October of a school year all

credentialed teachers have already been placed in a position in other schools.[51]

In New York State, 31 percent of new hires in urban districts lacked full credentials; in nonurban schools, it was 10 percent. (In one New York City elementary school in 1999, half the teachers were uncertified, in one junior high it was 44 percent, in another it was 39 percent.)[52] In 2001, in the multitrack high-poverty subdistrict in South Central Los Angeles of which Fremont High is a part—altogether, there are fourteen elementary and secondary schools with some fifty-five thousand students—49 percent of the track B teachers were uncredentialed.[53] In California overall, where a class size reduction program in the primary grades put particular stress on the system, and where a lot of qualified urban teachers left for suburbs that offered better pay, better conditions, better support, and fewer troubled kids, 30 percent of new hires in urban schools were uncredentialed; in the state as a whole it was 15 percent. Those numbers are particularly significant because high proportions of inexperienced and undertrained teachers produce a kind of critical mass that strains a whole school. Where more than 20 percent are inexperienced, in the judgment of Margaret Gaston and her colleagues at the Center on the Future of Teaching and Learning, "the school has little or no capacity to improve."[54]

The problem may be even more acute in the ranks of administrators. The high turnover and administrative chaos at Fremont was an outsize illustration of a nationally recognized problem, not an anomaly. According to a survey for the nation's two major principals' associations in 1998, there were shortages of qualified applicants for principals' jobs "among all kinds of schools (rural, urban, suburban) and among all levels" as well as high turnover rates. Fewer and fewer people wanted the job, in large part because of stress and lack of support. Not surprisingly, the toughest schools to staff were also the ones serving the highest percentage of poor and at-risk students. In New York City in November 1999, 212 principals' jobs were open, meaning that roughly one in five of New York's thousand-plus schools didn't have a permanent principal. The following year, 163 New York schools began the year with a substitute principal. Meanwhile, as a Los Angeles teacher said, "it is widely known that incompetent principals are routinely transferred from school and not removed from leadership roles."[55] In school administration, if the captain and officers of the *Titanic* can get themselves rescued, they're pretty certain of getting a new ship.

As should be obvious, the schools with the poorest students—and often the least experienced teachers, who need the most help—also tend to be those where books, materials, and other resources are scarcest and where curricula are thinnest. The differences the New Jersey Supreme Court listed in 1990 could apply to countless other states. In Princeton, students began a foreign language in the fifth grade and a second language in ninth grade; Paterson began its foreign language program in the tenth grade. Princeton (in 1989) had one computer for every eight students; East Orange had one for every forty-three and Camden one for every fifty-eight. In Princeton, the high school had seven science labs, "each with built-in equipment. . . . Many poorer districts offer science classes in labs built in the 1920s and 1930s, where sinks do not work, equipment such as microscopes is not available, supplies for chemistry and biology classes are insufficient, and hands-on investigative techniques cannot be taught."[56] In South Brunswick, the industrial arts program offered an automotive shop, a woodworking shop, a metal shop, a graphics shop, and a greenhouse for a course in horticulture; in Camden, "state-of-the-art equipment is not purchased; the old equipment in the classrooms is not maintained or repaired."

In Ohio in the early 1990s, according to Howard Fleeter of the School of Public Policy and Management at Ohio State University, the school districts ranked in the top 25 percent of assessed valuation per pupil offered an average of 399 Advanced Placement courses per district; the districts ranked in the bottom 25 percent offered 40 Advanced Placement courses. Jodi Altier, the valedictorian at Miller High School in Corning, Ohio—she had a 4.0 average—"applied to Notre Dame University, but was not accepted. When she went to be interviewed at Notre Dame, she was asked how many Advanced Placement courses she had taken. Jodi did not even know what Advanced Placement meant. No Advanced Placement courses are offered in the Miller High School."[57]

The many schools where teachers have only one set of books for several classes—if they have that—and where students therefore can't take books home have become almost a cliché. It's also a commonplace that where there are books and other necessary materials, they're often worn, covered with graffiti, and, like many library reference books, outdated. In the mid-1990s, when Alabama ACLU lawyer Adam Cohen traveled around the state, he found a Selma high school student "who told us he was having trouble keeping up in physics because his school could afford only four physics textbooks, and when he wanted to do homework, he had to call around to see if anyone was done with the book." And as have many people in other states, Cohen found ramshackle elementary school libraries with books that "cheerfully predicted that 'one day man will walk on the moon.'"[58] At Rainier Beach High in South Seattle, students walked out of school to protest the lack of textbooks to take home. The district said it was providing enough money; officials at the school said it was not, in part because with the high turnover in enrollment some students who left never returned their books. But that was hardly the fault of the students who remained and who were caught in the bureaucratic cracks. A school running out of textbooks, one student's grandmother told a reporter, was as unthinkable as McDonald's running out of hamburgers.[59]

In his testimony in November 1999 before North Carolina Superior Court Judge Howard W. Manning Jr., social studies teacher Michael Keim, one of the Hoke High School "roamers," showed a school globe—he estimated that it was twenty-five years old—that he uses in his history classes. "It's a little outdated," he said. "Rhodesia is visible on this map. . . . The Soviet Union is still intact. . . . Czechoslovakia is still one country. And I believe there aren't any problems in the Balkans because it's still just one huge Yugoslavia."

"How about Gaul?" asked the judge. "Is Gaul on there?"

"Gaul?"

(A few minutes later, perhaps trying to play off Manning's joke, a lawyer for the state, defending the status quo, asked whether, as a history teacher, Keim wouldn't prefer the old globe so students would know "the countries that used to be in place as opposed to the ones they now call themselves.")[60]

Teachers have come up with all sort of devices—copying pages from books to hand out as substitute homework resources, buying materials out of their own pockets, borrowing sets of books from other classes—to get around the book problem, which sometimes leads to genuinely bizarre results. At Belmont High in Los Angeles, for example, which was to be replaced by the toxin-plagued new Belmont Learning Center, Erika Cabrera and her classmates in tenth-grade U.S. history began the year with no books, either to take home or to use in the classroom. "Therefore, the teacher lectured all the time and put notes on the board," but because the teacher talked very fast and there were no other materials, the students complained they couldn't keep up. It wasn't her fault, the teacher shot back, that there were no books.

By the fifth week, the teacher did borrow some books from another class, though still not enough for students to take home for homework. "Then our teacher needed to return the books to the class where she got them, and we again had no books. Finally, the teacher borrowed books from another class, but again we did not have enough to take home with us. It was a real problem that we were using this second set of borrowed books, because they were really old—maybe ten years old or older. Also, the tests we took were based on material that was not in the second set of borrowed books. Therefore we had open-book tests, but [in another wonderful Catch-22] the textbooks were useless because the subjects of the tests were not in the books we had."[61] In a Rockefeller Foundation—

funded survey of teachers in 2002 used by the ACLU in its suit against the state of California, pollster Lou Harris found that nearly a third of teachers said they didn't have enough textbooks for their classes. (One Los Angeles high school puts gift certificates from Kinko's into new teachers' "goody baskets.")[62] From the survey data, Harris also concluded that 1.1 million of the state's 6 million students attended schools in which at least 20 percent of the teachers were undercredentialed, an estimate that jibes with other surveys, and that 1 million were in schools in which the bathrooms were not working or closed.[63]

IV

Nothing in this accumulation of statistics and stories, however, can fully describe the endemic chaos of the worst schools—a combination of high turnover in superintendents of the separate regional districts that big city systems like New York and Los Angeles are divided into and the corresponding turnover of teachers and administrators at the local sites, the endless breakdowns of physical facilities, student emergencies, complicated union work and seniority rules negotiated downtown, and rapidly changing programs and curricula, some dictated by districts, some handed down by legislators and state boards of education, a growing number by federal legislation. The rules imposed by bureaucracy and contract alone were enough to hamstring even the most dedicated principals, who in many districts were unable to hire the best teachers when others, through union seniority rules, had "bumping rights." In many cases, they couldn't hire anyone at all for a vacant spot until all teachers with seniority had gotten their chance at the job first, which sometimes took the process into midsummer, by which time the best people were gone.[64]

At times the book problem may be merely a problem of money, but as Maureen DiMarco, a senior executive at Houghton Mifflin, one of the country's leading textbook publishers, points out, in some districts there's a reluctance to commit textbook funds until the district is confident that there won't be another decree the next week that will force programs to change again. And when there are books, they often join school walls and toilet stalls as free-fire zones in the battles of the taggers. Because the infatuation in American education with fat, glossy texts crammed with full-color pictures and charts has driven up the cost of many books to $70 apiece, and sometimes more, it's even more understandable that districts shy from any attempt to deal books out too generously. At Fremont High in Los Angeles, when "an unknown sub" replaces a regular teacher for a few days, the regular teacher is asked to lock up the books while she's gone.[65]

Mixed in with all this are the elements of sheer incompetence, mismanagement, and sometimes outright corruption. In New York City in the 1980s and 1990s, well after backward little Kentucky tried to outlaw schoolhouse nepotism and cronyism, five of the decentralized city system's thirty-two "community"-controlled districts were nests of politics, cronyism, and at times outright theft by employees and board members. In certain districts in the Bronx and Brooklyn, where board members were sometimes described as godfathers or godmothers and administrators as the "pieces" they controlled, schools were regarded as personal fiefdoms, and school employees often expected to provide personal services to their godfather—principals working in a community board member's garden or rewiring his house. As described by Edward Stancik, special commissioner of investigation for the New York City School District:

> If you, as a Board member, name a principal at a particular school, you would refer to that principal as your piece. In other words you would say, for example, "I want that piece." Or, "I need more pieces." Or, "I've only got one piece." That would be referring to the principals that you named. Godfather and Godmother would refer to the particular Board member who was the benefactor of that principal. So a principal would say that his Godfather or Godmother was the Board member who appointed—not appointed officially, but who . . . was allowed to name—that principal.

> Q. And did those names indicate any particular type of relationship that existed between the Godfather, for example, and the piece?
> A. Well, the Board members had enormous control over the [principals] that they named.[66]

Every time Stancik and his people turned over a rock, there was another bit of slime. There was bribery, there were fancy dinners and parties for board members and their friends, there were "credit pools" where "a large number of bogus expenses are approved so that an amount of money is accumulated that is ready for disbursement on a moment's notice, but the supplies really [don't] exist so the money can go for whatever purposes the person in charge of it wishes and in some cases it was used to pay for trips. . . . [T]he credit pool was this sort of slush fund built up on phony vouchers which were put up for supplies that were never purchased."[67] The creators of the thirty-two semiautonomous community school districts, which have since been gradually stripped of their power and which the state scheduled for final dissolution by mid-2003, "did not intend to establish patronage mills where, every three years, teachers and administrators are forced to become foot soldiers in their bosses' campaigns and educational priorities take a back seat to political imperatives." But that's what some had become, with predictable consequences. In one district, Stancik found that because of the turmoil, there'd been five district superintendents in six and a half years, teacher turnover was "distressingly high," and its schools had "sunk to the very bottom of the citywide scores measuring performance in math and reading."[68] The kids had become an afterthought.

The Stancik investigation also turned up some genuinely creative career-enhancing strategies, particularly one cooked up by principal Marlene Lazar of Brandeis High School on Manhattan's Upper West Side and the school's chief of computer services, Hal Charney. Together they developed an automated system to inflate the school's attendance data by eliminating nearly half the student absences from the reports they sent downtown, thus ballooning her budget and teaching staff and earning special credit for herself for reducing truancy. Worse, says the investigator's report, which was issued in 2000, instead of using the extra teachers to improve instruction, Lazar relieved them of much classroom duty and assigned them to phony jobs with titles such as "cafeteria dean," thereby denying students 154 teaching periods a day. "Brandeis teachers," said Stancik's report, "viewed the comp time positions as perks, and these jobs were in high demand." By failing to report dropouts, or falsely showing they'd reenrolled, Lazar allegedly also created "phantom students" enrolled in phantom classes.[69]

The undercount of dropouts is almost universal, in part because it depends on district self-reporting, which tends to be sloppy anyway. And since districts try to keep their enrollment, and thus their state and federal funding, as high as possible, it makes it sloppier still. Every time a student leaves the rolls, it costs the school and district upward of $4,000 annually, and often a lot more. In district after district and state after state, therefore, official annual high school dropout rates of 1 to 4 percent simply don't make sense when ninth-grade rolls—the 1,573 at Fremont in Los Angeles, for example—are compared to twelfth-grade enrollment (of 438) three years later, much less to the number of graduates at the end of twelfth-grade. Even if one discounts the effects of ninth-grade classes swollen by students who are, in effect, being held back because they failed to master eighth-grade work in middle school, the difference is huge. In 1999, to use one striking example, the Texas Education Agency, trying to put luster on George W. Bush's education record—sometimes called the "Texas miracle"—issued numbers purporting to show that even as the state's test scores had been rising in the previous decade, dropout rates had been cut from an annual 6.1 percent in 1989–90 to an incredible 1.6 percent in 1998–9. But the state's own numbers also showed that while there were

266,000 seventh graders enrolled in Texas schools in 1992–3, only 197,000 (74 percent) graduated six years later. For Hispanics the attrition in grades seven through twelve was 40 percent. In California, which in 2002 claimed that 11 percent of its students had dropped out between grades nine and twelve in the prior three years, there were just under 366,000 students enrolled in twelfth-grade; there had been 468,000 in ninth grade in 1998–9.[70]

At times the dropout number-fudging becomes truly astounding. In 1996–7 the official seventh-grade enrollment of the class of 2002 in all of Los Angeles was 44,120. By 2001–2, there were 29,206 left. Of every three students, one was gone. Meanwhile, L.A.'s Manual Arts High School, an inner-city school that was 80 percent Latino, 20 percent black, and virtually all poor, claimed that it had a dropout rate approaching zero, that virtually all of its graduates had completed all the courses required for admission to the University of California, and that 80 percent were going on to college. That got the school's principal, Wendell Greer, a press conference with President Bill Clinton in 1999 in recognition of the school's distinguished accomplishment. Those claims, as subsequently disclosed by the rambunctious *LA Weekly*, turned out to be mostly phony. The only wonder was how Greer could have maintained the façade so long.[71]

Perhaps the saddest story of educational deterioration and insult— again, perhaps uniquely, from New York—is almost a footnote to the adequacy drama. But it's revealing nonetheless. From 1903, when the city's Public School Athletic League (PSAL) was founded, until about 1970, the city's schools maintained what was widely regarded as something approaching a model school sports and physical education program, with a wide array of sports and intense community interest in interscholastic competition in the major sports. In the generation between World War II and the early 1970s, games between schools like Brooklyn Tech or Lincoln and Erasmus, sometimes played at Ebbets Field, drew thousands of fans and, of course, intensified community cohesion and school loyalty. Along the way, those programs also produced some singularly gifted athletes. But in the thirty years since, the city's once-proud school sports and physical education programs have been starved and neglected, the PSAL's budget cut again and again. Fields and gyms were allowed to deteriorate to the point where some became unusable, and sports equipment became scarcer and scarcer—by 1999, the district had reduced its five-periods-per-week phys ed program to an average of two and a half periods and quit buying school gym equipment altogether. Teams were getting nothing for uniforms or transportation; sometimes coaches or school administrators would pass the hat among teachers to pay for the bus that would get the team to events.

In the system as a whole, there was one gym teacher for every 730 elementary school students, double the ratio in the rest of the state. At a time when there was more and more talk about the importance of physical fitness, when obesity was becoming an endemic problem among the young, and when it was widely believed that school sports were a major factor in encouraging adolescents to stay in school, New York, in the words of an angry *New York Times* report (1999), "all but walked off the field."[72] Since 1999, largely because of the *Times* story, some fields have been scheduled for restoration, in part with private funds raised through an independent group called Take the Field, but, according to Mary Musca, the organization's executive director, and a survey prepared for the reform group New Visions for Public Schools, New York's basic neglect of sports and phys ed continued. As of 2001, the survey showed, 41 percent of the city's elementary schools and 23 percent of high schools had no regular phys ed classes.[73] While nobody will claim that high school basketball, or maybe even gym class, is a constitutional right, as an indicator of neglect and indifference, this may be among the most telling.

IV

Within schools like Fremont in Los Angeles, it's a never-ending crisis even for the best people, whom, with some wonderful exceptions, those running our toughest schools often are not. Consider Margaret Roland, who'd just become principal at Fremont when her school became a leading exhibit in the suit against the state. Roland was the school's fifth principal in five years. Two years before, the district had sent in a team from downtown to help manage the school after students walked out in protest during the administration of Roland's predecessor's predecessor.[74] The protesting students said they wanted a principal, a subtlety that seems to have escaped some of the adults: Fremont, the adults said, had a principal.

Roland had been passed over several times in her pursuit of a principal-ship and she was surprised when she got this one, but by the end of her first year she'd barely come to know the place. In her deposition she said she didn't know how many of her 210 teachers lacked full credentials. And although she learned about the court case, with its string of complaints about the lack of books, inaccessible toilets, high-turnover teaching staffs, and overcrowding, soon after she got there, she didn't follow up and never conducted an investigation. Nor did she know her school's ranking on the state's Academic Performance Index—she knew it was low—or what the state expected from Fremont in terms of improvement. If she had more money, she said, she'd hire more counselors and buy more books: "novels, reading for pleasure." She, too, had been asked by students, and almost in the same words as had Patricia Gray in San Francisco, "Ms. Roland, are we going to get a permanent teacher?" The same, of course, could also be asked about administrators, even about principals. At the time Roland testified, the school had four assistant principals. One was a veteran, three were new that year, and one position was unfilled. At that point, even among its "permanent" teachers, between 25 and 30 percent were working on emergency permits.[75]

The sheer bureaucratic magnitude of the system itself was overwhelming, not just for Roland, but for the one assistant principal who had any real experience at the school: the reports, the ever-changing procedures and programs and committees, the negotiations with union representatives about things as mundane as the bell schedule, and of course the endless meetings—leadership council, SHAPO (the senior high assistant principals' organization), the local district meetings. Even labels changed: beginning in 2000, it was no longer permissible to have anything called reading classes in high school because it implied remedial reading for dummies. So in order not to put off students, the classes were renamed "academic literacy." In schools generally, euphemisms sprout like weeds. In Fremont people constantly "dialogue," busing is the "capacity adjustment program," and the box-like portable classrooms that are eating up acres and acres of playgrounds and other open space are called "bungalows." One administrator said she could tell that the most recent set of portables that arrived on her campus were extremely old because they had real wood in them.

At Fremont also, "one of the young ladies did have a problem with a rape situation." Euphemism, as always, functions to conceal conditions that would seem far more ugly—and would require quick intervention—if they were described candidly. No one knows how many rape "situations" and other violent acts aren't reported by school administrators, even in the face of parental demands, either out of fear they will get themselves in trouble or simply because they don't want another mess to deal with. Any number of students say they don't feel safe at school—for parents, safe schools is the highest priority—in part because school employees ignore as much as they can. In a Richmond, California, middle school, a student reported, "My friend was chased by other students who were throwing things and yelling at her. I tried to help my friend get away from the students who were harassing her so that she could get to the office for help. A security guard saw what was happening, but the guard did nothing."[76]

And, of course, there are the constant emergencies, from teachers who suddenly quit (and for whom no sub can immediately be rounded up by Sub Finder, the automated system downtown) to food fights in the cafeteria. "Sometimes we let our operational needs drive us," said Fremont assistant principal Marcia Hines. "We have emergencies with pipes, we have emergencies with floors, we have someone who needs to go home because they did something or other." Every day, the school had roughly five new substitutes, but since it wasn't the school's job to check on the subs' qualifications, no one in the main office was sure whether the algebra sub knew any math or the physics sub had ever heard of Newton or Galileo, and probably no one downtown did either. However, Fremont, trying to avoid damage to the equipment, did make it a practice never to put a computer class sub in a computer lab. That almost assured that the students would learn nothing.[77]

The multitrack schedule itself entailed endless juggling. This was not a September-June calendar with a breather in the summer; on this schedule, teachers and students were, as Hines said, "coming and going, coming and going, and doing a new master schedule every time a new track comes along." Within all this coming and going, a few teachers "rainbow" for extra money, meaning that they teach year-round. Quite a few more fill in, also for extra money, when they're off-track.[78]

Routine stuff: Would there be someone for the Spanish course when the A track returned at the end of August? Would the rooms that had to be converted for computer use be ready? Could a woman PE teacher be found for the girls' gym class? And since all that, and books as well, depended on the great bureaucratic maw downtown, there was no way to be sure. Even after a teacher was hired, it sometimes took four months to get a fingerprint check; until that was done, the hiree couldn't set foot in the classroom.[79] And the same went for almost everything else. Again and again administrators told teachers that they hoped the textbooks would arrive soon, if the order hadn't gotten lost in the long chain between the teacher, the school, the district purchasing department, the publisher, and the book clerk back at the school.[80] Ditto for the countless students who were on the rolls and simply didn't show up at the beginning of each new "mester." Nobody at school really knew what happened to them. Maybe they went to some other school or to some other district. It was supposed to be handled by the attendance office, but until the new person arrived, there'd be nobody to do it.[81] At one point during Hines's long deposition, one of the lawyers asked her to clarify something. Just then, had she been talking about the school year or the calendar year? "School year," she replied. "Is there any other kind? I have no life."

Schools like Fremont and the subdistrict it's located in crawl with consultants and outside experts—ed-school professors, motivational gurus, learning theorists, psychologists—running yet another professional development session or another clinic and pitching yet another jargon-rich program to downtown administrators who think this is the way to be creative or break the monotony. There were always a lot of them, but the new accountability systems and the call (and corresponding boosts in funding) for better in-service training for teachers have increased the pressure still further. And so some new plan is always just getting off the ground—training yet to come, details still to be explained. At the time Hines testified, Fremont had several, among them something called Academic Literacy Across the Curriculum for Achieving the Standards (the acronym, ALA-CASA, means "at home" in Spanish), run by a San Francisco State University teacher named Kate Kinsella, that appears to be focused primarily on Latino students whose primary language is Spanish. "Reading & Writing to Learn," says its Web site, "is the goal of ALACASA's ambitious professional development component for teachers [who] cycle through a series of seminars on topics related to developing academic literacy skills in all content areas." Fremont also was beginning something called Co-nect, which promised to show "schools and districts to use project-based learning and technology to support teachers, enhance the quality of student work, and integrate real-world projects into today's standards-based curriculum." But that, Hines said, was "just getting off the ground, too."

There are hundreds of such programs, few of them with much of a research base, if any, and who knows how many thousands of consultants ministering to desperate school district patients. But their real problem, aside from diverting money, time, and energy from other uses, is that they contribute to the school-site confusion created by endless change. In the past decade, school administrators have complained loudly about all the stuff that's foisted on them by politicians and state officials, but they're not shy about doing a lot of foisting themselves.

There is no foolproof gauge of the cumulative effects that dismal schools, with their filth, their lack of competent staffs, and their constant turmoil, have on the students who are stuck in them. Nor is there any measure of the demoralizing effects on the teachers and administrators who are trying to do conscientious jobs. But as countless students have testified, the insult is inescapable. Michelle Fine, a City University of New York social psychologist who runs structured focus groups with students, believes the impact is enormous, transforming "yearning for quality education into anger, pride into shame, and civic engagement into public alienation." Fine, who has done scores of such studies, was hired by the lawyers in the pending California suit to give her analysis:

The California schools in question [she reported] are educating poor and working-class youth, and youth of color, away from academic mastery and democracy and toward academic ignorance and civic alienation. Despite the fact that the youth are asking for clean and safe school environments, quality educators, and rigorous instruction, the evidence suggests that the more years they spend in their schools, the more shame, anger, and mistrust they develop; the more academic engagement declines; and the more our diverse democratic fabric frays. We can ill afford to have youth—particularly poor and working-class youth and youth of color, so in need of higher education—continue to decide early in their academic careers that schools are not designed for them.[82]

It takes no expert analyst to know that thousands of students survive those schools and go on to productive and happy lives, and sometimes careers of great distinction. American lore is crammed with their stories. But neither does it take much imagination to understand the depressing, alienating impact of our schools of disregard. Americans who can afford it do not choose high schools such as Fremont or Newtown or Hoke for their children; they run from them as hard as they can. "The conditions at Burbank," said teacher Mei-Ling Wiedmeyer, "make [the children] feel as if no one cares about their education. I can see them internalize the belief that if no one cares about their education, then they won't either." The only surprise about the Fine report is that anyone found it necessary to try to "prove" such things at all.

V

If all American schools were falling down around their teachers and students, if they all had rats in the halls and ratty books in the classrooms, if they all had squadrons of untrained teachers, and "if absolute equality were the constitutional mandate, and 'basic skills' sufficient to achieve that mandate," as the New Jersey Supreme Court said in 1990, "there would be little short of a revolution in the suburban districts when parents learned that basic skills is what their children were entitled to, limited to, and no more."[83] But of course that's not the case. In most, the roofs don't leak, the ceiling tiles aren't falling down, there's no coal dust on the desks, the playing fields don't flood with backed-up sewage, and most seventh graders graduate six years later and go on to college.

Yet even in the average school, the average teacher who majored in education as an undergraduate—and many still do—is likely to have scored lower in college admission tests than students in most other majors and intended professions, to make less money, and to work under conditions unpleasant enough to strain many people's dedication and idealism. (In

2001, SAT scores for entering college freshmen intending to be education majors were third from the bottom on a list of twenty-three majors, above only home economics and two grab-bag categories.)[84] In many states, the school isn't likely to have a full-time librarian, especially if it's an elementary school, or even a library at all. In many, the counselors barely have time to make certain that students take the courses required to meet the district (and increasingly the state) graduation requirements. Intelligent college and/or career planning is a relative luxury. First-class music and art programs are a rarity.

But with the exception of growing complaints about the lack of well-trained teachers—and with the questions about what is good training the subject of another controversy—probably the most pervasive belief about schools through much of the past generation, at least the schools attended by other people's children, was that they were too flabby. The most vocal critics, both in the business community and among think-tank conservatives, thought them too dominated by old progressive theory favoring such things as whole language and constructivist math, and suffused with bleeding-heart tenderness about self-esteem, at the expense of phonics, systematic learning of "math facts," direct instruction, and real achievement measured by honest, objective assessment. Along the way they were believed to have shunned, even demeaned, cultural literacy, as defined most prominently by E. D. Hirsch Jr., the University of Virginia professor of English and author of *Cultural Literacy*, the bestseller with the five-thousand-item list of what everybody should know.[85] (The kids have no idea even in what century the Civil War took place, can't tell Robert Frost from Jack, and think a soprano is a member of a mob family on television.) Meanwhile, Chester ("Checker") Finn and Diane Ravitch, both former federal education officials from the Reagan-Bush years and probably the country's most articulate educational conservatives, argued all through the 1980s and 1990s that, compared to that of students in other countries, American students' academic prowess was pretty dismal. We were suffering, they said, "from the tyranny of dogma."

Those conclusions were backed by the comparative scores on TIMSS, the Third International Math and Science Study, showing American students not testing as well (in eighth-grade math, for example) as students in Singapore, Korea, Taiwan, or even Bulgaria, Malaysia, and Hungary.[86] At the same time, American school districts claimed their students were doing fine and parents (for the most part) were smugly satisfied. Everybody thought they knew about the rotten schools attended by the black and Hispanic children across town, where many started kindergarten two or more years behind, got further behind every year they were in school, and often dropped out by the time they were sixteen (though in fact most of us knew far less than we thought). Although nobody much uses the phrase "the blackboard jungle" anymore—in the 1950s it was both a best-selling book and a movie—the image still lingers. But the schools on this side of the tracks were not like that; they were safe and the kids succeeded.

We were thus, in the view of people like Finn and Ravitch, all being hoodwinked by the spin called the Lake Wobegon effect—the reports from local schools, sometimes based on their own tests, that all their kids were above average even as standardized tests showed that they were not.[87] In one frequently cited report, Harold W. Stevenson and James W. Stigler also found that in Japan and China, where students outperformed their U.S. peers, parents and children rated effort as much more important in school success than U.S. parents. Conversely, in the United States, mothers believed natural ability more important than did mothers in China.[88] The parents of American students who were scoring below their overseas peers on those international comparisons thought their kids were doing much better than the parents of the kids in Japan who were getting higher scores. It was this observation that, more than anything else, set Checker Finn and a critical mass of American politicians on the pursuit of statewide testing systems that might inform parents how poorly their children were really doing.[89]

All those generalizations have set off huge battles about the validity of the international comparisons in light of major cultural differences, not to mention the average age difference between U.S. high school seniors and those abroad, and about the trade-offs between rote learning, known affec-tionately as drill-and-kill, and the relative pedagogical freedom in many U.S. schools that's said to foster creativity and critical thinking. In any society—Japan, say, or Taiwan—where few get to go to selective academic secondary schools and even fewer are admitted to good universities and get financial aid or low tuition, the academic competition may be far more intense than it is in this country, where almost any student can find a place in a college somewhere.[90] But the international tests have helped drive the accountability and testing movements and the push for higher standards, and in a totally unintended side effect, they have reinforced the adequacy argument. If the average school isn't good enough in Mason City, Boise, or Oswego, how could the average school in Harlem or South Central Los An-geles make the grade?

The conservative diagnosis—and often the diagnosis generally of legis-latures and businesspeople—is that the problem lies primarily in curricula, teaching methods, and establishment turf protection, and in many cases that's at least partly correct. Curricula and teaching techniques do matter, and often they're no better than uninspiring; sometimes they're awful. But when a school has a string of subs, no books to give the kids for homework, and constant shifting of classes and bodies, when it's bereft of functioning labs and counselors to deal with student crises, and when for one of many reasons the leaky roof doesn't get fixed, the chances of teaching anything well go down fast. Hamilton Lankford's perfect curve in New York showing that as the poverty level of a school goes up the training and measured ability of teachers goes down almost certainly has corollaries in most other school resources as well, had we only statistics to measure them—from rich curricula to the availability and quality of books and labs to the condition of the windows and the paint on the walls. In North Carolina, where high school students are expected to use graphing calculators on state tests (they cost about $100 each), teachers in poor schools had to borrow them on test days from other schools "and let students try to use the calculators on the tests without enough practice."[91] In some districts, parents are required to buy them for their children out of their own pockets. (The same is often true for team, band, and cheerleader uniforms, but those, at least, are not required for academic success.)

The Lankford curve also corresponds almost exactly to the similar curve that Marguerite Roza and Karen Hawley Miles, two researchers at the Center on Reinventing Public Education at the University of Washington, found when they looked at the disparities in intradistrict school funding in three U.S. cities: Seattle, Cincinnati, and Houston. While the districts claimed they were funding each of their schools at roughly the same level, they were doing it with a budgeting fiction that, because of wide discrepancies in the cost of teachers' salaries, subsidizes schools serving affluent kids at the expense of the schools serving the poorer kids. Seattle's Martin Luther King School, for example, where most students are poor enough to get free lunches, was budgeted to get $3,926 per student, but because of its inexperienced (and thus low-paid) teachers it got only $2,928. Meanwhile, the Wedgwood School, located in an affluent neighborhood, was budgeted at $3,731 per student but got $4,019.

> How is this possible? [Roza wrote.] While the district is careful to report its school-by-school budget figures, what you can't see from the reports is that these figures represent a sort of "play money"—schools are required to use the budgeted money to buy back artificially priced goods from the district.
>
> So in reality, the budgeted money is not the same as what it actually costs to operate the school. For example, the district charges schools a fixed false rate for all teachers, principals and other administrative staff, regardless of what these staff are actually paid by the

district. The district then pays out the real salaries—salaries that are not fixed but vary substantially with experience and other qualifications.

Schools such as Wedgewood, which can attract the best teachers (typically the most expensive teachers) can really benefit from this scheme. They don't use any extra play money to hire an expensive teacher than they do an inexpensive one. The district's budget reports don't even reflect that Wedgewood teachers are some of the most expensive in the district.[92]

Roza says the districts seemed not even to understand the discrepancies. They have since moved gradually, each in a different way, to adopt a modified form of student-based budgeting and thus reduce the discrepancies in some classes of funding. Houston, which has gone the farthest, appears even to be contemplating a cap where schools with high proportions of experienced teachers would be required eventually to hire only low-paid rookies. But that hasn't yet happened. In view of the likely uproar from the wealthy neighborhoods, no district is likely to eliminate the gaps in pay, and thus teacher quality, anytime soon.[93]

Of course there are exceptions, statistical outliers; they're clear both on Lankford's scatter diagrams and in the communities around us—middle-class schools that don't teach well, high-poverty schools that do and where students do well. The conservative Heritage Foundation, for one, is crazy about principals and teachers at schools full of minority kids whose test scores are high. It gives the school people awards and shows them off at its meetings and in its literature. Their achievement, often only grudgingly recognized by the establishment, not only seems to show that the right cares about black and Latino kids—and believes in their potential—as fervently as the left but also appears to demonstrate that some schools can raise test scores significantly, and that poor children can learn, without more money. And it seems to show that the main reason most public schools are failing (and thus that vouchers are necessary) is that the public system is stuck in its costly, self-serving, and politically correct futility: the tyranny of dogma.

In a lot of communities, test and accountability programs seem to be having an odd effect. Of course there are the well-known cram programs to which schools in states such as Texas devote nearly all their time in the two months before the test is given. There is fudging of numbers, either by hiding students who are not likely to test well, by putting them in classes for the handicapped, by temporarily redesignating high-achieving Anglos as Hispanic to bring up that group's scores, or simply by outright fraud. But for parents with kids with high scores (which, needless to say, may tell little

about either school quality or real achievement), testing has probably reinforced the Lake Wobegon effect. It strengthens the prior conviction that
the kids are doing okay and the schools are fine. It also drives up real estate
values handsomely. In Texas, and probably elsewhere, when local schools
get exemplary ratings from the state education agency—and quite a few
of them do—Realtors and developers post the ratings on billboards,
brochures, and Web sites.[94]

But Lankford's curve is still there. And so while students like Randell
Hasty are taught math and science by a string of subs and Alondra Jones
and Erika Cabrera aren't getting anything close to what the kids get in the
fancy suburbs or at selective public high schools like Lowell (much less
what they get at Marin Academy), there is no quantum break—the poor
kids on this side of the resource line, the rest on the other—which was the
moral basis of the equity suits of the 1970s. As long as everybody is in some
kind of school with some adult in the room, somebody could argue—as the
U.S. Supreme Court indeed did—that kids in underfunded schools were
not suffering anything dire enough to constitute denial of equal protection under the Fourteenth Amendment. Conversely, all through the 1990s
there were—and probably still are—schools in the comfortable California
suburbs, and elsewhere as well, where the roofs also leaked, where there
were too few counselors, no art program, no school nurse, no Internet-
connected computers, and where the books in the library also eagerly
awaited the day man would walk on the moon. At Ensign Intermediate
School in Newport Beach (among the state's plushest suburbs), "when it
rains, the library is off-limits because the roof and windows leak. At Costa
Mesa High, the gymnasium floor is riddled with holes. . . . Jagged metal
snags locker-room users. In the new state-funded computer lab, ceiling
tiles fall on students' heads."[95]

Once you make the adequacy argument, however, you may be able to
ride up the Lankford curve as easily as the system had ridden it down.
Maybe your local school is safe and well maintained, and maybe all the kids
in the neighborhood will eventually get into college. But maybe it could
also be better (and the value of your home could rise). If Alondra Jones
wasn't being served well, it's possible that some middle-class children
weren't being served adequately either. The trouble was that in most states,
nobody had ever bothered to find out, much less structure governance and
finance systems consistent with what it took to provide decent schooling
for the contemporary world. Until somebody began to measure what was
really needed, there was no way to know.

NOTES

1. *Williams et al. v. State of California,* Superior Court, City and County of San Francisco, No. 312236, deposition of Alondra Sharae Jones, May 16, 2001, 35–50.
2. This and all other California academic achievement data from California Department of Education Academic Performance Index (API) Reports, api.cde .ca.gov/reports.html.
3. *Williams,* declaration of Lawrence Poon, July 31, 2000.
4. Bernice Yeung, "Hard Lessons," *San Francisco Weekly,* Oct. 11, 2000.
5. Alondra Jones deposition, 116, 159. How did she know those were mouse droppings? she was asked in her deposition. "I hope it's a mouse," she answered. "Hope it's not more serious." Deposition, 128.
6. *Williams,* declaration of Alondra Jones, August 14, 2000.
7. Teacher CyberGuide, *A Raisin in the Sun,* www.nashville.k12.tn.us/Cyber-Guides; Shane Safir interview, August 22, 2002.
8. Paulo Freire, *Pedagogy of the Oppressed* (New York: Continuum, 1968, 1970), 33; Safir interview.
9. *Making the Grade,* KQED-TV documentary, 1999.
10. *Williams,* declaration of Shane Safir, June 27, 2000.
11. *Williams,* deposition of Alondra Jones, May 25, 2001, 393.
12. Patricia Gray interview at Balboa, June 6, 2002; Williams, deposition of Patricia Gray, July 18, 2001, 282–85.
13. Gray interview; *Williams,* deposition of Patricia Gray, July 18, 2001, 298, 323–25.
14. Alondra Jones deposition, 348–49. Lowell is San Francisco's elite public high school.
15. Interview with ACLU attorney Catherine E. Lhamon, who was present at the deposition, August 14, 2002.
16. Whack-a-mole is in fact more than a schoolhouse metaphor. In schools that have them, grass play areas are sometimes laced with gopher holes, which are dangerous for kids and thus require constant and rather costly efforts at what one former school board member called ole control. Maintenance crews don't whack them with mallets, but try to trap them and then destroy them. But it's a never-ending struggle.
17. *DeRolph v. State* (1997), 78 Ohio St. 3d 193.
18. Ibid., p. 84.
19. *Campaign for Fiscal Equity v. State of New York* (*CFE II,* 2001), Supreme Court, County of New York, Part 25, no. 111070/93, 68.
20. *Williams,* deposition of Carlos Ramirez, June 21, 2001, 320. Malabed herself said that when she started teaching at Bryant, the principal told her and other teachers to flush the pipes every day by letting the water run since "there was something unsafe in the pipes that kids should not drink." *Williams,* declaration of Lily Malabed, April 10, 2000; declaration of Cynthia Artiga-Faupusa, May 9, 2000.
21. List compiled from personal visits as well as various sources, including *Hoke County Board of Education v. State of North Carolina,* Wake County Superior

Court, 95 CVS-1158, plaintiffs' proposed findings of fact, pp. 430–40; *Bradford v. Maryland State Board of Education*, Circuit Court for Baltimore County, no. 94340058/CE189672; *Williams*, deposition of Marcia Hines, August 10, 2001, 465–66. "Sink" remark from *Williams*, declaration of Taoi Dao, July 21, 2000.

22. *Campaign for Fiscal Equity v. State of New York (CFE)*, trial transcript, October 13, 1999, 287, 284.

23. "Work Order Backlog," memo from Bruce Bender to Patricia Zedalis, May 21, 1997, CFE, plaintiff's exhibit, Px 1490.

24. "Meeting New York State's Crisis in School Facilities Today: Report of the [New York State] Regents Advisory Committee on School Facilities," August 30, 1996.

25. *Abbott v. Burke (Abbott II*, 1990) 119 N.J. 363.

26. *Williams*, declaration of Glauz Diego, August 9, 2000; declaration of Cindy Diego, August 9, 2000; declaration of D'Andre Lampkin, August 11, 2000, 1; deposition of Marcia Hines, June 18, 2001, 82. See also Erika Hayasaki, "Pupils Shunted to Vocational Ed Fear It Can Derail College Dreams," *Los Angeles Times*, March 27, 2002.

27. *Hoke*, trial transcript, November 15, 1999, 138; plaintiffs' proposed findings of fact, 426. In Los Angeles, the travelers schlep their stuff, but that's not a North Carolina word.

28. *Statewide Profile of the Educational System*, New York State Education Department, Albany, April 1999, 12.

29. *Campaign for Fiscal Equity v. State of New York (CFE)*, witness statement of John Lee, plaintiff's exhibit, 2855. Some schools, such as Midwood in Brooklyn, however, which was built for 2,300 and now enrolls 4,000, and which has been on triple shifts, continue to maintain an extraordinary level of academic intensity. In 1999 the school produced more finalists in the Intel Science Talent Search than any other school in the country.

30. After having nearly abandoned the project after spending $154 million, in 2002 the Los Angeles school board, desperate for space, voted to do a multi-million-dollar cleanup and finish the work. The ultimate price tag was to be about $220–240 million, making it the most expensive public school ever built in this country. But late in 2002, engineers found an earthquake fault under the site. No one knew whether it was active or not, but the project was suspended again. See, e.g., Andrew Trotter, "Los Angeles Revives Beleaguered Belmont Project," *Education Week*, March 20, 2002; Joetta L. Sack, "Romer Puts New Hold on Troubled Belmont Site," *Education Week*, January 8, 2003.

31. Data from Ronald W. Bennett, president of School Services of California, a private consulting and lobbying firm that analyzes fiscal data for school systems and other clients. In many cases, teachers prefer the newer portables because they are cleaner and have self-contained heating and air-conditioning that they can control.

32. *Williams*, declaration of Craig Gordon, August 29, 2001, 5; Balfanz telephone interview, August 22, 2002. Also, Robert Balfanz and Nettie Legters, "How Many Central City High Schools Have a Severe Dropout Problem, Where Are They Located, and Who Attends Them?" paper prepared for the Civil Rights

Project at the Harvard Graduate School of Education and Achieve, Inc., January 13, 2001. Also, Richard Lee Colvin, "A School Flails in a Sea of Chaos," *Los Angeles Times,* July 14, 2002.

33. Academic data from California Department of Education Academic Performance Index (API) reports. Description of track system and schedule from *Williams,* deposition of Margaret Rowland, June 20 and Aug. 2, 2001, and deposition of Marcia Hines, June 18 and August 10, 2001. Also Los Angeles Unified School District, "Key School Calendar Dates, 2002–03 School Year," www.lausd.k12.ca.us/lausd/offices/Office_of_Communications/dates.pdf.

34. *Williams,* declaration of Abraham Osuna, May 25, 2001.

35. Bachrach phone interview, June 3, 2002. Also, Hamilton Lankford, James Wyckoff, and Frank Papa, *The Labor Market for Public School Teachers: A Descriptive Analysis of New York State's Teacher Workforce* (New York: The Education Finance Research Consortium, 2000).

36. *Williams,* deposition of Marcia Hines, June 18, 2001, 138.

37. *Williams,* Roland deposition, 283.

38. Hamilton Lankford, "A Descriptive Analysis of the New York State and New York City Teaching Force," *Campaign for Fiscal Equity v. State of New York,* plaintiff's exhibit 1482. Also, Lankford, Wyckoff, and Papa, *The Labor Market.*

39. *CFE,* trial transcript, testimony of John Murphy, 17439.

40. *CFE,* testimony of Frank DeStefano, superintendent of Community School District 15 in Brooklyn, trial transcript, 5434–35; testimony of Kathleen Cashin, superintendent of Community School District 23 in Brooklyn, trial transcript, 333.

41. Stephanie Banchero and Ana Beatriz Cholo, "Many Uncertified Teachers Work in Worst Schools," *Chicago Tribune,* July 9, 2002.

42. For Maryland, *Bradford v. Maryland,* Circuit Court for Baltimore County Case no. 94340058/CE189672. For California, *The Status of the Teaching Profession, 2001* (Santa Cruz: The Center for the Future of Teaching and Learning, 2001), www.cftl.org/publications.html.

43. Craig D. Jerald, *All Talk, No Action: Putting an End to Out of Field Teaching* (Washington, DC: The Education Trust, 2002).

44. *Hoke,* trial transcript, September 28, 1999, 11–12.

45. *Hoke,* trial transcript, September 28, 1999, 26. In many schools, of course, subs have been a joke forever because students know that they're usually placeholders who probably don't know the subject; unless they've been briefed by the regular teacher, as some are, they won't have any idea what's been going on in class and can be manipulated to death. No one knows, of course, how many teachers there still are who think their students believe, as they do, that reading or writing is punishment.

46. *Hoke v. North Carolina,* 95 CVS 1158, plaintiffs' proposed findings of fact, § 232–33, 237, 258.

47. *Meeting the Highly Qualified Teachers Challenge* (Washington, DC: U.S. Department of Education, 2002), www.title2.org/secReport.htm.

48. On attrition, see, e.g., "Teacher Induction Programs," Policy Update, National Association of State Boards of Education, April 2000. On recruiting, David J. Hoff, "Urban Districts Employing More Aggressive Hiring Tactics," *Education Week,* October 3, 2001.

49. Arthur Levine, phone interview, October 12, 2002.

50. See, e.g., Peter Schrag, "California's 40,000 New 'Highly Qualified' Teachers," *Sacramento Bee*, August 7, 2002. The board has since negotiated a compromise with the U.S. Department of Education that seems to have conceded as much to California as California conceded to the feds. Catherine Gewertz, "City Districts Seek Teachers with Licenses," *Education Week*, September 11, 2002; Diana Jean Schemo, "Law Overhauling School Standards May Be Weakened," *New York Times*, October 15, 2002.

51. Quoted in Linda Darling-Hammond, "Access to Quality Teaching: An Analysis of Inequality in California's Public Schools," unpublished paper prepared for plaintiffs in *Williams*.

52. *CFE*, witness statement of Betty Rosa (a district superintendent in New York City), plaintiff's exhibit 2332A, pp. 12–13.

53. Interview with Russlyn Ali, executive director of the Education Trust-West, which calculated the number from data supplied by the Los Angeles school district, August 20, 2002.

54. Gaston interview, July 15, 2002; also *The Status of the Teaching Profession*, 8.

55. Kathryn Whitaker, "Where Are the Principal Candidates? Perceptions of Superintendents," *NAASP Bulletin* 85, no. 625 (May 2001): 82–92; *Williams*, declaration of Susan Carroll Boysal, July 27, 2000.

56. *Abbott v. Burke* (*Abbott II*, 1990), 119 N.J. 360, 361.

57. *DeRolph v. State*, Perry County Court of Common Pleas, Case 22043, findings of fact, conclusions of law, order and memorandum of the Perry County Court of Common Pleas, July 1, 1994, 9, 77. She subsequently graduated from Ohio University in 1996 with degrees in psychology and accounting. Doug Oplinger and Dennis J. Willard, "Slow to Build," *Akron Beacon Journal*, May 22, 1996.

58. Adam Cohen interview, September 19, 2002; Cohen, "After 10 Long Years, Alabama is Back Where It Started," *New York Times*, Mar. 11, 2002. Cohen is now a *Times* editorial writer. Jim Sanders, "For a Shabby Learning Experience, Try School Library," *Sacramento Bee*, January 21, 1990.

59. Keith Ervin, "Students Protest Lack of Textbooks," *Seattle Times*, May 31, 2002.

60. *Hoke*, transcript, Nov. 15, 1999, 149, 152.

61. *Williams*, declaration of Erika Cabrera, 1.

62. *Williams*, deposition of Marcia Hines, July 5, 2001, 201.

63. Lou Harris, "A Survey of the Status of Equality in Public Education in California," March 2002. In 2002, after many schools had eliminated student lockers as a security measure, the California legislature passed a bill that, in an effort to reduce the heavy loads that children had to carry in their backpacks, instructed the State Board of Education to find a way to limit the weight of textbooks.

64. In the past three or four years, some districts—Boston, for example—used what extra money they had to buy back some of the most restrictive seniority provisions in union contracts. In effect, they traded higher pay for contract modifications. Bess Keller, "Boston Contract: A Policy Blueprint," *Education Week*, November 13, 2002.

65. *Williams*, deposition of Marcia Hines, July 5, 2001, 235.

66. *Campaign for Fiscal Equity (CFE) v. State of New York*, New York Supreme Court, part 25, no. 93/111070, testimony of Edward Stancik, trial transcript, April

13, 2000, 20050. Also Lydia G. Segal et al., "Power, Politics and Patronage: Education in Community District 12," City of New York, April 1993.

67. *CFE,* Stancik testimony, transcript, 21466; Robert M. Brenner et al., "From Chaos to Corruption: An Investigation into the 1993 Community School Board Election," City of New York, the Special Commissioner of Investigation for the New York City School District, December 1993.

68. Sean Courtney et al., "Corruption in Community District 9 (Preliminary Report)," City of New York, the Special Commissioner of Investigation for the New York City School District, 1996.

69. Edward F. Stancik, "Grand Illusion: An Investigation into Enrollment and Attendance Manipulation at Brandeis High School," City of New York, the Special Commissioner of Investigation for the New York City School District, March 2000, 2. Also Lynette Holloway, "Principal Is Accused of Inflating Attendance to Aid Career," *New York Times,* March 17, 2000.

70. For a fuller discussion of Texas's claims, see Peter Schrag, "Too Good to Be True," *American Prospect,* January 3, 2000, 46–49. The California claims are from California State Department of Education press release #02-14, April 19, 2002. Official California data at data1.cde.ca.gov/dataquest/. The grade-to-grade calculations are also subject to error since students transfer and, in places like Texas and California, move back to Mexico. But in general, transfers in and transfers out should more or less balance.

71. Howard Blume and Dennis Dockstader, "Degrees of Deceit: How One Inner-City High School Played the Numbers Game and Made Its Dropout Rate Go Away," *LA Weekly,* July 19–25, 2002.

72. Kirk Johnson, "For New York, 25-Year Losing Streak," *New York Times,* January 13, 1999.

73. Mary Musca interview, September 4, 2002; Nancy Lederman, "Hit or Miss: Fitness and Sports Opportunities in the New York City Public Schools," Educational Frameworks, Inc. (for New Visions for Public Schools), 2001.

74. *Williams,* deposition of Marcia Hines, July 5, 2001, 348–51.

75. *Williams,* deposition of Margaret Roland, August 2, 2001, 322–23, 205; deposition of Marcia Hines, August 10, 2001, 507.

76. *Williams,* declaration of Magaly De Loza, May 5, 2000.

77. *Williams,* deposition of Marcia Hines, August 10, 2001, 614. Former *Los Angeles Times* reporter Richard Colvin, now the director of the Hechinger Center at Columbia University, also found that new computers "disappeared as quickly as they were unpacked," presumably because someone inside the school opened it to thieves.

78. *Williams,* deposition of Marcia Hines, June 18, 2001, 18, 109, and July 5, 2001, 225, 382.

79. *Williams,* deposition of Marcia Hines, June 18, 2001, 131.

80. Colvin (see note 77) says that when he visited the school in the spring of 2002, it was stuffed with books after the district superintendent, probably in response to the lawsuit against the state in which students complained about a lack of books, ordered Fremont to spend all its discretionary money on texts. But a lot of students still had no books because the teachers decided that the students couldn't read well enough to use the books. So why risk the damage and loss? Conversation with Colvin, August 28, 2002.

81. *Williams,* deposition of Marcia Hines, July 5, 2001, p. 403.

82. *Williams,* expert opinion of Michelle Fine, p. 4.

83. *Abbott v. Burke (Abbott II,* 1990), 119 N.J. 364.

84. *The College Bound Seniors: A Profile of SAT Program Test Takers* (New York: The College Board, 2001), www.collegeboard.com/sat/cbsenior/yr2001/pdf/ NATL.pdf.

85. E. D. Hirsch Jr., *Cultural Literacy: What Every American Needs to Know* (Boston: Houghton Mifflin, 1987).

86. The data here are from the most recent survey, done in 1999. *TIMSS 1999: International Mathematics Report: Findings from IEA's Repeat of the Third International Mathematics and Science Study at the Eighth Grade,* timss.bc.edu/timss 1999i/pdf/T99i_Math1.pdf. On Chester Finn and Diane Ravitch, *Educational Reform, 1995–96: A Report from the Educational Excellence Network to Its Education Policy Committee and the American People* (Indianapolis: The Hudson Institute, 1996). Also, Diane Ravitch and Chester Finn, *What Do Our 17-Year-Olds Know? A Report on the First National Assessment of History and Literature* (New York: Harper and Row, 1987).

87. The reference, of course, is to *A Prairie Home Companion,* radio host Garrison Keillor's gentle irony about the imaginary Minnesota town where, among many other wonderful things, all the kids are above average.

88. E.g., Chester Finn, "Federal Spending and Education Reform: How Sound an Investment?" testimony prepared for delivery to the Committee on the Budget, U.S. House of Representatives, March 16, 1995. See also Harold W. Stevenson and James W. Stigler, *The Learning Gap: Why Our Schools Are Failing and What We Can Learn from Japanese and Chinese Education* (New York: Summit Books, 1992), 100–101.

89. Various author conversations with Finn, 1985–2000.

90. See, for example, Gerald W. Bracey, "TIMSS, Rhymes With 'Dims,' as in 'Witted,' " *Phi Delta Kappan,* May 1998, 686–87; and Bracey, "Tinkering with TIMMS," *Phi Delta Kappan* (online article), 1998, www.pdkintl.org/kappan/kbra9809.htm.

91. *Hoke,* findings of fact, § 322.

92. Marguerite Roza, "Policy Inadvertently Robs Poor Schools to Benefit the Rich," *Seattle Post-Intelligencer,* September 24, 2000.

93. Telephone interview, Marguerite Roza, August 20, 2002. Paul Hill, Roza's colleague, who runs the Center on Reinventing Public Education at the University of Washington, says that if the federal government really enforced a policy that's supposed to prevent schools from using federal funds designed for high-poverty schools to replace underfunding from state and local sources, the schools with inexperienced teachers would at least get more funding to add staff or to buy other resources.

94. Author observation, Austin, November 1999; also, e.g., Altwood Homes, in Indian Springs: "Schools attended by Altwood families have received exemplary ratings, the highest rating awarded by the Texas Education Agency, every year since 1998" (www.altwoodhomes.com/neighborhood.html).

95. J. D. Sparks, "San Juan Argues Urgency of Bonds," *Sacramento Bee,* Neighbors sec., August 1, 2002 (about a middle-class suburban Sacramento school district where portable structures, some more than thirty years old, "are plagued by water damage, leaking roofs, insufficient electrical output for computers, ineffective or nonexistent heating and air-conditioning units, loose and miss-

ing floor tiles and worn carpeting." In one of the district's schools, where only 10 percent of the students are from poor families, and nearly all are native English speakers, "four portable classrooms . . . are racked with mold, water damage, split seams and shoddy roofs.") The quotes about Costa Mesa come from the *Orange County Register,* February 29, 2000.

17

Students for Sale:
Who Profits from Marketing in Schools?

Susan Linn

When my daughter was in third grade, her school's annual spring concert—usually a mix of jazz, folk, classical, or even rock music—was a program titled "An Evening of Disney." I was appalled. Instead of expanding their horizons even a little, my daughter and her schoolmates were devoting their year to learning the one body of music every eight-year-old in America is sold on a daily basis. Now it's being marketed to them in schools, along with videos and little mouse ears. I couldn't see how spending school time on Disney music expanded children's learning or enriched their musical lives. When I complained to the music teacher, she responded, "But the kids like it."

I didn't know it then, but the Disneyfication of my daughter's musical education was just a small sign of the times. It occurred only a year or so before Ed Winter, an enthusiast for marketing in schools who would have a profound effect on its nature, told *Business Week*, "Marketers have come to realize that all roads eventually lead to the schools."[1]

In-school advertising began escalating in earnest in 1990. It now includes (but isn't limited to) corporate-sponsored newscasts, field trips, classroom materials, vending machines, gymnasiums, walls, and whole buildings. Have you visited your child's school lately? Perhaps she's learning about energy production and consumption through the lens of companies like Exxon Mobil[2] or professional associations like the American Coal Foundation ("Unlocking Coal's Potential through Education").[3] Her inspiration for reading may be coming from Pizza Hut—complete with coupons to be redeemed at your local franchise.[4] She may be attending mandatory assemblies where she can learn about job interviewing from McDonalds.[5] If she lives in Washington, D.C., and wants to go into the hotel business, she might be attending the Marriott Hospitality Charter School.[6] If she's a kid in trouble, she could attend a Burger King Academy.[7]

If she's on a school athletic team, her shoes may come from Nike or Adidas.[8] Her school's scoreboard could owe its presence to the countless bottles of Coke or Pepsi she's bought from school vending machines and sport a company logo.[9] Access to her opinions and ideas might have been sold to a market research company.[10, 11] Her only exposure to current events might be brought to her courtesy of the aforementioned Ed Winter. He's the guy who thought of Channel One, the twelve-minute news program that includes two minutes of commercials that her school is obligated to show daily for 90 percent of the school days each year.[12]

Public schools have been venues for at least some corporate marketing since their inception. In fact, a 1929 report from the National Education Association published a treatise warning teachers about "free" corporate handouts, suggesting that corporate materials belonged in the classroom only if they were essential to a child's education.[13] In the 1930s schools became a battleground between corporations and the nascent consumer movement.[14] Students in the 1950s routinely saw corporate-sponsored "educational" films. By 1954, over 3.5 million students watched about 60,000 showings of films from the National Association of Manufacturers. By 1959, one in five corporations reported sponsoring educational materials.[15]

In the early 1990s the scope of commercialization of schools began escalating at an unprecedented rate. At the Commercialism in Education Research Unit at Arizona State University, Professor Alex Molnar has been tracking media mentions of school commercialism since the start of that decade. In 2002, he found 4,631—in contrast to the 991 found twelve years earlier.[16] As one marketing expert explained, "Ten years ago, schools were more or less acting as gatekeepers. . . . They were suspicious of manufacturers coming into schools to do business."[17] In 2000, a federal government report from the General Accounting Office (GAO) called marketing in schools a growth industry.[18]

Just as corporations and the free market are currently seen as models for solving health-care or other social problems,[19] they are also viewed as a solution for troubled public schools and school systems. To paraphrase the old corporate maxim, "If it's good for General Motors, it's good for education."

We are in the middle of a nationwide thrust to turn schools over to for-profit companies and Education Management Organizations (EMOs) such as Edison Schools, Inc. Even when cities and towns stop short of actually turning their children's education over to the business world, corporations have become models for running school systems.

Are corporations such great models? It seems like a bad joke to me that even as the heads of corporations like Enron, Worldcom, and Tyco are charged with cannibalizing their companies, the heads of major school systems, including those in Chicago and Philadelphia, are now called CEOs rather than superintendents.[20] The school department in the town of Brooklawn, New Jersey, even has a director of corporate development.[21] Though they are ultimately responsible for the *education* of millions of school children, many of the newest administrative appointees—whether they are called CEOs or superintendents—are not, and have never been, educators. The New York City schools are run by Joel Klein, the former American CEO of the German media conglomerate Bertelsmann.[22] In Seattle, an army general was replaced as superintendent by an investment banker[23] who recently resigned amid news that under his tenure the district overspent its budget by tens of millions of dollars.[24] In Philadelphia, the new CEO is the former city budget director for the city of Chicago and the former CEO of the Chicago Public Schools.[25] It has become the norm to measure a school's success only by its students' scores on standardized tests, just as a corporation is judged by its profits.

I've briefly mentioned the ongoing debates about restructuring public school management, school vouchers, and for-profit schools because such discussion is critical to the health of public schools. The push for school vouchers—which allocate to parents a certain amount of tuition dollars to spend wherever they want—applies the economics of the free market to education. However, these issues go way beyond the scope of this chapter. Since whole books have been devoted to them, I'll limit my discussion to more direct forms of advertising in schools—why it's happening, what forms it takes, and why it is a problem.

For corporations, of course, there is no downside. Because they are "contributing" to education, they look like good corporate citizens. They get to place their brand in the faces of students who, because of mandatory schooling laws, can't escape from it. To quote Joel Babbit, former president of Channel One, the commercially based news program mentioned earlier, "The advertiser gets kids who cannot go to the bathroom, cannot change the station, who cannot listen to their mother yell in the background, who cannot be playing Nintendo."[26]

The notion that marketing in schools is a reflection of good corporate citizenship is debatable. Since when do acts of good citizenship necessitate a *quid pro quo*? If you believe, as I do, that all of us—including corporate executives—benefit from a well-educated populace, the following questions come to mind: Why should your child's education be tied to someone else's monetary gain? Don't we all have an obligation to support public schools?

Those in the education trenches who allow, if not embrace, corporate marketing in their schools—superintendents, principals, teachers, and school board members—don't justify it on philosophical, political, or educational grounds, nor do they suggest that it is in the best interest of children to use school as a marketplace. For them, it comes down to money.

In 2003, my own state of Massachusetts cut its school budget for the first time in a decade.[27] Last year, legislators raised the school budget only 1 percent as opposed to the annual increase of 10 percent that had become common.[28] During the same legislative session in which this minuscule increase was passed, legislators also passed a law allowing schools to sell the sides of school buses to advertisers. According to one legislator, "We saw it as a way of getting a few more dollars in the door."[29] Massachusetts is not an exception. When school personnel look to commercialize their students' school experience, they almost always plead poverty.

In 2001, when the Brooklawn, New Jersey, high school announced that it would call its new school gymnasium "Shop Rite" after the local supermarket chain agreed to put up $100,000 ($5,000 a year for twenty years) to help pay for it, the school board hadn't asked for a tax increase for thirty years. Almost half of Brooklawn residents are senior citizens. "We don't want to bankrupt our seniors," the school board president explained, but the school superintendent added, "It's the privatization of public responsibility. . . . We'll be the first school district to be branded with a corporate logo. You hope children can become sophisticated enough to deal with it."[30]

Groundwork for the current iteration of corporate involvement in schools was laid in the Reagan years. Under Ronald Reagan, the federal government began to cut back the money states received for public programs, and the privatization of public services began to be seen as a solution for everything from prisons to garbage collection. In 1982, Reagan's Education Task force put out a treatise called *A Nation at Risk,* a rallying cry to business to get involved in schools.[31] At the same time, the federal government began to cut back on money for state programs, including those for education. These days, the federal government is responsible for only about 6 percent of school funding. But states and local communities have always borne the brunt of paying for educating their children. At its height, the federal government was responsible for only 10 percent of school costs.[32]

It's true that, at least until 2003, even taking inflation into account, school budgets have been rising over the past two decades. Even so, over the past fifteen years—which have seen a great escalation in school commercialization—they have not kept pace with growing populations.[33] Nor have budgets risen in proportion to the costs of federally mandated programs for which local school systems are responsible. Schools are obligated by law to meet the costs of special education programs and, more recently, to meet standards for achievement in certain subjects. In 2002, the Association of School Administrators estimated that testing mandates would cost states more than $7 billion over the next seven years[34]—at a time when forty states faced budget deficits.[35]

Before the current cuts, money that might have gone for equipment, maintenance, and classroom materials was already being spent for other things. Now the situation is even more dire. Wealthier communities might pass tax overrides to raise money for school buildings or to maintain certain programs. But poorer communities, or wealthy communities that don't make education a priority, are in a terrible bind. Schools with poorer students already receive less state and local aid than other schools.[36]

For corporations competing to sell children products, the current budget crunch is a gift. "Tight budgets opened doors," enthused a writer for *Promo* this year. Quoting an executive from the youth division of Alloy— a teen clothing catalogue-cum-web portal/magazine publisher—the article explained that administrators "are becoming more open to commercialism and thinking about how they can reduce budgetary problems." As a result, "brands are learning to create curriculum-based programs when possible or appropriate, bring mobile tours to schools, infiltrate locker rooms and sports fields, and sample, sample, sample."[37]

So what's the problem? How is marketing to children in schools harming them? If, as I'm arguing, it's harmful in their leisure time, it's certainly harmful during the hours they spend in school. Worries about advertising's impact on childhood obesity and nutrition, for instance, apply in any venue. But when products are advertised in school, there is an implicit message to students that the school supports the product. Whatever feelings children have about school—whether it is a positive or a negative force in their lives—there is an expectation that what they are learning there is good for them, in the same way that eating vegetables is good for them. At the very least, children believe that the adults involved in schools believe that what's happening there is good for kids.

We cannot expect kids to separate the message from the messenger. So when, as a mother reported recently, her fifth-grade daughter was handed a deodorant sample during health class, it carried a stamp of official approval. When a teacher in a local junior high decorated his wall with a poster of World Wrestling stars exhorting the joys of reading, he was endorsing violence as well as literacy. When a cafeteria in an elementary school in Superior, Wisconsin, featured a life-size cutout of teen pop star Britney Spears (who shills for Pepsico) as a "Got Milk" promotion (complete with information about how to get her latest CD), the school simultaneously endorsed milk, Pepsi, the teen singer, and whatever values she promotes in her music.

Dorothy Wolden, whose seven-year-old daughter attended the school at the time, was furious about the cutout and has this to say about her attempts to get it removed:

> In the cardboard stand-up, she [Britney] is wearing a short black t-shirt and black leather pants with studs, exposing about 3 or 4 inches of her tum. Between her feet, below the "Got Milk?" and her "signature," is an ad with a picture of her then-latest CD cover that says "Get Britney's new album 'Oops I Did It Again' on Jive CDs and tapes IN STORES NOW." The same ad was on the 3 by 3 poster of Britney on the cafeteria wall.
>
> One of the silliest stories about the whole thing was that someone decided my problem must be Britney's tummy and pasted a hand-lettered sign over her skin that said "Drink Milk!" (but left the album ad exposed). The superintendent in a phone conversation wondered if my issue was with the leather or the studs if not the skin. He told me, "Some schools are coloring in that stomach area with black marker; would that satisfy you?" [38]

The implicit endorsement of products and of commercialism itself is concerning, but marketing in schools raises other major worries. Critics believe that it interferes with the fabric of the public school system and, most important, with learning. In 1929, the National Education Association's position that corporate-sponsored classroom materials undermined democratic control of school curriculum was based on the fact that presentation of such material bypassed review by the school board members elected from the community. [39] More recently, others have expressed, and continue to express, concerns about content.

The only goal for creating classroom materials should be furthering the education of students using that material. Once a goal becomes imprinting brands into students' consciousness, or creating a positive association to a product, education is likely to take a back seat. [40] Is, for instance, a corporation likely to be unbiased in its presentation of subjects in which it has a vested interest? According to Consumer Union's 1995 review of seventy-seven corporate-sponsored classroom kits that claimed to be educational, the answer is "no." Nearly 80 percent were found to be biased or incomplete, "promoting a viewpoint that favors consumption of the sponsor's product or service or a position that favors the company or its economic agenda. A few contained significant inaccuracies." [41] Materials from energy companies and professional organizations such as Exxon (now Exxon

Mobil) or the American Coal Foundation, for instance, were found to be biased in their presentations of the pros and cons of reliance on fossil fuel. Through the American Petroleum Institute, the oil and gas industries produce classroom materials about energy. These can be downloaded at a site called classroom-energy.org.[42] In addition to the Institute's own materials, the site includes links to science lessons produced by oil and gas companies.

Why do teachers use corporate-sponsored materials? For one thing, schools have cut back on the amount of funding available for classroom materials.[43] Not only that, corporate materials are often slick-looking, with interesting graphics. Many teachers I know complain about using dreary out-of-date textbooks. However, even if teachers don't reject materials because they are dotted with corporate logos, the materials they use in the classroom should be vetted for bias or inaccuracies by curriculum specialists.

In recent years, much of the public outrage about marketing in schools has focused primarily on Channel One, which is a daily video program consisting of ten minutes of news interspersed with two minutes of commercials designed specifically for schools.

Channel One came into being in 1989 under the auspices of Tennessee entrepreneur Chris Whittle, who was the first to take advantage of the development of cable and satellite technology for the purpose of marketing to children in school. According to Channel One's web site, the program is fed to 12,000 middle, junior, and high schools around the country, and is viewed by more than eight million students.[44] Schools that sign on with Channel One contract to show the broadcast on 90 percent of school days and in 80 percent of their classrooms.[45] Teachers are required to show the program in its entirety, including the commercials.

What do schools get in exchange for broadcasting Channel One? For the duration of their relationship, the company provides every school with a color television monitor for every twenty-three students, VCRs as part of a central control unit, blank video tapes, a fixed satellite dish on the school roof, and free installation of cable wiring.[46] The value of this equipment has been estimated variously at $25,000[47] TO $50,000.[48] Except for the wiring, all of the equipment is removed when Channel One's contract is terminated. The catch is, this equipment isn't really free. In the course of a school year, students spend the equivalent of five instructional days watching Channel One. The teaching time lost to the ads alone is equivalent to one entire school day per year.[49] The school time lost to Channel One costs tax payers $1.8 billion dollars per year, and $300 million pays for time spent watching commercials. Advertising space on Channel One currently sells for roughly $200,000 per day for a thirty-second spot.[50]

A study examining which kinds of schools tend to use Channel One found that schools in poor neighborhoods are more likely to have it. These are the schools that frequently spend less money on their students. In fact, schools that spend the least amount on teaching materials are three times as likely to have Channel One than schools that spend more. The study's author concluded that in schools with scarce resources, Channel One is often used instead of "traditional" kinds of instructional materials—like books.[51]

People frequently ask about the quality of the news on Channel One. Is it educational? The reviews are mixed. There are studies showing that students who have Channel One know slightly more about current events than students who don't have the program.[52] Others show no difference.[53] While students watching Channel One may have a better recollection of current events than their nonviewing peers, they don't seem to have an increased understanding of the events they remember.[54] I don't know of any studies that measure the educational value of Channel One against twelve minutes of current events taught by a good teacher, or against twelve minutes spent reading a credible newspaper each day, or, for that matter, twelve minutes spent watching a noncommercial newscast.

In his eloquent essay, "How to Be Stupid: The Lessons of Channel One," New York University professor Mark Crispin Miller makes the point that the news as seen on Channel One is "even more compressed and superficial than the stuff the networks give us: big accidents and major snowstorms, non-stories about the Super Bowl, horse-race coverage of domestic politics, bloody images of foreign terrorism, the occasional nerve-wracking and largely unenlightening visit to some scary place like Haiti or Tibet, and features—either grim or inspirational—on teens suffering from various high-profile torments (cancer, AIDS, addiction)."[55]

A 1997 study analyzed thirty-six Channel One programs and found that only 20 percent of the program featured stories about recent political, social, or cultural events. The other 80 percent was devoted to sports, weather, natural disasters, features and profiles, and self-promotion of Channel One.[56] In 1998, Channel One hired an education director.[57] A review in the *Columbia Journalism Review* two years later suggested that the news quality had improved somewhat.[58] At this point, there is no education director listed on the company's web site,[59] and when I called the company, the person I spoke to said that there was no such position.

In any case, discussions about the quality of Channel One's news are distracting. Even aside from the commercials, Channel One represents a corporate intrusion into the lives of children—taking a total of five instructional days' worth of school time over the course of the year—in which one corporation dictates the content of "lessons" for eight million students without review from their teachers, principals, superintendents, or school boards. Teachers are allowed to preview programs and can opt not to show them—but the number of programs they can reject is limited to 10 percent of the whole.

While the effectiveness of the news content is debatable, the commercials seem to be a great success. To quote Dr. Miller again:

> The ads on Channel One would seem to be especially powerful, however, because they thrive by contrast not just with the news before and after them, but with the whole boring, regimented context of the school itself. . . . Imagine, or remember, what it's like to have to sit there at your desk, listening to your teacher droning on, with hours to go until you can get out of there, your mind rebelling and your hormones raging. It must be a relief when Channel One takes over, so you can lose yourself in its really cool graphics and its tantalizing bursts of rock music—and in the advertisers' mind-blowing little fantasies of power: power through Pepsi, Taco Bell, McDonald's, Fruit-A-Burst and/or Gatorade ("Life Is a Sport. Drink It Up!"), power through Head 'n' Shoulders, Oxy-10 and/or Pantene Pro-V Mousse (". . . a stronger sense of style!"), power through Donkey Kong and/or Killer Instinct ("PLAY IT LOUD!") and/or power through Reebok ("This is my planet!").[60]

The effectiveness of advertising on Channel One has been documented in qualitative[61] and quantitative studies.[62] When University of Missouri communications professor Ray Fox studied 200 students who viewed the Channel One newscast on a daily basis, he found, not surprisingly, that students clearly remembered the ads. He also found that the ads entered the fabric of their lives. Students incorporated Channel One into their creative writing and even reported dreaming about some of the ads.[63]

A study that compared two schools that were matched in every way except for the presence of Channel One found that kids who watched Channel One in school showed more of a preference for products on it than kids in schools that didn't show the program. Of even more concern is that students exposed to Channel One showed more inclination toward materialistic values than those who weren't exposed. The study found that regular viewers of Channel One were more likely to agree that: money is everything; a nice car is more important than school; designer labels make a difference; wealthy people are happier than poor people.[64]

These findings run counter to the argument of proponents of Channel One, and of any marketing in schools, that in-school advertising has little impact on children because they are exposed to advertising in all aspects of their lives. This study suggests that the ads on Channel One (and presumably other advertising in schools) have more of an impact—not just on brand preferences but also on students' values—because they are seen in the classroom at the behest of school officials and are integrated into the whole gestalt of "school" and what is taught there.

Running neck and neck with Channel One in arousing public ire is the phenomenon of "pouring-rights" contracts, in which a major beverage company, usually Coca Cola or Pepsico, buys the exclusive right to market their products within a school or school system. Since increased soda consumption is linked to the growing epidemic of childhood obesity, pouring-rights contracts have been coming under increasing scrutiny in recent years.

When Kelly Brownell, director of the Center for Eating and Weight Disorders at Yale and an outspoken critic of selling soda or any kind of junk food in schools, visited his son's public high school, he counted thirteen soft-drink machines—providing students with a total of 170 options to buy a beverage. Only one of those buttons yielded a container of 100-percent juice. Eleven were for water. The other 158 choices were for soft drinks. Describing the contents of a vending machine dominated by a big Minute Maid juice logo, Brownell reports in his book, *Food Fight,* that the buttons on that particular machine yielded no containers of 100-percent juice and that four of the buttons were for Yoohoo, a sweetened chocolate drink.[65]

A look at some facts about soda consumption lends credibility to the concerns of health-care providers:

- Per capita, Americans are consuming almost five times as much soda pop as they were fifty years ago.[66]
- According to a study at Boston Children's Hospital conducted with children aged seven to eleven, the odds of becoming obese increase for each additional can of sugar-sweetened drink consumed each day, as does BMI (Body Mass Index), which measures weight in proportion to height.[67]
- A twenty-ounce bottle of soda contains 260 calories.[68]
- For people already meeting their caloric needs, one twenty-ounce soda a day for a year could increase their weight twenty-seven pounds.
- A healthy teenager weighing 120 pounds, who exercises regularly, would have to walk at a moderate pace for two hours to burn off one twenty-ounce bottle of soda.[69]

The U.S. General Accounting Office's report identified beverage contracts as the most lucrative of all marketing done in schools.[70] It's certainly profitable for the beverage companies, who are also building brand loyalty.

The amount of money schools get for selling these rights, and what they give away to get that money, varies from district to district and sometimes from school to school. It seems to depend on the bargaining acumen of whoever is negotiating the contract. Often, but not always, the amount schools get is tied to commissions on the amount that students drink.

For instance, the West Ashley School in Charleston, South Carolina, gets $ 0.40 for every dollar plunked in a vending machine.[71] The school, which has about 2,100 students, now has approximately one vending machine per fifty students[72] and is realizing about $3,000 per month.[73] Figuring a nine-month school year, they are gaining about $13.00 per student. Per person, students spend about $3.57 each month in those vending machines, or about $32.00 per year. In other words, the students are paying almost $32.00 for $13.00 worth of whatever the school buys with their "extra" money.

The argument is that kids would be buying soda anyway, so they might as well spend that money in school. That may be, but if schools had no vending machines, the inconvenience of obtaining soda during school might enable students to cut down on their consumption. The fact that the vending machines are tied to school funds makes using them that much more attractive. The covert message is "Drink soda and support your school." Sometimes the message isn't all that covert. Some contracts even include quotas—the students are required to drink a certain amount each year. A Colorado Springs superintendent gained notoriety a few years ago when someone leaked a memo he wrote suggesting that students weren't buying enough cola. In order to receive payments ranging from $5,000 to $25,000 per school, the district had to meet a quota of 70,000 cases a year.[74]

A report published by the California Endowment provides insight into pouring-rights contracts. Of five districts involved, commissions ranged from 39 to 56 percent from vending machine sales. Districts received one-time bonuses ranging from $25,000 to $1,000,000. One district signing an exclusive contract also agreed that the corporation's logo could appear on all fountain cups used throughout the district. Those cups had to be purchased from the company. In addition, the company's advertisements would appear on all scoreboards, marquees, and in gymnasiums, and the company had exclusive advertising rights at any events held throughout the school district.

Another contract gave the beverage company "the exclusive right to make beverages available for sale and distribution on campus, including rights to install and operate all equipment that dispenses beverages from any location, to offer fruit drinks, packaged waters and other products in the cafeteria lines of all schools, and to provide all beverages sold at ath-

letic contests, booster club activities and all other special events conducted
at any location on the campus."[75] In this contract, "campus" referred to
"every school and facility owned or operated by the School District, now or
in the future, including all elementary, middle, high and alternative
schools, athletic facilities, and concession stands, and, for each building,
the grounds, parking lots, dining facilities, food service outlets and vending areas."[76]

The number of vending machines placed in schools almost always increases. In Edison, New Jersey, most schools didn't have soda machines
(and those that did had only two) until they signed their exclusive agreement with Coke. After the agreement, all of the high schools had four,
most junior highs had three, and most elementary schools had one.[77]

The problem with sending all of these vending machines to school is
nicely summed up in a 2001 U.S. Department of Agriculture report to
Congress titled, "Food Sold in Competition with USDA Meal Programs."
The report says, "When children are taught in the classroom about good
nutrition and the value of healthy food choices but are surrounded by
vending machines, snack bars, school stores, and a la carte sales offering
low nutrient-density options, they receive the message that good nutrition
is merely an academic exercise that is not supported by the school administration and is therefore not important to their health or education."[78]

In 2001, Coca Cola announced that it was responding to public concern
about obesity and changing its exclusive contracts with some schools.[79]
However, Coke has continued to negotiate exclusive deals with schools.[80]
Bolstering Coke's presence in the public education system, the company's
biggest bottler, Coca Cola Enterprises, is now an official sponsor of the national Parent-Teacher Association. One of its executives sits on the PTA's
board of directors.[81]

Candy and other snacks are also sold to students in vending machines.
Legislation that would authorize the Department of Agriculture to prohibit sales of foods like soda and candy in schools have been proposed repeatedly to Congress. It's not surprising that the bills have been blocked by
lobbyists from the soft drink and sugar industries. What's sad, however, is
that they have been joined by the National School Boards Association and
the National Association of Secondary School Principals, who say that the
loss of funds to schools would do more harm than the costs to children's
health.[82] How are children going to thrive when educators are pitted
against health-care professionals and nutritionists, forcing us to choose between their health and their education?

Pouring-rights contracts can also have an impact on aspects of children's lives other than obesity. I recently received the following e-mail
from an understandably irate father whose daughter was prevented by Pep-

sico from embarking on a fund-raising endeavor that involved selling bot-
tled water named after her school teams:

> My name is Gary K. Boyes Sr. I am the Father of Andrea Boyes, the
> cheerleader whose fund-raising intentions with custom labeled bot-
> tled water have been banned from the public school grounds by
> Pepsi. We are in Salem, Oregon. She is allowed to market her Titan
> water anywhere but where it was designed for. . . .
> My daughter was asked for a fund-raising idea. She worked out
> almost the whole thing herself. She chose a healthy consumable as
> the product for repeat sales. She designed the label and made all
> arrangements for production of the new West Salem Titan water. All
> I did was pick up the first order when completed. She essentially set
> up a small business to continually provide funding. In addition to this
> planned legacy from the first cheerleading squad at the new school,
> she had an as yet unpublished private goal that she kept under wraps
> until seeing the sales rates. She was hopeful that it could support a
> scholarship program so that a student that wanted to be a cheer-
> leader could try out without regard to their parents' ability to cover
> the high cost of making the squad. Many are forced to forgo even try-
> ing, and she wanted it to become possible for everyone based on
> their skills. At 15, she worked one day a week through the summer as
> an office manager for a local construction company and paid all of
> her cheerleading costs herself. She didn't have to, she wanted to.
> I have been getting a quick education on what I was generally apa-
> thetic about before. I can tell you I'm pretty ticked off with what I've
> found out.[83]

The Salem Keiser school district where Mr. Boyes's daughter is a student
has an exclusive ten-year, $5-million contract with Pepsi. The district also
has exclusive contracts with food service, furniture, athletic equipment,
and computer dealers.[84]

Both Channel One and beverage contracts are major commercial intru-
sions into the educational lives of children, but they are by no means the
only culprits. Less well known but equally pernicious is the degree to
which—often under pressure from administrators to turn more profit—
school food services have been selling fast food to their students during
lunch.[85] The presence of fast food and fast-food chains is most common in
high schools,[86] but by the mid-1990s, Pizza Hut, Taco Bell, and Domino
Pizza were gaining popularity in elementary schools as well.[87] A school in
San Lorenzo, California, has a student-staffed Burger King right on its
campus.[88]

What's troubling is that many nutritionists, including those within public education systems, seem to accept and even embrace food marketing in schools. A survey of nutrition professionals showed that while most of the respondents agreed that a product should have nutritional value to be marketed in schools, they did not feel that the underlying goal of food marketing—to create customers—is incompatible with the public-service aspect of their profession.[89]

Meanwhile, food marketing in schools abounds: Kellogg's has created nutrition education kits that promote Pop Tarts. General Mills has the "Big G Box Tops for Education" program that encourages sale of their products by donating money based on the number of product box tops the kids collect. Branded snacks are sold by students for fund-raisers. The Sampling Corporation of America helps companies distribute and promote products in elementary schools. Cafeteria posters may celebrate candy.[90]

A school principal sent me an "educational" poster about nutrition put out by the Frito-Lay company. A rather small representation of the USDA food pyramid is almost dwarfed by Frito-Lay products (as well as an enormous image of Pokémon characters). The poster exhorts kids to "Snack for Power, Snack for Fun!" "Did you know," the poster says, "Cheetos, Doritos and other Frito-Lay snacks give you the bread/brain power that the food guide pyramid says you need? That means that you can include Frito-Lay snacks along with toast, spaghetti, rice and crackers as part of a nutritious diet!" A picture depicts a bag of Doritos and a glass of milk with the caption, "That's some powerful snack."

The poster arrived at the school accompanied by the following note:

Dear Cafeteria Manager:
Frito-Lay is tapping into the popularity of Pokémon for its latest promotion, and we want you to benefit from it. Enclosed you'll find a colorful poster for your cafeteria—with a nutrition message for kids about the Food Guide Pyramid.

The poster uses the Pokémon characters to capture kids' attention, and then lets them know that Frito-Lay products can be an important part of snacking right—as in the familiar Food Pyramid—because Frito-Lay snacks can help them meet their daily Bread/Grain requirements.

Display this poster in your cafeteria. It'll make the lunchroom a more fun and interesting place for your students, tell a story about nutrition and help build your cafeteria sales.

Given growing concern about childhood obesity, the more optimistic among us can hope that the days of junk-food lunches and vending machines littering schools are on the wane. Thanks to the hard work of parents and advocacy groups, districts across the country are beginning to cut back on the ways the food industry can market to kids in schools. Both the outcry and the decline, however, seem to be focused on marketing unhealthy food, not on marketing per se. Those young children who manage to avoid marketing in their preschools are likely to be hit with some kind of advertising from the moment they start kindergarten. Here's one mother's experience:

> I am the mother of three children, aged 18 months, 3 years and 5 years. My oldest child is currently enrolled in kindergarten, so I am at the beginning of an 18 year (at least!) relationship with our town's public school system.
>
> Last month my son came home with his "Scholastic Book Fair order form," to be completed and sent back in with a check for total amount purchased. I recall filling these out as a child and bringing them back to school (after my mother made each of us erase the joke/riddle book choices and choose a "real" book instead—ha-ha). I was informed that the children would be bringing the orders to the library at school and would bring the books home that same afternoon.
>
> While I was annoyed that a child who may not be able to afford a purchase would be singled out in front of his peers, my irritation was soon twofold. My son told me about a book that he wished he had purchased because he knew it was very funny. When I asked how he knew, he told me that "it was in the movie we saw." Upon further investigation, I have since found out that each class sits through a 5–10-minute "movie" (i.e., commercial) which highlights the Scholastic books available for purchase, during library class time.
>
> While I am irate, I am discomforted at the prospect of charging into the administration office and causing a stir during my son's first three months of school . . . [91]

Ordering books from Scholastic and Scholastic Book Fairs are time-honored traditions in many schools. While these practices certainly are a form of marketing, many people concerned about advertising in schools have looked the other way because they seemed like a harmless way to get books into children's hands. Now, however, Scholastic sends out a video highlighting some of the books available to schools planning a fair. As this e-mail illustrates, the videos are extremely effective in convincing the kids who watch them to select certain books. Children's book choices are not guided by teachers, or by what looks interesting to them as they peruse se-

lections at the fair, but by commercials. They are buying what the corporation wants to sell at that time.

A few months ago, I got a call from a television producer who was doing
a story on the Field Trip Factory, a company that links schools with corporations who "donate" field trips to their stores or factories. For instance,
the mega pet-store chain Petco sends students to their store, where an employee shows them various kinds of pets. The kids go home with coupons
for goldfish and Petco stickers for their notebooks, all in a giant Petco
bag.[92] For a "Fitness and Safety in Sports" trip, kids get to go to a Sports Authority store. The trademarked "Be a Sports Authority" trip is described as
a "Free 60- to 90-minute trip through the aisles of the Sports Authority."
The web site even shows how teachers can meet national education standards in physical education.[93] The children also go home with a goody
bag—including a store coupon worth five dollars.[94]

These field trips are a slippery slope. Growing up in Detroit, I have fond
memories of going to the Wonder Bread factory and the Vernors soda pop
plant. But I also remember field trips to the zoo, the historical museum
and the Detroit Symphony youth concerts. Field trips are often among the
first casualties in a budget crunch.[95] Schools participating in Field Trip Factory trips seem to do so because they are free; it may be their only chance to
get students out of the classroom. That means that they are taking students
to Petco, for instance, *instead* of to the zoo.

Trips to the Sports Authority are positioned as taking the place of physical education classes, which are no longer routinely offered in schools. According to a Sports Authority vice president, "Children today need more
initiatives to get out and play . . . If the Sports Authority can provide that,
especially considering the cutbacks in P.E., I think it is appropriate for
companies to take up the slack. And what better organization to do this but
a sporting goods store?"[96]

In addition to bringing companies together with schools, the Field Trip
Factory provides scripts for store personnel charged with handling the
trips. However, they can't script every interaction, so when a reporter from
National Public Radio's *Marketplace* accompanied a class on one of the
Sports Authority trips, an employee ended the trip with the following
speech, "There's a little lunch bag in here and a coupon for you to give to
your parents to bring them back in here, so they can buy all of the stuff that
we talked about today. How's that sound? You like shopping here, right?"[97]

The Field Trip Factory describes its mission as providing free field trips
to "cash-strapped schools." Since the most impoverished schools are usually attended by impoverished children, I can't help but wonder what kind
of family stress is fomented when children come home with coupons and
urge their parents to go back and buy "all the stuff" they talked about on

the field trip. One parent, quoted in the *Washington Post,* felt his daughter's class trip to Petco was positive, but called it "cruel and unusual punishment for parents." He added, "We'll have to deal with the fallout. . . . She'll be wanting to buy cats [and] parakeets for the next two weeks."[98]

In answer to concerns about promoting commercialism, a Field Trip Factory executive claimed that the trips helped kids become educated consumers.[99] However, when reached by phone, she explained that the trips to grocery stores helped children become educated consumers because they taught children to look at different prices within the store. When I asked if the trips ever talked about comparison shopping at other grocery stores as part of learning to be educated consumers, she said that they did not. The executive emphasized that the trips were designed to educate, not to sell products. She mentioned a trip to a Saturn dealership as an example through which children learned about automobile safety. She explained that her company did not tell kids to go home and talk to their parents about products. That message does not seem to be getting through to employees of at least some of the Field Trip Factory destinations. A spokesperson for a Saturn dealership in Illinois was quoted as saying, "We get to market to local areas, to local schools. This becomes, you know, dinner conversation. 'What did you do today?' 'Well, we went to Saturn . . . ' "[100]

As de facto funding for public schools continues to decrease, it's likely that, without more public outcry, corporations will continue to be more than willing to leap into the breach—at a cost. Instructional time, access to accurate information, and the chance to develop critical thinking skills may all be lost as corporations take an increasing role in public education. The most concrete cost to children and to the pocketbooks of American taxpayers is the contribution marketing in schools makes to childhood obesity, but marketing anything to children in public schools compromises their education.

NOTES

1. Ed Winter, quoted in Pat Wechsler, "This Lesson Is Brought to You By . . ." *Business Week,* June 30, 1997, 68.
2. Kate Zernike, "Coke to Dilute Push in Schools for Its Products," *New York Times,* March 14, 2001, sec. A, p. 14.
3. American Coal Foundation, "Unlocking Coal's Potential Through Education: Our Mission," available at http://www.afc-coal.org/ (accessed September 11, 2003).
4. Pizza Hut, "Book It! Time for Kids," available at http://www.bookitprogram.com (accessed September 11, 2003).
5. Susan Campbell, "The Hazards of Learning to Speak for Yourself," *Hartford Courant,* June 19, 2001, Life, D2.

6. Project 2000, Inc., "Mariott Hospitality Public Charter High School," available at http://project2000inc.org/mariott.htm (accessed September 11, 2003).

7. Francis Beckett, "Schools, United States—Schools with High Hopes for Low Achievers: Francis Beckett Finds Determined US Efforts to Lure the Truants Back," *The Guardian*, October 26, 1992, E4.

8. Alex Molnar, "What's in a Name? The Corporate Branding of America's Schools: Year 2001–2002," in *Fifth Annual Report on Trends in Schoolhouse Commercialism* (Tempe, AZ: Commercialism in Education Research Unit [CERU], Education Policy Studies Laboratory, University of Arizona, 2002), 29.

9. Ryan Kim, "Schools May Sell Naming Rights: District Considers Proposal to Raise Funds."

10. Enola Aird, "Reading, Writing, 'Rithmetic—and Marketing," *Newsday*, June 12, 2001, A39.

11. It's important to note that until 2002 schools did not even need parental permission to allow market research firms to mine students for their ideas. That changed with a provision in the federal No Child Left Behind Act, which reauthorized the Elementary and Secondary Education Act ("Student Privacy Protections Added in ESEA Reauthorization Bill," *Education Technology News* 19, no. 2 (January 16, 2002).

12. Wechsler, "This Lesson Is Brought to You."

13. Alex Molnar, *Giving Kids the Business: The Commercialization of America's Schools* (Boulder, CO: Westview Press, 1996), 39.

14. Inger L. Stole, "Advertisers in the Classroom: A Historical Perspective," paper presented at the Association for Consumer Research annual conference, Columbus, OH, 1999.

15. Elizabeth A. Fones-Wolf, *Selling Free Enterprise: The Business Assault on Labor and Liberalism, 1945–60* (Urbana: University of Illinois Press, 1994), 204. She cites the *New York Times*, January 4, 1959, and others.

16. Molnar, "What's in a Name?" 5.

17. Rod Taylor, senior vice president at CoActive Marketing, Great Neck, NY, quoted in Carrie MacMillan, "Readin', Writin', and Sellin'," *Promo* 15, no. 10 (September 1, 2002): 24.

18. General Accounting Office, *Public Education: Commercial Activities in Schools—Report to Congressional Requesters* (Washington, DC: United States General Accounting Office, 2000), 26.

19. For a full discussion of this, see Robert Kuttner, *Everything for Sale: The Virtues and Limits of Markets* (Chicago: University of Chicago Press, 1996).

20. Jen Lin-Liu, "Hornbeck Steps Down as Superintendent, Two Take Over," Associated Press State and Local Wire, August 14, 2000.

21. Dan Russakoff, "Finding the Wrongs in Naming Rights: School Gym Sponsorship Sparks Furor," *Washington Post*, December 16, 2001, A3.

22. Alison Gendar and David Saltonstall, "Lawyer Picked as Chancellor: Joel Klein has Federal, Business Background," *New York Daily News*, July 30, 2002, 3.

23. Gail Russell Chaddock, "Corporate Ways Invade Schools," *Christian Science Monitor*, August 4, 2000, 1.

24. Linda Shaw and Keith Ervin, "Olchefske Facing a Crisis That's Not Just About Money; Cool Businesslike Superintendent Must Balance the Books—and

Regain Trust," *Seattle Times*, November 17, 2002, A1; Linda Shaw and Keith Ervin, "Under Fire, Olchefske Steps Down: Seattle Superintendent Quits Amid Financial Upheaval," *Seattle Times*, April 15, 2003, A1.

25. "Chicago's Budget Director Taking Schools Post in Philadelphia," Associated Press State and Local Wire, July 13, 2002.

26. Joel Babbit quoted in Ralph Nader, *Children First: A Parent's Guide to Fighting Corporate Predators* (Washington, DC: Children First, 1996), 64.

27. Joan Vennochi, "Budget Punishes Schools' Success," *Boston Globe*, July 17, 2003, A19.

28. Rick Collins, "Coming to Your Town Soon: A Debate Over Advertising on School Buses," *State House News Service*, August 5, 2002, available at www.statehousenews.com.

29. Representative Bradley Jones quoted in ibid.

30. Russakoff, "Finding the Wrongs."

31. Molnar, *Giving Kids the Business*, 1.

32. Richard Rothstein, "When States Spend More," *American Prospect 9*, no. 36 (January 1, 1998–February 1, 1998): 72–79.

33. Ibid.

34. National Association of State Boards of Education, "Cost of President's Testing Mandate Estimated As High As $7 Billion," National Association of State Boards of Education, Washington, DC, April 25, 2001, available at http://www.nasbe.org/Archives/cost.html (accessed July 20, 2003).

35. National Governors Association and National Associations of State Budget Officers, "Executive Summary," *Fiscal Survey of States*, May 2002, ix.

36. Jean Brennan, ed., *The Funding Gap* (Washington, DC: The Education Trust, August 2002).

37. Derek White, executive vice president of Alloy, quoted in MacMillan, "Readin', Writin', and Sellin'," 24.

38. Personal e-mail communication from Dorothy Wolden, November 20, 2000.

39. Alex Molnar, "Corporate Involvement in Schools: Time for a More Critical Look," Education Policy Studies Laboratory (EPSL), National Association of States Board of Education, Washington, DC, Winter 2001, available at http://www.asu.edu/educ/epsl/CERU/Documents/cace-01-01.html.

40. Deron Boyles, *American Education and Corporations: The Free Market Goes to School* (New York: Garland Publishing, 1998).

41. Consumers Union, "Evaluations," in *Captive Kids: A Report on Commercial Pressures on Kids in School* (Washington, DC: Consumers Union, 1998), 3, available at www.consumersunion.org/other/captivekids/evaluations.

42. American Petroleum Institute, "Classroom Energy! Lesson Plans," available at http://www.classroom-energy.org/teachers/plans/index.html (accessed November 12, 2002).

43. Consumers Union, "Evaluations."

44. Channel One, "About Channel One," available at http://www.channelone.com/common/about/ (accessed September 14, 2003).

45. Consumer Union, "Evaluations."

46. Steven Manning, "The Television News Show Kids Watch Most," *Columbia Journalism Review 38*, no. 6 (2000): 55–57.

47. Ibid.

48. Janice M. Barrett, "Participants Provide Mixed Reports About Learning from

Channel One," *Journalism and Mass Communication Educator* 53, no. 2 (1998): 54–67.

49. Center for Commercial-Free Public Education, "Education Industry: What's on Channel One?" July 8, 1998, available at http://www.corpwatch.org/issues/PID.jsp?articleid=888 (accessed May 21, 2003).

50. Max B. Sawicky and Alex Molnar, "The Hidden Costs of Channel One: Estimates for the Fifty States," Education Policy Studies Laboratory (EPSL), Arizona State University, April 1998, available at http://www.asu.edu/educ/epsl/CERU/Documents/cace-98-02/CACE-98-02.htm.

51. Michael Morgan, "Channel One in the Public Schools: Widening the Gap," research report prepared for UNPLUG, University of Massachusetts at Amherst, Department of Communication, October 13, 1993.

52. Drew Tienne, "Exploring the Effectiveness of Channel One School Telecasts," *Educational Technology* 33, no. 5 (1993): 26–42.

53. Nancy Nelson Knupfer and Peter Hayes, "The Effects of the Channel One Broadcast on Students' Knowledge of Current Events," in *Watching Channel One*, ed. Ann DeVaney (Albany: State University of New York Press, 1994), 42–60.

54. Ibid.

55. Mark Miller, "How to Be Stupid: The Teachings of Channel One," paper prepared for Fairness and Accuracy in Reporting (FAIR), January 1997, 1, available at http://www.fair.org/extra/9705/ch1-miller.html.

56. William Hoynes, "News for a Captive Audience: An Analysis of Channel One," *Extra!* (published by FAIR), May/June 1997, 11–17.

57. Manning, "The Television News Show Kids Watch Most."

58. Ibid.

59. Channel One, "About Channel One."

60. Miller, "How to Be Stupid."

61. Roy F. Fox, "How Do Kids Respond to Commercials?" in *Harvesting Minds: How TV Commercials Control Kids* (Westport, CT: Praeger, 1996), 39–59.

62. Bradley S. Greenberg and Jeffrey E. Brand, "Television News Advertising in Schools: The 'Channel One' Controversy," *Journal of Communication* 43, no. 1 (1993): 143–51.

63. Fox, "How Do Kids Respond," 92.

64. Jeffrey E. Brand and Bradley S. Greenberg, "Commercials in the Classroom: The Impact of Channel One Advertising," *Journal of Advertising Research* 34, no. 1 (1994): 18–21.

65. Kelly D. Brownell and Katherine Battle Horgen, *Food Fight: The Inside Story of the Food Industry, America's Obesity Crisis, and What We Can Do About It* (New York: Contemporary Books, 2004).

66. Judith Jones Putnam and Jane E. Allshouse, "In 1945, Americans Drank More Than Four Times as Much Milk as Carbonated Soft Drinks; in 1997, They Downed Nearly Two and a Half Times More Soda Than Milk," figure 8 in *Food Consumption Prices and Expenditures, 1970–1997* (Washington, DC: Food and Rural Economics Division, Economics Research Services, U.S. Department of Agriculture, 1999), 49.

67. David S. Ludwig, Karen E. Peterson, and Steven L. Gortmaker, "Relation Between Consumption of Sugar-Sweetened Drinks and Childhood Obesity: A Prospective, Observational Analysis," *The Lancet* 357 (February 17, 2001): 505–8.

68. Amanda Purcell, "Prevalence and Specifics of District-Wide Beverage Contracts in California's Largest School Districts," report commissioned by the California Endowment, April 2002, 3.
69. Ibid.
70. General Accounting Office, "Public Education," 4.
71. National Public Radio (NPR), Morning Edition, "Analysis: Soda Machines Used to Raise Money for Schools," NPR transcript for October 18, 2002.
72. Mindy Spar, "Local School Focus of 'Now,' " *Post and Courier* (Charleston, SC), October 18, 2002, TV3.
73. NPR, "Analysis: Soda Machines."
74. Steven Manning, "Counting Cokes and Candy Bars," Cleveland *Plain Dealer*, March 25, 1999, 9B; Zernike, "Coke to Dilute Push in Schools."
75. Purcell, "Prevalence and Specifics," 9.
76. Ibid.
77. Marc Kaufman, "Fighting the Cola Wars in Schools," *Washington Post*, March 23, 1999, Z12.
78. U.S. Department of Agriculture, "Food Sold in Competition with USDA Meal Programs: A Report to Congress," January 12, 2001, available at http://www.fris.usda.gov/end/lunch/CompetitiveFoods/report_congress.htm (accessed November 15, 2002).
79. Zernike, "Coke to Dilute Push in Schools."
80. "Sports Authority: Soft Drink Deal Reached," *Pittsburgh Post Gazette*, June 28, 2003, D5.
81. Sherri Day, "Coke Moves with Caution to Remain in Schools," *New York Times*, September 3, 2003, sec. C, p. 1.
82. Richard Rothstein, "Lessons: For Schools' Ills, the Sugar Pill," *New York Times*, August 21, 2002, sec. B, p. 8.
83. E-mail correspondence with Gary Boyes, November/December 2002.
84. "West Salem Cheerleader in Hot Water with Pepsi," Associated Press State and Local Wire, November 3, 2002.
85. Marion Nestle addresses in depth the commercialization of school food services and the other ways food marketers target children in school in her book *Food Politics: How the Food Industry Influences Nutrition and Health* (Berkeley: University of California Press, 2002), 188–95.
86. Diane Brockett, "School Cafeterias Selling Brand-Name Junk Food: Who Deserves a Break Today?" *Education Digest* 64, no. 2 (1998): 56–59.
87. Jane Levine, "Food Industry Marketing in Elementary Schools: Implications for School Health Professionals," *Journal of School Health* 69, no. 7 (1999): 290–91.
88. "Battle of the Bulge; Fast Food Is King at Arroyo High," editorial, *San Francisco Chronicle*, July 29, 2003, D4.
89. Jane Levine and Joan Gussow, "Nutrition Professionals' Knowledge of and Attitudes Toward the Food Industry's Education and Marketing Programs in Elementary Schools," *Journal of the American Dietetic Association* 8 (1999): 973–76.
90. Levine, "Nutrition Professionals' Knowledge."
91. Personal communication.
92. ABC News, World News Saturday, "Profile: Controversy Over Company Sponsored School Field Trips," May 11, 2002, transcript from Factiva, July 22, 2003.

93. Field Trip Factory, "Be a Sports Authority: Fitness, Safety & Teamwork," available at http://www.fieldtripfactory.com/tsa/ (accessed July 22, 2003).

94. Alisa Hauser Kraft, "Buy, Baby Bunting," *Chicago Reader* 32, no. 37 (June 13, 2003): 1, 20–22.

95. Julia Silverman, "When Strapped Schools Can't Pay for Field Trips, Corporations Step In," Associated Press Newswire, October 15, 2002.

96. Ibid.

97. Pete Johnson, Sports Authority sales manager, quoted in Minnesota Public Radio, Marketplace Morning Report, "Profile: School Field Trips to Stores and Shopping Centers," September 4, 2002, transcript from Factiva, May 22, 2003.

98. Caroline E. Mayer, "A Growing Market Strategy: Get 'Em While They're Young; Firms Sponsor School Activities and Books," *Washington Post,* June 3, 2002, A1.

99. "In-School Marketing Programs Focus on Educating Rather Than Selling," *Youth Markets Alert 1* 14, no. 4 (April 1, 2002): 1.

100. ABC News, "Profile: Controversy Over Company-Sponsored School Field Trips."

IV

Parent, Family, and Community Involvement: The Key to Success

18

Involving Parents and the Community

Anne Wheelock

Communicating with Parents:
Promoting Understanding of Untracking

First of all, I'm in favor of mixed-ability grouping. But my concern is that we can do it only if we hold down class size, which we can do next year. But what about the year after? If we have to increase class size, will that make this move unrealistic?

I hope with this program we try to get as much academic excellence as we can. What consideration was given to opening up algebra to all students but keeping an accelerated group? The assumptions I've heard are not realistic. You're asking the teachers to bite off an awful lot, and the kids at both ends of the spectrum may be hurt.

It is a winter night in New England, and the large lecture hall at the Wellesley Middle School is filled with parents of the school's seventh-grade students. Armed with the kinds of questions that parents typically ask when they are worried that change may threaten the well-being of their children, these parents have come out tonight because the school's teachers have told principal John D'Auria that they are ready to try heterogeneous grouping in the eighth grade. In response, D'Auria has figured out a plan that will allow the school to pilot this approach in the coming year. Average class size will be reduced from twenty-nine to twenty-one, and the sharing of the school's teachers with the high school will be eliminated.

Because this class size cannot be guaranteed in subsequent years, D'Auria and superintendent Karla Deletis have decided to move more quickly than usual. Although they have received preliminary approval from the school board, they have had time to tell only those parents most active in the school's PTO of the change. As a result, many parents are suspicious that something is being put over on them; some even plan to protest at the next school committee meeting.

Prior to the meeting, D'Auria has sent a letter to all parents describing the proposed changes. The letter outlines the school's plan to adopt a core science, English, and social-studies curriculum for all eighth-grade students along with heterogeneous grouping that mirrors arrangements already in place in the sixth and seventh grades. The letter also describes the school's proposal to continue offering three eighth-grade math levels; a "Level 3" pre-algebra course; a "Level 2" transitional algebra course based on the University of Chicago Mathematics Project's textbook series, which focuses on probability, statistics, and geometry; and a traditional algebra course offered as an accelerated course. In the letter, D'Auria also notes:

> The staff is eagerly anticipating these changes in curriculum and grouping format. We think these revisions will benefit *all* our students—from our most confident to our least confident learners. I view these recommendations as outgrowths of our core value work and our experiences in developing ways to challenge every student in heterogeneous settings. . . . We have seen considerable success in these settings. We have examined the research. . . . We have looked to our middle school neighbors. . . . This evidence encourages us to offer all our eighth-grade students the rich curricular experiences that once were available to only a few. . . . Our judgment is reflective of the needs of middle school–age students.

Parents have come here tonight for further discussion of this letter and the four agenda items that D'Auria flashes on the overhead projector at the outset:

1. Exact nature of changes
2. Context for these changes
3. Gain for students
4. How we plan to assess the outcomes of these curricular and instructional modifications

Parents listen carefully as D'Auria reviews the school's core objectives and values related to teacher expectations and student effort. He lists the new skills that teachers have developed in preparation for heterogeneous grouping—cooperative learning, mastery learning, and the use of instructional technology. He describes how students have risen to higher expectations and how, as a result, teachers have recommended fewer students for "Level 3" courses, obviating the need to offer such courses. He concludes, "We think these changes will bring our goals off the pages and into the daily lives of all our students."

> *My daughters are very confident and fast talkers, and I love the attitude of the teachers here. But I'm still concerned about teachers' being able to handle a wide range of differences and build self-esteem among students who are not so good at organizing their work. Won't this affect the quality of classroom atmosphere?*

> *I have very serious concerns. I have trouble with a teacher teaching something and gearing it to all students. . . . After all, you can learn cooperation and respect in extracurricular activities. This came too fast. . . .*

The parents have legitimate questions, many best answered by the teachers who chair each department: Linda Smith, social studies; Peggy Mongiello, English; and Bill Atherton, science and math. In turn, Smith, Mongiello, and Atherton provide an overview of the curriculum and describe the enthusiasm of their colleagues for heterogeneous grouping and a more interesting curriculum for all. Teachers in the audience nod when Smith observes that heterogeneous grouping and curricular changes in the earlier grades have resulted in better instruction. "Students do better in school when they're invested in their work and in inherently challenging assignments," she concludes. Mongiello adds, to more nodding, "Good teaching is based on a situation that challenges all students."

What do challenging assignments for students of diverse abilities look like? The teachers provide examples:

- In English: Students studying the autobiographical form in literature and experimenting with different writing styles read Roald Dahl's *Boy* and are then asked to write their own autobiography in a similar anecdotal form, covering any experiences that they choose. Given no limits, one "Level 1" student wrote seven pages; one "Level 2" student submitted thirty-five pages.
- In social studies: Using nothing but information gleaned from a variety of maps, students research habitats of Africa. With assignments requiring them to work out scale, distance, and travel time, students analyze and synthesize information, develop hypotheses about climate, terrain, and ethnic groups, and ultimately write postcards to their friends and family about their "trips."
- In science: According to Atherton, "What is different is the routine

you get youngsters into. Every kid will be at a lab station, working with a partner. I work all year on making myself superfluous while kids learn to form questions and solve problems. Sometimes I surprise them and drop an old eyeball preserved in formaldehyde in their beakers. They have to figure out what it is. These are not special things. All kids can do it!"

Teachers all emphasize that parents' concerns are those that any educator would share, whether for the least or the most confident students. They explain that they take into account the needs of slower learners, not by watering down the curriculum, but by preparing students for assignments, structuring assignments clearly, and applying mastery concepts for skills so that those who do not achieve 80 percent mastery are rechecked until they do. They note also that they consciously provide gifted students with extra opportunities to excel through independent assignments and contracts for honors work.

I came here really negative. Now I'm only indifferent. I'm concerned we're diluting the education of our top students. I think you're sacrificing the most motivated for the good of the rest of the class. How do you take the kids and give everyone a sense of achievement without diluting the achievement of the "high" kids? It seems to me that the more kids compete with each other, the harder they'll work.

I'm beginning to understand why I have a problem with this. If you carry the logic to its extreme, if average kids can benefit from a more challenging curriculum than they're getting now, why can't the "high" kids benefit from a curriculum that's harder for them?

What gains do Wellesley staff envision for all students? D'Auria wants everyone to understand that improvement is significant at all levels, and he projects the anticipated gains for "Level 1" students onto the screen:

1. Students will learn more varied and diverse problem-solving strategies: At the Wellesley Middle School, staff work on helping all students think about alternative solutions to many problems.
2. What students learn will be more lasting: When students explain their answers and point of view to others, they integrate their learning in a more lasting way. Learning theory demonstrates that students retain ten times more information from a discussion-group format than from a lecture.

3. Students will be supported in greater risk taking: In a tracked setting, "high" students frequently come to believe that asking questions is a sign of stupidity and fear that their placement in the top group has been a mistake or that if they show uncertainty, they will be removed from their group.

4. Students will have more opportunity to unlearn some self-limiting beliefs such as "If I can't learn it quickly, then I'm not good at it"; "If I can't learn it quickly, then it's not worth doing"; and "Being smart means being able to learn many ideas quickly and lots of facts." These are not beliefs that will help one in life. We want students to know that achievement derives more from consistent effort than anything else.

5. Students will learn greater acceptance and appreciation for others: we want students who can identify, describe, and view the world from the perspective of others.

Reviewing gains for students at other levels, D'Auria presents similar advantages such as the benefits derived from exposure to curriculum that is rich and challenging, developing different and diverse ways of thinking, and the opportunity to unlearn self-limiting beliefs. Noting that in tracked schools "children in the middle can sometimes feel a little lost," he acknowledges concerns of parents of average learners. By encouraging risk taking among *all* students, he points out, greater confidence and more adventurous learning has emerged most dramatically in mixed-ability groups.

> *Even after all this discussion, I can't help but think there's benefit to homogeneous grouping in certain settings and certain times. I know I benefited from both. Is there some way to make sure that students have the benefits of working in homogeneous grouping from time to time?*

> *What I'm concerned about is that with this new heterogeneous grouping in grade eight, kids won't be prepared for the levels they encounter in high school. What I want to know is whether elimination of levels at grade eight will make the transition to high school more difficult.*

The questions continue—all of them reasonable, all reflecting the kinds of concerns that most parents have for their children. The superintendent, who has been in the audience, assures parents that the proposed plan does not reflect a "hidden agenda" to eliminate levels at the high school. Classroom teachers, specialists, and counselors in the audience further respond:

> Yes, we can regroup kids in smaller groups when that's appropriate, and we can give kids extra-credit assignments.
>
> In fact, there's enormous variability in every class, even ones you think are homogeneous. You can't really rank children on a continuum in every skill at every level. The more we use different alternatives, the more we can accomodate the variability.
>
> We will always be calling on the guidance counselor to help out. It will be her job to make sure our high school staff is clear about the tasks at the different high-school levels. Then our students can decide how much they want to stretch. When they leave our school, they will know they have been successful learners. Their choice will have to do with their own interests. But for eleven-, twelve-, and thirteen-year-olds, we'd like to be sure that options are not foreclosed for them.

It is 11:00. John D'Auria concludes:

> We have a challenge in front of us to make sure we provide intellectual challenges for all kids. A core curriculum means teachers can develop the best of the strategies that will bring out the best in kids—the best cooperative learning activities, the best assignments. We need the support of parents, and we need to hear from parents about what's working and what's not so we can better and better match what we do to what your child needs; so we can challenge kids appropriately, but not confuse coverage for depth; so they can learn ideas, concepts, substance.

The meeting is over. After a two-hour presentation and an hour and a half of questions and discussion, a few parents still feel unsure; even the best answers have not taken away all their misgivings. But most seem satisfied; everyone is better informed; and the support is so substantial that although the discussion continues at the subsequent school-board meeting, the proposals pass community review and are approved for implementation the fall.

Gaining Parent Support for Untracking

You have to give parents the guarantee that their child is not going to be harmed. Parents ask, "Can you be sure my child is not going to be worse off?" I can say "She won't be worse off, and we hope she will be better off."

—Janet Pearson, teacher, Kammerer Middle School,
Louisville, Kentucky

As schools embark on the process of untracking, all parents want to know how grouping changes are going to affect their children. Parents of students with disabilities need to know that someone has been thinking about how newly designed grouping arrangements will promote success for their children without overwhelming them. Parents of academically confident children need to know that heterogeneous classes do not result in "dumbed down" curriculum or instruction geared to "the middle." Parents of "average" children need to know that their children will not be lost in classrooms that allocate most of the teachers' attention to students at the extreme ends of the learning spectrum.

Not too long ago, grouping practices at Kammerer Middle School in Louisville, Kentucky, strictly mirrored district policy: advanced placement was determined by standardized testing across the district; placement in honors and comprehensive classes was determined at the school level. Given the force of habit and tradition, it had never occurred to many teachers or parents that alternatives to this approach existed.

However, not everyone at the school level was entirely comfortable with tracking, particularly when it seemed to result in in-school segregation. As Kammerer's language-arts teacher Claudia Runge reports:

> Many of us were concerned that our "comprehensive" classes were racially identifiable. We had concerns about labeling. With ability grouping in the elementary grades, by the time the kids got to us, they weren't doing the work they should have been doing. We were getting kids who had a pretty low self-concept, and we weren't doing anything to help that.

At Kammerer, teachers and parents never set out *intentionally* to adopt alternatives to tracking. Rather, untracking—and parent participation in that process—evolved as an outgrowth of the school's overall policy of parent involvement. In 1986, principal Nancy Weber had convened a Parent Roundtable simply as a way for teachers and parents to meet to talk about the needs of middle-grades youngsters. Meeting monthly with two or three school staff, the Parent Roundtable provided a forum for reacting to various articles and reports, including the Carnegie Commission's *Turning Points*, about young adolescents and middle schools.

Tracking *per se* was never on the agenda, explains Runge. But, she says,

"If you read a lot of middle-school material, you're bound to come across the topic. It popped up in everything we read. After two years of the Roundtable, tracking became an issue. We just kept coming back to it."

By early 1989, teachers on one of the school's two sixth-grade teams were eager to pilot the academic integration of students from all levels. At the same time, as a result of the Parent Roundtable, school staff had developed a positive relationship with a small core group of influential parents who, says Runge, "didn't necessarily support the idea of untracking but were at least familiar with the material." And so, in August 1989, Weber sent a letter to all parents describing how the school's process for academic integration would be implemented to reflect current recommendations for improving middle schools, including the elimination of tracking.

Even with such preparation, the introduction of academic integration at Kammerer did not move forward without a hitch. In fact, says Janet Pearson, sixth-grade team leader, "We were convinced that in order for all students to achieve at the highest levels we needed heterogeneous classes. But we misread our constituency. In the minds of our parents, this was an experimental program." Even a special orientation meeting designed to present information to in-coming sixth-grade parents did not fully allay fears. Pearson relates, "I began to realize that unless we had one-to-one meetings with parents to tell them about our intentions, they were not going to listen. Over the next four weeks, I personally spent hours and hours on the telephone and in personal conferences with tearful parents. Many wanted to do this, but it was an agonizing decision for them when they feared they were removing their child from the 'protected surroundings' of the track."

During that first year, the pilot sixth-grade team combined one regular, one honors, and two advanced-placement classes, maintaining this ability-grouping proportion both in each science and social-studies class as a whole and within small in-class groups in those subjects. Although students were randomly mixed for allied-arts and physical-education classes, in math and language arts the team continued to offer separate AP classes to conform with district policy.

This approach paid off. That first year, according to Pearson, "While some parents requested the transfer of their children to the second sixth-grade team that had retained tracking, most stayed with us." Throughout that year, teachers continued to make themselves available for questions and provided progress reports to parents through a team newsletter distributed every four to five weeks.

Tracking continued to be the focus of discussion at Parent Roundtable meetings where teachers reported on the progress of new approaches, entertained questions, and were able to assure parents that:

Instruction is directed to the highest level, encouraging expression of a variety of perspectives among students. . . . Discipline problems are definitely reduced in all groups on all levels, and . . . previously lower-performing students have new role models, and find they can compete.

By April 1990, parents and teachers meeting together at the Roundtable reflected positively on the year's progress, reporting in the group's minutes that "this discussion group itself is amazing in that teachers, parents, and administrators are discussing alternatives in schools. This could not have been predicted a few years ago." As Pearson notes, "The Roundtable at first was a place for open, philosophical discussions. Once we jumped into the change, the Roundtable was a vehicle to help implement our plans."

Teachers at Kammerer took the lessons of parent involvement seriously as they moved to advance their program. Prior to the second year of integration, staff set up spring meetings at each of the feeder elementary schools to explain the program to parents. Again, not all parents were persuaded of the wisdom of heterogeneous grouping, and when some registered complaints with the central administration, school staff adapted their approach by offering the choice of a heterogeneously grouped team or a tracked team in both the sixth and seventh grades. Staff and parents also planned for an initial orientation for parents, additional Roundtable discussions about tracking, and a continuation of the parent newsletter with regular reports on the progress of academic integration. Pearson says, "This time we knew we were not going to drop a bomb. We knew what parents were looking for."

The efforts worked. Of the 120 sixth-grade students moving on to seventh grade, parents of all but one chose to continue on the "blended" team, and the team had to draw up a waiting list. By the start of the third year, 104 of the 116 student places on the heterogeneously grouped team in the sixth grade had been spoken for by the initial sign-up deadline, and the heterogeneous teams in the upper grades had waiting lists of students from all levels—including one whose parent had been an early and vocal opponent of the pilot program. This high level of parent enthusiasm, Pearson emphasizes, comes from being open to working with parents at every step of the process. "We're not trying to put anything over on anyone. No one feels coerced," she says.

Guidelines for Involving Parents in the Untracking Process

> Principals aren't trained to be politicians, yet this is a political issue. I
> learned you need to be politically savvy.
> —Sue Galletti, principal, Islander Middle School,
> Mercer Island, Washington

The experiences of schools where untracking has been successful offer suggested guidelines for involving parents in the untracking process:

- Be aware that parents need to be involved in the change process. Even though you have a plan that you are certain is a good one, don't hesitate to talk it over with everyone who is going to be affected, in large groups if necessary, but especially in small groups and in individual parent conferences.
- In communicating with parents, be sure that you can articulate the expected outcomes of innovative grouping practices in terms of benefits to all children. Understand that the word *restructuring* without further elaboration can imply undirected experimentation, and that few parents will willingly allow their children to be guinea pigs in such an experiment.
- Be prepared for the possibility that not all parents will endorse proposed alternatives to tracking. If, even after extended discussions, some parents continue to object, school staff may decide that, as teacher Claudia Runge says, "You just have to take the plunge." In such situations, phasing in heterogeneous grouping and monitoring outcomes may help resolve concerns of parents who are likely to complain to district decision makers.
- Be sure to maintain a high level of instruction for all students. Explain changes in terms of how you have strengthened curriculum and instruction for all students. Assure parents that children will not be experiencing a "watered-down" curriculum—with the "same old basal readers" simply adopted in mixed-ability classes—by providing them with specific examples of individualized assignments that enrich learning.
- Don't abandon efforts to communicate with parents after the initial stages of implementation. Keep parents informed through regular progress reports, newsletters, meetings, and formal and informal evaluations. Involve them in staff development related to new curriculum. Let parents know about academic successes and changes in discipline and student attitudes.

Above all, successful parent involvement in untracking requires a sincere and ongoing invitation to parents to raise questions and make suggestions—with school staff sharing research findings, information about state-of-the-art classroom practices, the developmental needs of students, and learning theory to create a consensus about the school's responsibility to all students. As Kammerer parents and teachers noted after their first year, "Teachers and parents must believe that all students can learn well and base action on this." A successful partnership between parents and schools engaged in untracking can flourish on the strength of this belief.

Preparing for Tough Questions: What Do You Say When . . . ?

> The change process is anxiety-producing. This anxiety surfaces in numerous ways: questions are raised, resistance is generated, unrelated issues surface, and rumors abound. Recognizing that each of these will occur is the first step in addressing them.
> —Ron Williamson and J. Howard Johnson, *Planning for Success: Successful Implementation of Middle Level Reorganization,* 1991

Like many institutions, untracking schools have constituencies that resist change, including parents. These schools have learned some lessons from their experience of listening and responding to teachers, parents, and community constituencies who would prefer to leave traditional grouping practices untouched. Educators in these schools advise being prepared with research findings and examples from experience when addressing concerns of skeptics. Here are some responses to some tough questions:

"IT SEEMS TO ME THAT MIXING GROUPS OF STUDENTS
TOGETHER IS GOING TO HOLD BACK THE LEARNING
OF THE SMARTER STUDENTS."

Of the hundreds of research studies conducted on heterogeneous groups, the vast majority conclude that high-achieving students do not lose ground in diverse-ability classes. In almost every case, classroom environment is found to be far more important than student enrollment. When curriculum and instruction are engaging, students of all levels benefit, including the most confident learners.

These findings apply even to the "top" 3 percent of students. In a recent study Robert Slavin and Robert Stevens of Johns Hopkins University compared student progress in heterogeneous classes that were using the Cooperative Integrated Reading and Composition (CIRC) curriculum with that in homogeneously grouped classes. Students rated among the top 33 percent, 10 percent, and 3 to 5 percent were examined. The result was that, in fact, the reading and writing performance of the heterogeneously grouped students surpassed that of the homogeneously grouped ones at all levels.

Educators emphasize that attention be paid to these findings. As Jake Burks of Maryland's Harford County Public School District, reminds parents:

> We need to make educational decisions based on the best knowledge available; we have to have research inform everything we do. I want *all* parents to say, "Meet my child's needs." That's their job. But in our job, we're not in the business of educating one group of students. As professionals we're responsible for educating everyone, and there are things that we must not do. That's a moral and professional issue.

Teachers' own experiences also contradict the notion that more confident learners are held back in heterogeneous classes. As teacher Suzy Ronfeldt of the Albany Unified School District in California explained to Nancy Kreinberg and Harriet Nathan in *Teachers' Voices, Teachers' Wisdom:*

> During our first untracked year when we also did more cooperative learning, some parents felt their children were just helping others to learn. They felt their children might be losing out, and they missed being able to say "My Sally is in the top math group."
>
> I had to talk about several of the positive aspects of untracked classrooms. First of all, when a child has to explain her thinking and reasoning so another child understands it, she clarifies her thoughts and really learns what she is trying to teach. Second, you begin to realize that each child has his or her own way of conceptualizing. Third, if you are able to put yourself in the other person's shoes and see how he thinks and interprets, your own understanding is enriched.
>
> In a classroom that honors children's thinking and problem solving, tracking is too narrowing. How do you track children as they try to figure out which is longer—the length of the fifth-grade hall or the height of the school building? As my class worked in groups of four on this problem one of them had posed, they arrived at a rich variety of strategies.
>
> One group used the large outside blocks on the building to figure the height. Another group used string tied to a piece of tanbark and threw it from one roof level to another to measure the height. An-

other group got hold of the blueprints for the building. Still another group measured the two levels of stairs using each step to figure some of the building height. Another group simply went outside and held their hands as blinders on each side of their head then sighted in on the length of the hall, turned their heads and sighted in on the height of the building. The last group took down the architects's drawing from the office wall and measured the length and height from that. Do you label one of these strategies as the "gifted" approach or are they all "gifted" approaches?

In Albany, I have not had questions about tracking from the parents in the last three years. They seem to feel their children are being challenged.

"WON'T 'SLOWER' STUDENTS FEEL OVERWHELMED BY THEIR 'SMARTER' COUNTERPARTS IN HETEROGENEOUS CLASSES?"

Children with learning disabilities or others who benefit from different kinds of explanations may derive the most noticeable benefits from heterogeneous grouping. Exposed to grade-level curriculum, instruction that conveys high expectations for their learning, and concrete support, these students make significant gains that can narrow achievement gaps between their performance and the accomplishments of the more confident learners. Self-esteem also improves as students experience access to learning in heterogeneous groups that have no stigma attached to them.

According to Darcy Yearley, Director of Guidance and Student Support Services at the Wellesley Middle School:

One of the most important lessons we've come to learn is that good instruction in regular classes is good for kids with learning disabilities. After we began integrating special education students in heterogeneous classes, we had only one "D" the first term and two "D"s the second term. In only two cases did children achieve less than satisfactory.

Remember, for these kids, school has always been a risk. These are the kids who always have to say, "I don't get it." We've been exhilarated by the tenacity these students have shown in going after knowledge now that they have the chance.

We've also realized that the major reasons special education students don't achieve has more to do with the failures of adults than of students. We've been able to make heterogeneous grouping work for these kids as well as other kids because we've improved our communication between regular education and special education teachers, and we've improved our communication between school and home.

"I'VE READ ALL THE RESEARCH DOCUMENTING THE HARMS OF TRACKING, BUT I'M STILL NOT SURE WHETHER IT'S TRACKING ITSELF THAT HARMS STUDENTS OR THE INFERIOR TEACHING AND CURRICULUM OFFERED IN THE LOW TRACK. COULDN'T WE JUST WORK HARDER TO MAKE THE LOWER TRACKS BETTER?"

Principal John D'Auria of Wellesley Middle School has this to say:

> If we want students to learn only facts and information, perhaps up-grading the lower tracks will be adequate. But if we want all students to become intellectual risk-takers and learn the skills necessary for lifelong learning, heterogeneous grouping is superior to homogeneous grouping no matter how good each track is.
>
> Let's look at a question from a standardized I.Q. test as an example. Here's an analogy: "A book is to an empty bookcase as what? Take your pick from four alternative answers—Three eggs is to a basket? A carton of eggs is to a refrigerator? An egg is to a rooster? An egg is to a frying pan?" Only one of these answers is considered "right."
>
> If we track our students, we will end up with all the students who choose the "right" answer to questions like these in one class called the "high" class. But several of the "wrong" answers could be very good answers depending on how you think about them. We want all our students to learn as many varied and diverse strategies for solving problems as they can, and we think that the way to do this is to expose them to different ways of thinking so that they learn that there is more than one way to process information and create new knowledge.
>
> Many of our classes spend time thinking about thinking. They consider questions such as "If thinking were like Lincoln Logs, what would thinking be like?" and "If thinking were like Tinker Toys, what would thinking be like?" The answers come slowly to questions like these, and often the kids who get the ball rolling are the kids who are willing to take risks and who don't have the experience of worrying that a "wrong" answer will knock them out of the top group.
>
> Students interacting with a diverse group of peers learn to develop equally diverse ways of communicating ideas. Students who learn that everyone has something to contribute to understanding a problem develop skills in asking for help when they need it. Students working on assignments which require contributions from all students learn

that effort often matters as much as ability. In short, heterogeneous groups offer students valuable learning experiences which tracked settings cannot provide no matter how good they may be.

Promoting Parent Knowledge about Tracking

Entrance to school brings with it forms and releases and assessments . . . and somehow the results of my tests got confused with those of another student. . . . I was placed in the vocational track, a euphemism for the bottom level. Neither I nor my parents realized what this meant. We had no sense that business math, typing, and English-Level D were dead ends. The current spate of reports on the schools criticizes parents for not involving themselves in the education of their children. But how would someone like Tommy Rose, with his two years of Italian schooling, know what to ask? And what sort of pressure could an exhausted waitress apply? The error went undetected, and I remained in the vocational track for two years.
    —Mike Rose, *Lives on the Boundary: The Struggles and Achievements of America's Underprepared,* 1989

If, in principle, *all* parents need to be informed about school grouping practices, too often only a few of them are familiar with unspoken norms that *seem* unremarkable but may have enormous impact on the future of their children. For example many parents believe that math 8 is the only eighth-grade math course, whereas in reality it may be the lowest track in a particular school's math sequence. Other parents may not realize that enrollment in certain "gatekeeping" courses, such as pre-algebra and algebra in the middle grades, predetermines later access to enrollment in higher-level courses at the high-school level.

When sociologist Elizabeth Useem reviewed district and school placement policies and interviewed parents of seventh graders about their children's course placement in math, she discovered that access to "high" levels of math in the middle grades varies considerably from district to district. In some districts fewer than 15 percent of eighth graders are placed in algebra, compared with 50 percent in others, with more highly educated parents favoring enrollments in advanced math.

Useem also found that patterns of enrollment vary with the degree of school tolerance for parent involvement, and that schools use a variety of policies to discourage parents who seek to enroll their children in higher-level math courses. In particular, in districts with the lowest enrollments in "gatekeeping" courses, Useem found that:

- Many schools do not give parents all the information that they need about course sequences and their implications to enable them to make wise choices.
- Some schools tell parents that enrollment in the "high" curriculum will "mess up" a student's schedule, particularly if, after trying the course, a student decides to drop down a level.
- Course-planning materials for parents and students often use language discouraging enrollment at the high level. Courses are described as "fast paced and rigorous" or for students who are "mathematically talented" or have "exceptional ability," rather than simply "able" or "interested."
- Standardized test scores are often used as a rigid "cut-off" mechanism. When standardized tests are not the sole criterion for course selection, local tests are used to persuade parents that their children are not qualified for high-level groupings in *that* district.
- Parents are discouraged from pushing for "overrides" of school-placement decisions by requiring school conferences with teachers or requesting that parents sign waivers according to which they assume full responsibility for any future failure of their children in accelerated courses.

The ability of parents to be involved in decisions about course assignment depends largely on the school's belief in the capacity of all students to learn. Moreover, parents' access to decision making varies dramatically according to social status. For example, when there *is* parental involvement in course-placement decisions, parents of African-American and Latino students are involved only half as often as those of white students.

As the National Urban League and the Educational Testing Service found in surveys of thousands of parents in six cities, parents do believe that the level at which a student is placed makes a difference in learning, especially in math, and many expressed a desire to be involved in placement decisions. Like the low-income parents in Elizabeth Useem's study, however, few urban parents know that there is any choice of math available to eighth graders, even when they are aware of the existence of different course levels, ranging from "basic" through "honors." Moreover, few parents, outside of some whose children attend magnet schools, know how schools decide which students will be placed in gatekeeping eighth-grade math courses; and although some believe that schools can be responsive "if you push the issue," generally they observe that schools make their decisions first, leaving parents to review those decisions after the fact.

Information for Parents and Citizens about Tracking

All parents need and have the right to the facts about tracking in their schools. Educators can go a long way toward providing this information by making clear both the formal and informal mechanisms that underlie tracking arrangements in each school. In *Making the Best of Schools: A Handbook for Parents, Teachers, and Policymakers,* Jeannie Oakes and Martin Lipton make suggestions about general information that parents should have in order to establish a common ground for discussion with schools about tracking. They recommend that schools make public:

- The scope of the tracking policy, whether determined by the district or defined within the school
- How decisions are made about track placement
- How teachers are assigned to classrooms
- The number of classes in which subjects and grades are tracked
- All curriculum choices available in each subject
- The kinds of material in each curriculum
- The number of children moving from low tracks onto higher levels each year
- The percentage of students enrolled in each track by race and grade compared with those percentages overall
- Expectations for the future of students in each curriculum

Answers to these questions can be gathered through interviews, observations, questionnaires, or an analysis of school records. Sometimes the process of asking such questions can in itself begin a positive dialogue; at other times, the process may reveal strong fears of and resistance to change. But the sharing of such information is a critical step toward defining and addressing the problem of educational inequity resulting from tracking.

The Challenge for Parents: Asking the "Right Questions"

Low-income parents are constantly discovering—through the experience of their children—the fault lines in public education, but how does their knowledge inform both research and practice? How can we link what parents know at critical junctures to what researchers

name as the problem? What might happen if researchers and educators could learn more about the benchmarks along the path toward
educational failure as observed by parents and if parents could name
the manifestations of the problems the experts use to predict the
same outcome?

—Dan Rothstein, The Right Question Project

Whereas upper-income parents frequently understand the implications of
a placement decision and also have the skills to negotiate about a situation
that may be detrimental to their children, low-income parents may not
have these advantages. Some parents, for example, may not know the
"right questions" to ask or feel confident about asking any questions at all,
even when they intuitively understand that their children's future is at
stake. The Right Question Project works with low-income parents in urban
school districts to develop and create strategies for engaging them in deci-
sion-making processes that affect their children.

Through a series of community-based workshops, the project endeavors
to translate the formal parlance of educators such as "tracking" and "academic placement" into a language that helps parents "name" the matter at
hand in their own terms. After having attended the workshops they can say
to themselves, "That's pretty clear why that's an important issue for my kid"
and "Now I have some ideas about what I can do about it." Rothstein, project director, describes how a workshop on tracking focuses on the impact
of grouping on children:

We give each participant two sheets of paper stapled together. On the
first page we write: "What Your Child Should Learn: The Curriculum
for All the District's Schoolchildren." Underneath is a drawing (an
original by a six-year-old) of a boy and a girl sharing a book, standing
under a smiling sun.

On the second page we write: "The full curriculum is 100 pages
long." On half of the papers we hand out a second page that reads:
"Your child will be taught the full 100 pages." The other half of the
papers state: "Your child will be taught only the first 50 pages."

We then ask parents what they received. (We ask for volunteers because if some parents cannot read, they will also be able to participate
fully.) When the parents who received a curriculum that states that
their child will be taught only the first 50 pages hear that others are
being taught the full 100 pages, they ask:

Why is my child only being taught 50 pages?
What does it mean that he's only taught 50?

Who made that decision?
When was it made?
Why is this important?
If I want to know, is this something I have a right to know?
Am I supposed to be involved? Can I be?

On a few of the papers we put down some grades in English and math. The grades were all "A"s. We ask what kinds of questions the parents have about the grades. Here are some:

What does the "A" mean?
Does it mean the same for the 100- and 50-page curriculum?
Do they tell us somehow on the report card which curriculum it belongs to?

We then ask them to reflect on the significance of the grades. One father said: "If I didn't know that there are different programs, then I'd be happy if my son brought home "A"s. But I'd be pretty upset if I knew there was a 25-page curriculum, a 50-page curriculum, and a 100-page curriculum."

Parents' newfound awareness of the consequences of placement decisions and differential curriculum for their children leads to further questions. Frequently African-American, Latino, and low-income parents may begin to wonder about the likelihood of their children being assigned to the "low" classes, and decide to take action to change that placement. Understanding the implications of tracking can also become the basis for parent-initiated review of systemwide placement practices and collective action for change.

Community-Based Pressure for Untracking

Reformers who emphasize "quality," and who mean by it higher expectations for all, will be tolerated only to the point where they can find a willing audience; beyond that point they will be resisted.
—Arthur G. Powell, Eleanor Farrar, and David K. Cohen,
The Shopping Mall High School, 1985

Resistance to change is not the exclusive province of parents. In fact, in some districts, expanded consciousness about tracking is leading to the formation of citizen groups seeking to challenge grouping practices in schools where educators themselves resist untracking. Sometimes these groups are composed of parents alone. Sometimes they are made up of parents in coalition with teachers and other citizens with a common concern about improving the quality of education for all students. These groups can be a powerful force for untracking.

Building a Constituency for Change Through Information-Gathering and Education

Parent advocacy for particular placements traditionally benefits individual students, but parents collaborating together may challenge tracking practices for an entire school or district. In fact, educators who support change may have no stronger allies than parents and citizens knowledgeable about the extent and harm of tracking. Community-education efforts that raise the level of public awareness about grouping practices can create a positive context for change.

In Albany, New York, the Albany Citizens for Education (ACE) has developed a context within which alternatives to tracking can be discussed openly. Founded in the throes of an electoral campaign designed to endorse a set of independent, nonmachine candidates for the Albany School Board, ACE is made up of parents and citizens intent on improving education for all students in that urban district. Over several years, citizens have succeeded in electing a reform-minded majority to the school board. At the same time, with more openness on the board, ACE members have worked closely with board committees, including one mandated to develop a Strategic Plan for Albany Public Schools. Included in that plan, approved by the board in 1990, is a recommendation that the tracking system at every level in Albany schools be replaced or modified.

ACE's early information-gathering efforts that led to this recommendation raised key questions pertaining to districtwide grouping practices. In a letter to the superintendent, ACE began its research by asking for data on students placed in the district's "academically talented" classrooms, background on procedures used for selecting students for these classes, and information about curriculum differences between that program and "regular" classrooms. After a long waiting period, district staff responded with information that enabled ACE to clarify district tracking policies for parents.

With the district's tracking policies finally available in writing, ACE moved forward to make placement policies more widely known through public forums and school-board meetings. But ACE members also wanted to put out the message that alternatives to tracking could improve schooling across the board and that all children could benefit from curriculum and instruction currently offered to only the most able students. Therefore, during the school year 1990–91, ACE joined with the Urban League of the

Albany Area, the Albany NAACP, and the City School District of Albany it-self to sponsor a Saturday conference "to promote a long-term, broad-based effort to enrich, diversify, and strengthen education in Albany."

Despite cold winter weather, approximately two hundred people joined ACE and its partners at the all-day conference. The theme "Tapping Every Talent: Expanding Achievement Opportunities for All Students" conveyed the belief that education must and could be improved in heterogeneous settings. Reinforcing the theme that *all* students have gifts and talents to be developed, workshops highlighted research on tracking, effective instruc-tional strategies, and successful programs. In addition, a local attorney of-fered a workshop called "Advocating for Your Child in a Tracked System," which focused on the kinds of decisions used to place children in academic tracks and techniques for obtaining standardized test scores. With the en-ergy level still high at the end of the day, participants convened in the school cafeteria to collect recommendations from each workshop. Several participants advocated specific programs. Others, with heightened aware-ness of the variety of alternatives available, expressed a sense of urgency about pressing for more general tracking reforms.

ACE has begun to see some results from these efforts. In 1991, the dis-trict moved to reduce the number of tracks from four to three and adopted a transitional math curriculum to replace the practice of introducing alge-bra to a selected group of "high" students in seventh grade. While public debate continued at Albany School Board meetings, the School Depart-ment formed several committees including parents, teachers, and admin-istrators to research alternative approaches. After several months of meetings and investigation, including field trips to other communities, committee members became excited about "Project Opportunity"—a promising model that they observed in Ithaca, New York, which encom-passed both curriculum enrichment in heterogeneous classes and built-in opportunities for strengthening teachers' skills. Although change will begin in the elementary grades, parents will not stop there. As Joan Eken-gren, a parent member of ACE, reports, "We just have to keep persevering and hammering away at the issue, it seems. We hope that people will real-ize we're not going to drop this. It's too important!"

Challenging Resegregation in Tracked Schools

A desegregated school system does not necessarily provide equal educa-tion for everyone. In Selma, Alabama, the resegregation of the schools through a tracking system has become the focus of parent and citizen pres-sure mobilized through a citizen organization called the Best Educational Support Team (BEST). BEST works to address inequities in a district where materials and facilities in predominantly African-American elementary schools are demonstrably inferior to those of white schools and where, in the high school in 1988, only 3 percent of the African-American students were enrolled in the highest track, known as Level 1.

Since its inception, BEST has worked to reform the tracking system and its effect of resegregating African-American and white students into virtually separate within-school systems. Assignment to tracks was based solely on teacher recommendation without clear criteria for making selections. Thus it was possible for African-American students who were as capable as whites to be excluded from such Level 1 courses as algebra 1, biology 1, or computer sciences—and the future opportunities inherent in them.

BEST's arguments against tracking, bolstered by data demonstrating its discriminatory effects, resulted in changes in criteria for placement in Level 1, with grade-point averages and test scores replacing teacher recommendations. This change alone boosted the enrollment of African-Americans in the highest track to 10 percent. However, protests by white parents also followed, and in December 1989, the school board's white majority voted not to renew the contract of Selma's African-American superintendent, Dr. Norward Roussell. As BEST member Rose Sanders said, "Only when [Dr. Roussell] moved to get rid of the tracking system, did they move to get rid of him."

Since that time, citizen boycotts and student sit-ins have marked Selma's community protests. Both white and African-American students increasingly realize the impact of tracking on their lives. As student Malika Sanders, a member of Students Marching Against Racial Tracking (SMART), the students' counterpart to BEST, told *Rethinking Schools*:

> I think a lot of Level 1 students are beginning to understand that everyone should get a chance to take Level 1 courses. In Level 2 and 3 they don't give you college preparatory courses, they just give you the basics. . . . The Level system has leveled the confidence of the students. But it's not true that they can't do the work. I've taken some Level 1 courses, and I can tell you that they are not that hard. Everyone should have a choice whether they want to take these courses or not.

In addition, BEST members have taken to the road to speak out against tracking at community forums across the country. As BEST member Connie Tucker says, "The powers that be think we will get tired, but folks are not willing to let this die."

Community "Consciousness-Raising" for Citizens and Educators
At the eastern end of Long Island, New York, the National Association for the Advancement of Colored People (NAACP) has a long history of concern about the educational achievement of African-American students in

the schools of the region. In 1990, some branch members started to wonder: "Has public education, 'the great equalizer' in the words of Horace Mann, become the great tranquilizer instead?" "To keep things quiet, are troublesome students shunted to separate classrooms or even buildings under the guise of special education?" "Are some students on the low-ability track, the one that rarely leads to college, put there simply because they are members of minorities?"

To explore these issues, the group's Education Committee sought information through a series of letters and freedom-of-information requests about what kinds of programs the students that they represented were experiencing. What they learned was disturbing. As similar inquiries have revealed, African-Americans at East End schools were overrepresented in special education and underrepresented in high-level honors classes. Given this pattern, it is not surprising that almost half of the white graduates went to four-year colleges, whereas only 16 percent of the African-Americans did so.

With these data in hand, the organization initiated a series of informational meetings to raise awareness about unequal educational opportunity and discuss remedies. First, they invited York College education professor James C. Hall, Jr., to speak to branch members, teachers, and parents about the benefits of mixing children of disparate abilities and backgrounds in classrooms at all levels. Second, the committee prodded the Suffolk County Chief School Administrators Association and the local Board of Cooperative Educational Services (BOCES) into cosponsoring an afternoon "awareness" conference for educators to expand understanding of both research related to tracking and alternatives.

Along with an official from New York State's Department of Education and several Long Island school principals, the panel of speakers included Dr. Dominic Annacone, former superintendent of the Sag Harbor School District. Dr. Annacone described how Pierson High School's planning process had included "at least ten meetings" with parents to discuss concerns that curriculum would be "watered down" for the most confident students and that special education students would be in "over their heads." These concerns, he explained, were addressed over and over in packed meetings prior to the opening of the new school year. But once parents had seen changes for themselves, they were enthusiastic. Two months into the school year, Dr. Annacone reported, only four parents turned out for a review meeting.

Community-School Partnerships for School Reform
In California, The Achievement Council, an organization dedicated to increasing academic achievement among Latino, African-American, and

low-income students of all ethnic groups, is demonstrating how community-based organizations can work effectively with schools to forge a vision of schoolwide improvement dedicated to closing the achievement gap between these students and other young people. Part of that vision is the untracking of curriculum in order to open college-preparatory opportunities to underrepresented students. Another goal is to change conditions that reinforce patterns of low student achievement, including categorical programs that sort students into separate groups with different curricular and instructional approaches.

The council's framework for change begins with an analysis of the *culture* of each school—the values, attitudes, and norms that influence behavior, relationships, and expectations. In assessing school culture, the council follows key principles that shape each of its projects: the principles that 1) "all students deserve a rigorous core curriculum, rich in concepts and ideas, drawing on the best sources to stimulate both analysis and awareness of the underpinnings of world culture"; and 2) that "all students benefit from heterogeneous groups for most learning activities." The Achievement Council also acts on the belief that educators, students, and parents together form a community of interest for school improvement, with school staff exercising professional responsibilities to translate the vision into a cooperative action plan. These core beliefs are critical to guiding the council's projects for improving student achievement for the state's most vulnerable students.

There are four central elements in the Achievement Council's strategy to implement change in low-performing schools: 1) expanding the accountability system and improving professional performance; 2) implementing a rigorous curriculum for all students; 3) developing staff-development and school-improvement programs in low-performing schools; and 4) undertaking an aggressive statewide initiative to address low student achievement. This four-pronged strategy generates such activities as a statewide Principals' Institute, which is designed to identify effective approaches to school improvement while pairing principals who have been successful in turning around their schools with others who want assistance to develop a blueprint for change. A Guidance Counselors' Infusion Model has also been fashioned to support counselors as change agents in their schools so that the number of students who enter college-level courses may be increased, the college pipeline may be opened early in a student's career, and teacher expectations may be modified.

Other activities of the council involve promotion of a challenging curriculum for all students, especially in mathematics; an emerging parent involvement project; and a concerted effort to link the needs of staff in urban schools with resources to nurture and sustain school-based reform and professional growth. Working with low-performing schools in Los Angeles and San Francisco, the council's ultimate objective is to enlarge the pool of college-eligible Latino and African-American students by strengthening their preparation for and access to college preparatory courses.

Ultimately, says Jean Adenika of The Achievement Council, real school reform requires providing access to educational opportunities that are equal to those offered in the "best" schools. By fostering school-community partnerships for change, The Achievement Council develops institutional efforts that go beyond those of individual guidance counselors, teachers, or community groups to contribute valuable community-based support and resources for school changes, including untracking, to close achievement gaps schoolwide.

National Citizens' Organizations

Citizens' groups and student-advocacy organizations increasingly realize that tracking undermines the achievement of most students. Organizations such as the National Coalition of Advocates for Students, Quality Education for Minorities Project, and the Hispanic Policy Development Project have taken strong positions against tracking. In addition, as attention to the issue of tracking intensifies, citizens' organizations outside of traditional educational circles have also become involved. These include the National Coalition of Education Activists, a multiracial organization of parents, teachers, and citizens working for fundamental school reform including high-quality heterogeneous classes; Schools Are for Everyone, a national coalition of families, consumers, and advocates united in the belief that "all children learn best in heterogeneous classrooms where individual differences are celebrated"; and Rethinking Schools, a working group of teachers and citizens, which publishes a bimonthly newspaper concerned with issues of democracy and equity in education, including tracking and multiculturalism. Each of these organizations promotes educational materials and events to support a growing network of activist teachers, citizens, and parents seeking alternatives to tracking.

Parents, Teachers, and the Community: Together Is Better

Untracking proceeds more smoothly when everyone affected is informed and involved. In some communities, it is parents who first raise doubts about the compatibility of tracking with the goal of excellent education for all students. Parent concerns provoke educators to explore their own capacity for change, examine their beliefs about the nature of intelligence, assess their preparation for working with academically integrated classrooms, and launch "catch-up" efforts to learn about effective teaching approaches for heterogeneous classes.

In other school districts, principals and teachers are eager to adopt innovative approaches for heterogeneous classrooms, whereas parents are the ones who worry that losses of the "safer" traditional classrooms will outweigh promised gains or that the end of tracking will result in fewer supports or challenges for their children. In these communities, parents first need information about the nature of proposed changes to increase their willingness to work with school staff and strengthen their confidence that a school-parent partnership represents an honest alliance to support the learning of all children.

RESOURCES

The Achievement Council, 4055 Wilshire Blvd., Suite 350, Los Angeles, CA 90010; (213) 487-3194; Linda Wong, Executive Director; Jean Adenika, Southern California Director; Phyllis Hart, Manager of School Services.

Albany Citizens for Education (ACE), P.O. Box 6934, Fort Orange Station, 450 Central Ave., Albany, NY 12206; (518) 447-5877.

BEST Education Support Team, P.O. Box 1305, Selma, AL 36702.

Educational Testing Service, Princeton, NJ 08541-0001; (609) 734-5308.

Hispanic Policy Development Project, 36 E. 22nd St., New York, NY 10010; (212) 529-9323; Siobhan Nicolau, Executive Director.

Kammerer Middle School, 7315 Wesboro Rd., Louisville, KY 40222; (502) 473-8279; Nancy A. Weber, Principal.

Kreinberg, Nancy, and Harriet Nathan, eds. *Teachers' voices, teachers' wisdom: Seven adventurous teachers think aloud.* Berkeley, CA: EQUALS, 1991. Available from EQUALS, Lawrence Hall of Science, University of California, Berkeley, CA 94720; (510) 642-1823.

Levine, David. Selma confronts tracking. *Rethinking Schools* 4, no. 3 (March/April 1990).

National Association for the Advancement of Colored People (NAACP), Eastern Long Island Branch, P.O. Box 338, East Hampton, NY 11937; Louis Ware, President; Lyla Hoffman, Education Committee.

National Coalition of Advocates for Students, 100 Boylston St., Boston, MA 02116; (617) 357-8507.

National Coalition of Education Activists, P.O. Box 405, Rosendale, NY 12472; (914) 658-8115; Debi Duke, Executive Director.

National Urban League, 500 East 62nd St., New York, NY 10021; (212) 310-9000.

Oakes, Jeannie, and Martin Lipton. *Making the best of schools: A handbook for parents, teachers, and policymakers.* New Haven, CT: Yale University Press, 1990.

On the right track: What can parents do to help their children succeed in school? Available from the National Urban League.

On the right track: What students should know to succeed in school. Available from the National Urban League.

People About Changing Schools (PACE), 79 Leonard St., New York, NY 10013.

Quality Education for Minorities Network, 1818 N St., NW, Suite 350, Washington, DC 20036; (202) 659-1818.

Rethinking Schools, 1001 E. Keefe Ave., Milwaukee, WI 53212; (414) 964-9646.

Rose, Mike. *Lives on the boundary: The struggles and achievements of America's underprepared.* New York: Free Press, 1989.

Schools Are for Everyone (SAFE), P.O. Box 583, Syracuse, NY 13210.

School Voices, 79 Leonard St., New York, NY 10013.

The Right Question Project, Inc., 167 Holland St., Somerville, MA 02144; (617) 628-4070; Dan Rothstein, Director.

Useem, Elizabeth L. "You're good, but you're not good enough": Tracking students out of advanced mathematics." *American Educator,* Fall 1990.

Wellesley Middle School, 50 Kingsbury St., Wellesley, MA 02181; (617) 446-6235; John D'Auria, Principal.

Williamson, Ron, and J. Howard Johnston. *Planning for success: Successful implementation of middle level reorganization.* Reston, VA National Association of Secondary School Principals, 1991.

19

Is Your Child Being Tracked?

National Coalition of Education Activists

You may not immediately recognize tracking in your school, or your school system may claim that it does not use tracking. However, if you answer *no* to any of the questions below, you may want to talk with other parents or teachers about your concerns and investigate further.

1. Do most classes have a racial and ethnic mix similar to the school as a whole? For instance, if the school is two-thirds black and one-third white, are most of the classes the same or are some 90 percent black and others 90 percent white?
2. Do most classes have roughly equal numbers of boys and girls?
3. Do students in most classes have backgrounds similar to those found in the school as a whole? For example, do there seem to be classes where most students' parents are professionals and others where most students come from poor or working-class families?
4. Can you see that your children are progressing? Grades may not be the best indicator; notice whether children are reading and writing more or better, moving beyond basic math skills, expressing more complicated ideas, taking on more responsibility, developing skills or talents, and so on.
5. Do your children's teachers seem to know your children's weaknesses and strengths and have a plan for addressing them?
6. When you attend school programs or extracurricular activities, do the participating students seem to reflect the racial, ethnic, and class mix found in the school as a whole?

7. If your school or school system has special programs or schools, do the students who are part of them seem to reflect the mix found in the school or system as a whole?

8. Do your children receive meaningful homework assignments? Ask questions if they:
   - have no homework;
   - get many worksheet drills;
   - are reading and answering questions on paragraphs instead of whole stories and books;
   - have lots of multiple choice questions rather than thoughtful writing assignments.

9. Is your child enrolled in algebra by the ninth grade? This is an important "gateway" course. Students who do not have access to algebra by Grade 9 will have trouble fitting in math courses they need for college, trades, and many jobs.

10. Do your child's classes focus on regular coursework in English, mathematics, reading, et cetera? Or do they focus primarily on basic skills to pass a "competency test" or similar test?

20

Organizing and Teaching

William Ayers

In the mid 1960s I became an organizer for the East Side Community Union in the Lakeview section of Cleveland, Ohio. The Community Union was an extension of the Southern civil rights movement into the North—a grassroots effort to organize disenfranchised and marginalized citizens of the ghetto into a powerful force capable of effectively fighting for their own needs and aspirations. Our buttons read "Let the People Decide," and "Build an Interracial Movement of the Poor." The other organizers and I believed then that legitimate and just social change should be led by those who had been pushed down and locked out, and that struggling in the interest of the most oppressed people in society held the key to a fundamental transformation that would ultimately benefit all people. We saw our political work as also ethical work—organizing and righteousness. I was twenty years old.

Our first job was to become part of the community, to listen hard to what people told us, to be respectful neighbors. We knocked on doors, talked around kitchen tables, hung out on stoops, and went to barbeques in the park. We were identifiable outsiders, of course, and we lived here by choice and with a larger purpose, but we were mindful of the fact that our agenda meant nothing unless it could be realized in light of the particular agendas of the people of Lakeview. We knew, too, that we did not want to build a "career" here, that the point of our work was to somehow, as we said at the time, "organize ourselves out of a job." We could perhaps be catalysts for change, but we could never substitute for indigenous, community leadership. We wanted to create organizations of, by, and for the poor.

I remember the day we knocked on Dolores Hill's door. "Oh, you're the civil rights kids from down the block," she exclaimed with a big welcoming smile. "I've been waiting for you. Come on in." We talked into the night about kids, welfare, schools, crime, dope, rent, gangs. It was the beginning of a beautiful friendship.

Dolores Hill was a natural leader, widely known and deeply respected. Perceptive, articulate, hard-working, honest, and tough, she had grown up on the block and was now raising her own children here. Active in her church and PTA, she was a person others looked to for guidance and help. When a child was hit by a car on Lakeview Avenue, it was Dolores Hill who called a meeting in her living room to press the city to install a stoplight; when a back-to-school welfare allowance was cut, Dolores Hill organized the protest; when a rat bit a youngster while she slept in her apartment, Dolores Hill thought up the rather dramatic tactic of taking a few rats with us downtown to the protest picket line, as well as the memorable accompanying slogan, "Get the rats out of Lakeview and City Hall." She was the first president of the Community Union.

Mrs. Hill opened meetings with a prayer. We would invariably sing a few songs—"Will the Circle Be Unbroken?" "This Little Light of Mine," "Oh Freedom!" Singing brought us together as a group of people, helped remind us of our common purpose, and made us all feel a little stronger. When Dolores Hill began to set the agenda, she would usually interject her own words of wisdom as introduction and frame: "Tonight we'll be talking about welfare rights. Now remember, just because you're poor and on welfare doesn't mean you're not a citizen, and citizens have rights"; or, "Now we'll move on to figuring out about starting a Children's Community preschool. Our children are poor, true, but that doesn't mean they don't have fine minds. We have to think about how to stimulate those minds."

Within a couple of years the East Side Community Union had become a vital part of the neighborhood. There was a large, dynamic welfare rights project affiliated with a national organization; there was a housing and rent strike committee organizing building by building, demanding fair rents and reasonable upkeep and repairs; there was a community health project led by two young doctors; there was a storefront office where people could drop in for coffee and conversation; and there was a preschool operating out of a church basement. All of these projects were built on the energy and intelligence of the people of Lakeview—energy and intelligence the society had largely ignored, locked up, and kept down. Dolores Hill never missed an opportunity to underline the point: "I'm poor because I haven't got any money. I'm not mentally ill! I'm not lazy! I'm not stupid!"

The Community Union lived for only a few years. It was founded shortly after Reverend Bruce Klinger was run over by an earth-mover and killed during a sit-in at the Lakeview Avenue construction site of what would become another segregated and marginalized school. It was gone by the time

Ahmed Evans and a group of young nationalists engaged in a deadly shoot-out with the Cleveland police in a Lakeview Avenue apartment. In between there was struggle, hope, possibility, occasional heroism, and perhaps the most loving attempt we will ever see to change all that is glaringly wrong in our society.

In the midst of our efforts and in what some have called a cynical response to the massive upheaval among African-Americans, agents of government-sponsored poverty programs began to appear. Their first efforts involved a "community needs assessment" in which they surveyed neighborhood people in an attempt to define problems and craft solutions. They used a "scientifically" developed instrument, a questionnaire that could be easily quantified and rated. Instead of searching for the strengths and capacities in the community, they looked exclusively at deficiencies; instead of focusing on problems as shared and social, they probed individual deficits; instead of uncovering root causes and building focused strategies and tactics to bring about change, they stopped short of collective action. In brief, while they learned and applied the rhetoric of the civil rights movement, they shared none of its spirit or larger ethical and political purposes. Their approach was narrow, myopic, and certain to fail.

Dolores Hill, in the eyes of the poverty program workers, was a vast collection of ills. She had dropped out of high school, become pregnant at nineteen, and was a single mother with three young children, one of whom needed expensive glasses. She had been arrested once as a teenager for shoplifting, and had hung out at that time with a group of Lakeview Avenue youngsters who called themselves the Street Demons. Now she was on welfare, and she occasionally worked cleaning white people's houses while her oldest boy watched the children. She also took cash from the children's father, a long-distance truck driver who sometimes spent the night at her apartment. In other words Dolores Hill, by their account, represented the whole litany of behaviors that add up to a "culture of poverty" or a "tangle of pathologies": welfare cheat, gang member, criminal, unwed mother, neglectful parent, pregnant teen, high school drop-out, and so on. They were fairly drooling over her.

This kind of portrait was rather easily sketched of many people in Lakeview. It is, of course, a false picture—incomplete, negative, pretentious, self-fulfilling. It fails to see human life as embedded, dynamic, complex, and contradictory—powered by chance as well as choice, directed by mind and meaning as much as punishment and reward. It highlights certain isolated incidents in a life at the expense of other incidents. It attributes explanatory power to those incidents, a procedure that would never be allowed if the subjects were white and well-off. I (and many others I know and have known) could be tagged and stuck with several of these labels depending on how the observer looked and where the action was stopped—let's see . . . gang member, criminal, drug involved, drop-out. But I would never be tarred as representing a "culture of poverty"—the privileges of race and background that accrue to me by accident and chance.

The pathology portrait of the poor conveniently lumps those few selected items and incidents together to fit a preconceived, stereotyped view. Embraced by conservatives and liberals alike, this facile view assumes that the existing social system and structure is fundamentally fine, any problems related to race and class are relics of the past, and anyone should be able to do well now unless plagued by some complex, difficult to change, *internal* psychocultural effects. In other words "we've done too much already" (conservatives) or "we've done as much as we can" (liberals) and we'll all hope for *"those people"* to get it together or somehow disappear.

Not surprisingly, the programs proposed as a result of this kind of shoddy, suspect analysis tend to be unhelpful at best, often debilitating or even harmful. They offer services rather than solidarity. They turn people into clients rather than assisting them to become agents. They perpetuate dangerous generalities and degrading stereotypes about individuals, and, most important, they fail to identify or uncover any underlying structural causes that might generate the problems in the first place—they find no enemies except those posited, presumed traits within poor people themselves.

In those years I was both an organizer and a teacher—roles I found complementary and analogous. Whether knocking on doors or teaching a class, I began with an attempt to see the person, to hear him or her, to understand what she was going through. Each vocation is rooted, after all, in relationship and an abiding faith in the human capacity to grow and learn—a facility that is natural, inherent, and intense. Each is built upon a belief that all people—kids, parents, teachers, citizens—bring an intelligence with them to the school or the community meeting, and that intelligence is the starting point for action and further learning. These are basic democratic values, values that we fought for then, and are still fighting for now. To talk of irreversibility or the irredeemable, to talk of bell curves and absolute deficiencies, to talk of hopelessness is to raise bells of alarm in every fiber of an organizer's or a teacher's being.

I taught at the Children's Community, our church basement preschool, and I worked with Head Start, one of the few truly hopeful programs emerging from the War on Poverty. Attacked by conservatives at its inception as a communist plot, the socializing of child-rearing, and a frontal assault on family values, Head Start has become sanctified as a symbol of doing something good for the poor (even as it is constantly and quietly eroded, menaced, and cut back). But it is worth remembering that liberals justified Head Start as a program that would create a "level playing field" for youngsters, without questioning the meritocratic and hierarchic realities of schools and society, and that once again the poor were blamed for their situations. The first brochures explaining Head Start to parents and staff described the poor as living in "islands of nothingness." It was from this nothingness that children were to be lifted up and brought into the "human family." This is not policy that loves or supports families or parents or children. It is not policy that understands or builds upon strengths. Rather this kind of policy makes the cost of participation acceptance of degrading and self-denying generalizations.

Like the organizer, the fundamental message of the teacher is this: you can change your life. Whoever you are, wherever you've been, whatever you've done, the teacher invites you to a second chance, another round, perhaps a different conclusion. The teacher posits possibility, openness, and alternative; the teacher points to what could be, but is not yet. The teacher beckons you to change your path, and so she has but one basic rule, which is to reach.

But of course the teacher can only create a context, set a stage, open a curtain. The teacher's task is excruciatingly complex precisely because it is idiosyncratic and improvisational—as inexact as a person's mind or a human heart, as unique and inventive as a friendship or falling in love. The teacher's work is all about background, environment, setting, surround, position, situation, connection. And relationship. It is about having one eye on the students before you—three-dimensional, complex, trembling, and real—and one eye on the world we share—dynamic, complex, in need of repair. As Martin Heidegger said, teaching is tougher than learning in one respect: teaching requires the teacher to *let learn*. Learning requires action, choice, and assent from the student. Teaching, then, is undertaken with hope, but without guarantees. Teaching, like organizing, is an act of faith.

About the Contributors

William Ayers is a Distinguished Professor of Education and Senior University Scholar at the University of Illinois at Chicago. He is founder of the Center for Youth and Society, co-director of the Small Schools Workshop, co-founder of the Annenberg Challenge, and co-chair of the Chicago School Reform Collaborative.

Robert Coles is a child psychiatrist, Pulitzer Prize–winning author, professor at Harvard Medical School, and a recipient of the Presidential Medal of Freedom.

Kathleen Cushman is the author of *Fires in the Bathroom: Advice for Teachers from High School Students* (The New Press) and *What We Can't Tell You: Teenagers Talk to the Adults in Their Lives* (Next Generation Press, 2005). As a writer for the nonprofit organization What Kids Can Do, Inc., she works to bring forward the voices of youth around the nation. She lives in New York City.

Lisa Delpit is an Eminent Scholar and Executive Director of the Center for Urban Education and Innovation at Florida International University in Miami, where she lives. Her work is dedicated to providing excellent education for marginalized communities in the United States and abroad.

Patricia Ford is a lecturer at the University of Illinois at Chicago and a community organizer. She is the co-director of the urban school reform organization Small Schools Workshop with William Ayers.

Michael Thomas Ford is the author of several books, essays, and articles on gay and lesbian issues.

Michele Foster is an educational anthropologist and sociolinguist who focuses on the social, cultural, and linguistic context of education. She has been a faculty member of several institutions, including Claremont Graduate University, the University of California at Davis, and the University of Pennsylvania, and is a frequent contributor to journals and books on education.

Herbert Kohl is the author of more than forty books, including the best-selling *36 Children* and the classic *"I Won't Learn From You"* (The New Press). A recipient of the Robert F. Kennedy Book Award, he was the founder and first director of the Teachers and Writers Collaborative in New York City and established the PEN West Center in San Francisco, where he lives.

Susan Linn is Instructor in Psychiatry at Harvard Medical School and Associate Director of the Media Center at Judge Baker Children's Center in Boston. An award-winning producer and ventriloquist, she is internationally known for her pioneering work using puppets as therapeutic tools with children and is a co-founder of the coalition Stop Commercial Exploitation of Children.

Daniel Moulthrop is a radio reporter for WCPN, Cleveland's NPR affiliate. **Nínive Clements Calegari** is the founding executive director of 826 Valencia, a nonprofit organization providing free literacy and literary arts services to young people. Both are former classroom teachers. **Dave Eggers** is the founder of 826 Valencia, as well as the founder of *McSweeney's* and the author of several novels.

David Mura is a poet, critic, playwright, and performance artist.

The **National Coalition of Education Activists (NCEA)** is a multiracial network of education activists working for equity and social justice in America's schools.

Dr. Laurie Olsen is the director of California Tomorrow, a nonprofit policy research, advocacy, and technical assistance organization catalyzing school reform around issues of diversity. She lives in Berkeley, California.

Gary Orfield is Professor of Education and Social Policy at the Harvard Graduate School of Education. He is the co-founder and director of the Civil Rights Project at Harvard University, an initiative that is developing and publishing a new generation of research on multiracial civil rights issues.

Mica Pollock, Associate Professor at the Harvard Graduate School of Education, studies youth and adults struggling to talk about, think about, and address fundamental questions of racialized inequality and diversity in their daily lives. An anthropologist of education, she examines disputes over difference, discrimination, and inequality in both school and community settings.

Victoria Purcell-Gates, formerly a professor of teacher education at Michigan State University, currently serves as the Canada Research Chair for Early Childhood Literacy at the University of British Columbia, where she is a professor in the Department of Language and Literacy Education.

Judith Rényi is Senior Vice President for Academic Partnerships at American College of Education. Formerly the president of the NEA Foundation, she has helped to make high-quality, effective professional development part of every teacher's working life.

Peter Schrag has written books about schools and other social and political issues for more than four decades. He is the author of *Paradise Lost* (The New Press), a *New York Times* Notable Book, and lives in Oakland, California.

Studs Terkel is the author of twelve books of oral history, including *Working* and the Pulitzer Prize–winning *"The Good War"* (both available from The New Press). He is a member of the Academy of Arts and Letters and a recipient of a Presidential National Humanities Medal, the National Book Foundation Medal for Distinguished Contribution to American Letters, a George Polk Career Award, and the National Book Critics Circle Ivan Sandrof Lifetime Achievement Award.

Anne Wheelock is an independent education writer and policy analyst based in Massachusetts. She is the author of several books on dropout prevention and public school reform.

Sources

Ayers, William and Patricia Ford, eds. *City Kids, City Teachers: Reports from the Front Row.* New York: The New Press, 1996.

Ben Jelloun, Tahar. *Racism Explained to My Daughter.* With responses from William Ayers, Lisa Delpit, David Mura, and Patricia Williams. New York: The New Press, 1997.

Calegari, Nínive Clements, Daniel Moulthrop, and Dave Eggers. *Teachers Have It Easy: The Big Sacrifices and Small Salaries of America's Teachers.* New York: The New Press, 2005.

Coles, Robert, and Randy Testa with Michael Coles, eds. *Growing Up Poor: A Literary Anthology.* New York: The New Press, 2001.

Cushman, Kathleen. *Fires in the Bathroom: Advice for Teachers from High School Students.* New York: The New Press, 2003.

Delpit, Lisa. *Other People's Children: Cultural Conflict in the Classroom.* With essays by Herbert Kohl, Charles M. Payne, and Patricia Lesesne. New York: The New Press, 2006.

Delpit, Lisa and Joanne Kilgour Dowdy, eds. *The Skin That We Speak: Thoughts on Language and Culture in the Classroom.* New York: The New Press, 2001.

Ford, Michael Thomas. *The World Out There: Becoming Part of the Lesbian and Gay Community.* New York: The New Press, 1996.

Foster, Michele. *Black Teachers on Teaching.* New York: The New Press, 1997.

Kohl, Herbert. *Teaching for Social Justice: A* Democracy and Education *Reader.* Ed. William Ayers, Jean Ann Hunt, and Therese Quinn. New York: The New Press/Teachers College Press, 1998.

Linn, Susan. *Consuming Kids: The Hostile Takeover of Childhood.* New York: The New Press, 2004.

National Coalition of Education Activists (NCEA). From *Rethinking Schools: An Agenda for Change.* Ed. David Levine, Robert Lowe, Bob Peterson, and Rita Tenorio. New York: The New Press, 1995.

Olsen, Laurie. *Made in America: Immigrant Students in Our Public Schools.* New York: The New Press, 1997.

Orfield, Gary, Susan E. Eaton, and the Harvard Project on School Desegregation. *Dismantling Desegregation: The Quiet Reversal of* Brown v. Board of Education. New York: The New Press, 1996.

Pollock, Mica. Excerpt from "Everyday Antiracism in Education." *Anthropology News* 47, no. 2 (February 2006): 9–10. Copyright © 2006 by the

American Anthropological Association. Not for sale or further reproduction.

Rényi, Judith. *Going Public: Schooling for a Diverse Democracy.* New York: The New Press, 1994.

Schrag, Peter. *Final Test: The Battle for Adequacy in America's Schools.* New York: The New Press, 2003.

Terkel, Studs. *Working: People Talk About What They Do All Day and How They Feel About What They Do.* New York: The New Press, *Working: People Talk About What They Do All Day and How They Feel About What They Do.* New York: The New Press, 1997.

Wheelock, Anne. *Crossing the Tracks: How "Untracking" Can Save America's Schools.* New York: The New Press, 1992.

All of these titles are available at www.thenewpress.com or by calling 1–800–233–4830.

Also Available from The New Press

Zero Tolerance: Resisting the Drive for Punishment in Our Schools
Edited by Bill Ayers, Bernardine Dohrn, and Rick Ayers
CURRENT AFFAIRS/EDUCATION
A clear-eyed collection that takes aim at the replacement of teaching with punishment in America's schools.
Paperback, $17.95, 288 pages
ISBN: 978-1-56584-666-1

Math and Science Across Cultures: Activities and Investigations from the Exploratorium
Maurice Barin, Modesto Tamez, and The Exploratorium Teacher Institute
EDUCATION
Innovative, hands-on math and science activities of many cultures, from one of the world's foremost science museums.
Paperback, $19.95, 192 pages
ISBN: 978-1-56584-541-1

Growing Up Gay/Growing Up Lesbian: A Literary Anthology
Edited by Bennett Singer
GAY & LESBIAN STUDIES/YOUNG ADULT
An award-winning collection of over fifty gay and lesbian coming-of-age stories. A free teaching guide is available.
Paperback, $14.95, 336 pages
ISBN: 978-1-56584-103-1

Coming of Age in America: A Multicultural Anthology
Edited by Mary Frosch
FICTION
The acne and ecstasy of adolescence, a multicultural collection of short stories and fiction excerpts that *Library Journal* calls "wonderfully diverse from the standard fare."
Paperback. $15.95, 288 pages
ISBN: 978-1-56584-147-5

Coming of Age Around the World: A Multicultural Anthology
Edited by Mary Frosch
FICTION/LITERATURE
Twenty-four stories by renowned international authors chronicle the modern struggle for identity among young people around the globe.
Paperback, $16.95, 320 pages
ISBN: 978-1-59558-080-1

Beyond the Bake Sale: The Essential Guide to Family-School Partnerships
Anne T. Henderson, Karen L. Mapp, Vivian R. Johnson, and Don Davies
EDUCATION
A practical, hands-on guide to helping schools and families work better together.
Paperback, $18.95, 288 pages
ISBN: 978-1-56584-888-7

Should We Burn Babar?: Essays On Children's Literature and the Power of Stories
Herbert Kohl
Fiction/Literature
The prizewinning educator's thoughts on the politics of children's literature.
Paperback, $14.95, 240 pages
ISBN: 978-1-59558-130-3

Lies My Teacher Told Me: Everything Your American History Textbook Got Wrong
James W. Loewen
AMERICAN HISTORY/EDUCATION
The bestselling, award-winning, iconoclastic look at the errors, misrepresentations, and omissions in the leading American history textbooks.
Hardcover, $27.95, 416 pages
ISBN: 978-1-56584-100-0

Lies My Teacher Told Me About Christopher Columbus:
What Your History Books Got Wrong
James W. Loewen
AMERICAN HISTORY/EDUCATION
A provocative educational poster and booklet that draws on recent scholarship to debunk the myths and discover the man.
Paperback/Poster, $14.95, 48 pages
ISBN: 978-1-56584-008-9

CityWorks: Exploring Your Community: A Workbook
Adria Steinberg and David Stephen
EDUCATION
An innovative way for young people to understand their communities.
Paperback, $19.95, 176 pages
ISBN: 978-1-56584-416-2

Studs Terkel's Working: *A Teaching Guide*
Rick Ayers
EDUCATION/SOCIOLOGY
An invaluable educational resource for introducing Studs Terkel's classic
work of oral history to today's students.
Paperback, $14.95, 224 pages
ISBN: 978-1-56584-626-5

History Lessons: How Textbooks from Around the World Portray U.S. History
Kyle Ward
HISTORY
Now in paperback, an eye-opening compilation showing how very differ-
ent U.S. history looks when viewed by the rest of the world.
Paperback, $17.95, 432 pages
ISBN: 978-1-59558-082-5

A People's History of the United States: Abridged Teaching Edition
Howard Zinn
AMERICAN HISTORY/EDUCATION
More than five hundred years of American social and cultural history.
Paperback, $19.95, 640 pages
ISBN: 978-1-56584-826-9

A People's History of the United States: Wall Charts
Howard Zinn and George Kirschner
AMERICAN HISTORY/EDUCATION
Two oversized posters based on Zinn's bestselling social history.
Paperback/Poster, $25.00, 48 pages
ISBN: 978-1-56584-171-0

*She Would Not Be Moved: How We Tell the Story of Rosa Parks and the Montgomery
Bus Boycott*
Herbert Kohl
Introduction by Marian Wright Edelman
AFRICAN AMERICAN STUDIES/EDUCATION
The prizewinning educator's brilliant and timely meditation on the mis-
leading ways in which we teach the story of Rosa Parks.
Paperback, $14.95, 144 pages
ISBN: 978-1-59558-127-3

Teachers Have It Easy: The Big Sacrifices and Small Salaries of America's Teachers
Daniel Moulthrop, Nínive Clements Calegari, and Dave Eggers
EDUCATION
The bestselling call to action for improving the working lives of public school teachers—and improving our classrooms along the way.
Paperback, $16.95, 384 pages
ISBN: 978-1-59558-128-0

History in the Making: An Absorbing Look at How American History Has Changed in the Telling over the Last 200 Years
Kyle Ward
HISTORY/EDUCATION
From the widely acclaimed co-author of *History Lessons*, an examination of how the way we tell the story of our country has changed over time.
Hardcover, $26.95, 400 pages
ISBN: 978-1-59558-044-3

Other People's Children: Cultural Conflict in the Classroom
With a new introduction by the author
Lisa Delpit
EDUCATION/AFRICAN AMERICAN STUDIES
A new edition of the classic revolutionary analysis of the role of race in the classroom with framing essays by Herbert Kohl, Charles M. Payne, and Patricia Lesesne.
Paperback, $17.95, 256 pages
ISBN: 978-1-59558-074-0

Fires in the Bathroom: Advice for Teachers from High School Students
Kathleen Cushman
EDUCATION
The acclaimed book of practical advice from students to their teachers.
Paperback, $18.95, 224 pages
ISBN: 978-1-56584-996-9

Please visit www.thenewpress.com to browse the full catalog.